Android System Programming

Porting, customizing, and debugging Android HAL

Roger Ye

BIRMINGHAM - MUMBAI

Android System Programming

First published: May 2017

Production reference: 1290517

Published by Packt Publishing Ltd.
Livery Place
35 Livery Street
Birmingham
B3 2PB, UK.
ISBN 978-1-78712-536-0

www.packtpub.com

Credits

Author
Roger Ye

Reviewers
Bin Chen
Chih-Wei Huang
Shen Liu
Nanik Tolaram

Commissioning Editor
Amarabha Banerjee

Acquisition Editor
Shweta Pant

Content Development Editor
Arun Nadar

Technical Editor
Prajakta Mhatre

Copy Editor
Safis Editing

Project Coordinator
Ritika Manoj

Proofreader
Safis Editing

Indexer
Mariammal Chettiyar

Production Coordinator
Nilesh Mohite

About the Author

Roger Ye has worked in the area of embedded system programming for more than 10 years. He has worked on system programming for mobile devices, home gateways, and telecommunication systems for various companies, such as Motorola, Emerson, and Intersil.

Most recently, he has worked as an engineering manager, leading a team of Android engineers to develop mobile security applications at Intel Security. With extensive knowledge and experience in the areas of embedded systems and mobile device development, he published a book called *Embedded Programming with Android, Addison-Wesley*, in 2015.

I would like to thank my dearest wife, Bo Quan, and my lovely daughter, Yuxin Ye, for enduring me to spend significant time on this book over the weekends. They have been very encouraging and always give me support to work on the things that I am interested in.

About the Reviewers

Bin Chen is a senior engineer from Linaro. He has worked on various Android-based products since 2010: TV, STB, Galaxy Tab, Nexus Player, and Google Project Ara, in that order, and now AOSP 96Boards. He occasionally blogs and speaks about all things Android. He lives in Sydney, Australia.

Chih-Wei Huang is a developer and promoter of free software who lives in Taiwan. He is famous for his work in the VoIP and internationalization and localization fields in Greater China.

Huang graduated from National Taiwan University (NTU) in 1993 with a bachelor's degree in physics, and attained a master's degree in the electrical engineering department of NTU in 2000. Huang currently works as a chief engineer of Tsinghua Tongfang Co., Ltd. for the OPENTHOS project. He is one of the founding members of the Software Liberty Association of Taiwan (SLAT).

Chih-Wei Huang is the founder and coordinator of the Chinese Linux Documentation Project (CLDP). He is also the second coordinator of the Chinese Linux Extensions (CLE) and a core developer of GNU Gatekeeper (from 2001 to 2003).

He is a contributor to pyDict, OpenH323, Asterisk, GStreamer, and more. He is working on a way to leverage the ASUS Eee PC with the power of the free software community and aims to provide a complete solution for Android on the x86 platform. The Eee PC, VirtualBox, and QEMU have been tested and are OK.

Chih-Wei Huang and Yi Sun started the Android-x86 open source project in 2009. The project aims to bring Android to the x86 platform.

About the Reviewers

Shen Liu is a senior engineer, working at Intel China. He used to work at McAfee LLC, Broadcom Corporation, and Huawei Technologies. He has over 10 years of work experience on Linux/Android and embedded systems, in different roles. He had taken manager, architect, and engineer roles during his career. He is mainly responsible for the Android framework, but is not limited to it, and he has a lot of passion for software design. On top of that, he loves reading technical books.

Nanik Tolaram works as a senior Android platform engineer for BlocksGlobal in Australia, where he is responsible for developing Screener (`screener.digital`) and Lumin (`mylumin.org`). He is passionate about Android and is very active within both the local and international Android developer communities--from talks and teaching to writing articles for ODROID open source magazine (`magazine.odroid.com`). In his spare time, he loves to tinker with electronics and study human psychology and behavior. He lives in Sydney, Australia, with his lovely wife and two beautiful boys.

www.PacktPub.com

For support files and downloads related to your book, please visit `www.PacktPub.com`.

Did you know that Packt offers eBook versions of every book published, with PDF and ePub files available? You can upgrade to the eBook version at `www.PacktPub.com` and as a print book customer, you are entitled to a discount on the eBook copy. Get in touch with us at `service@packtpub.com` for more details.

At `www.PacktPub.com`, you can also read a collection of free technical articles, sign up for a range of free newsletters and receive exclusive discounts and offers on Packt books and eBooks.

`https://www.packtpub.com/mapt`

Get the most in-demand software skills with Mapt. Mapt gives you full access to all Packt books and video courses, as well as industry-leading tools to help you plan your personal development and advance your career.

Why subscribe?

- Fully searchable across every book published by Packt
- Copy and paste, print, and bookmark content
- On demand and accessible via a web browser

Customer Feedback

Thanks for purchasing this Packt book. At Packt, quality is at the heart of our editorial process. To help us improve, please leave us an honest review on this book's Amazon page at `www.amazon.com/dp/178712536X`.

If you'd like to join our team of regular reviewers, you can e-mail us at `customerreviews@packtpub.com`. We award our regular reviewers with free eBooks and videos in exchange for their valuable feedback. Help us be relentless in improving our products!

Table of Contents

Preface

Android is the most popular mobile operating system in the world. Since 2013, Android has around 80% market share worldwide, while the second largest mobile operating system, iOS, has less than 20% market share. Due to the popularity of Android, there are many books about Android programming in the market. Most of them are targeted at Android application developers, which are the largest community in the world of Android development.

There is also another group of people working on the layer beneath the Android framework. Many people call them Android system developers. Comparing to Android application developers, Android system developers use the C/C++ languages, or even assembly language, to develop system services or device drivers. The scope and the definition of Android system development is much more vague than comparing to Android application development. For Android application development, the development environment and tools are very clear: the Android SDK and Android Studio from Google should be used and the programming language is Java.

For Android system development, we may use the Android NDK to develop Android system services or native applications. Many people refer to development based on the Android Open Source Project (AOSP) as Android system development. Nevertheless, Android system development encompasses the activities that produces native applications, services, or device drivers for a particular hardware platform. It closer to the hardware and the operating system, whereas Android application development is more general and hardware-independent.

Due to the hardware and operating system dependencies, it is more difficult to teach Android system programming than Android application programming. From the number of books in the market, we can see this. It is much easier to teach Android application development using specific examples. The readers of application programming books can follow the examples and can test them on most available Android devices. However, most Android system programming book can only talk about general concepts or ideas. When the authors want to use examples, they must pertain to a particular hardware platform and Android version. This makes it difficult for readers to repeat the same process.

Virtual hardware platforms

To make the discussion more general and overcome the issue of specific hardware platforms, I use virtual hardware platforms to demonstrate the work at the Android system level.

Before this book, I made an attempt to use a virtual hardware platform to explain how we can learn embedded system programming using an Android emulator in my previous book, *Embedded Programming with Android*. It seems many readers liked the idea, because they can explore the code examples much more easily on a virtual hardware platform that is available for everyone.

Android version used in this book

Android is still changing at a very fast pace. When I completed the book *Embedded Programming with Android*, we were still using Android 5 (Lollipop), and Android 6 (Marshmallow) was on the way to market with preview releases. Now while I am working on this book, Android 7 devices are available on the market and the next release of Android 8 has been announced with preview releases. We will use Android 7 (Nougat) to build all source code used in this book.

What this book covers

In this book, we discuss the Android system programming practices. We will use two projects (x86emu and x86vbox) to teach essential knowledge of Android system programming. The book is split into includes two parts.

The first part of this book talks about how to customize, extend, and port an Android system. We will use an Android emulator as the virtual hardware platform to demonstrate how to customize and extend an Android system. You will learn how to integrate an ARM translator (Houdini) into the Intel x86-based emulator and how to add Wi-Fi support to an Android emulator. We will use an x86emu device to learn these topics. After that, we will learn how to port an Android system to a new platform using VirtualBox. You will learn how to boot Android in the PXE/NFS environment, how to enable the graphics system, and how to integrate VirtualBox Guest Additions into the Android system. We will use x86vbox device to learn these topics.

In the second part of this book, we will learn how to update or patch a released system using recovery. In this part, we will provide a general introduction to recovery first. After that, we will explore how to build recovery for x86vbox device. With recovery for x86vbox device, we will demonstrate how to flash an update package to change the system image. We will use examples such as the Gapps and xposed recovery packages to demonstrate how to update an Android system image using third-party recovery packages.

Chapter 1, *Introduction to Android System Programming*, covers a general introduction of Android system programming. It also explains the scope of this book.

Chapter 2, *Setting Up the Development Environment*, provides details of the development environment setup for AOSP programming. After we set up the development environment, we will build an Android emulator image to test our setup. Other than the environment setup, we specifically discuss how to create your own source code mirror of AOSP from GitHub to help your quickly switch between different configurations.

Chapter 3, *Discovering Kernel, HAL, and Virtual Hardware*, covers an introduction to the Linux kernel, Hardware Abstraction Layer, and virtual hardware. In this chapter, we look at all the layers in the Android system software stack related to porting. We also take a in-depth look at the internals of the virtual hardware that we are going to use in this book.

Chapter 4, *Customizing the Android Emulator*, covers the development of a new device, x86emu. We will learn how to customize and extend this device in the next few chapters.

Chapter 5, *Enabling the ARM Translator and Introducing Native Bridge*, explores a new feature introduced in Android 5--Native Bridge. Since we created an x86-based device, x86emu, we have to integrate the ARM translator module (Houdini) into our device so that most ARM-native applications can run on it.

Chapter 6, *Debugging the Boot Up Process Using a Customized ramdisk*, introduces an advanced debugging skill to troubleshoot issues during the boot up stage. The famous Android-x86 project uses a special ramdisk to start the boot up process. It helps to troubleshoot device driver and init process issues very easily.

Chapter 7, *Enabling Wi-Fi on the Android Emulator*, presents details of how to enable Wi-Fi on our Android emulator. The Android emulator only supports an emulated 3G data connection, but many applications are aware of data and the Wi-Fi connection. We demonstrate how to enable Wi-Fi in the Android emulator in this chapter.

Chapter 8, *Creating Your Own Device on VirtualBox*, explores how to port Android on VirtualBox by introducing a new device x86vbox. The x86emu device is used to demonstrate how to customize an existing implementation, while x86vbox is used to demonstrate how to port Android to a new hardware platform.

Chapter 9, *Booting Up x86vbox Using PXE/NFS*, explains how to boot up Android on VirtualBox using PXE/NFS. Since VirtualBox is a general virtual hardware, the first problem that we meet is we need a bootloader to boot the system. We will use the PXE/NFS boot to solve this issue. This is an advanced debugging skills which can be used in your own project.

To discuss a more advanced case about the PXE/NFS setup using an external DHCP/TFTP server running in the host-only network environment, I have written an article, which you can find at https://www.packtpub.com/books/content/booting-android-system-using -pxenfs.

Chapter 10, *Enabling Graphics*, covers the Android graphic system. We introduce the Android graphics architecture and how to enable it on the x86vbox device.

Chapter 11, *Enabling VirtualBox-Specific Hardware Interfaces*, explains how to integrate the device drivers in VirtualBox Guest Additions into the Android system.

Chapter 12, *Introducing Recovery*, provides an introduction to recovery. We will learn how to customize and port recovery to a new hardware platform by building a recovery for the x86vbox device.

Chapter 13, *Creating OTA Packages*, covers the scripting language used by recovery: Edify. We will learn how to build and test OTA updates.

Chapter 14, *Customizing and Debugging Recovery*, expands on the concepts we learned about recovery and OTA packages. We will customize both recovery and updater for x86vbox device. We will test third-party OTA packages from Gapps and Xposed using our own recovery.

What you need for this book

To read this book, you should have essential knowledge of embedded operating systems and C/C++ programming language.

Who this book is for

Before we talk about who should read this book, we should ask who are the people that usually do Android system programming in the real world? There are potentially quite a lot. Here, I can give a few general categories. Firstly, there are a large number of engineers at Google working on the Android system itself, since Android is a product from Google. Google usually work with silicon vendors to enable Android on various hardware platforms.

There are many engineers at silicon chip companies, such as Qualcomm, MTK, or Intel to enable Android on their platform. They develop HAL layer components or device drivers to enable hardware platforms. The hardware platforms are usually called reference platforms, which are provided to OEM/ODM to build the actual products. Then, the engineers at OEM/ODM companies usually customize the reference platform hardware and software to add unique features to their products. All these engineers form the major groups working on system-level programming. Thus, if you are working in any of these areas, you may want to read this book.

Besides the previously mentioned categories, it is also possible that you are a developer working for an embedded system company. You may work on projects such as embedded system for automobile, video surveillance, or smart home. Many of these systems use Android nowadays. One of the fastest growing areas in embedded systems is Internet of Things (IoT) devices. Google announced Brillo as the operating system for IoT devices. Brillo is a simplified embedded operating system based on Android. The source code of Brillo is also included in the AOSP. This book is also relevant to people who use Brillo.

For Android application developers, system-level knowledge can help you to resolve complex issues as well. If you are working on projects that involve new hardware features, you may want to extend your knowledge to the system level.

This book is also useful for people teaching Android system programming or embedded system programming. There is plenty of source code in this book that can be used to form your own lesson plans.

Conventions

In this book, you will find a number of text styles that distinguish between different kinds of information. Here are some examples of these styles and an explanation of their meaning.

Code words in text, database table names, folder names, filenames, file extensions, pathnames, dummy URLs, user input, and Twitter handles are shown as follows: "The general Android kernel source code is in the `kernel/common` folder , which looks very much like the Vanilla kernel."

A block of code is set as follows:

```
static struct hw_module_methods_t lights_module_methods = {
  .open = open_lights,
};
```

Any command-line input or output is written as follows:

```
$ ls
Light.java LightsManager.java LightsService.java
```

New terms and **important words** are shown in bold. Words that you see on the screen, for example, in menus or dialog boxes, appear in the text like this: "We should set the launch type to **Standard Create Process Launcher**."

Warnings or important notes appear in a box like this.

Tips and tricks appear like this.

Reader feedback

Feedback from our readers is always welcome. Let us know what you think about this book-what you liked or disliked. Reader feedback is important for us as it helps us develop titles that you will really get the most out of.

To send us general feedback, simply e-mail feedback@packtpub.com, and mention the book's title in the subject of your message.

If there is a topic that you have expertise in and you are interested in either writing or contributing to a book, see our author guide at www.packtpub.com/authors.

Customer support

Now that you are the proud owner of a Packt book, we have a number of things to help you to get the most from your purchase.

Downloading the example code

You can download the example code files for this book from your account at http://www.packtpub.com. If you purchased this book elsewhere, you can visit http://www.packtpub.com/support and register to have the files e-mailed directly to you.

You can download the code files by following these steps:

1. Log in or register to our website using your e-mail address and password.
2. Hover the mouse pointer on the **SUPPORT** tab at the top.
3. Click on **Code Downloads & Errata**.
4. Enter the name of the book in the **Search** box.
5. Select the book for which you're looking to download the code files.
6. Choose from the drop-down menu where you purchased this book from.
7. Click on **Code Download**.

Once the file is downloaded, please make sure that you unzip or extract the folder using the latest version of:

- WinRAR / 7-Zip for Windows
- Zipeg / iZip / UnRarX for Mac
- 7-Zip / PeaZip for Linux

The code bundle for the book is also hosted on GitHub at https://github.com/PacktPublishing/Android-System-Programming. We also have other code bundles from our rich catalog of books and videos available at https://github.com/PacktPublishing/. Check them out!

Errata

Although we have taken every care to ensure the accuracy of our content, mistakes do happen. If you find a mistake in one of our books-maybe a mistake in the text or the code- we would be grateful if you could report this to us. By doing so, you can save other readers from frustration and help us improve subsequent versions of this book. If you find any errata, please report them by visiting `http://www.packtpub.com/submit-errata`, selecting your book, clicking on the **Errata Submission Form** link, and entering the details of your errata. Once your errata are verified, your submission will be accepted and the errata will be uploaded to our website or added to any list of existing errata under the Errata section of that title.

To view the previously submitted errata, go to `https://www.packtpub.com/books/content/support`and enter the name of the book in the search field. The required information will appear under the **Errata** section.

Piracy

Piracy of copyrighted material on the Internet is an ongoing problem across all media. At Packt, we take the protection of our copyright and licenses very seriously. If you come across any illegal copies of our works in any form on the Internet, please provide us with the location address or website name immediately so that we can pursue a remedy.

Please contact us at `copyright@packtpub.com` with a link to the suspected pirated material.

We appreciate your help in protecting our authors and our ability to bring you valuable content.

Questions

If you have a problem with any aspect of this book, you can contact us at `questions@packtpub.com`, and we will do our best to address the problem.

1
Introduction to Android System Programming

This book is about Android system programming. In this chapter, we will start with a discussion on system programming and the scope of Android system programming (to give a high-level view of this book). After that, we will look at the Android system architecture. From the architecture, we can see the layers that we will focus on in this book. We will also talk about the virtual hardware platforms and third-party open source projects that we will use in this book. In summary, we will cover the following topics in this chapter:

- Introduction to Android system programming
- Overview of the Android system architecture
- Introduction to the third-party projects used in this book
- Introduction to virtual hardware platforms

What is system programming?

When we talk about what system programming is, we can start with the definition of system programming in Wikipedia:

> *"System programming (or systems programming) is the activity of programming system software. The primary distinguishing characteristic of systems programming when compared to application programming is that application programming aims to produce software which provides services to the user (e.g. word processor), whereas systems programming aims to produce software and software platforms which provide services to other software, are performance constrained, or both (e.g. operating systems, computational science applications, game engines and AAA video games, industrial automation, and software as a service applications). "*

From the preceding definition, we can see that when we talk about system programming we actually deal with the building blocks of the computer system itself. We may depict the system architecture and how it looks like inside the system. As an example, we can refer to system programming books for Windows or Linux. The book *Linux System Programming* published by O'Reilly Media, Inc. includes topics about *file I/O*, *process management*, *memory management*, *interrupt handling*, and so on. There is another book called *Windows System Programming* published by Addison-Wesley Professional that includes very similar topics to its Linux counterpart.

You may expect similar content in this book for Android, but you will find that the topics in this book are quite different from the classic system programming book. First of all, it doesn't really make sense to have a system programming book for Android talk about file I/O, process management, or memory management, because the *Linux System Programming* book can cover almost the same topics for Android (Android uses Linux kernels and device driver models).

When you want to explore kernel space system programming, you can read books such as *Linux Device Drivers* by O'Reilly or *Essential Linux Device Drivers* from Prentice Hall. When you want to explore user space system programming, you can read the book that I mentioned before, *Linux System Programming* by O'Reilly. Then you may wonder, Do we need an *Android System Programming* book in this case? To answer this question, it depends on how we look at system programming for Android. Or in other words, it depends on which angle we look at *Android System Programming* from. We can tell people different things about the same world from different perspectives. In that sense, we may need more than one book to talk about Android system programming.

To talk about Android system programming, we can talk about it theoretically or practically. In this book, we will do it practically with a few actual projects and hands-on examples. Our focus will be how to customize the Android system and how to port it to a new platform.

What is the scope of this book?

As we know, there are two kinds of programming for Android: application programming and system programming.

Usually, it is hard to draw a line between system programming and application programming, especially for C language-based operating systems, such as Linux and all kinds of Unix system. With the Android framework, the application layer is separated nicely from the rest of the system. You may know that Android application programming uses the Java language and Android system programming using Java, C/C++, or assembly languages. To make it simple, we can treat everything other than application programming in the Android world as the scope of system programming. In this sense, the Android framework is also in the scope of system programming.

From the perspective of the audiences of this book, they may want to learn more about the layers they may touch on in their project work. The Android framework is a layer that will be changed by Google only in most cases. From this point of view, we won't spend too much time talking about the framework itself. Instead, we will focus on how to port the system including the Android framework from the standard platforms in **Android Open Source Project** (**AOSP**) to other platforms. We will focus on the layers that need to be changed during the porting process in this book.

After we have done the porting work, a new Android system will be available. One thing that we need to do for the new system is deliver the changes for the new system to the end users from time to time. It could be a major system update or bug fixing. This is supported by **over-the-air** (**OTA**) updates in Android. This is also one of the topics in this book.

Traditionally, all Unix programming was system-level programming. Unix or Linux programming is built around three cornerstones, which are system calls, the C library, and the C compiler. This is true for Android system programming as well. On top of the system calls and C library, Android has an additional layer of abstraction for the Android application level. This is the Android framework and Java virtual machine.

In that sense, most Android applications are built using Android SDK and Java language. You may be wondering whether it is possible to do Android application development using C/C++ or even do system level programming using Java. Yes, all these are possible. Besides Android SDK, we can also develop native applications using Android NDK. There are also a lot of Android framework components developed using the Java language. We can even develop Android applications using C# with Visual Studio (Xamarin). However, we won't go to that kind of complexity in this book. We will focus on the layers below the application framework. Again, the focus will be on customizing and extending the existing system or porting the entire system to a new hardware platform.

The reason why we will focus on the porting of Android systems and the customization of Android systems is because these are what most people working on the Android system level will do. After Google releases a new version of Android, silicon vendors need to port the new version to their reference platform. When OEM/ODM companies get the reference platform, they have to customize the reference platform to their products. The customization includes the build of the initial system itself and the deployment of the updates to the deployed system. In the first part of this book, we will discuss the porting of Android systems. In the second part of this book, we will discuss how to update the existing system.

If we consider the architecture of Android in the right-hand side of the following figure, we can see that most porting work will focus on the **Kernel** and **Hardware Abstraction Layer** (**HAL**) in the Android system architecture. This is true for other Android derivatives as well. The knowledge and concepts in this book can apply to Android wearables and Brillo as well. The left-hand side of the following figure, it shows the architecture diagram of **Brillo**. **Brillo** is the IoT operating system from Google for IoT devices. It is a simpler and smaller version of Android for IoT devices. However, the porting layer is still the same as Android.

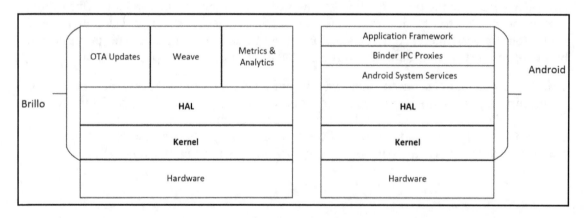

Comparison of Android and Brillo system architecture

The Brillo/Weave architecture diagram on the left-hand side is created by referring to the presentation by Bruce Beare, from OpenIoT Summit. Thanks, Bruce Beare for the great presentation and video on YouTube, which gives a very comprehensive introduction to the Brillo/Weave architecture.

Overview of the Android system

As we can see from the architecture diagram, the architecture layers of Android include **Application Framework**, **Android System Services**, **HAL**, and **Kernel**. Binder IPC is used as a mechanism for inter-process communication. We will cover each of them in this section. Since recovery is also part of the system programming scope, we will also give an overview of recovery in this section.

 You can find more information about key porting layers and system architecture internals at the following Google website:
`http://source.android.com/devices/index.html`

Kernel

As we know, Android uses the Linux kernel. Linux was developed by Linus Torvalds in 1991. The current Linux kernel is maintained by the Linux Kernel Organization Inc. The latest mainline kernel releases can be found at `https://www.kernel.org`.

Android uses a slightly customized Linux kernel. The following is a concise list of the changes to the Linux kernel:

- **ashmem (Android Shared Memory)**: A file-based shared memory system to user space
- **Binder**: An **interprocess communication (IPC)** and **remote procedure call (RPC)** system
- **logger**: A high-speed in-kernel logging mechanism optimized for writes
- **paranoid networking**: A mechanism to restrict network I/O to certain processes
- **pmem (physical memory)**: A driver for mapping large chunks of physical memory into user space

- **Viking Killer**: A replacement OOM killer that implements Android's "kill least recently used process" logic under low-memory conditions
- **wakelocks**: Android's unique power management solution, in which the default state of the device is sleep and explicit action is required (via a wakelock) to prevent that

Most of the changes were implemented as device drivers with little or no changes necessary to the core kernel code. The only significant subsystem-spanning change is wakelocks.

There are many Android patches accepted by the mainline Linux kernel today. The mainline kernel can even boot up Android directly. There is a blog from Linaro about how to boot Nexus 7 running a mainline kernel. If you want to try it, you can find the instructions at https://wiki.linaro.org/LMG/Kernel/FormFactorEnablement.

If a Linux device driver is available for a hardware device, it usually can work on Android as well. The development of device drivers is the same as the development of a typical Linux device driver. If you want to find out the merges on the mainline kernel related to Android, you can check the kernel release notes at https://kernelnewbies.org/LinuxVersions.

The Android kernel source code is usually provided by SoC vendors, such as Qualcomm or MTK. The kernel source code for Google devices can be found at https://android.googlesource.com/kernel/.

Google devices use SoC from various vendors so that you can find kernel source code from different vendors here. For example, the kernel source of QualComm SoC is under kernel/msm and the kernel source of Mediatek is under kernel/mediatek. The general Android kernel source code is in the folder kernel/common, which looks much like the Vanilla kernel.

The default build of AOSP is for various devices from Google, such as Nexus or Pixel. It started to include some reference boards from silicon vendors as well recently, such as hikey-linaro, and so on. If you need a vendor-specific Android kernel for your reference platform, you should get the kernel source code from your platform vendors.

There are also open source communities maintaining Android kernels. For example, the kernel for the ARM architecture can be found at Linaro for many reference boards. For Intel x86 architecture, you can find various versions of kernels in the Android-x86 project. As you can see from the following Linaro Linux Kernel status website, the linaro-android tree is a forward port of the out-of-tree AOSP patches. It provides a preview of what Google's next AOSP kernel/common.git tree "might" look like.

The Linaro Android kernel tree can be found at `https://android.git.li` `naro.org/gitweb/kernel/linaro-android.git`. The status of this kernel tree can be seen at `https://wiki.linaro.org/LMG/Kernel/Upstreaming`.

HAL

HAL defines a standard interface for hardware vendors to implement and allows Android to be agnostic about lower-level driver implementations. HAL allows you to implement functionality without affecting or modifying the higher level system. HAL implementations are packaged into module (`.so`) files and loaded by the Android system at the appropriate time. This is one of the focuses for porting Android systems to a new platform. We will discover more about HAL in Chapter 3, *Discovering Kernel, HAL, and Virtual Hardware*. Throughout this book, I will give a very detailed analysis of the HAL layer for various hardware interfaces.

Android system services

Functionality exposed by application framework APIs communicates with system services to access the underlying hardware. There are two groups of services that application developers may interact mostly with. They are **system** (services such as window manager and notification manager) and **media** (services involved in playing and recording media). These are the services that provide application interfaces as part of the Android framework.

Besides these services, there are also native services supporting these system services, such as SurfaceFlinger, netd, logcatd, rild, and so on. Many of them are very similar to Linux daemons that you may find in a Linux distribution. In a complicated hardware module, such as graphic, both system services and native services need to access HAL in order to provide the framework API to the application layer. We will talk about system services when we debug the init process in Chapter 6, *Enabling Wi-Fi on the Android Emulator* to Chapter 9, *Booting Up x86vbox Using PXE/NFS*.

Binder IPC

The Binder IPC mechanism allows the application framework to cross process boundaries and call into the Android system services code. This enables high-level framework APIs to interact with Android system services. An Android application usually runs in its own process space. It doesn't have the ability to access system resources or the underlying hardware directly. It has to talk to system services through Binder IPC to access the system resource. Since applications and system services run in different processes, the Binder IPC provides a mechanism for this purpose.

The Binder IPC proxies are the channel by which the application framework can access system services in different process spaces. It does not mean it is a layer between the application framework and system services. Binder IPC is the inter-process communication mechanism that can be used by any process that wants to talk to another process. For example, system services can use Binder IPC to talk to each other as well.

Application framework

The application framework provides APIs to the applications. It is used most often by application developers. After an interface is invoked by the applications, application frameworks talk to the system services through the Binder IPC mechanism. An Android application framework is not just a set of libraries for the application developers to use. It provides much more than that.

The break-through technology that the Android application framework brought to the developer community is a very nice separation between application layers and system layers. As we know Android application development uses the Java language and Android applications run in an environment similar to the Java virtual machine. In this kind of setup, the application layer is separated from the system layer very clearly.

The Android application framework also provides a unique programming model together with a tight integration with the **integrated development environment** (IDE) from Google. With this programming model and related tools, Android developers can work on application development with great efficiency and productivity. All these are key reasons why Android has gained so much traction in the mobile device world.

I have given an overall introduction to all the layers in the previous Android system architecture diagram. As I mentioned about the scope of Android system programming before, we can consider all programming in Android systems as within the scope of system programming other than application programming. With this concept in mind, we actually missed one piece in the previous architecture diagram, which is recovery.

Recovery

In this chapter, we want to have a brief look at recovery as well, since we have three chapters about it in the second part of this book.

Recovery is a tool that can be used to upgrade or reinstall Android systems. It is part of the AOSP source code. The source code for recovery can be found at `$AOSP/bootable/recovery`.

The unique point about recovery compared to the other parts of Android is that it is a self-contained system by itself. We can look at recovery using the following diagram, and compare it to the Android and Brillo architectures that we talked about before:

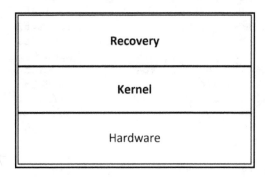

Recovery is a separate system from Android that shares the same kernel with the Android system that it supports. We can treat it as a mini operating system or an embedded application that we can find in many embedded devices. It is a dedicated application running on top of the same Linux kernel as Android and it performs a single task, which is to update the current Android system.

When the system boots to recovery mode, it boots from a dedicated partition in the flash. This partition includes the recovery image that includes a Linux kernel and a special ramdisk image. If we look at Nexus 5 partitions, we will see the following list:

```
# parted /dev/block/mmcblk0
parted /dev/block/mmcblk0
GNU Parted 1.8.8.1.179-aef3
Using /dev/block/mmcblk0
Welcome to GNU Parted! Type 'help' to view a list of commands.
(parted) print
print
print
Model: MMC SEM32G (sd/mmc)
Disk /dev/block/mmcblk0: 31.3GB
Sector size (logical/physical): 512B/512B
```

```
Partition Table: gpt
```

Number	Start	End	Size	File system	Name	Flags
1	524kB	67.6MB	67.1MB	fat16	modem	
2	67.6MB	68.7MB	1049kB		sbl1	
3	68.7MB	69.2MB	524kB		rpm	
4	69.2MB	69.7MB	524kB		tz	
5	69.7MB	70.3MB	524kB		sdi	
6	70.3MB	70.8MB	524kB		aboot	
7	70.8MB	72.9MB	2097kB		pad	
8	72.9MB	73.9MB	1049kB		sbl1b	
9	73.9MB	74.4MB	524kB		tzb	
10	74.4MB	75.0MB	524kB		rpmb	
11	75.0MB	75.5MB	524kB		abootb	
12	75.5MB	78.6MB	3146kB		modemst1	
13	78.6MB	81.8MB	3146kB		modemst2	
14	81.8MB	82.3MB	524kB		metadata	
15	82.3MB	99.1MB	16.8MB		misc	
16	99.1MB	116MB	16.8MB	ext4	persist	
17	116MB	119MB	3146kB		imgdata	
18	119MB	142MB	23.1MB		laf	
19	142MB	165MB	23.1MB		boot	
20	165MB	188MB	23.1MB		recovery	
21	188MB	191MB	3146kB		fsg	
22	191MB	192MB	524kB		fsc	
23	192MB	192MB	524kB		ssd	
24	192MB	193MB	524kB		DDR	
25	193MB	1267MB	1074MB	ext4	system	
26	1267MB	1298MB	31.5MB		crypto	
27	1298MB	2032MB	734MB	ext4	cache	
28	2032MB	31.3GB	29.2GB	ext4	userdata	
29	31.3GB	31.3GB	5632B		grow	

The list includes 29 partitions and recovery partition is one of them. The recovery ramdisk of recovery, it has a similar directory structure to the normal ramdisk. In the init script of recovery ramdisk, init starts the recovery program and it is the main process of the recovery mode. The recovery itself is the same as other native daemons in the Android system. The programming for recovery is part of the scope of Android system programming. The programming language and debug method for recovery is also the same as native Android applications. We will discuss this in more depth in the second part of this book.

The third-party open source projects derived from AOSP

As we know, AOSP source code is the major source that we can start to work with in system-level programming. Various silicon vendors usually work with Google to enable their reference platforms. This is a huge effort and they won't publish everything to the world except for their customers. This brings a limitation to the open source world. Since the AOSP source code is mainly for Google devices, such as emulator, Nexus, or Pixel series, there is no problem for developers who use Nexus devices as hardware reference platforms. How about other devices? Manufacturers may release the kernel source code for their devices, but nothing else. In the open source world, several third-party organizations provide solutions for this situation. We will have a brief look at the ones that we used in this book in the following sections.

LineageOS (CyanogenMod)

LineageOS is a community providing aftermarket firmware distribution for many popular Android devices. It is the successor to the highly popular CyanogenMod. If you cannot build the ROM for your devices from AOSP source code, you may look at LineageOS source code. Because there are many devices supported by LineageOS, many major third-party ROM images are built on top of its predecessor CyanogenMod. From the famous MIUI in China to the latest OnePlus device, they all use CyanogenMod source code as the base start from. The major contributions of LineageOS/CyanogenMod to the open source world are the adaptation of the Linux kernel and HAL to various Android devices.

 The source code of LineageOS is maintained in GitHub and you can find it at https://github.com/LineageOS.

To build LineageOS source code for your device, the overall build process is similar to the AOSP build. The key difference is the large number of devices supported by LineageOS. For each device, there is a web page to give information about how to build for a device. We use Nexus 5 as an example. You can go to the following page for detailed information:

https://wiki.lineageos.org/devices/hammerhead

In the information page, you can find information about how to download the ROM image, how to install the image, and how to build the image. There is a build guide for devices and we can find the build guide for Nexus 5 at `https://wiki.lineageos.org/devices/hammer head/build`.

To build LineageOS for Nexus 5, the two key elements are **Kernel** and **Device.** The Kernel includes the Linux kernel and Nexus 5-specific device drivers, while the Device includes the major part of the device-specific HAL code. The naming convention for both the Kernel and Device folder is `android_kernel/device_{manufacturer}_{code name}`.

The code name for Nexus 5 is **hammerhead** and the manufacturer is **lge,** which is LG.

We can find the following two Git repositories for Kernel and Device:
`https://github.com/LineageOS/android_kernel_lge_hammerhead`
`https://github.com/LineageOS/android_device_lge_hammerhead`

Other than the Kernel and Device, other important information is the LineageOS version. You may find it on the same device information page. For Nexus 5, the versions that can be used are 11, 12, 12.1, 13, and 14.1. You may be wondering how to match LineageOS versions to AOSP versions.

The information can be found at the following two pages at Wikipedia about CyanogenMod and LineageOS:
`https://en.wikipedia.org/wiki/CyanogenMod#Version_history`
`https://en.wikipedia.org/wiki/LineageOS#Version_history`

The LineageOS/CyanogenMod and AOSP versions supported for Nexus 5 are CM11 (Android 4.4), CM 12 (Android 5.0), CM 12.1 (Android 5.1), CM 13 (Android 6.0), and CM 14.1 (Android 7.1.1).

You will not be able to access the links related to CyanogenMod while you read this book, since the infrastructure behind CyanogenMod has been shut down recently. You can read the following post to find out more:
`https://plus.google.com/+CyanogenMod/posts/RYBfQ9rTjEH`

Nevertheless, the idea from the preceding configuration is that the key pieces of code to differentiate one device from another are the Kernel and Device. It is possible to share the rest of the code across devices. This is one of the goals for the projects in this book. We try to keep the changes for different hardware platforms within the Kernel and the Device, while keeping the rest of the AOSP source code untouched. This is not 100% possible, but we can try to do it as much as possible. The benefit is that we can keep our code separated from AOSP code and it is much easier to update to a new AOSP version.

Android-x86

While LineageOS/CyanogenMod provides excellent support for a large number of Android devices, many of these devices are ARM-based devices from various silicon vendors, such as Qualcomm, Samsung, MTK, and so on. Similarly, there is an open source community for Intel-based Android devices as well. This is another famous open source project, Android-x86. Even though the number of Intel x86-based Android devices on the market cannot compare to the number of ARM-based devices, there is another market using the Intel x86 Android build extensively. This is the Android emulator market. For commercial Android emulator products, you can find AMI DuOS, Genymotion, Andy, and so on.

The project Android-x86 uses a very different approach to support various Intel x86-based devices compared to LineageOS/CyanogenMod. Its goal is to provide **Board Support Package** (**BSP**) for any Intel x86 devices. It is similar to how you install Microsoft Windows or Linux on your PC. You have only one copy of the release and you can install it on any Intel PCs. There is no special build of Windows or Linux for each different PC or laptop.

To achieve this goal on Android, Android-x86 customized the Android boot up process significantly. There are two stages of boot up process in Android-x86. The first stage is booting up a minimal Linux environment using a special ramdisk--`initrd.img`. After the system can boot up to this Linux environment, it starts the second stage through the `chroot` or `switch_root` command. In this stage, it will boot up the actual Android system.

This is a very smart way to resolve the new challenge using existing technology. Essentially, we try to resolve the problem in two steps. In the first stage of the boot up process, since both Windows and Linux can boot on Intel x86 PCs without a dedicated build, you should be able to boot Linux on an Intel device without too much effort. This is exactly what the first stage of Android-x86 boot up does. After the minimal Linux system can run properly, this means the minimum set of hardware devices is initialized and you are able to debug or boot the rest of the system using this minimal Linux environment. In the second stage, a common Android image for Intel x86 can be started with limited hardware initialization. This approach can be used in the debugging of hardware devices as well. We will show how we can do the same thing on the Android emulator in this book.

The official website of the Android-x86 project is `http://www.android-x86.org/`. You can find the information about the Android-x86 project there. To build Android-x86, it is a little tricky to get the source code. The original source code was hosted at `http://git.android-x86.org` and it was maintained by volunteers from **Taiwan Linux User Group** (**TLUG**). It was valid for several years. However, it ceased to work from April 2015.

You can always find the latest status from the Google discussion group at `https://groups.google.com/forum/#!forum/android-x86`. There is an official announcement about the issue of `git.android-x86.org` at the discussion group from the maintainer Chih-Wei Huang. Later, the hosting was moved to SourceForge for a short period. However, issues retrieving source code from SourceForge have been reported again since July 2016. Currently, the source code is hosted at OSDN and you can search the announcement from Chih-Wei Huang on September 8, 2016 at the Android-x86 discussion group. Since most open source projects are maintained by volunteers, they may be up and down from time to time. It is always good to keep your own mirror of the projects that you work on. We will discuss this issue in this book as well so that you can have full control of your own work.

We know that many open source projects are related to each other and this is true for both Android-x86 and LineageOS/CyanogenMod as well. Starting from January 2016, Jaap Jan Meijer did the initial porting of CyanogenMod to Android-x86 and this makes CyanogenMod available on most Intel devices. If you are interested in this topic, you can search for `CM porting plan` in the Android-x86 discussion group.

CWM/CMR/TWRP

As a part of system-level programming, we introduced recovery in the previous section. The original recovery from AOSP only supports very limited functionalities so there are many third-party recovery projects.

ClockworkMod recovery (**CWM**) is one of the famous open source recovery projects, written by Koushik Dutta. Even though many people still use ClockworkMod recovery now, this project ceased development some time ago.

Another recovery project is **CyanogenMod recovery** (**CMR**). CMR is maintained by the CyanogenMod team and it is quite similar to ClockworkMod recovery.

TWRP or **TeamWin Recovery Project** is another very widely used custom recovery. It is fully touch-driven and has one of the most complete feature sets available. TWRP is the default recovery of OmniROM and its source code is hosted in GitHub as part of OmniROM at `https://github.com/omnirom/android_bootable_recovery/`.

Strategy of integration

In the preceding sections, we talked about Android architecture, AOSP, and third-party open source projects for Android. The software industry has been there for decades. There are so many existing source codes that can be reused and the need to create something from scratch is very rare. The porting and customization for a new platform is basically art of integration.

In this book, we will use the AOSP source code as the foundation and try to build everything on top of it. However, we may not be able to rely on AOSP source code only. In fact, we want to demonstrate how to support a platform that is not supported by AOSP. How are we going to do this? Do we create something from scratch? The answer is no. We will demonstrate how we can integrate all existing projects together to create a new platform. That's the reason why we discuss third-party open source projects.

In our case, VirtualBox is not supported by AOSP and we are going to enable it using AOSP and Android-x86. We need to use projects from both AOSP and Android-x86 to build a system for VirtualBox. However, our goal is to create a new build system for VirtualBox with minimal changes to the AOSP source code tree. This is also the goal of many other projects based on AOSP.

Based on the previous understanding, we have four categories of projects in our integration process:

- **The original unmodified AOSP projects**: In these kinds of projects, we will use AOSP projects without any changes.
- **The third-party projects**: In this category, the projects are added by the third-party projects and are not part of AOSP, so there are no changes involved as well.
- **Projects modified by both AOSP and one of the third-party projects**: This is complicated. We need to review the third-party changes and decide whether we want to include them in our system or not.
- **Projects modified by multiple open source projects and AOSP**: This is the most complicated case that we should avoid to integrate or change.

It is very easy to understand that we should try to reuse projects in category 1 and 2 as much as possible. The challenges and major work will be in category 3, while we should try to avoid category 4 whenever possible.

Virtual hardware reference platforms

The new Android releases usually come with two reference platforms. Developers can test the new Android releases on Android emulator first. This can be very useful in the preview stages. After the official release, the Google hardware platforms, such as Nexus or Pixel, usually become the devices for developers. The emulator and Nexus/Pixel builds are the earliest builds available in AOSP.

In this book, we will use Android emulator as the virtual hardware reference platform for our topics. Since the Android emulator build is already available in AOSP, you may wonder what we can do with it. Actually, we can customize an existing platform by adding new features to it. This is what OEM/ODM companies usually do using a reference platform from a silicon vendor. With Android emulator, we will demonstrate how to create a new device so that we can customize it. If you know any commercial emulator products, such as Genymotion and AMI DuOS, then you may know what features these products added to the emulator. We will extend Android emulator in a very similar way.

After we explore the topics about the customization of a new device, we will explore more advanced topics about porting. The major work with porting is the changes to the kernel and HAL. To discuss advanced topics about porting and debugging, we will also use VirtualBox as another virtual hardware reference platform. Even though VirtualBox has been used by many commercial emulator products, such as Genymotion, AMI DuOS, Leapdroid, and so on, it is not supported by AOSP directly. Most Android emulators for the PC are based on VirtualBox and they are designed for gamers to run Android games. In this book, we will learn how to create a similar build using various open source resources.

Introduction to the x86-based Android emulator

Android emulator has been changed dramatically as well in Android 4, 5, 6, and 7. Before Android 5, Android emulator was built on a virtual hardware reference board called goldfish.

The hardware specification of the goldfish virtual hardware platform can be found in the AOSP source tree at `$AOSP/platform/external/qemu/docs/GOLDFISH-VIRTUAL-HARDWARE.TXT`. In this book, we will refer to the AOSP root directory as `$AOSP`.

The goldfish virtual hardware platform was built on QEMU 1.x to emulate ARM devices on the x86 environment. The x86 host environments could be a Windows, Linux, or macOS X computer. Since the target device architecture is emulated using QEMU, the performance is poor. The emulator is very slow and difficult to use for application developers. However, QEMU is actively developed on the x86 architecture and widely used together with various virtualization technologies, such as VT-x, AMD-V, and so on.

Since Android 4.x, Intel developed an x86-based Android emulator using KVM on Linux and Intel HAXM for Windows and macOS X. With the introduction of virtualization technology to the emulator, the Intel x86-based emulator is much faster than the emulated one for the ARM or MIPS architecture. For the sake of Android application developers, Google officially integrated the Intel x86-based Android emulator to Android SDK. The Intel x86-based Android emulator has become the recommended choice for developers to test their Android applications.

Introduction to ranchu

With the introduction of Android 5 (Lollipop), the 64-bit hardware architecture is available for both ARM and Intel platforms. However, 64-bit hardware devices for Android were still under development at that time. The only choice for developers was to get a hardware reference platform from silicon vendors.

To help developers test their applications on 64-bit architecture, the engineers at Linaro did an excellent job enabling a virtual hardware platform on QEMU to test ARMv8-A 64-bit architecture. They gave this virtual hardware platform a code name, **ranchu**. You may refer to the blog at Linaro by Alex Bennée at `https://www.linaro.org/blog/core-dump/running-64bit-android-l-qemu/`.

This change was adopted by Google later and was used as the hardware reference platform for the next generation of Android emulators. If you install the Android SDK images, you can see two kernel images starting from Android 5. The kernel image `kernel-qemu` is the image to be used with the goldfish virtual hardware platform and the image `kernel-ranchu` is the image to be used with the ranchu virtual hardware platform.

To respond to this change, both Intel and MIPS worked on their architectures to support their 64-bit hardware emulation in ranchu. You can refer to the group discussions at `https://groups.google.com/forum/#!topic/android-emulator-dev/dltBnUW_HzU`.

The ranchu hardware platform is based on a newer QEMU version and the architecture is changed to have less dependency on Google modification and goldfish-specific devices. For example, it uses virtio-block devices to emulate the NAND and SD card. This has the potential of providing much better performance and also makes it possible to utilize the features provided by the latest QEMU code base. The ranchu kernel is built on a new version in the `android-goldfish-3.10` branch, while the latest goldfish kernel is in the `android-goldfish-3.4` branch. You can notice this difference by running your Android virtual device using different kernels from Android SDK.

VirtualBox-based Android emulators

With the ever evolving nature of virtualization technology, there are many commercial Android emulator products developed on the market as well. You may have heard of some of them such as Genymotion, AMIDuOS, Andy, BlueStacks, and so on. Many of them are built using VirtualBox from Oracle, such as Genymotion, AMIDuOS, and Andy. The reason that VirtualBox is used instead of other solutions such as VMware is because VirtualBox is an open source solution.

To achieve the best performance and user experience, both host and target need to be customized in the commercial emulator products. Besides Android emulator, we will also use VirtualBox as the virtual hardware platform to demonstrate how to port Android to a new platform. The reason that we need another virtual hardware platform in this book is because Android emulator is already supported in AOSP. We will use Android emulator as a platform to teach how to extend and customize an existing platform. While VirtualBox is not supported in AOSP, it can be used as a target platform to teach how to port Android to a new platform. Even though Android has been ported to VirtualBox by Genymotion, AMI, and others, none of them are open source products.

Summary

In this chapter, we discussed what Android system programming is and the scope involved in system-level programming in this book. After that, we took an overview of the Android system architecture and talked about the layers that we will focus on in this book. We also discussed the virtual hardware platforms that we use in this book. In this book, we use the code from various third-party projects, so we also took a brief overview of each of them in this chapter. In the next chapter, we will start to learn about the development environment setup for Android system programming. This includes both development tools and the source code repository setup.

2
Setting Up the Development Environment

After the introduction about system programming in the last chapter, we need to set up a development environment first before we can go further. We need to know how to build and test **Android Open Source Project** (**AOSP**) while we explore various Android system programming topics in this book. We will cover the following topics in this chapter:

- Installing the Android SDK and setting up an Android Virtual Device
- Setting up the AOSP build environment and building a testing image
- Creating your own source code repository mirror

Summary of Android versions

Since we will use Android emulator as one of the virtual hardware platforms, we need to use one particular Android version throughout this book. At the time of writing, the latest Android version is Android 7 (Nougat). We will use Android 7 throughout the book. I started work on this book with Android 6, so the source code for Android 6 is also available in my GitHub repository at `https://github.com/shugaoye`.

From the first release to Android 7, both the development environment and the AOSP source code have been changed a lot. We will have a brief look at various Android versions first before we talk about the development environment setup.

To set up the AOSP build environment, there are two things that you need to pay special attention to the host environment and Java SDK. Even though the recommended host environment is Ubuntu running on Intel architecture, the hardware architecture and Ubuntu versions have changed from release to release. You can always refer to the following URL at Google for the latest AOSP build environment setup:

```
https://source.android.com/source/index.html
```

For Gingerbread (2.3.x) and above, a 64-bit build environment is required. For older versions, the build environment is 32-bit systems.

The Ubuntu versions used range from Ubuntu 10.04 to 14.04, but for each release there is a recommended Ubuntu version. If it is a new setup, it is suggested to use the recommended Ubuntu version to make the job easier. However, there are no hard requirements here. You should be able to use any Ubuntu version higher than the recommended Ubuntu version. There are also many articles about how to set up the AOSP build using a different Linux distribution such as RedHat or Debain.

Oracle JDK was used to build AOSP until Lollipop. From Lollipop and the above, OpenJDK was used instead of Oracle JDK.

The following table summarizes all Android releases, required hosts, and JDK environments until Nougat; you can refer to it for full details.

AOSP releases:

Nickname	AOSP	SDK API level	Host	JDK	OS/Ubuntu	Goldfish	Ranchu
Cupcake	1.5	3	x86	Oracle JDK 5	10.04	x	
Donut	1.6	4	x86	Oracle JDK 5	10.04	x	
Eclair	2.0/2.1	5	x86	Oracle JDK 5	10.04	x	
Eclair	2.0.1	6	x86	Oracle JDK 5	10.04	x	
Eclair	2.1	7	x86	Oracle JDK 5	10.04	x	
Froyo	2.2	8	x86	Oracle JDK 5	10.04	x	
Gingerbread	2.3.1	9	x64	Oracle JDK 6	12.04	x	
Gingerbread	2.3.3	10	x64	Oracle JDK 6	12.04	x	
Honeycomb	3.0	11	x64	Oracle JDK 6	12.04	x	

Honeycomb	3.1	12	x64	Oracle JDK 6	12.04	x	
Honeycomb	3.2	13	x64	Oracle JDK 6	12.04	x	
Ice Cream Sandwich	4.0	14	x64	Oracle JDK 6	12.04	x	
Ice Cream Sandwich	4.0.3	15	x64	Oracle JDK 6	12.04	x	
Jelly Bean	4.1.2	16	x64	Oracle JDK 6	12.04	x	
Jelly Bean	4.2.2	17	x64	Oracle JDK 6	12.04	x	
Jelly Bean	4.3.1	18	x64	Oracle JDK 6	12.04	x	
KitKat	4.4.2	19	x64	Oracle JDK 6	12.04	x	x
KitKat	4.4W.2	20	x64	Oracle JDK 6	12.04	x	x
Lollipop	5.0.1	21	x64	Open JDK 7	12.04	x	x
Lollipop	5.1.1	22	x64	Open JDK 7	12.04	x	x
Mashmallow	6.0	23	x64	Open JDK 7	14.04	x	x
Nougat	7.0.x	24	x64	Open JDK 8	14.04	x	x
Nougat	7.1.1	25	x64	Open JDK 8	14.04	x	x

From the preceding table, you can see that the ranchu emulator is supported by KitKat and the others. If you install and download the system image of Kitkat or the others on Android SDK, you should be able to find two kernel files, `kernel-qemu` and `kernel-ranchu`.

There are two API levels in the Nougat releases. Android 7.0.0 and 7.1.0 are API level 24. Android 7.1.1 and 7.1.2 are API level 25. All source code in this book can support up to API level 25.

 The code name of the original Android emulator is goldfish. It is based on an older version of QEMU. A new Android emulator version was released based on QEMU 2.x in 2016. The code name of this new emulator is ranchu. It is supported by KitKat and the others.

Installing Android SDK and setting up an Android Virtual Device

Ideally, if you have an AOSP build environment, you can build everything including Android SDK from scratch. However, it is much more convenient to have an Android SDK installation to help with virtual device creation or running emulator images.

You can always download the latest Android SDK from the following website:

```
https://developer.android.com/index.html
```

The host environment that we use in this book is Ubuntu 14.04. Download the Android SDK for Linux and decompress it to a folder in your Home directory.

The tools in Android SDK have been changed since API level 25. You may use an older version of Android SDK or the latest Android SDK so I gave the instructions for both cases here.

Creating AVD in an older version of SDK

For the older version of SDK, such as `android-sdk_r24.4.1-linux.tgz`, it includes all necessary components and we can use it after decompression. We can find the following contents after decompressing:

```
$ ls android-sdk-linux
add-ons        platforms       SDK Readme.txt  temp
build-tools    platform-tools  system-images   tools
```

You can add the `platform-tools` and `tools` directory to your `PATH` environment variable.

We will use a virtual device based on API level 25 in this book to test our image.

To create a virtual device, we can launch **Android Virtual Device** (**AVD**) Manager using the following command, as shown in the following screenshot:

```
$ android avd
```

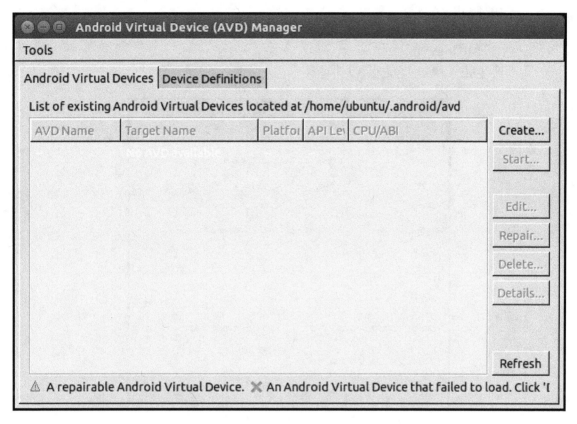

AVD Manager

Click the **Create...** button in AVD Manager and create a new virtual device named `a25x86` with the following configuration, as shown in the following screenshot:

- Android 7.1.1 - API level 25
- 1024 MB RAM
- 400 MB SD card
- 400 MB internal storage
- Display size at 480 x 800: hdpi

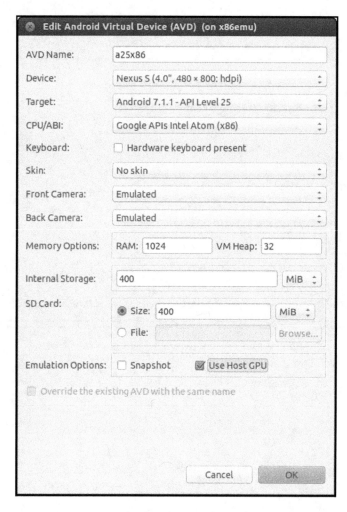

Android Virtual Device a25x86

Creating AVD in the latest version of SDK

For the newer versions, there is only SDK command-line tools available for download. For example, if you download the command-line tools for r25, such as `tools_r25.2.3-linux.zip`, you can find the `tools` folder only. In this case, you need to use Android SDK Manager at `tools/bin/sdkmanager` to download the rest of SDK components. To download the rest of SDK components, you can use the following command:

```
$ sdkmanager --update
```

If you use the latest version of Android SDK, you may get the following error message, if you follow the previous instructions:

```
$ android avd
********************************************************************
The "android" command is deprecated.
For manual SDK, AVD, and project management, please use Android Studio.
For command-line tools, use tools/bin/sdkmanager and tools/bin/avdmanager
********************************************************************
Invalid or unsupported command "avd"

Supported commands are:
android list target
android list avd
android list device
android create avd
android move avd
android delete avd
android list sdk
android update sdk
```

In this case, you can create AVD using the following command.

```
$ avdmanager create avd -n a25x86 --tag google_apis -k 'system-
images;android-25;google_apis;x86'
Auto-selecting single ABI x86
Do you wish to create a custom hardware profile? [no]
```

Testing the goldfish emulator

In Android 7, both the ranchu and goldfish emulators are supported. Let's test the goldfish emulator first. We can run this virtual device in the goldfish emulator using the following command:

```
$ emulator @a25x86 -verbose -show-kernel -shell -engine classic
```

```
emulator:Found AVD name 'a25x86'
emulator:Found AVD target architecture: x86
emulator:Looking for emulator-x86 to emulate 'x86' CPU
. . .
   kernel.path = /home/roger/android-sdk-linux/system-images/android-
   25/default/x86/kernel-qemu
. . .
```

To monitor the status of a virtual device, we can use the following Android emulator options:

- `-verbose`: Shows the emulator debug information.
- `-show-kernel`: Shows kernel debug information.
- `-shell`: Uses `stdio` as the command line prompt.
- `-engine`: Selects the emulator engine. The choice can be `auto`, `classic`, or `qemu2`. The `classic` option is to use the goldfish emulator and the `qemu2` option is to use the ranchu emulator. If the option is `auto` or without the `engine` option, the system will check the environment and try to launch ranchu first. If it fails, it will fall back to goldfish.

From the preceding log, we can see that the `kernel-qemu` kernel file is used for the goldfish emulator.

Both the ranchu and goldfish emulators are developed on top of QEMU, but they use different kernel and QEMU versions. We can verify the QEMU version used for either goldfish or ranchu using the following emulator commands.

To verify the QEMU version used by goldfish, we can run the following command:

```
$ emulator -engine classic -qemu -version
QEMU PC emulator version 0.10.50 Android, Copyright (c) 2003-2008 Fabrice
Bellard
```

From the preceding output, we can see that QEMU version 0.10.50 is used for the goldfish emulator.

For the latest emulator version, it seems there is a bug with regard to handling the classic engine. You may get the following error message, when you execute the preceding command:

```
$ emulator -engine classic -qemu -version
emulator: ERROR: android_qemud_get_serial_line: can't create charpipe to
serial port
```

The emulator command is a wrapper for QEMU. Any command-line options after –qemu are passed to QEMU as the command lines of QEMU directly.

To find out the emulator version, we can use the following command:

`$ emulator -version`

The following command will show the QEMU version:

`$ emulator -qemu -version`

After the Android device has started successfully, from the Android UI, we can go to **Settings -> About Phone** and see the screen shown in the following screenshot:

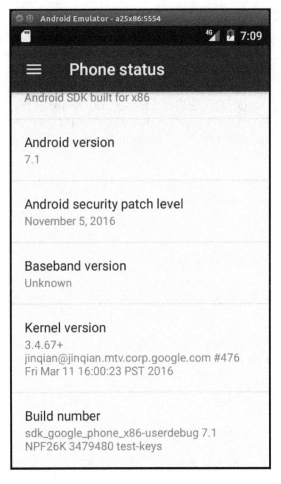

Android kernel version of goldfish

Pay attention to the following information on the **About Phone** screen:

- **Android version: 7.1**
- **Kernel version: 3.4.67**
- **Build number: sdk_google_phone_x86-userdebug 7.1 NPF26K 3479480 test-keys**

As we can see from the preceding information, the kernel version is 3.4.67 and the filesystem build number is sdk_google_phone_x86-userdebug 7.1 NPF26K 3479480 test-keys for goldfish emulator. In the next section, we can see that ranchu emulator uses a different kernel version, even though both emulators share the same filesystem.

The Android system build includes two parts: the AOSP system and an Android-compatible Linux kernel. The build result of the AOSP system includes all image files for the Android system except the kernel image. They are built separately and are also under difference licenses. The preferred license for the AOSP is the Apache Software License, while the Linux kernel is under the GPLv2 License. Be aware of this difference. It also means that the AOSP build doesn't include the kernel build. We have to build the kernel separately. We can also use different kernel images with the same filesystem as in the test of the goldfish and ranchu emulator.

When we talk about the Android version, we have to look into the details of the kernel version and filesystem build number.

Testing ranchu emulator

We can test ranchu emulator as well with the same virtual device. We can use a similar command without the -engine option or with the -engine qemu2 option to start ranchu emulator:

```
$ emulator @a25x86 -verbose -show-kernel -shell
emulator:Found AVD name 'a25x86'
emulator:Found AVD target architecture: x86
emulator:  Found directory: /home/roger/android-sdk-linux/system-
images/android-25/default/x86/

emulator:Probing for /home/roger/android-sdk-linux/system-
images/android-25/default/x86//kernel-ranchu: file exists
emulator:Auto-config: -engine qemu2 (based on configuration)
emulator:Found target-specific 64-bit emulator binary: /home/roger/android-
sdk-linux/tools/qemu/linux-x86_64/qemu-system-i386
...
```

From the preceding log, we can see that the kernel file `kernel-ranchu` is used in ranchu emulator.

We can also verify the QEMU version used by ranchu emulator using the following command:

```
$ emulator -qemu -version
QEMU emulator version 2.2.0 , Copyright (c) 2003-2008 Fabrice Bellard
```

We can see that ranchu uses a much newer QEMU version that can support many new features, which we will discuss later in this book.

Again, let's review the version information in **Settings** as we did for goldfish emulator; refer to the following screenshot:

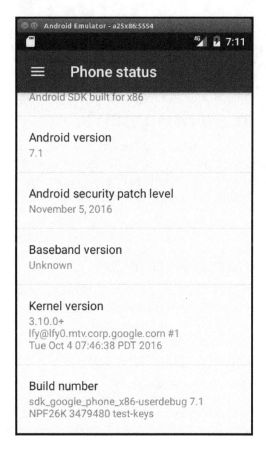

Android kernel version of ranchu

We can see that the ranchu emulator uses the kernel version 3.10.0, which is different from the goldfish emulator. The filesystem build is the same as for the goldfish emulator.

The AOSP build environment and the Android emulator build

In order to create our own Android system, we have to set up the AOSP build environment and build our own AOSP target for the Android emulator. Since Android is under rapid development, the build process and environment setup can change from time to time. You can always refer to Google's website for the latest information, `https://source.android.com/source/building.html`.

While the Google website and other sources can give general guidelines and procedures about the AOSP build, in this section we will look specifically at how to build AOSP for Android emulator image for API level 25.

The AOSP build environment

Since we want to set up a build environment for API level 25, you can refer to the table of AOSP releases for the basic requirements about the host and JDK. It is recommended to use the Ubuntu 14.04 64-bit host with Open JDK 8. For the hardware requirement, you may want to have a powerful enough computer with at least 8 GB RAM and 500 GB hard disk space.

Installing the required packages

We use the Ubuntu 14.04 64-bit version as our host operating system. After installing Ubuntu 14.04, the first thing you have to do is to install all necessary software packages as follows. If you use a different Linux distribution, you can refer to Google's website or search on the Internet for the relevant setup procedures. Let's execute the following commands to install all necessary packages for Ubuntu 14.04:

```
$ sudo apt-get install git-core gnupg flex bison gperf build-essential\
  zip curl zlib1g-dev gcc-multilib g++-multilib libc6-dev-i386\
  lib32ncurses5-dev x11proto-core-dev libx11-dev lib32z-dev ccache\
  libgl1-mesa-dev libxml2-utils xsltproc unzip
```

Installing Open JDK 7 and 8

We will install both Open JDK 7 and 8 so we can build both Android 6 and 7 in our build environment.

To build Android API level 23, we need to install OpenJDK 7. We can execute the following commands from the Linux console to install OpenJDK 7:

```
$ sudo apt-get update
$ sudo apt-get install openjdk-7-jdk
```

For Android 7, we need to use OpenJDK 8 to build. There are no available supported OpenJDK 8 packages for Ubuntu 14.04 yet, but the Ubuntu 15.04 OpenJDK 8 packages have been used successfully with Ubuntu 14.04. We need to install OpenJDK 8 on Ubuntu 14.04 using the following instructions.

Download the .deb packages for 64-bit architecture from archive.ubuntu.com:

```
openjdk-8-jre-headless_8u45-b14-1_amd64.deb with SHA256
0f5aba8db39088283b51e00054813063173a4d8809f70033976f83e214ab56c0
openjdk-8-jre_8u45-b14-1_amd64.deb with SHA256
9ef76c4562d39432b69baf6c18f199707c5c56a5b4566847df908b7d74e15849
openjdk-8-jdk_8u45-b14-1_amd64.deb with SHA256
6e47215cf6205aa829e6a0a64985075bd29d1f428a4006a80c9db371c2fc3c4c
```

Optionally, confirm the checksums of the downloaded files against the SHA256 string listed with each preceding package.

For example, with the *sha256sum* tool:

```
$ sha256sum {downloaded.deb file}
```

Install the packages:

```
$ sudo apt-get update
```

Run dpkg for each of the .deb files you downloaded. It may produce errors due to missing dependencies:

```
$ sudo dpkg -i {downloaded.deb file}
```

To fix missing dependencies:

```
$ sudo apt-get -f install
```

With both OpenJDK 7 and 8 installed, we can update the default Java version by running the following commands:

```
$ sudo update-alternatives --config java
$ sudo update-alternatives --config javac
```

We have a build environment ready now. You may want to refer to Google's website to set up other things. For example, we may want to use cache to speed up the build or set up a separate output directory out of the AOSP tree.

Downloading the AOSP source

Once we have a build environment ready, we need to get the AOSP source code. Again, refer to Google's website or the Internet to get more information.

You need to download the Android 7 source code from `source.android.com`.

Installing repo

AOSP consists of a large number of Git repositories, and we have to use the repo tool to manage these Git repositories. To download and install repo, we can use the following commands:

```
$ mkdir ~/bin
$ PATH=~/bin:$PATH
$ curl https://storage.googleapis.com/git-repo-downloads/repo > ~/bin/repo
$ chmod a+x ~/bin/repo
```

Initializing a repo client and downloading the AOSP source tree

After we have the repo tool, we can initialize the repo and download the AOSP source tree by executing the following commands:

```
$ repo init -u https://android.googlesource.com/platform/manifest -b
android-7.1.1_r4
$ repo sync
```

Pay attention to the AOSP tag `android-7.1.1_r4` here. This is the version of AOSP source code that we use throughout this book.

It will take quite a long time to get the AOSP source tree. After we get the source tree, let's take a look at the top level folders:

```
$ ls -F
abi/        cts/         docs/        libcore/           packages/  tools/
art/        dalvik/      external/    libnativehelper/   pdk/
bionic      developers   filelist     Makefile           prebuilts
bootable    development  frameworks   ndk                sdk
build       device       hardware     out                system
```

I won't explore the details about the source tree here; we will cover this in `Chapter 3`, *Discovering Kernel, HAL, and Virtual Hardware*.

Building AOSP Android emulator images

In this book, we will use x86-based emulators. The x86-based emulator can use virtualization technology on the host, so it is much faster than the ARM emulator. We want to build the one that comes with the AOSP source code first. To create an Android emulator build, we can execute the following commands from the AOSP top-level folder:

```
$ . build/envsetup.sh
including device/generic/mini-emulator-arm64/vendorsetup.sh
including device/generic/mini-emulator-armv7-a-neon/vendorsetup.sh
including device/generic/mini-emulator-mips/vendorsetup.sh
including device/generic/mini-emulator-x86_64/vendorsetup.sh
including device/generic/mini-emulator-x86/vendorsetup.sh
including sdk/bash_completion/adb.bash
$ lunch

You're building on Linux

Lunch menu... pick a combo:
     1. aosp_arm-eng
     2. aosp_arm64-eng
     3. aosp_mips-eng
     4. aosp_mips64-eng
     5. aosp_x86-eng
     6. aosp_x86_64-eng
     7. mini_emulator_arm64-userdebug
     8. m_e_arm-userdebug
     9. mini_emulator_mips-userdebug
    10. mini_emulator_x86_64-userdebug
    11. mini_emulator_x86-userdebug

Which would you like? [aosp_arm-eng] 5
```

```
================================================
PLATFORM_VERSION_CODENAME=REL
PLATFORM_VERSION=7.1.1
TARGET_PRODUCT=aosp_x86
TARGET_BUILD_VARIANT=eng
TARGET_BUILD_TYPE=release
TARGET_BUILD_APPS=
TARGET_ARCH=x86
TARGET_ARCH_VARIANT=x86
TARGET_CPU_VARIANT=
TARGET_2ND_ARCH=
TARGET_2ND_ARCH_VARIANT=
TARGET_2ND_CPU_VARIANT=
HOST_ARCH=x86_64
HOST_2ND_ARCH=x86
HOST_OS=linux
HOST_OS_EXTRA=Linux-4.2.0-27-generic-x86_64-with-Ubuntu-14.04-trusty
HOST_CROSS_OS=windows
HOST_CROSS_ARCH=x86
HOST_CROSS_2ND_ARCH=x86_64
HOST_BUILD_TYPE=release
BUILD_ID=NMF260
OUT_DIR=out
================================================
```

We set up the environment variables first using the startup script `envsetup.sh`. After that, we execute the command `lunch` to choose a build target. To build for the Android-x86 emulator, we can choose the target `aosp_x86-eng`, which will build an Android emulator version for x86. To learn more about the script file `envsetup.sh` and command `lunch`, refer to the Google website at `https://source.android.com`.

The actual build is started after we execute the following `make` command:

```
$ make -j4
================================================
PLATFORM_VERSION_CODENAME=REL
PLATFORM_VERSION=7.1.1
TARGET_PRODUCT=aosp_x86
TARGET_BUILD_VARIANT=eng
TARGET_BUILD_TYPE=release
TARGET_BUILD_APPS=
TARGET_ARCH=x86
TARGET_ARCH_VARIANT=x86
TARGET_CPU_VARIANT=
TARGET_2ND_ARCH=
TARGET_2ND_ARCH_VARIANT=
TARGET_2ND_CPU_VARIANT=
```

```
HOST_ARCH=x86_64
HOST_OS=linux
HOST_OS_EXTRA=Linux-4.2.0-27-generic-x86_64-with-Ubuntu-14.04-trusty
HOST_BUILD_TYPE=release
BUILD_ID=MOB30M
OUT_DIR=out
============================================
including ./abi/cpp/Android.mk ...
including ./art/Android.mk ...
...
make_ext4fs -S out/target/product/generic_x86/root/file_contexts -l
576716800 -a system
out/target/product/generic_x86/obj/PACKAGING/systemimage_intermediates/syst
em.img out/target/product/generic_x86/system
+ make_ext4fs -S out/target/product/generic_x86/root/file_contexts -l
576716800 -a system
out/target/product/generic_x86/obj/PACKAGING/systemimage_intermediates/syst
em.img out/target/product/generic_x86/system
Creating filesystem with parameters:
    Size: 576716800
    Block size: 4096
    Blocks per group: 32768
    Inodes per group: 7040
    Inode size: 256
    Journal blocks: 2200
    Label:
    Blocks: 140800
    Block groups: 5
    Reserved block group size: 39
Created filesystem with 1277/35200 inodes and 82235/140800 blocks
+ '[' 0 -ne 0 ']'
Install system fs image: out/target/product/generic_x86/system.img
out/target/product/generic_x86/system.img+ maxsize=588791808 blocksize=2112
    total=576716800 reserve=5947392
```

The entire build time is dependent on your hardware configuration. Even on a high-end CORE i7 Intel processor, it may take about 40 minutes. The option −j4 starts the parallel build using four processor cores. You can choose the number according to your computer hardware.

Testing AOSP images

After the build is completed, we find all images in the output folder, as shown in the following screenshot:

```
 ● ● ●    sgye@x86emu: ~/vol1/android
TARGET_CPU_VARIANT=
TARGET_2ND_ARCH=
TARGET_2ND_ARCH_VARIANT=
TARGET_2ND_CPU_VARIANT=
HOST_ARCH=x86_64
HOST_2ND_ARCH=x86
HOST_OS=linux
HOST_OS_EXTRA=Linux-4.2.0-27-generic-x86_64-with-Ubuntu-14.04-trusty
HOST_CROSS_OS=windows
HOST_CROSS_ARCH=x86
HOST_CROSS_2ND_ARCH=x86_64
HOST_BUILD_TYPE=release
BUILD_ID=NMF26O
OUT_DIR=out
============================================
sgye@x86emu:~/vol1/android$ ls $OUT
android-info.txt       gen                      root
build_fingerprint.txt  installed-files.txt      symbols
cache                  module-info.json         system
cache.img              obj                      system.img
clean_steps.mk         previous_build_config.mk userdata.img
data                   ramdisk.img
dex_bootjars           recovery
sgye@x86emu:~/vol1/android$ █
```

Build output of generic_x86

The AOSP build output is stored under the $AOSP/out folder. This folder includes the build results for both target and host. The build results for different devices are stored separately at $AOSP/out/target/product/{device name}. In our case, it is $AOSP/out/target/product/generic_x86.

The images system.img, userdata.img, and ramdisk.img are necessary to run the emulator, but as you can see there is no kernel image. We will discuss kernel builds later in this book. For now, we will use the kernel image from Android SDK to test our AOSP build.

To test using our AOSP images, we can create a script as follows:

```
#!/bin/sh

emulator @a25x86 -verbose -show-kernel -system $OUT/system.img -ramdisk
$OUT/ramdisk.img -initdata $OUT/userdata.img
```

We can put this script `test_aosp.sh` in the `$HOME/bin` folder. Usually, we can add `$HOME/bin` to the executable search `path` variable so that we can run this script `test_aosp.sh` from the command line as follows:

```
$ test_aosp.sh
```

If you test your AOSP build using Android 6 or earlier, you need to use classic engines instead of ranchu. The ranchu build has a problem in the Android 6 AOSP build, but this issue has been fixed in the Android 7 build. To support ranchu in the 6.0.1 AOSP build, we have to change the manifest to include the latest emulator device. The Android SDK release doesn't have this issue. Google fixed this issue internally, but didn't publish the fixes until Android 7.

After the emulator starts, we can check the version information as we did before. In the following screenshot, we can see the version information in AOSP images:

Android version of AOSP image

As we can see, kernel version 3.10.0 is used; this is because we use the ranchu emulator. Let's compare the information with SDK images that we tested before. From the following table, we can see that the model number is **AOSP on IA Emulator** instead of **sdk**. The Android version is 7.1 for SDK and 7.1.1 for AOSP. The AOSP image build number is the build target `aosp_x86-eng`, which we chose previously, and this also includes the date and time of the build.

SDK and AOSP versions:

	SDK (goldfish)	SDK (ranchu)	AOSP
Model	sdk	sdk	AOSP on IA Emulator
Android version	7.1	7.1	7.1.1
Kernel version	3.4.67	3.10.0	3.10.0
Build number	sdk_google_phone_x86-userdebug 7.1 NPF26K 3479480 test-keys	sdk_google_phone_x86-userdebug 7.1 NPF26K 3479480 test-keys	aosp_x86-eng 7.1.1 NMF26O eng.sgye 20170126.183237 test-keys

Creating your own repository mirror

It usually takes a very long time to download the AOSP source code. After you have downloaded the AOSP source code, you have actually downloaded a specific version of the AOSP source code from the remote repository. You may have to test different configurations or versions in your development work. It is a very time-consuming task to switch to a different version or create a new copy of the AOSP source code.

In this book, we will use the AOSP source code as the base for our development. To reuse some of the existing open source projects that are not included in AOSP, we have to modify the repo manifest from time to time. This involves changing the repo configuration. To work more efficiently, we can use a local mirror. It can save a lot of time to create a local mirror instead of downloading source code from remote repositories for all configuration changes. It may take hours to change a configuration from a remote repository, but it will need just a few minutes with the local repository.

When we work with open source projects, the server to host the project may change from time to time. It is always good to have your own mirror so that we won't rely too much on the remote repositories. With a local mirror, we can still work without too much impact even though the remote server may be not available for a certain period. This is exactly the issue that I face when I try to integrate Android-x86 projects in the later part of this book.

I will explain how to create a mixed local mirror of AOSP, Android-x86, and GitHub in this section.

Repo and manifest

To create and manage repository mirrors, we need to understand the `repo` command and the directory structure managed by `repo` a little more. The `repo` command deals with a XML file manifest and it stores everything in a folder called `.repo`.

After we run the `repo init` command as we did in the previous section, a `.repo` folder is created under the current folder. If we take a look at the `.repo` folder, we can see the following contents:

```
$ ls -F .repo
manifests/  manifests.git/  manifest.xml@  repo/
```

Three folders and a symbolic link are created. The following is an explanation of each:

- `manifests`: This is a working copy of the Git repository of the manifest itself.
- `manifests.git`: This is the Git repository of the manifest. The manifest itself is under the version control using Git.
- `manifest.xml`: This is a symbolic link to the file `.repo/manifests/default.xml`. This file is the main configuration file used by `repo`. We will look into the details later.
- `repo`: The repo tool itself is written in the Python language. Python scripts are stored in this folder.

After we run the `repo init` command to initialize the repo data structure, we can run the `repo sync` command to retrieve a working copy. If we look at the `.repo` folder again after the `repo sync` command, we can see that there are two project related folders created:

```
$ ls -F .repo
manifests/       manifest.xml@  project-objects/  repo/
manifests.git/   project.list   projects/
```

The following is an explanation of the newly created file and folders:

- `project.list`: This is a list of all projects downloaded.
- `project-objects`: This is a copy of the remote repository.
- `projects`: This is the repository hierarchy matching the working copy. The path may be rearranged after a repository is copied to local. The contents in this folder are symbolic links to the items in `project-objects`.

The most important file in the `.repo` folder is `.repo/manifests/default.xml` or its symbolic link `manifest.xml`. The detailed specification of this file can be found in the document under the `.repo` folder at `.repo/repo/docs/manifest-format.txt`. We won't go into any details, but let's take look at the most commonly used elements.

```xml
<?xml version="1.0" encoding="UTF-8"?>
<manifest>

  <remote   name="aosp"
            fetch=".." />
  <default  revision="refs/tags/android-7.1.1_r4"
            remote="aosp"
            sync-j="4" />

  <project path="build" name="platform/build" groups="pdk" >
    <copyfile src="core/root.mk" dest="Makefile" />
  </project>
  <project path="abi/cpp" name="platform/abi/cpp" groups="pdk" />
  <project path="art" name="platform/art" groups="pdk" />
  <project path="bionic" name="platform/bionic" groups="pdk" />
...
</manifest>
```

In the preceding code snippet, we can see that there are three XML elements inside manifest:

- `remote`: The `remote` element provides the details about remote repository. We can give it a name such as `aosp`. The URL of the remote repository can be specified in the `fetch` field. It can be a relative path or a full path.
- `default`: There are multiple `remote` elements that can be specified in manifest. The `default` element defines which `remote` is the default one.

- `project`: Each `project` element defines a Git repository. The `path` field supplies the local path after it is downloaded. The `name` field supplies the remote path of the Git repository. The `revision` field supplies the branch that we want to get and the `remote` field tells us which remote server we use to get the Git repository.

There are other XML elements that can be used in manifest as well. You can find out what they are by looking at the preceding specification yourself.

Using a local mirror for AOSP

If you refer to the article from the Google website about downloading the source, you can find a section called *Using a local mirror*. It reveals that if you need two different configurations of the AOSP build environment, the download for two clients is larger than the size of a full mirror of the repository. It is very simple to set up a mirror as follows:

```
$ mkdir -p /usr/local/mirror/aosp
$ cd /usr/local/mirror/aosp
$ repo init -u https://android.googlesource.com/mirror/manifest --mirror
$ repo sync
```

From the preceding commands, we can see that we actually use a different manifest to create a mirror. If we look at the content of the manifest for a mirror, we can see the following XML code:

```
<?xml version="1.0" encoding="UTF-8"?>
<manifest>
  <remote  name="aosp"
           fetch=".." />
  <default revision="master"
           remote="aosp"
           sync-j="4" />
  <project name="accessories/manifest" />
  <project name="brillo/manifest" />
...
</manifest>
```

We can see that for all projects, there are only the project names without other information in each project item. This is because we actually copy each Git repository to the local as a bare Git repository. We won't check out a working copy, so we don't need to worry about the version.

If we look at the manifest to check out a working copy, we will see the following:

```
<?xml version="1.0" encoding="UTF-8"?>
<manifest>

  <remote  name="aosp"
           fetch=".." />
  <default revision="refs/tags/android-6.0.1_r61"
           remote="aosp"
           sync-j="4" />

  <project path="build" name="platform/build" groups="pdk" >
    <copyfile src="core/root.mk" dest="Makefile" />
  </project>
  <project path="abi/cpp" name="platform/abi/cpp" groups="pdk" />
  <project path="art" name="platform/art" groups="pdk" />
...
</manifest>
```

It includes more items than the one to create a mirror. The name field specifies the path at the remote repository and the path field specifies the local path after the repository is downloaded to the local. We also need to specify revision that we want to retrieve.

After we have a mirror, we can check out a copy of the AOSP source from that mirror as follows:

```
$ mkdir -p $HOME/aosp/master
$ cd $HOME/aosp/master
$ repo init -u /usr/local/mirror/aosp/platform/manifest.git
$ repo sync
```

If you need, you can check out multiple copies from the local mirror. No matter if you check out multiple copies or you change to a different version, you can save a lot of time compared to checking out from a remote repository.

When you work on a system-level project, you may need projects out of the AOSP source. For example, in this book, we use multiple projects from CyanogenMod, Android-x86, and my own projects in GitHub. In this case, we can actually create our own manifest to mix all projects that we need together from our local mirror. Our local mirror will become a superset of the public mirror. We can create branches and tags from time to time in local repositories, but we only push the baselines that we want to release to the public repositories. This is exactly what the Google development team does in their private repositories.

Creating your own mirror of GitHub

All source code used in this book is stored in GitHub. We also use source from other projects in GitHub, because many open source projects are hosted on GitHub, such as CyanogenMod, OmniROM, Team Win Recovery, and so on. We can create a mirror for all projects that we have used in local storage so that we can commit any changes and create our own baselines. If you want to make changes to any projects that are not owned by yourself, you can create your own copy using the **Fork** function of GitHub.

To create your own manifest for GitHub, you can create a repository in GitHub, call it `mirror`, and then add an XML file called `default.xml` to it as follows:

```xml
<?xml version="1.0" encoding="UTF-8"?>
<manifest>

  <remote   name="cm"
            fetch="git://github.com/CyanogenMod"
            review="review.cyanogenmod.org"
            revision="refs/heads/cm-13.0" />

  <remote   name="twrp"
            fetch="git://github.com/TeamWin"
            revision="master" />

  <remote   name="omnirom"
            fetch="https://github.com/omnirom" />

  <remote   name="github"
            fetch=".." />
  <default revision="master"
            remote="github"
            sync-j="4" />

  <!-- configuration of github repositories v1.0 -->
  <project name="manifests" />
  <project name="manifest" />
  <project name="mirror" />
  <project name="local_manifests" />
...
  <!-- CyanogenMod -->
  <project name="android_bootable_recovery" remote="cm" />
  <project name="android_external_busybox" remote="cm" />
  <project name="android" remote="cm" />

  <!-- Team Win Recovery Project -->
  <project name="Team-Win-Recovery-Project" remote="twrp" />
  <project name="android_device_emulator_twrp" remote="twrp" />
```

```
<project name="android_device_emulator_twrpx86" remote="twrp" />
<project name="android_device_emulator_twrpx8664" remote="twrp" />

<!-- omnirom -->
<project path="external/lz4" name="android_external_lz4" remote="omnirom"
revision="android-6.0" groups="pdk-cw-fs,pdk-fs" />

<!-- from original Android repositories -->
...
</manifest>
```

From the preceding `default.xml`, we can see that we actually fetch multiple projects from CyanogenMod, TWRP, OmniROM, and our own GitHub repositories using a single XML file. We put all of them together to form our own GitHub local mirror.

To create the local mirror, we can use the following commands:

```
$ mkdir -p /media/aosp-mirror/github
$ cd /media/aosp-mirror/github
$ repo init -u https://github.com/shugaoye/mirror.git --mirror
$ repo sync
```

After we have created the local mirror, we can check what we have downloaded via the following screen:

Content of the local mirror

From the preceding screenshot, we can see that all Git repositories that we specified in `default.xml` are copied to our local storage. The manifest file for the local mirror that I use in this book can be found at `https://github.com/shugaoye/mirror`.

Fetching Git repositories outside GitHub

As we can see from the preceding example, we created our manifest repository for the GitHub mirror. After that, we use it to initialize our mirror repo. Then we use the `repo sync` command to fetch all Git repositories from GitHub to our local mirror.

How about repositories that we don't have write access to? In this book, we use a lot of projects from Android-x86. However, we don't have write permission to Android-x86 repositories. The Android-x86 project also doesn't have a mirror manifest available for use.

We can actually create a mirror manifest file from the original Android-x86 manifest. We can refer to the document at the following link for how to get Android-x86 source code:

`http://www.android-x86.org/getsourcecode`

The previous document mentioned that we can use the following command to initialize and sync repo from the Android-x86 repository:

```
$ mkdir android-x86
$ cd android-x86
$ repo init -u git://git.osdn.net/gitroot/android-x86/manifest -b $branch
$ repo sync
```

We can clone the preceding Android-x86 manifest repository to a folder and analyze it:

```
$ git clone git://git.osdn.net/gitroot/android-x86/manifest -b marshmallow-x86
$ ls
cm.xml   default.xml
```

After we clone it, we can find the preceding two files. `default.xml` is used to initialize the Android-x86 repo and `cm.xml` is used to initialize Android-x86 for the CyanogenMod build.

If we look at the content of `default.xml`, we can see the following code snippet:

```xml
<?xml version="1.0" encoding="UTF-8"?>
<manifest>

  <remote  name="aosp"
           fetch="https://android.googlesource.com/" />
  <remote  name="x86"
           fetch="." />
  <default revision="refs/tags/android-6.0.1_r61"
           remote="aosp"
           sync-c="true"
           sync-j="4" />

  <!-- from x86 port repositories -->
  <project path="build" name="platform/build" groups="pdk" remote="x86"
  revision="marshmallow-x86" >
    <copyfile src="core/root.mk" dest="Makefile" />
  </project>
  <project path="kernel" name="kernel/common" remote="x86"
  revision="kernel-4.4" />
  <project path="art" name="platform/art" groups="pdk" remote="x86"
  revision="marshmallow-x86" />
...
  <!-- from original Android repositories -->
  <project path="abi/cpp" name="platform/abi/cpp" groups="pdk" />
  <project path="bootable/recovery" name="platform/bootable/recovery"
  groups="pdk" />
...
</manifest>
```

We can see that the Android-x86 manifest includes two parts. The first part is Android-x86, its own repositories, and the rest are the original AOSP repositories.

We can retrieve the first part and compose a mirror manifest for Android-x86. Where should we put this file? We can put it in a branch of the same mirror manifest repository in our GitHub.

In the working copy of our GitHub mirror repository, we can create a branch called
`android-x86`. We can replace `default.xml` in our GitHub mirror with the first part in
Android-x86 manifest and we get the one in the following listing:

```xml
<?xml version="1.0" encoding="UTF-8"?>
<manifest>

   <remote   name="github"
             fetch=".." />

   <remote   name="x86"
             fetch=" git://git.osdn.net/gitroot/android-x86/" />

   <default  revision="android-x86"
             remote="github"
             sync-j="4" />

   <!-- from x86 port repositories -->
   <project name="manifest" remote="x86" />
   <project name="platform/build" remote="x86" />
   <project name="kernel/common" remote="x86" />
   <project name="platform/art" remote="x86" />
...
   <project name="platform/system/extras" remote="x86" />
   <project name="platform/system/vold" remote="x86" />

</manifest>
```

As we can see from the preceding listing, we removed unnecessary fields such as `path` or
`groups`, and so on. With this manifest for the Android-x86 mirror, we can create a local
mirror for Android-x86 now as follows:

```
$ mkdir -p /media/aosp-mirror/android-x86
$ cd /media/aosp-mirror/android-x86
$ repo init -u https://github.com/shugaoye/mirror.git -b android_x86 --
mirror
$ repo sync
```

After we download all Git repositories, we can see the content as follows:

```
sgye@x86vbox: /media/aosp-mirror/android-x86
sgye@x86vbox:~$ cd /media/aosp-mirror/android-x86
sgye@x86vbox:/media/aosp-mirror/android-x86$ ls -F
device/  github/  git-repo.git/  kernel/  manifest.git/  mirror.git/  platform/
sgye@x86vbox:/media/aosp-mirror/android-x86$ ls -F platform/
art.git/     bootable/   external/    hardware/  system/
bionic.git/  build.git/  frameworks/  packages/
sgye@x86vbox:/media/aosp-mirror/android-x86$
```

Local mirror of android-x86

Creating your own manifest for client download

With all local mirrors, we can create our own manifest to check out our source code now. We can put it in our GitHub in a new repository called `manifests`. In this repository, we can create an XML file, `default.xml`, as follows:

```xml
<?xml version="1.0" encoding="UTF-8"?>
<manifest>

  <remote  name="github"
           fetch="." />

  <remote  name="aosp"
           fetch="../android" />

  <remote  name="x86"
           fetch="../android-x86" />
```

```
<default revision="refs/tags/android-7.1.1_r4"
         remote="aosp"
         sync-c="true"
         sync-j="4" />

<!-- android-x86 -->
<project path="bootable/newinstaller"
name="platform/bootable/newinstaller"
remote="x86" revision="nougat-x86" />
...
<!-- GitHub -->
<project path="external/busybox" name="android_external_busybox"
remote="github" revision="cm-14.0" />
...
<!-- TWRP, use the below repositories for TWRP build -->
<project path="bootable/recovery" name="Team-Win-Recovery-Project"
remote="github" groups="pdk"  revision="android-7.0" />
...
<!-- AOSP -->
<project path="build" name="platform/build" groups="pdk" >
  <copyfile src="core/root.mk" dest="Makefile" />
</project>
<project path="abi/cpp" name="platform/abi/cpp" groups="pdk" />
...
<project path="tools/swt" name="platform/tools/swt"
groups="notdefault,tools" />
<project path="tools/tradefederation"
name="platform/tools/tradefederation"
groups="notdefault,tradefed" />

</manifest>
```

In the preceding listing, this is a manifest modified based on the AOSP release android-7.1.1_r4 manifest. In this file, we combined multiple projects from AOSP, Android-x86, TWRP, and our own GitHub projects into one. Usually, we have to do this using local_manifests to fetch all non-AOSP projects into our local copy. This approach usually takes a very long time and it is difficult to create baselines for our own configurations.

 The local_manifests file can be used to overwrite the configuration of the manifest file temporarily. You can refer to *Appendix B* of *Embedded Programming with Android* to find out more details.

With a local mirror and our own manifest, we can find a clean way to do this. When you have one copy for AOSP and one copy for Android-x86, you have a lot of duplicated projects in your storage because Android-x86 manifests include many original projects from AOSP. With the preceding setup, there are no duplicated projects in your local mirror.

To check out a working copy, we can use the following commands:

```
$ mkdir -p $HOME/aosp/android
$ cd $HOME/aosp/android
$ repo init -u /usr/local/mirror/github/manifests.git
$ repo sync
```

If we want to check out a build of Android-x86, it becomes a different configuration instead of a totally different repository now:

```
$ cd $HOME/aosp/android
$ repo init -u /usr/local/mirror/github/manifests.git -b nougat-x86
$ repo sync
```

Since we have our own local mirror, we can use the `sync-c="true"` option in the manifest, as we can see in the previous listing. With this option, the `repo` command will only check out the version we need in our working copy instead of creating the Git repositories with all revisions. This can save a lot of space for the working copy. However, this is not recommended without a local mirror, because it will take even longer when you switch to a different version.

You can find the manifest to check out a working copy at my GitHub `https://github.com/shugaoye/manifests`.

We will use this to manage all different build configurations in this book.

I introduced two kinds of manifest files here:

- To create a local mirror, you can refer to the manifest file at `https://github.com/shugaoye/mirror`
- To check out a working copy, you can refer to the manifest file at `https://github.com/shugaoye/manifests`

Summary

In this chapter, we set up the environment for SDK and AOSP. We built the Android emulator images for AOSP. We also tested and compared the Android images in Android SDK and AOSP. All these steps are necessary before we continue exploring how to create our own Android system later. We also spent some time discussing how to set up our own repo mirror. This tip can help us later, when we start to create projects from multiple open source projects. In the next chapter, we will start to explore the architecture of Android. We will look into the details of layers related to the porting and customization of the Android system.

3
Discovering Kernel, HAL, and Virtual Hardware

Once we set up the development environment and get the source code ready to use. We can start to explore the Android system architecture in more depth. We will look at the AOSP source tree first. After that, we will study the virtual hardware platforms that we are going to use in this book. Based on our understanding of the virtual hardware, we will look at the layers related to the system customization. In this chapter, we will cover the following topics:

- Deep analysis of Android HAL using the goldfish lights service
- Review the hardware specification for goldfish
- Overview about QEMU pipe implementation in the goldfish kernel

What is inside the AOSP?

Before we move to the details, let's take a look at the top level of the AOSP source code tree again:

```
sgye@x86vbox: ~/vol1/android-x86emu
sgye@x86vbox:~/vol1/android-x86emu$ ls -F
abi/             build/          docs/          libnativehelper/  platform_testing/
Android.bp@      cts/            external/      Makefile          prebuilts/
art/             dalvik/         frameworks/    ndk/              sdk/
bionic/          developers/     hardware/      out/              system/
bootable/        development/    kernel/        packages/         toolchain/
bootstrap.bash@  device/         libcore/       pdk/              tools/
sgye@x86vbox:~/vol1/android-x86emu$
```

The following table gives a brief description about each folder. We will look at some of them throughout this book:

Directory	Description
packages	Stock Android applications.
libcore	Core Java library. Apache Harmony is used before Nougat. OpenJDK is used with Nougat. Some features of Java 8 are used in Nougat.
frameworks/*	Android framework core components.
frameworks/base/services	Android system services.
art	Android runtime.
dalvik	Dalvik virtual machine.
libnativehelper	Helper functions for use with JNI.
system/*	Native services and libraries.
system/core	A minimal Linux system to boot Android.
bionic	C library.
external	External projects imported into the AOSP. It includes both the HAL layer and system services.

hardware	HAL and hardware libraries.
device	Device-specific files and components.
bootable	Recovery and bootloader.
abi	Minimal C++ runtime type information support.
build	Build system and Makefiles.
sdk	Android SDK.
cts	Compatibility test suite.
development	Development tools.
ndk	Android NDK.
tools	Various IDE tools.
prebuilts	Prebuilt images and binaries.

For a particular module or component, we may have to dig into multiple levels of subfolders to figure out what is included in it. This is especially true for the frameworks, system, and external folders. The subfolders in frameworks include Android framework layer code, but Android system services also reside in frameworks/base/services and we will look at them later in this session. The same is true for the contents in the system and external folders.

Android emulator HAL

We built the Android emulator in Chapter 2, *Setting Up the Development Environment*. In order to have an overview of Android emulator HAL, we can take a look at the $OUT/system/lib/hw folder as follows:

```
sgye@x86vbox: ~ (on x86vbox)
sgye@x86vbox:~$ ls -F $OUT/system/lib/hw
audio_policy.default.so*     fingerprint.ranchu.so*     local_time.default.so*
audio.primary.default.so*    gps.goldfish.so*           power.default.so*
audio.primary.goldfish.so*   gralloc.default.so*        power.goldfish.so*
bluetooth.default.so*        gralloc.goldfish.so*       sensors.goldfish.so*
camera.goldfish.jpeg.so*     gralloc.ranchu.so*         sensors.ranchu.so*
camera.goldfish.so*          keystore.default.so*       vibrator.default.so*
fingerprint.goldfish.so*     lights.goldfish.so*        vibrator.goldfish.so*
sgye@x86vbox:~$
```

We can see that there is a list of shared libraries. These are the shared libraries of goldfish HAL. The source code of the preceding shared libraries can be found in the `device/generic/goldfish` folder. The following table shows the relationship between the shared library, device node, and hardware module:

Hardware	Device	Lib (HAL)
audio	/dev/eac	audio.primary.goldfish.so
camera	/dev/qemu_pipe	camera.goldfish.jpeg.so camera.goldfish.so
fingerprint	/dev/qemu_pipe	fingerprint.goldfish.so
gps	/dev/qemu_pipe	gps.goldfish.so
lights	/dev/qemu_pipe	lights.goldfish.so
power	/dev/qemu_pipe	power.goldfish.so
sensors	/dev/qemu_pipe	sensors.goldfish.so
vibrator	/dev/qemu_pipe	vibrator.goldfish.so
graphics	/dev/qemu_pipe	gralloc.goldfish.so
serial	/dev/ttyS[0 - 2]	simple device don't need a separate shared library

As we can see from the preceding table, except for the serial port and audio, all the other hardware modules use a device node `/dev/qemu_pipe` to talk to the kernel. The QEMU pipe device provides a bridge between emulated devices and Android emulator. Since the QEMU pipe is an important device for the emulator, we will introduce it later in this chapter.

Usually, the HAL implementation is a shared library and it will be loaded by system service at runtime. It actually depends on the complexity of the hardware itself when it comes to deciding the actual implementation. For example, there is no separate shared library for simple hardware such as serial ports. The system service implementation of a serial port accesses the device node directly.

For more complicated hardware devices, such as graphics, there is a dedicated daemon SurfaceFlinger running in the background as well as multiple shared libraries associated with it.

In this chapter, we will analyze the HAL of device goldfish lights and use it as an example to understand the relationship between frameworks, system servers, and HAL implementation. After that, we will go through the hardware interface for goldfish devices. Finally, we will analyze the QEMU pipe implementation in the goldfish kernel.

Calling sequence

We will use the lights hardware interface as an example to explain how HAL, system services, and hardware managers work together.

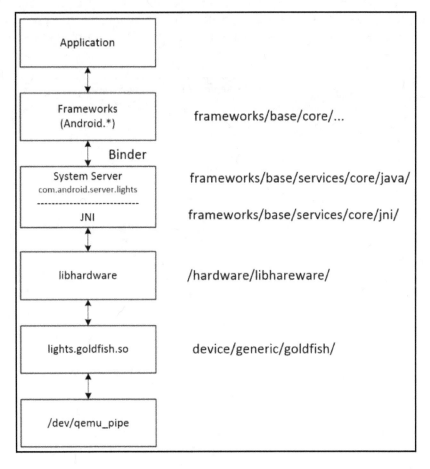

Lights HAL, system service, and hardware manager

As shown in the preceding figure, when an application wants to access hardware resources, it has to get an instance of the hardware manager first. For goldfish lights, the code in the application may look as follows:

```
LightsManager lights =
LocalServices.getService(LightsManager.class);
mBacklight = lights.getLight(LightsManager.LIGHT_ID_BACKLIGHT);
mBacklight.setBrightness(brightness);
```

The hardware manager talks to the system service to get hardware access. Usually, the hardware manager is implemented in Java. It calls to the system service using a binder interface since the hardware manager and system service run in different process spaces. The upper layer of the system service also implements in Java. After the system service gets the request, it will call to HAL library using JNI since the HAL is implemented using C or C++ usually.

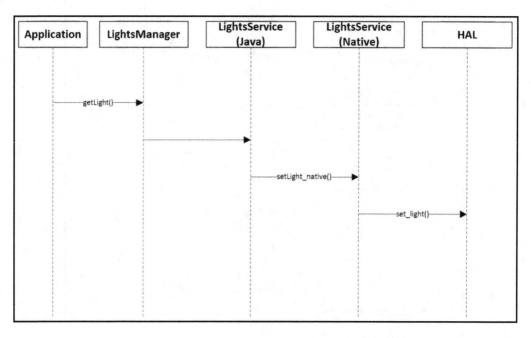

Calling sequence of lights service

The preceding figure shows the calling sequence when an application wants to change the light on the device. We will use a bottom-up approach in this section to look at the calling sequence from HAL to the application layer.

Goldfish lights HAL

The goldfish lights HAL implementation can be found in the
`$AOSP/device/generic/goldfish/lights` folder. To implement the HAL layer, the
hardware vendor usually needs to implement the following three data structures:

```
struct hw_module_t;
struct hw_module_methods_t;
struct hw_device_t;
```

All the preceding three data structures are implemented in the `lights_qemu.c` file for
goldfish. In the HAL implementation, we need to define `struct hw_module_t` named
`HAL_MODULE_INFO_SYM` first as follows. This registers the hardware module ID
`LIGHTS_HARDWARE_MODULE_ID` in the system. After this, lights system service can get the
module using the `hw_get_module` function:

```
/*
 * The emulator lights Module
 */
struct hw_module_t HAL_MODULE_INFO_SYM = {
    .tag = HARDWARE_MODULE_TAG,
    .version_major = 1,
    .version_minor = 0,
    .id = LIGHTS_HARDWARE_MODULE_ID,
    .name = "Goldfish lights Module",
    .author = "The Android Open Source Project",
    .methods = &lights_module_methods,
};
```

You may notice that the `method` field has a pointer of `lights_module_methods` inside the
preceding data structure. It is defined as follows:

```
static struct hw_module_methods_t lights_module_methods = {
    .open =  open_lights,
};
```

This defines the second HAL data structure `hw_module_methods_t`. Inside this data
structure, it defines an `open_lights` method, which is the HAL function to initialize the
hardware. Let's take a look at this function as follows:

```
/** Open a new instance of a lights device using name */
static int
open_lights( const struct hw_module_t* module, char const *name,
struct hw_device_t **device )
{
    void* set_light;
```

```
      if (0 == strcmp( LIGHT_ID_BACKLIGHT, name )) {
        set_light = set_light_backlight;
      } else if (0 == strcmp( LIGHT_ID_KEYBOARD, name )) {
        set_light = set_light_keyboard;
      } else if (0 == strcmp( LIGHT_ID_BUTTONS, name )) {
        set_light = set_light_buttons;
      } else if (0 == strcmp( LIGHT_ID_BATTERY, name )) {
        set_light = set_light_battery;
      } else if (0 == strcmp( LIGHT_ID_NOTIFICATIONS, name )) {
        set_light = set_light_notifications;
      } else if (0 == strcmp( LIGHT_ID_ATTENTION, name )) {
        set_light = set_light_attention;
      } else {
          D( "%s: %s light isn't supported yet.", __FUNCTION__, name );
          return -EINVAL;
      }

  struct light_device_t *dev =
      malloc( sizeof(struct light_device_t) );
      if (dev == NULL) {
          return -EINVAL;
      }
      memset( dev, 0, sizeof(*dev) );

      dev->common.tag = HARDWARE_DEVICE_TAG;
      dev->common.version = 0;
      dev->common.module = (struct hw_module_t*)module;
      dev->common.close = (int (*)(struct hw_device_t*))close_lights;
      dev->set_light = set_light;

      *device = (struct hw_device_t*)dev;
      return 0;
  }
```

Inside open_lights, it allocates the memory for the light_device_t data structure, which inherits the third HAL data structure, hw_device_t. When it initializing the data structure light_device_t, it registers two functions, close_lights and set_light, so the system service can call these functions to change the light or close the device. The function pointer set_light is set to a specific function according to the type of light.

Inside each `set_light_xxx` function, it talks to the kernel space through the QEMU pipe device `/dev/qemu_pipe`. For example, we can take a look at `set_light_backlight`:

```
static int
set_light_backlight( struct light_device_t* dev, struct light_state_t
const* state )
{
    /* Get Lights service. */
    intfd = qemud_channel_open( LIGHTS_SERVICE_NAME );

    if (fd < 0) {
      ...

    /* send backlight command to perform the backlight setting. */
    if (qemud_channel_send( fd, buffer, -1 ) < 0) {
        E( "%s: could not query lcd_backlight: %s",
        __FUNCTION__, strerror(errno) );
        close( fd );
        return -1;
    }

    close( fd );
    return 0;
}
```

Inside the `set_light_backlight` function, it calls `qemud_channel_open` and `qemud_channel_send` to do the actual work. Both functions use the QEMU pipe device `/dev/qemu_pipe` eventually.

The system service and hardware manager

To analyze how the application accesses light hardware, refer to the figure of the lights service calling sequence. In an application, what calls the `getService(LightsManager.class)` function to get an instance of `LightsManager` as follows:

```
LightsManager lights =
LocalServices.getService(LightsManager.class);
mBacklight = lights.getLight(LightsManager.LIGHT_ID_BACKLIGHT);
```

Usually the hardware manager and system service are implemented in different processes for most hardware interfaces. However, the hardware of the light is so simple, so both the system service and hardware manager are implemented in the same process.

The system service includes two parts: Java and JNI. The JNI implementation can be found at `frameworks/base/services/core/jni`, while the Java implementation can be found at `frameworks/base/services/core/java/com/android/server`. Both `LightsManager` and `LightsService` are implemented in `frameworks/base/services/core/java/com/android/server/lights`.

There are three files in this folder as follows. They implement both `LightsManager` and `LightsService`:

```
$ ls
Light.java   LightsManager.java   LightsService.java
```

Let's look at `LightsManager` first. We can see from the following snippet that `LightsManager` only returns an abstract class, `Light`, to the caller:

```java
package com.android.server.lights;

public abstract class LightsManager {
    public static final intLIGHT_ID_BACKLIGHT = 0;
    public static final intLIGHT_ID_KEYBOARD = 1;
    public static final intLIGHT_ID_BUTTONS = 2;
    public static final intLIGHT_ID_BATTERY = 3;
    public static final intLIGHT_ID_NOTIFICATIONS = 4;
    public static final intLIGHT_ID_ATTENTION = 5;
    public static final intLIGHT_ID_BLUETOOTH = 6;
    public static final intLIGHT_ID_WIFI = 7;
    public static final intLIGHT_ID_COUNT = 8;

    public abstract Light getLight(int id);
}
```

Let's follow the code to look at the abstract class `Light`. In the abstract class `Light`, it defines a list of functions that have to be implemented for `Light`. These functions are implemented in the `LightsService` class:

```java
package com.android.server.lights;

public abstract class Light {
    public static final intLIGHT_FLASH_NONE = 0;
    public static final intLIGHT_FLASH_TIMED = 1;
    public static final intLIGHT_FLASH_HARDWARE = 2;

    /**
     * Light brightness is managed by a user setting.
     */
    public static final intBRIGHTNESS_MODE_USER = 0;
```

```
/**
 * Light brightness is managed by a light sensor.
 */
public static final intBRIGHTNESS_MODE_SENSOR = 1;

public abstract void setBrightness(int brightness);
public abstract void setBrightness(int brightness,
intbrightnessMode);
public abstract void setColor(int color);
public abstract void setFlashing(int color, int mode, intonMS,
intoffMS);
public abstract void pulse();
public abstract void pulse(int color, intonMS);
public abstract void turnOff();
}
```

In `LightsService.java` in the following snippet, it implements the list of functions defined by the `Light` class:

```
...
private final class LightImpl extends Light {

        private LightImpl(int id) {
            mId = id;
        }

        @Override
        public void setBrightness(int brightness) {
            setBrightness(brightness, BRIGHTNESS_MODE_USER);
        }
...
```

This set of functions in the abstract class `Light` calls a `setLightLocked` function to do the actual work. In this function, it calls a native function, `setLight_native`, to invoke the native part of `LightsService`:

```
private void setLightLocked(int color, int mode, int onMS, int offMS, int
brightnessMode) {
        if (color != mColor || mode != mMode || onMS != mOnMS
    || offMS != mOffMS) {
            if (DEBUG) Slog.v(TAG, "setLight #" + mId + ": color=#"
                    + Integer.toHexString(color));
            mColor = color;
            mMode = mode;
            mOnMS = onMS;
            mOffMS = offMS;
            Trace.traceBegin(Trace.TRACE_TAG_POWER,
            "setLight(" + mId + ", 0x" +
```

```
        Integer.toHexString(color) + ")");
        try {
            setLight_native(mNativePointer,
            mId, color, mode, onMS, offMS,
            brightnessMode);
        } finally {
            Trace.traceEnd(Trace.TRACE_TAG_POWER);
        }
    }
}
```

Besides setLight_native, LightService also calls two more native functions, init_native and finalize_native. We can see this in the following code snippet. These two functions call to the HAL layer functions, as we discussed in the previous section:

```
public LightsService(Context context) {
    super(context);

    mNativePointer = init_native();

    for (inti = 0;  i<LightsManager.LIGHT_ID_COUNT;  i++) {
      mLights[i] = new LightImpl(i);
    }
}

...

@Override
protected void finalize() throws Throwable {
    finalize_native(mNativePointer);
    super.finalize();
}

...

private static native long init_native();
private static native void finalize_native(long ptr);

static native void setLight_native(long ptr, int light, int color, int
mode, int onMS, int offMS, int brightnessMode);
```

We have looked at the implementation of LightsManager and the Java implementation of LightsService. Now let's explore the JNI part of the LightsService implementation. The JNI part is implemented in com_android_server_lights_LightsService.cpp, which can be found in the $AOSP/frameworks/base/services/core/jni folder. We will look at how these three native functions used in LightsService are connected to the HAL layer:

```cpp
static jlong init_native(JNIEnv* /* env */, jobject /* clazz */)
{
    int err;
    hw_module_t* module;
    Devices* devices;

    devices = (Devices*)malloc(sizeof(Devices));

    err = hw_get_module(LIGHTS_HARDWARE_MODULE_ID,
        (hw_module_tconst**)&module);
    if (err == 0) {
        devices->lights[LIGHT_INDEX_BACKLIGHT]
                = get_device(module, LIGHT_ID_BACKLIGHT);
        devices->lights[LIGHT_INDEX_KEYBOARD]
                = get_device(module, LIGHT_ID_KEYBOARD);
        devices->lights[LIGHT_INDEX_BUTTONS]
                = get_device(module, LIGHT_ID_BUTTONS);
        devices->lights[LIGHT_INDEX_BATTERY]
                = get_device(module, LIGHT_ID_BATTERY);
        devices->lights[LIGHT_INDEX_NOTIFICATIONS]
                = get_device(module, LIGHT_ID_NOTIFICATIONS);
        devices->lights[LIGHT_INDEX_ATTENTION]
                = get_device(module, LIGHT_ID_ATTENTION);
        devices->lights[LIGHT_INDEX_BLUETOOTH]
                = get_device(module, LIGHT_ID_BLUETOOTH);
        devices->lights[LIGHT_INDEX_WIFI]
                = get_device(module, LIGHT_ID_WIFI);
    } else {
        memset(devices, 0, sizeof(Devices));
    }

    return (jlong)devices;
}
```

In the `init_native` function, it calls the `hw_get_module` function to get the light HAL module using `LIGHTS_HARDWARE_MODULE_ID` as the hardware ID. If you look back, it is defined in the HAL. This function loads the shared library of HAL implementations. In this case, it loads `lights.goldfish.so`. After loading the shared library, it calls `get_device` to initialize all the light devices. We can see the implementation of `get_device` in the following snippet:

```
static light_device_t* get_device(hw_module_t* module, char const* name)
{
    int err;
    hw_device_t* device;
    err = module->methods->open(module, name, &device);
    if (err == 0) {
        return (light_device_t*)device;
    } else {
        return NULL;
    }
}
```

In `get_device`, it invokes the `open` method and gets the instance of HAL data structure `hw_device_t`. We discussed the `open` method in the goldfish lights HAL.

Now let's look at another native function, `setLight_native`:

```
static void setLight_native(JNIEnv* /* env */, jobject /* clazz */, jlong
ptr, jint light, jint colorARGB, jint flashMode, jint onMS, jint offMS,
jint brightnessMode)
{
    Devices* devices = (Devices*)ptr;
    light_state_t state;

    if (light < 0 || light >= LIGHT_COUNT || devices->lights[light] ==
NULL) {
        return ;
    }

    memset(&state, 0, sizeof(light_state_t));
    state.color = colorARGB;
    state.flashMode = flashMode;
    state.flashOnMS = onMS;
    state.flashOffMS = offMS;
    state.brightnessMode = brightnessMode;

    {
        ALOGD_IF_SLOW(50, "Excessive delay setting light");
        devices->lights[light]->set_light(devices->lights[light],
        &state);
```

```
        }
    }
```

In the `setLight_native` function, it gets the pointer of the data structure `Devices` first. After that, it calls the HAL function `set_light` to do the actual work.

Finally, let's look at the implementation of the native method, `finalize_native`:

```
static void finalize_native(JNIEnv* /* env */, jobject /* clazz */, jlong
ptr)
{
    Devices* devices = (Devices*)ptr;
    if (devices == NULL) {
        return;
    }

    free(devices);
}
```

We can see that the `finalize_native` function just frees all resources used.

Android emulator kernel and hardware

We use goldfish lights as an example to perform the calling sequence analysis from an application to the goldfish HAL. Now we can look at the kernel layer and the underlying hardware. We can also take an overview from the top to the bottom again to understand how the entire system works.

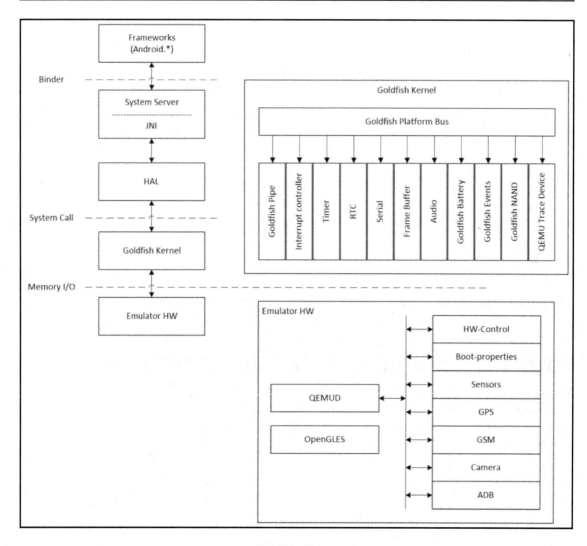

The goldfish architecture

We use the preceding figure to explain goldfish kernel and hardware in detail. As you can see, the preceding figure is similar to the architecture diagram that we saw in Chapter 1, *Introduction to Android System Programming*. This architecture diagram is the general architecture diagram for Android, but the preceding figure is specific to goldfish.

From the diagram, we can see the parts that we are interested in the goldfish kernel and emulator hardware. From the top to the bottom, the application utilizes the Android framework to implement functionalities and access the hardware. The framework usually resides in a different process from the system service layer, so they use Binder IPC to communicate with each other. The system service talks to the **HAL** using **JNI**, since **HAL** usually implements in the native language. The **HAL** is the user space implementation of hardware control and it communicates to the device driver in the kernel space through system calls. In the case of the goldfish hardware, the device driver accesses the virtual hardware through memory I/O registers, as we will see in the following section on Android emulator hardware.

Android emulator hardware

Unlike real hardware, most Android emulator hardware interfaces are emulated using QEMU, which is a popular open source emulator engine used by many open source projects. The Android development team customized QEMU and added a virtual hardware platform called goldfish. As we mentioned in `Chapter 2`, *Setting Up the Development Environment*, there are currently two versions of Android emulator available in the latest SDK. The code name for the original Android emulator is goldfish and the new one is ranchu. However, the virtual hardware code base for device emulation in QEMU is the same for both versions.

Detailed information about goldfish hardware interfaces can be found in the document `GOLDFISH-VIRTUAL-HARDWARE.TXT`. This document can be found in the AOSP source code at `$AOSP/platform/external/qemu/docs/GOLDFISH-VIRTUAL-HARDWARE.TXT`.

For different kernel versions, the hardware interfaces may have some differences. In this book, we will look at the Intel x86-based ranchu virtual hardware, which uses Android Linux version 3.10.0. Let's look at the goldfish devices that we will discuss in this chapter.

Goldfish platform bus

In the architecture diagram for goldfish, we have a detailed diagram for the kernel and goldfish hardware. We can see that all goldfish devices are enumerated through the goldfish platform bus. The platform bus is a special device that is capable of enumerating other platform devices found on the system to the kernel. This flexibility allows us to customize which virtual devices are available when running a given emulated system configuration. The following table defines goldfish platform bus registers.

Goldfish platform bus 32-bit I/O registers:

Offset	Name	Abstract
0x00	BUS_OP	R: Iterate to the next device in enumeration. W: Start device enumeration.
0x04	GET_NAME	W: Copy device name to kernel memory.
0x08	NAME_LEN	R: Read length of current device's name.
0x0c	ID	R: Read ID of the current device.
0x10	IO_BASE	R: Read I/O base address of the current device.
0x14	IO_SIZE	R: Read I/O base size of the current device.
0x18	IRQ_BASE	R: Read base IRQ of the current device.
0x1c	IRQ_COUNT	R: Read IRQ count of the current device.
0x20	NAME_ADDR_HIGH	# For 64-bit guest architectures only: W: Write high 32-bit of kernel address of name buffer used by GET_NAME. Must be written to before the GET_NAME write.

QEMU pipe device

One of the most important emulated devices in goldfish hardware is the QEMU pipe device. This is a special device that is totally specific to QEMU, but allows guest processes to communicate directly with the emulator with extremely high performance. This is achieved by avoiding any in-kernel memory copies, relying on the fact that QEMU can access guest memory at runtime (under proper conditions controlled by the kernel). As we can see from the goldfish architecture diagram, many other hardware interfaces, such as GPS, sensors, basebands, cameras, and so on, are emulated through the QEMU pipe. The following table defines QEMU pipe device registers.

QEMU pipe device registers:

Offset	Name	Abstract
0x00	COMMAND	W: Write to perform command (see the following).
0x04	STATUS	R: Read status.
0x08	CHANNEL	RW: Read or set current channel ID.
0x0c	SIZE	RW: Read or set current buffer size.

0x10	ADDRESS	RW: Read or set current buffer physical address.
0x14	WAKES	R: Read wake flags.
0x18	PARAMS_ADDR_LOW	RW: Read/set low bytes of parameter's block address.
0x1c	PARAMS_ADDR_HIGH	RW: Read/set high bytes of parameter's block address.
0x20	ACCESS_PARAMS	W: Perform access with parameter block.

Refer to the AOSP document ANDROID-QEMU-PIPE.TXT for details about the device's operations.

Goldfish audio device

The goldfish audio device implements a virtual sound card with the following properties:

- Stereo output at fixed 44.1 kHz frequency, using signed 16-bit samples. This is mandatory.
- Mono input at fixed 8 kHz frequency, using signed 16-bit samples. This is optional.

The following table defines goldfish audio device registers:

Offset	Name	Abstract
0x00	INT_STATUS	
0x04	INT_ENABLE	
0x08	SET_WRITE_BUFFER_1	W: Set address of first kernel output buffer.
0x0c	SET_WRITE_BUFFER_2	W: Set address of second kernel output buffer.
0x10	WRITE_BUFFER_1	W: Send first kernel buffer samples to output.
0x14	WRITE_BUFFER_2	W: Send second kernel buffer samples to output.
0x18	READ_SUPPORTED	R: Reads 1 if input is supported, 0 otherwise.
0x1c	SET_READ_BUFFER	
0x20	START_READ	
0x24	READ_BUFFER_AVAILABLE	

`0x28`	`SET_WRITE_BUFFER_1_HIGH`	# For 64-bit guest CPUs: W: Set high 32 bits of the first kernel output buffer address.
`0x30`	`SET_WRITE_BUFFER_2_HIGH`	# For 64-bit guest CPUs: W: Set high 32 bits of second kernel output buffer address.
`0x34`	`SET_READ_BUFFER_HIGH`	# For 64-bit guest CPUs: W: Set high 32 bits of kernel input buffer address.

Goldfish serial port

Android emulator has its own implementation of a virtual serial port. It always reserves the first two virtual serial ports:

- The first one is used to receive kernel messages. This is done by adding the `console=ttyS0` parameter to the kernel command line.
- The second one is used to set up the legacy `qemud` channel, used on older Android platform revisions. This is done by adding `android.qemud=ttyS1` on the kernel command line. The `qemud` channel is implemented as a Linux daemon process used as a channel between the guest and emulator. In the latest emulator version, a QEMU pipe is used instead of `qemud`.

The following table defines goldfish serial port registers:

Offset	Name	Abstract
`0x00`	`PUT_CHAR`	W: Write a single 8-bit value to the serial port.
`0x04`	`BYTES_READY`	R: Read the number of available buffered input bytes.
`0x08`	`CMD`	W: Send command (see the following).
`0x10`	`DATA_PTR`	W: Write kernel buffer address.
`0x14`	`DATA_LEN`	W: Write kernel buffer size.
`0x18`	`DATA_PTR_HIGH`	# For 64-bit guest CPUs only: W: Write high 32 bits of kernel buffer address.

The CMD I/O register is used to send various commands to the device, identified by the following values:

```
0x00 CMD_INT_DISABLE    Disable device.
0x01 CMD_INT_ENABLE     Enable device.
0x02 CMD_WRITE_BUFFER   Write buffer from kernel to device.
0x03 CMD_READ_BUFFER    Read buffer from device to kernel.
```

Each device instance uses one IRQ, raised to indicate that there is incoming/buffered data to read.

Goldfish kernel

Goldfish kernel can be downloaded from the AOSP source repository. You can download and build the kernel source code using the following command:

```
$ git clone https://android.googlesource.com/kernel/goldfish.git
$ cd goldfish
$ git checkout -b android-goldfish-3.10 origin/android-goldfish-3.10
$ make i386_ranchu_defconfig
$ make
```

The following table is a list of goldfish device drivers. This is based on kernel version 3.10.0. At the moment, kernel version 3.10.0 is for ranchu and 3.4.67 is for goldfish. The following table lists some goldfish specific devices. In ranchu, Virtio devices are used as block devices to simulate EMMC. Virtio devices are paravirtualized devices in QEMU that have better performance than emulated hardware devices.

Device	Path
goldfish platform bus	drivers/platform/goldfish/pdev_bus.c
QEMU pipe	drivers/platform/goldfish/goldfish_pipe.c
Frame buffer	drivers/video/goldfishfb.c
goldfish audio	drivers/staging/goldfish/goldfish_audio.c
goldfish NAND	drivers/staging/goldfish/goldfish_nand.c
goldfish battery	drivers/power/goldfish_battery.c
goldfish events	drivers/input/keyboard/goldfish_events.c
goldfish MMC	drivers/mmc/host/android-goldfish.c
goldfish serial	drivers/tty/goldfish.c

QEMU pipe

Since QEMU pipe is used as a channel to emulate many goldfish devices, we can review one of the major functions, `goldfish_pipe_read_write`, to understand data transmission between guest and host:

```
static ssize_t goldfish_pipe_read_write(struct file *filp, char __user
*buffer, size_t bufflen, int is_write)
{
...
    /* Now, try to transfer the bytes in the current page */
    spin_lock_irqsave(&dev->lock, irq_flags);
    if (access_with_param(dev, is_write ? CMD_WRITE_BUFFER :
    CMD_READ_BUFFER, xaddr, avail, pipe, &status)) {
      writel((u32)(u64)pipe, dev->base + PIPE_REG_CHANNEL);
#ifdef CONFIG_64BIT
      writel((u32)((u64)pipe >> 32), dev->base + PIPE_REG_CHANNEL_HIGH);
#endif
      writel(avail, dev->base + PIPE_REG_SIZE);
      writel(xaddr, dev->base + PIPE_REG_ADDRESS);
#ifdef CONFIG_64BIT
      writel((u32)((u64)xaddr>> 32), dev->base + PIPE_REG_ADDRESS_HIGH);
#endif
      writel(is_write ? CMD_WRITE_BUFFER : CMD_READ_BUFFER,
        dev->base + PIPE_REG_COMMAND);
      status = readl(dev->base + PIPE_REG_STATUS);
}
    spin_unlock_irqrestore(&dev->lock, irq_flags);

if (status > 0 && !is_write)
    set_page_dirty(page);
put_page(page);
...
```

As we can see from the preceding code, it invokes the `access_with_param` function first. This is the fastest way to transfer data between the guest and emulator using shared memory. With this method, the goldfish kernel allocates a piece of memory at boot time. The guest and emulator will use this shared memory to transfer parameters between them. If the `access_with_param` function fails, it will use the following sequence to transfer data through the QEMU pipe device:

```
write_channel(<channel>)
write_address(<buffer-address>)
REG_SIZE     = <buffer-size>
REG_CMD      = CMD_WRITE_BUFFER/CMD_READ_BUFFER
status = REG_STATUS
```

Now let's take a look at the `access_with_param` function as follows:

```
/* A value that will not be set by qemu emulator */
#define INITIAL_BATCH_RESULT (0xdeadbeaf)
static int access_with_param(struct goldfish_pipe_dev *dev, const int cmd,
unsigned long address, unsigned long avail, struct goldfish_pipe *pipe, int
*status)
{
    struct access_params *aps = dev->aps;

    if (aps == NULL)
        return -1;

    aps->result = INITIAL_BATCH_RESULT;
    aps->channel = (unsigned long)pipe;
    aps->size = avail;
    aps->address = address;
    aps->cmd = cmd;
    writel(cmd, dev->base + PIPE_REG_ACCESS_PARAMS);
    /*
     * If the aps->result has not changed, that means
     * that the batch command failed
     */
    if (aps->result == INITIAL_BATCH_RESULT)
        return -1;
    *status = aps->result;
    return 0;
}
```

The address of `aps` is the pre-allocated shared memory between the guest and emulator. All data structures that need to be used for a single operation are filled in this data structure `aps`. The command will be written to register `PIPE_REG_ACCESS_PARAMS`. The write to `PIPE_REG_ACCESS_PARAMS` will trigger the operation. QEMU will read the content of the `access_params` block, use its fields to perform the operation, and then write back the return value into `aps->result`. The difference between shared memory `aps` and the QEMU pipe device is similar to DMA and register-based device I/O. The shared memory or DMA is much more efficient in large blocks of memory access.

You can explore the rest of the goldfish device drivers by yourself.

Summary

In this chapter, we introduced the content of the AOSP source code. After that, we used goldfish lights HAL as an example to analyze the calling sequence from the application to HAL. Finally, we reviewed the Android architecture again using the Android system for the emulator. We also reviewed goldfish kernel and hardware to understand how they work together with the rest of the software stacks. In the next chapter, we will start to work on our own x86emu device and use it to explore how to extend an emulator to support additional functionalities.

4
Customizing the Android Emulator

In the last chapter, we spent some time exploring the details of the Android system architecture. With our knowledge about kernel, HAL, and system service, we can start to customize the Android system ourselves. In this chapter, we will cover the following topics:

- Why customize the Android emulator?
- Creating a new x86emu device
- Building and testing the new x86emu device

Why customize the Android emulator

You may be wondering why we want to customize Android emulator. Google already provides it in the Android SDK and we can just use it without any additional effort. However, as a developer, you may find that it may not be good enough to meet your expectations. For example, in the most recent Android Studio or SDK releases, the Intel x86 emulator is recommended for developers, since it is much faster than the ARM version. One problem with using the Intel x86 emulator is that many Android applications with native code cannot run properly, because the x86 native library is not built into these applications.

To resolve this issue, we can integrate Houdini libraries from Intel to the emulator. With Houdini libraries, we can execute ARM native code on the Intel x86 platform. Another common request for Android emulator is that **Google Mobile Services** (**GMS**) is not included in it. Many developers develop applications with the assumption that GMS should be available on the device. In the next few chapters, we will learn how to create a x86emu device to customize Android emulator so that we can integrate components such as Houdini or enable additional hardware interfaces, such as Wi-Fi, in Android emulator.

Armed with the knowledge about how to create the x86emu device, you can create your own Android emulator to meet your requirements.

It is possible, we always avoid changing too much AOSP code directly. This is because the more we change, the harder it is for us to port it to the latest version of Android. Google constantly releases new Android code from time to time. Sometime, new releases may be difficult to merge because of the architecture change.

From this chapter to Chapter 7, *Enabling Wi-Fi on the Android Emulator*, we will teach a way to customize existing devices with minimal changes to the AOSP source code. From Chapter 8, *Creating Your Own Device on VirtualBox* to Chapter 11, *Enabling VirtualBox-Specific Hardware Interfaces*, we will discuss the porting to a new platform that we have to change to AOSP code directly. Even in that case, we still have to plan and consider the merge effort to a new Android release.

Understanding build layers

The AOSP build system includes the abstraction layers to build a device. After we understand the ideas behind these layers, it will help us to understand the relationship of the various Makefiles for a device. It is always good to refer to the original Google document at the following URL, when you start to create a new device. The information will usually be updated when a new Android release is available: `http://source.android.com/source/add-device.html`.

In this section, we will apply the information from the previous Google document to the specific Android emulator virtual hardware that we are going to work on. In this way, we can derive all device-specific Makefiles according to the general guidance from the previous Google document. Throughout the process from generic to specific, we can apply the inheritance of object-oriented concepts to the Makefile system.

There are three layers, **Product**, **Board/Device**, and **Architecture**, in the device build system. These layers can be considered as different dimensions to measure the characteristic of a product. Each layer relates to the one above it in a one-to-many relationship, which is similar to the inheritance or composition relationship in the object-oriented terms. For example, one kind of hardware architecture can have more than one board and each board can have more than one product. We will see how this method works when we create a new device in this chapter later.

The following table is a list of layers used in an AOSP build system. I created this table by modifying the one from the Google document and added my comments specific to the x86emu device, which we are going to work on in this chapter.

Layer	Description
Product	The Product layer defines the feature specifications of the shipping product such as the modules to build, locales supported, and the configuration for various locales. In other words, this is the name of the overall product. Product-specific variables are defined in **product definition Makefiles**. A product can inherit from other product definitions, which simplifies maintenance. A common method is to create a base product that contains features that apply for all products, then creating product variants based on that base product. In this chapter, we inherit from a generic device for an Android emulator in AOSP to create our x86emu device. For the x86emu device, we can also create two products that differ only by their architecture variants (we can have different builds for x86 or x86_64).
Board/Device	The Board/Device layer represents the physical layer of plastic on the device (that is, the industrial design of the device). For example, North American devices probably include QWERTY keyboards, whereas devices sold in France probably include AZERTY keyboards. This layer also represents the bare schematics of a product. These include the peripherals on the board and their configuration. In the x86emu device, we need to define the size of the filesystem, the graphics hardware and camera, and so on. In Chapter 7, *Enabling Wi-Fi on the Android Emulator*, we want to support Wi-Fi in the emulator. We need to specify it in the board configuration file.
Arch	The Architecture layer describes the processor configuration and **Application Binary Interface** (**ABI**) running on the board.

Build variants

When building for a particular product, it's often useful to have minor variations on what is ultimately the final release build. By using different build variants, it can help the different parties in the product development cycle. There are primarily three kinds of build variant in the AOSP so far. The **engineering build** is the default one and is suitable for development work. In this type of build, the product security policy is not fully enforced and the debugging mechanisms are turned on. It is easy for engineers to test and fix issues with an engineering build.

The second flavor is **user build**, which is used for the final release. All debugging mechanisms are turned off and the product security policy is fully enforced. The third flavor is **userdebug,** which is in between the engineering build and user build. This type of build can be used in the field test, which is also used by the end users.

All components in the AOSP build are called **modules**. In a module definition, the module can specify tags with `LOCAL_MODULE_TAGS`, which can be one or more values of `optional` (default), `debug`, or `eng`. With a tag, we can define the usage of a module. For example, all debug tools will only be included in the engineering build.

If a module doesn't specify a tag (by `LOCAL_MODULE_TAGS`), its tag defaults to `optional`. An `optional` module is installed only if it is required by product configuration with `PRODUCT_PACKAGES`. We usually specify packages needed by a product in the device Makefile using the `PRODUCT_PACKAGES` variable. This way, we can easily define modules that are only suitable for a particular build.

The following table shows the AOSP-defined build variants documented in the preceding Google URL:

Build variants	Description
eng	This is the default flavor: • Installs modules tagged with: `eng` and/or `debug` • Installs modules according to the product definition files, in addition to tagged modules • `ro.secure=0` • `ro.debuggable=1` • `ro.kernel.android.checkjni=1` • `adb` is enabled by default

user	This is the flavor intended to be the final release: • Installs modules tagged with `user` • Installs modules according to the product definition files, in addition to tagged modules. • `ro.secure=1` • `ro.debuggable=0` • `adb` is disabled by default
userdebug	The same as `user`, except: • Also installs modules tagged with `debug` • `ro.debuggable=1` • `adb` is enabled by default

Creating a new x86emu device

To customize Android emulator, we need to create a new device based on Android emulator and make our customization on this new device. We will work on this from the original AOSP source code.

Checking out from the AOSP

As I mentioned before, I try to avoid unnecessary changes to the AOSP source code as much as I can. In this chapter, in order to set up the build environment, you can check out the `android-7.1.1_r4` version of the AOSP source code and clone the kernel and x86emu source to the AOSP source tree as follows:

```
$ mkdir android-x86emu
$ cd android-x86emu
$ repo init -u https://android.googlesource.com/platform/manifest -b
android-7.1.1_r4
$ repo sync
$ git clone https://github.com/shugaoye/goldfish.git -b
android-7.1.1_r4_x86emu_ch04_r1 kernel
$ cd device/generic
$ git clone https://github.com/shugaoye/x86emu.git -b
android-7.1.1_r4_x86emu_ch04_r1
```

Now we have retrieved the source code step by step. The project x86emu is the new device that we create in this chapter and can be used to customize Android emulator in the next few chapters. The goldfish project is the kernel that I forked from the AOSP goldfish kernel: `https://android.googlesource.com/kernel/goldfish/`.

The `android-7.1.1_r4_x86emu_ch04_r1` tag is the baseline of this chapter's source code release. All source code created or changed in this book is baselined using the naming convention `{Android version}_{project}_{chapter number}_{release number}`. Here is the explanation of this naming convention:

- `Android version` is the original AOSP version number
- `project` can be x86emu or x86vbox
- `chapter number` is what chapter we create a baseline for the source code
- `release number` is used to indicate the number of releases

These can work in the simple configuration of this chapter. This method is not good enough when we use source code from multiple sources as we will do in other chapters later in this book. We will use our own manifest file to manage the source code in this book.

Checking out from a local mirror

To use our own manifest file, we can use either a local mirror or a remote repository. If we use a local mirror, we have to change `manifest.xml` of `android-7.1.1_r4` a little to make our own. We copy `.repo/manifest.xml` to our `manifests/default.xml` and make the following changes:

```xml
<?xml version="1.0" encoding="UTF-8"?>
<manifest>

  <remote   name="github"
         fetch="." />
  <remote   name="aosp"
         fetch="../android" />
  <default revision="refs/tags/android-7.1.1_r4"
         remote="aosp"
         sync-j="4" />

  <!-- github/shugaoye -->
  <project path="kernel" name="goldfish"
  remote="github" revision="refs/tags/
  android-7.1.1_r4_x86emu_ch04_r1" />
  <project path="device/generic/x86emu" name="x86emu" remote="github"
  revision="refs/tags/android-7.1.1_r4_x86emu_ch04_r1" />
  <!-- AOSP -->
  <project path="build" name="platform/build" groups="pdk" >
    <copyfile src="core/root.mk" dest="Makefile" />
  </project>
  <project path="abi/cpp" name="platform/abi/cpp" groups="pdk" />
```

```
...
</manifest>
```

This manifest file has an assumption that our local mirror has the following directory structure:

```
$ ls -F
android/   android-x86/   github/
```

The AOSP mirror is created under the `android` folder. GitHub mirror is created under the `github` folder. We need to use android-x86 source code as well later. We can put it under the `android-x86` folder. Our own manifest is stored at `github/manifests` and the preceding manifest file is `github/manifests/default.xml`. In this file, we add additional lines to retrieve the Android kernel and x86emu device from GitHub.

With this manifest, we can get the source code using the following command:

```
$ mkdir android-x86emu
$ cd android-x86emu
$ repo init -u {your mirror URL}/github/manifests.git -b
android-7.1.1_r4_ch04
$ repo sync
```

We can also retrieve all source code from the remote repository directly using our own manifest file. With that, we need to change the manifest file a little as follows:

```xml
<?xml version="1.0" encoding="UTF-8"?>
<manifest>

  <remote   name="github"
            fetch="." />

  <remote   name="aosp"
            fetch="https://android.googlesource.com/" />
  <default revision="refs/tags/android-7.1.1_r4"
           remote="aosp"
           sync-c="true"
           sync-j="1" />

  <!-- github/shugaoye -->
  <project path="kernel" name="goldfish" remote="github"
   revision="refs/tags/android-7.1.1_r4_x86emu_ch04_r1" />
  <project path="device/generic/x86emu" name="x86emu" remote="github"
   revision="refs/tags/android-7.1.1_r4_x86emu_ch04_r1" />

  <!-- aosp -->
  <project path="build" name="platform/build" groups="pdk,tradefed" >
```

```
      <copyfile src="core/root.mk" dest="Makefile" />
    </project>
  . . .
```

As you can see, we changed the URL of the remote `aosp` to use the absolute path in this revision of the manifest file. To check out the source code using this revision, we can run the following commands:

```
$ mkdir android-x86emu
$ cd android-x86emu
$ repo init -u https://github.com/shugaoye/manifests -b
android-7.1.1_r4_ch04_aosp
$ repo sync
```

Because there are multiple repositories involved in this book, I strongly encourage you to use a local mirror. This can make the build and debug process more efficient.

 It is also possible to use `local_manifests` to set up your workspace. You can refer to Appendix B, *Using Repo in This Book*, in the book *Embedded Programming with Android*. A sample file can be found at `https://github.com/shugaoye/build/blob/master/local_manifest.xml`.

In this book, I use branches for the manifest file to manage the different versions of source code. To create a baseline of the source code in a chapter, I use the following naming convention:

`{Android version}_{chapter number}_{remote (optional)}`

- `Android version` is the original AOSP version number
- `chapter number` is what chapter we create a baseline for the source code
- `remote` is used to indicate how to check out the source code from the remote repositories

For example, from the following screenshot, we can see that the branch `android-7.1.1_r4_ch04` is used to check out the source code of chapter 4 from a local mirror. The branch `android-7.1.1_r4_ch04_aosp` is used to check out the source code for chapter 4 from the remote repository. Since I am in China, I don't have access to the AOSP source code all the time. I created revisions (`android-7.1.1_r4_ch04_tuna` and `android-7.1.1_r4_ch04_ustc`) for chapter 4 to check out the source code from AOSP mirrors in China and GitHub. You may change the manifest file according to your needs.

Creating x86emu device

After we check out the source code, we can look at how to create a new x86emu device in the $AOSP/device folder. The hierarchy in the device folder is in the vendor-name/device-name format. For example, the Nexus S from Samsung can be found in the samsung/crespo folder. The device name of Nexus S is crespo. We can create our device under a common folder, generic, as follows. The folder name for our device is generic/x86emu:

```
$ cd device/generic
$ mkdir x86emu
```

This is the project that we create in this chapter and you can find the source code at `https://github.com/shugaoye/x86emu.git`.

We will create a list of Makefiles in this folder to build the device. Refer to the build layers in the previous section. Here is a list of Makefiles that need to be included in the device skeleton:

- `AndroidProducts.mk`: This is a Makefile to describe the various products that can be built for this device
- `BoardConfig.mk`: This is a board configuration Makefile for the hardware board
- `device.mk`: This is the device Makefile that is used to declare the files and modules needed for the device
- `vendorsetup.sh`: This is a shell script that can be used to add your product (a "lunch combo") to the build along with a build variant separated by a dash
- `{Product Makefile}.mk`: This is the product definition Makefile and it is used to create a specific product based on the device

Now we can create Makefiles for our device one by one according to the preceding list.

AndroidProducts.mk

We included all product definition Makefiles in this file. The AOSP build system will start to search all product definitions using this file. The following is the content of `AndroidProducts.mk`:

```
PRODUCT_MAKEFILES := \
    $(LOCAL_DIR)/x86emu_x86.mk \
    $(LOCAL_DIR)/x86emu_x86_64.mk \
```

As we can see, we defined two product variants for x86 and x86_64 builds.

Both `x86emu_x86.mk` and `x86emu_x86_64.mk` are very similar. They define the same set of product definition variables for 32 bit and 64 bit.

The following table compares the product definition Makefiles for 32-bit and 64-bit build:

x86emu_x86.mk	x86emu_x86_64.mk

`$(call inherit-product, device/generic/x86emu/device.mk)`
`$(call inherit-product, $(SRC_TARGET_DIR)/product/full.mk)`
`# Overrides`
`PRODUCT_BRAND := x86emu_x86`
`PRODUCT_NAME := x86emu_x86`
`PRODUCT_DEVICE = x86emu`
`PRODUCT_MODEL := x86emu_x86_ch4`
`TARGET_ARCH := x86`
`TARGET_KERNEL_CONFIG := i386_ranchu_defconfig`
`$(call inherit-product, $(LOCAL_PATH)/x86emu_base.mk)`
	`$(call inherit-product, device/generic/x86emu/device.mk)`
	`$(call inherit-product, $(SRC_TARGET_DIR)/product/full_x86_64.mk)`
	`# Overrides`
	`PRODUCT_BRAND := x86emu_x86_64`
	`PRODUCT_NAME := x86emu_x86_64`
	`PRODUCT_DEVICE = x86emu`
	`PRODUCT_MODEL := x86emu_x86_64_ch4`
	`TARGET_SUPPORTS_32_BIT_APPS := true`
	`TARGET_SUPPORTS_64_BIT_APPS := true`
	`TARGET_ARCH := x86_64`
	`TARGET_KERNEL_CONFIG := x86_64_ranchu_defconfig`
	`$(call inherit-product, $(LOCAL_PATH)/x86emu_base.mk)`

You may notice that we inherit the common product definition files for 32-bit and 64-bit first at the beginning:

```
$(call inherit-product, $(SRC_TARGET_DIR)/product/full.mk)
```

And:

```
$(call inherit-product, $(SRC_TARGET_DIR)/product/full_x86_64.mk)
```

There are many generic product definitions defined by the AOSP build system. You can find them at `$AOSP/build/target/product`:

```
$ ls build/target/product
AndroidProducts.mk      full_base.mk              sdk_base.mk
aosp_arm64.mk           full_base_telephony.mk    sdk_mips.mk
aosp_arm.mk             full_mips64.mk            sdk.mk
aosp_base.mk            full_mips.mk              sdk_phone_arm64.mk
aosp_base_telephony.mk  full.mk                   sdk_phone_armv7.mk
aosp_mips64.mk          full_x86_64.mk            sdk_phone_mips64.mk
aosp_mips.mk            full_x86.mk               sdk_phone_mips.mk
aosp_x86_64.mk          generic_armv5.mk          sdk_phone_x86_64.mk
aosp_x86.mk             generic_mips.mk           sdk_phone_x86.mk
base.mk                 generic.mk                sdk_x86_64.mk
core_64_bit.mk          generic_no_telephony.mk   sdk_x86.mk
core_base.mk            generic_x86.mk            security
core_minimal.mk         languages_full.mk         telephony.mk
core.mk                 languages_small.mk        vboot.mk
```

```
core_tiny.mk          locales_full.mk          verity.mk
embedded.mk           runtime_libart.mk
emulator.mk           sdk_arm64.mk
```

After that, a set of product definition variables PRODUCT_BRAND, PRODUCT_NAME, PRODUCT_DEVICE, and PRODUCT_MODEL are defined with different values. TARGET_ARCH and TARGET_KERNEL_CONFIG are also defined for 32 bit and 64 bit separately. Pay attention to PRODUCT_MODEL. Since we will change Makefiles in each chapter, in this book we use PRODUCT_MODEL to indicate the build for each chapter. In this chapter, we define PRODUCT_MODEL as x86emu_x86_ch4 for the build in this chapter. At the end of the file, we also include a common Makefile x86emu_base.mk for both 32-bit and 64-bit products. This file includes additional configurations for the kernel build:

```
TARGET_KERNEL_SOURCE := kernel

PRODUCT_OUT ?= out/target/product/x86emu

include $(TARGET_KERNEL_SOURCE)/AndroidKernel.mk

# define build targets for kernel
.PHONY: $(TARGET_PREBUILT_KERNEL)

LOCAL_KERNEL := $(TARGET_PREBUILT_KERNEL)

PRODUCT_COPY_FILES += \
    $(LOCAL_KERNEL):kernel \
```

The kernel build is usually not included in the AOSP build. You have to build them separately according to the instructions from Google. In this book, we integrate the kernel build in our own Makefile here. The kernel AndroidKernel.mk Makefile is created based on the Makefile of the Qualcomm kernel source at https://android.googlesource.com/kernel/msm/.

There are many product definition variables used in the preceding Makefiles. Let's review the product definition variables that we used here. Refer to the Google documents for the complete list:

- PRODUCT_BRAND: This is the brand that the software is customized for. We just defined it as our device name.
- PRODUCT_NAME: This is the product name that we give to the device. We set it to x86emu_x86 in this book. It is also the prefix that we can select in the lunch combo, such as x86emu_x86-eng. The suffix is the build variants.

- PRODUCT_DEVICE: The name of the actual product. TARGET_DEVICE derives from this variable. This is also the board name that the build system uses to locate BoardConfig.mk. It is the x86emu for our device and it is also the directory name of our device at $AOSP/device/generic/x86emu.
- PRODUCT_MODEL: This is the name that we can see in the settings in **Model**. As I mentioned earlier, we use this variable to differentiate the build of each chapter in this book.
- PRODUCT_OUT: This is the output folder of the build result. It is the same as the environment variable $OUT.
- PRODUCT_COPY_FILES: This is a list of specific files that we would like to copy to the target's filesystem. The list of words looks like source_path:destination_path. The file at the source path should be copied to the destination path during the build process.

BoardConfig.mk

BoardConfig.mk defines the board-specific configurations. We define CPU/ABI, the target architecture, OpenGLES configurations, and so on in this file. We also define the image file size, format, and so on:

```
TARGET_NO_BOOTLOADER := true
TARGET_NO_KERNEL := true
TARGET_CPU_ABI := x86
TARGET_ARCH := x86
TARGET_ARCH_VARIANT := x86
TARGET_PRELINK_MODULE := false

# The IA emulator (qemu) uses the Goldfish devices
HAVE_HTC_AUDIO_DRIVER := true
BOARD_USES_GENERIC_AUDIO := true

# no hardware camera
USE_CAMERA_STUB := true

# customize the malloced address to be 16-byte aligned
BOARD_MALLOC_ALIGNMENT := 16

# Enable dex-preoptimization to speed up the first boot sequence
# of an SDK AVD. Note that this operation only works on Linux for now
ifeq ($(HOST_OS),linux)
WITH_DEXPREOPT := true
endif
```

```
# Build OpenGLES emulation host and guest libraries
BUILD_EMULATOR_OPENGL := true

# Build and enable the OpenGL ES View renderer. When running on the
emulator,
# the GLES renderer disables itself if host GL acceleration isn't
available.
USE_OPENGL_RENDERER := true


TARGET_USERIMAGES_USE_EXT4 := true
BOARD_SYSTEMIMAGE_PARTITION_SIZE := 1342177280
BOARD_USERDATAIMAGE_PARTITION_SIZE := 576716800
BOARD_CACHEIMAGE_PARTITION_SIZE := 69206016
BOARD_CACHEIMAGE_FILE_SYSTEM_TYPE := ext4
BOARD_FLASH_BLOCK_SIZE := 512
TARGET_USERIMAGES_SPARSE_EXT_DISABLED := true


BOARD_SEPOLICY_DIRS += \
        build/target/board/generic/sepolicy \
        build/target/board/generic_x86/sepolicy
```

This file is copied from a predefined AOSP board configuration at
`$AOSP/build/target/board/generic_x86/BoardConfig.mk` **with minor changes.**

We can also use the system-defined board configuration directly and overwrite predefined
variables as follows:

```
include $(SRC_TARGET_DIR)/board/generic_x86/BoardConfig.mk

#
# Overwrite predefined variables.
#

TARGET_USERIMAGES_USE_EXT4 := true
BOARD_SYSTEMIMAGE_PARTITION_SIZE := 1610612736
BOARD_USERDATAIMAGE_PARTITION_SIZE := 576716800
BOARD_CACHEIMAGE_PARTITION_SIZE := 69206016
BOARD_CACHEIMAGE_FILE_SYSTEM_TYPE := ext4
BOARD_FLASH_BLOCK_SIZE := 512
TARGET_USERIMAGES_SPARSE_EXT_DISABLED := true

BOARD_KERNEL_CMDLINE += androidboot.selinux=permissive
```

If we look at the folder of `$AOSP/build/target/board/generic_x86`, it contains a few
other files:

```
$ ls -F
BoardConfig.mk  device.mk  README.txt  sepolicy/  system.prop
```

We need to copy `system.prop` to our `device` folder as well, since this file defines the
Radio Interface Layer (RIL) configuration for the emulator as follows:

```
rild.libpath=/system/lib/libreference-ril.so
rild.libargs=-d /dev/ttyS0
```

Without this, you will find that the data connection cannot work properly in the build.

device.mk

You may notice that there is a `device.mk` file in the `generic_x86` folder. Yes, we can reuse
that file directly. The following is our `device.mk` file:

```
$(call inherit-product, $(SRC_TARGET_DIR)/board/generic_x86/device.mk)
```

As we can see, in our `device.mk` file, we simply inherit the common `device.mk` from the
`generic_x86` device.

We can look at the `device.mk` file for the `generic_x86` device as follows:

```
PRODUCT_PROPERTY_OVERRIDES := \
    ro.ril.hsxpa=1 \
    ro.ril.gprsclass=10 \
    ro.adb.qemud=1

PRODUCT_COPY_FILES := \
device/generic/goldfish/data/etc/apns-conf.xml:system/etc/
apns-conf.xml \
device/generic/goldfish/camera/media_profiles.xml:system/etc/
media_profiles.xml \
frameworks/av/media/libstagefright/data/media_codecs_google_audio.xml:syste
m/etc/media_codecs_google_audio.xml \
frameworks/av/media/libstagefright/data/media_codecs_google_telephony.xml:s
ystem/etc/media_codecs_google_telephony.xml \
frameworks/av/media/libstagefright/data/media_codecs_google_video.xml:syste
m/etc/media_codecs_google_video.xml \
device/generic/goldfish/camera/media_codecs.xml:system/etc/media_codecs.xml

PRODUCT_PACKAGES := \
    audio.primary.goldfish \
    vibrator.goldfish
```

In the preceding `device.mk` file for the `generic_x86` device, it overwrites a few properties
and copies configuration files to the `system` folder. It also includes the HAL layers for the
goldfish device.

Now we can add our device build to the build system using the following command:

```
$ add_lunch_combo <product_name>-<build_variant>
$ lunch <product_name>-<build_variant>
```

Such as:

```
$ add_lunch_combo x86emu_x86-eng
$ lunch x86emu_x86-eng
```

To automatically add this to the build system, we can add a script `vendorsetup.sh`. In this script, we can create all the build variants for `x86emu_x86`:

```
for i in eng userdebug user; do
        add_lunch_combo x86emu_x86-${i}
done
```

 Be aware that the 64-bit build for the x86emu device is not tested in this book. You must make the necessary changes by yourself if you want to test a 64-bit build.

In this section, besides product-level variables as I explained before, there are also variables for the target device and board-level variables. The following is a list of variables for the target devices that are defined in `BoardConfig.mk`, `device.mk`, or product definition Makefiles:

- `TARGET_ARCH`: This is the architecture of the device. It is usually something such as `arm`, `x86`, and so on.
- `TARGET_USERIMAGES_USE_EXT4`: This variable needs to be set as `true` to build a filesystem in ext4 format. The filesystem can be built into other formats such as yaffs2 in the older Android version prior to Android 4.4.
- `TARGET_KERNEL_SOURCE`: This is the path for the kernel source code. In our case, the kernel source code can be found at `$AOSP/kernel`.
- `TARGET_KERNEL_CONFIG` : The kernel configuration file that we use to build the kernel source.

The following is a list of board-level variables that we used in this chapter:

- `BOARD_SYSTEMIMAGE_PARTITION_SIZE`: The size of the filesystem partition for the system image (`system.img`)

- BOARD_USERDATAIMAGE_PARTITION_SIZE: The size of the filesystem partition for the user data (userdata.img)
- BOARD_CACHEIMAGE_FILE_SYSTEM_TYPE: The filesystem format of cache partition
- BOARD_FLASH_BLOCK_SIZE: The block size of the flash device

Building and testing x86emu

Once we have the source code, we can start to build and test our x86emu device in this section.

Building x86emu

Before we start to build x86emu, let's have a quick look at the Android build system first. The major difference between the Android build system from other make-based build systems is that the Android build system doesn't rely on recursive Makefiles. Android Makefiles end in the extension .mk; the main Makefile for a particular source directory is named Android.mk. The build system imports all Android.mk from various folders to create one large Makefile to start the build, as we can see from the following code snippet:

```
$ make -j4
============================================
PLATFORM_VERSION_CODENAME=REL
PLATFORM_VERSION=7.1.1
TARGET_PRODUCT=x86emu
TARGET_BUILD_VARIANT=eng
TARGET_BUILD_TYPE=release
TARGET_BUILD_APPS=
...
HOST_BUILD_TYPE=release
BUILD_ID=MOB30Z
OUT_DIR=out
============================================
including ./abi/cpp/Android.mk ...
including ./art/Android.mk ...
including ./bionic/Android.mk ...
...
```

Before we start the build, we must set up the build environment first. The Android build system provides a `build/envsetup.sh` script for the build environment setup. We can set up the build environment by running the following command:

```
$ source build/envsetup.sh
```

After this, we need to specify the target that we want to build. In Android build system terms, this is called a lunch-combo. We can specify a lunch-combo directly:

```
$ lunch x86emu_x86-eng
```

Or select it from a list in a menu:

```
$ lunch

You're building on Linux

Lunch menu... pick a combo:
     1. aosp_arm-eng
     2. aosp_arm64-eng
     3. aosp_mips-eng
     4. aosp_mips64-eng
     5. aosp_x86-eng
     6. aosp_x86_64-eng
     7. x86emu_x86-eng
     8. x86emu_x86-userdebug
     9. x86emu_x86-user

Which would you like? [aosp_arm-eng] 7

================================================
PLATFORM_VERSION_CODENAME=REL
PLATFORM_VERSION=7.1.1
TARGET_PRODUCT=x86emu_x86
TARGET_BUILD_VARIANT=eng
TARGET_BUILD_TYPE=release
TARGET_BUILD_APPS=
TARGET_ARCH=x86
TARGET_ARCH_VARIANT=x86
TARGET_CPU_VARIANT=
TARGET_2ND_ARCH=
TARGET_2ND_ARCH_VARIANT=
TARGET_2ND_CPU_VARIANT=
HOST_ARCH=x86_64
HOST_2ND_ARCH=x86
HOST_OS=linux
HOST_OS_EXTRA=Linux-4.2.0-27-generic-x86_64-with-Ubuntu-14.04-trusty
HOST_CROSS_OS=windows
```

```
HOST_CROSS_ARCH=x86
HOST_CROSS_2ND_ARCH=x86_64
HOST_BUILD_TYPE=release
BUILD_ID=NMF260
OUT_DIR=out
===============================================
```

We learnt this in `Chapter 2`, *Setting Up the Development Environment,* when we built the Android emulator image. You may notice that the difference here in the menu items is that the menu includes the device configurations added by us in this chapter.

The lunch-combo that we select here is `x86emu_x86-eng`. We can start to build the target now using the following command:

```
$ make -j4
```

Or:

```
$ m -j4
```

The `-j4` option is used to specify the number of concurrent make sessions. It is related to the number of CPU cores that you have on your system, for example, you may choose `-j8` in a more powerful hardware platform. The `m` command is available after we execute `source build/envsetup.sh`. It is equivalent to `croot; make -j4`.

If you want to see the actual commands in the build, you can use the `showcommands` option on the command line:

```
$ make -j4 showcommands
```

You may use other frequently used build targets. Here is a list of them that you may refer to in your build:

- `make sdk`: Build the tools that are part of an SDK (`adb`, `fastboot`, and so on).
- `make snod`: Build the system image from the current software binaries.
- `make all`: Make everything, whether it is included in the product definition or not.
- `make clean`: Remove all built files (prepare for a new build). It is the same as `rm -rf out/<configuration>/`.
- `make modules`: Shows a list of submodules that can be built (a list of all `LOCAL_MODULE` definitions).
- `make <local_module>`: Make a specific module (note that this is not the same as the directory name. It is the `LOCAL_MODULE` definition in the `Android.mk` file).

- make clean-<local_module>: Clean a specific module.
- make bootimage TARGET_PREBUILT_KERNEL=/path/to/bzImage: Create a new boot image with custom bzImage.
- make recoveryimage: Make the recovery in bootable/recovery/.

Besides the build targets, there are some helper macros and functions that are installed when you source envsetup.sh. You can find out what they are by using the hmm command:

```
$ hmm
Invoke ". build/envsetup.sh" from your shell to add the following functions
to your environment:
- lunch:    lunch <product_name>-<build_variant>
- tapas:    tapas [<App1> <App2> ...]
[arm|x86|mips|armv5|arm64|x86_64|mips64] [eng|userdebug|user]
- croot:    Changes directory to the top of the tree.
- m:        Makes from the top of the tree.
- mm:       Builds all of the modules in the current directory, but not
their dependencies.
- mmm:      Builds all of the modules in the supplied directories, but not
their dependencies.
            To limit the modules being built use the syntax: mmm
dir/:target1,target2.
- mma:      Builds all of the modules in the current directory, and their
dependencies.
- mmma:     Builds all of the modules in the supplied directories, and their
dependencies.
- cgrep:    Greps on all local C/C++ files.
- ggrep:    Greps on all local Gradle files.
- jgrep:    Greps on all local Java files.
- resgrep:  Greps on all local res/*.xml files.
- mangrep:  Greps on all local AndroidManifest.xml files.
- sepgrep:  Greps on all local sepolicy files.
- sgrep:    Greps on all local source files.
- godir:    Go to the directory containing a file.

Environemnt options:
- SANITIZE_HOST: Set to 'true' to use ASAN for all host modules. Note that
                 ASAN_OPTIONS=detect_leaks=0 will be set by default until
                 the build is leak-check clean.

Look at the source to view more functions. The complete list is:
addcompletions add_lunch_combo cgrep check_product check_variant
choosecombo chooseproduct choosetype choosevariant core coredump_enable
coredump_setup cproj croot findmakefile get_abs_build_var getbugreports
get_build_var getdriver getlastscreenshot get_make_command getprebuilt
```

```
getscreenshotpath getsdcardpath gettargetarch gettop ggrep godir hmm is
isviewserverstarted jgrep key_back key_home key_menu lunch _lunch m make
mangrep mgrep mm mma mmm mmma pez pid printconfig print_lunch_menu qpid
rcgrep resgrep runhat runtest sepgrep set_java_home setpaths
set_sequence_number set_stuff_for_environment settitle sgrep smoketest
stacks startviewserver stopviewserver systemstack tapas tracedmdump
treegrep
```

After we build the target successfully, we can find the images at
`out/target/product/x86emu` in our case. We can also use the environment variable
`$OUT` as follows to list the build output:

```
$ ls -F $OUT
Android-info.txt   dex_bootjars/                      ramdisk.img              symbols/
boot.img           gen/                               ramdisk-recovery.img     system/
cache/             installed-files.txt                recovery/
system.img
cache.img          kernel                             recovery.id
userdata.img
clean_steps.mk     obj/                               recovery.img
data/              previous_build_config.mk           root/
```

Testing x86emu

To test x86emu, we can use the AVD `a25x86` that we created in `Chapter 2`, *Setting Up the
Development Environment*. To use our own system images, we can create a shell script
`~/bin/test-ch04.sh` as follows:

```
#!/bin/sh

emulator @a25x86 -verbose -show-kernel -shell -selinux disabled -system
${OUT}/system.img -ramdisk ${OUT}/ramdisk.img -initdata ${OUT}/userdata.img
-kernel ${OUT}/kernel
```

You can see from the preceding shell script that the images for x86emu are used to start the
AVD `a25x86`. You need to set your Android SDK path so you can use the emulator from
Android SDK:

```
$ test-ch04.sh
```

After you start the emulator, you can go to **Settings** | **About phone** to check the build information, as shown in the following screenshot:

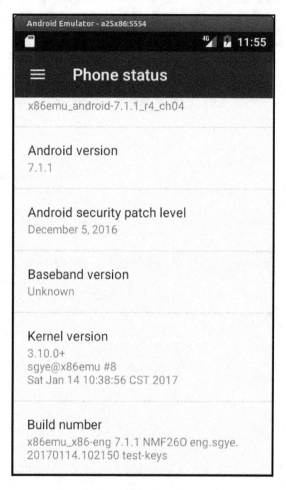

x86emu build information

We can see from **About phone** that **Model** is **x86emu_android-7.1.1_r4_ch04**, which we specified in the product definition Makefile `x86emu_x86.mk`. **Kernel version** is **3.10.0** and **Build number** is the build target **x86emu_x86-eng**.

If you want to test the images in this chapter without setting up your own build, you can download the images from SourceForge at `https://sourceforge.net/projects/Android-system-programming/files/android-7/ch04/`.

Integrating with Eclipse

You may use an **Integrated Development Environment (IDE)** for your development work. It is possible to integrate the AOSP build environment and selected projects into your favorite IDE. Here, I will use Eclipse as an example to explain how to integrate our projects and AOSP build environment in Eclipse. Be aware that since AOSP can only be built in the Linux environment, this can only work for Linux as well.

Even though Android Studio is the default IDE for Android application development, I prefer Eclipse for Android system programming. With Eclipse, we can build both native and Java applications. We can also integrate AOSP builds in Eclipse projects.

To set up the Eclipse environment, you can use the latest Eclipse with ADT plugin or you can download an old ADT bundle from Google.

For Linux x86 or x86_64:

- http://dl.google.com/Android/adt/adt-bundle-linux-x86_64-20140702.zip
- http://dl.google.com/Android/adt/adt-bundle-linux-x86-20140702.zip

To use Eclipse, we need to create a Makefile for our x86emu device build as follows:

```
all:
    cd ../../..;make -j8 showcommands 2>&1 | tee x86emu-`date +%Y%m%d`.txt

x86emu:
    cd ../../..;make -j4

snod:
    cd ../../..;make snod

initrd:
    cd ../../..;make initrd USE_SQUASHFS=0

ramdisk:
    cd ../../..;make -j4

clean-ramdisk:
    rm ${OUT}/ramdisk.img
    rm -rf ${OUT}/root

clean-initrd:
    rm ${OUT}/initrd.img
    rm -rf ${OUT}/installer
```

We need to define a few build targets that can be used in Eclipse. Let's see how to import an x86emu device build into the Eclipse project. We will use Eclipse from the ADT bundle to explain the process. To integrate the AOSP build with Eclipse, we must launch Eclipse in the AOSP build environment. Let's start Eclipse as follows:

```
$ source build/envsetup.sh
$ lunch x86emu_x86-eng
${SDK_ROOT}/eclipse/eclipse
```

After we have installed the ADT bundle, we can find Eclipse in the preceding directory under the SDK installation path. After we launch Eclipse, select the **C/C++** Perspective, as shown in the following screenshot:

Select the C/C++ perspective

We can import the x86emu directory as an existing Makefile project to Eclipse by selecting **File | Import... | Existing Code as Makefile Project**, as shown in the following screenshot:

Importing existing code as a Makefile project

Click on **Next** and navigate to the `$AOSP/device/generic/x86emu` folder to import the source code, as shown in the following screenshot:

Import existing code

Once we import the project, we should be able to see that all files under the x86emu folder are shown on the right-hand side in **Project Explorer**, as we can see in the following screenshot. Then we can click the right mouse button to see the menu list for the project and select **Make Targets | Create... | Create Make Target**. We can add the build target that we defined in the Makefile in the **Target name** field. If we define the default build target all, the default build in Eclipse will trigger the build target all in our Makefile. This is what we defined for build target all:

```
all:
    cd ../../..;make -j8 showcommands 2>&1 | tee x86emu-`date +%Y%m%d`.txt
```

What we do here is launch the AOSP build at the AOSP root directory. We also generate a log file for the build using a naming convention, x86emu-{$DATE}.txt, and you can find this log file at the AOSP root folder after the build is completed.

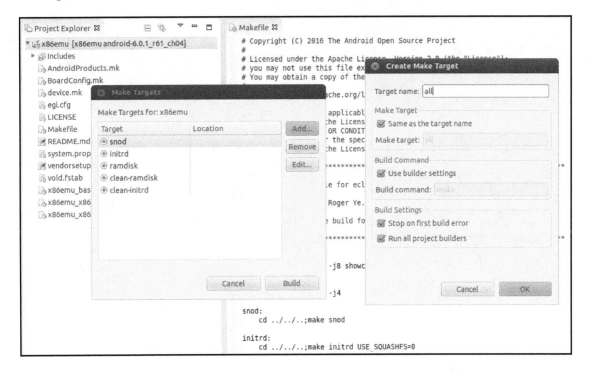

Creating a Make Target in Eclipse

After we create all build targets, we can build AOSP from Eclipse by selecting **Project | Build All** or use the shortcut *Ctrl + B* to launch the build.

Summary

In this chapter, we learnt how to create a new device based on the Android emulator build for Intel x86 architecture. We explained the different build layers in the AOSP built system and how these build layers associate with Makefiles for a device. After that, we build and tested the new x86emu device. Finally, to improve the efficiency of development work, we integrated the AOSP build in Eclipse. In the next chapter, we will extend Android emulator to support ARM binary translation using the x86emu device.

5
Enabling the ARM Translator and Introducing Native Bridge

We created a new x86emu device in the last chapter. This is the foundation of further customization and extension. As we know, if the application includes native libraries, it cannot run on a different processor architecture. Most Android applications are built for the ARM platform. We usually have problems with running these applications with ARM native libraries on Intel x86 platform. However, Google provides a solution for this situation from Android 5 and above called **Native Bridge**. We will delve into the Native Bridge and Intel Houdini implementation to extend x86emu to support the ARM native application in this chapter. In this chapter, we will cover the following topics:

- Introducing Native Bridge
- Integrating the Houdini library to the x86emu device
- Building and testing the image with Houdini integration

Introducing Native Bridge

Native Bridge is implemented as a part of **Android Runtime** (**ART**) in the Android architecture. It is used to support running native libraries in a different processor architecture so that an application with native libraries can run on a broader range of devices. The Intel ARM translator called Houdini is one of the use cases of Native Bridge. In ART, there are two stages for the Native Bridge to be initialized:

1. In the first stage, the Native Bridge is loaded in the system as part of the ART initialization process. This is common for all applications.

2. In the second stage, when an application with native libraries is started, it will be forked from Zygote. At this time, the Native Bridge will be initialized and ready to be used for the application. This is a process that is specific for individual applications. For example, if there are no native libraries being used, Native Bridge won't be initialized for this application.

Zygote
Android at its core has a process they call the Zygote, which starts up at init. This process is a "warmed-up" process, which means it's a process that's been initialized and has all the core libraries linked in. When you start an application, the Zygote is forked to create the new process. The real speedup is achieved by *not* copying the shared libraries. This memory will only be copied if the new process tries to modify it. This means that all of the core libraries can exist in a single place because they are read-only.

When the application starts to load a native library from a different processor architecture, the Native Bridge will help to resolve the loading of this library. For example, when we load an ARM library on Intel the x86 architecture, the Native Bridge will use Houdini to load and execute this ARM library in the Intel x86 environment.

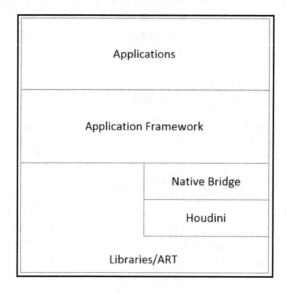

Native Bridge in Android architecture

Native Bridge is built as a `libnativebridge.so` shared library as part of the Android system libraries, as shown in the preceding diagram. The implementation can be found at `$AOSP/system/core/libnativebridge`. Within the Native Bridge implementation, it has five states defined in `native_bridge.cc`, as follows:

```
enum class NativeBridgeState {
    kNotSetup,              // Initial state.
    kOpened,                // After successful dlopen.
    kPreInitialized,        // After successful pre-initialization.
    kInitialized,           // After successful initialization.
    kClosed                 // Closed or errors.
};
```

When the Android system has just started, Native Bridge is in a `kNotSetup` state. During the initialization of ART, it will be loaded into the system and the stage changes to `kOpened`.

These two states are in the first stage of the Native Bridge initialization. When the user starts an application with native libraries, the system will fork a new process from Zygote. At this time, the system will do some pre-initialization work for Native Bridge, and we will see this later in this chapter. The state changes to `kPreInitialized` at this time. After the process is forked from Zygote, Native Bridge is initialized as part of the process creation and its state becomes `kInitialized`. The `kClosed` state is usually not used unless there is an error and Native Bridge is closed. These three states fall into the second stage of the Native Bridge initialization.

With the overview about Native Bridge in Android system architecture, we will have to delve into the details of each stage about Native Bridge used at runtime.

Setting up Native Bridge as part of the ART initialization

First of all, let's take a look at how Native Bridge is loaded in the system. Native Bridge is loaded as part of the initialization of ART. As shown in the following diagram, it includes function calls from **ART** to the **Native Bridge** implementation. At the end of this stage, the state of **Native Bridge** will be set to kOpened.

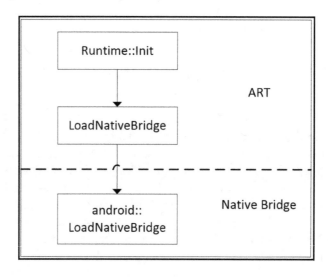

Loading Native Bridge

When the system is initializing ART, the Runtime::Init function is called. Inside Runtime::Init, a LoadNativeBridge function is invoked to load the Native Bridge shared library. We can see this in the following code snippet:

```
bool Runtime::Init(const RuntimeOptions& raw_options, bool
ignore_unrecognized) {
  ATRACE_BEGIN("Runtime::Init");
  CHECK_EQ(sysconf(_SC_PAGE_SIZE), kPageSize);
  ...
    std::string native_bridge_file_name =
    runtime_options.ReleaseOrDefault(Opt::NativeBridge);
    is_native_bridge_loaded_ =
    LoadNativeBridge(native_bridge_file_name);
    ...
}
```

This `LoadNativeBridge` function is part of ART and it is implemented in the `native_bridge_art_interface.cc` file, as shown in the following snippet. This function simply calls to another function, `android::LoadNativeBridge`, in the namespace `android`, while it itself is in the namespace of `art`. The functions in the namespace of `android` are part of the Native Bridge implementation, as shown in the preceding diagram, and we will see more of this later in this chapter. We can see the implementation of `LoadNativeBridge` in the following code snippet:

```
static android::NativeBridgeRuntimeCallbacks native_bridge_art_callbacks_ {
  GetMethodShorty, GetNativeMethodCount, GetNativeMethods
};

bool LoadNativeBridge(std::string& native_bridge_library_filename) {
  VLOG(startup) << "Runtime::Setup native bridge library: "
      << (native_bridge_library_filename.empty() ? "(empty)" :
      native_bridge_library_filename);
  return android::LoadNativeBridge(native_bridge_library_filename.c_str(),
                                   &native_bridge_art_callbacks_);
}
```

The `android::LoadNativeBridge` function in the `android` namespace has an extra `native_bridge_art_callbacks` parameter compared to the `art:LoadNativeBridge` function in the `art` namespace. The type of this parameter is a pointer of `struct NativeBridgeRuntimeCallbacks`, which is defined in `native_bridge.h`. In `struct NativeBridgeRuntimeCallbacks`, it defines three callback methods as follows:

```
// Runtime interfaces to native bridge.
struct NativeBridgeRuntimeCallbacks {
  // Get shorty of a Java method. The shorty is supposed to be
  persistent in
  // memory.
  //
  // Parameters:
  //   env [IN] pointer to JNIenv.
  //   mid [IN] Java methodID.
  // Returns:
  //   short descriptor for method.
  const char* (*getMethodShorty)(JNIEnv* env, jmethodID mid);

  // Get number of native methods for specified class.
  //
  // Parameters:
  //   env [IN] pointer to JNIenv.
  //   clazz [IN] Java class object.
  // Returns:
  //   number of native methods.
```

```
    uint32_t (*getNativeMethodCount)(JNIEnv* env, jclass clazz);

    // Get at most 'method_count' native methods for specified class
    'clazz'.
    // Results are outputed
    // via 'methods' [OUT]. The signature pointer in JNINativeMethod is
    reused
    // as the method shorty.
    //
    // Parameters:
    //    env [IN] pointer to JNIenv.
    //    clazz [IN] Java class object.
    //    methods [OUT] array of method with the name, shorty, and fnPtr.
    //    method_count [IN] max number of elements in methods.
    // Returns:
    //    number of method it actually wrote to methods.
    uint32_t (*getNativeMethods)(JNIEnv* env, jclass clazz,
    JNINativeMethod* methods, uint32_t method_count);
};
```

These three callback functions that are part of ART are implemented in the
`native_bridge_art_interface.cc` file. These callback functions provide a way for
native methods to call JNI native functions. We will see how this callback data structure is
passed to the actual Native Bridge implementation later. In our case, the actual
implementation is the Houdini library.

The `native_bridge.h` file defines another callback function data structure,
`NativeBridgeCallbacks`, which is used as the Native Bridge interface of its actual
implementation. In our case, this implementation is the Houdini library. The Houdini
library needs to implement these callback functions and pass the pointers to Native Bridge
so that ART can use them. The following figure depicts the relationship between these two
groups of callback functions:

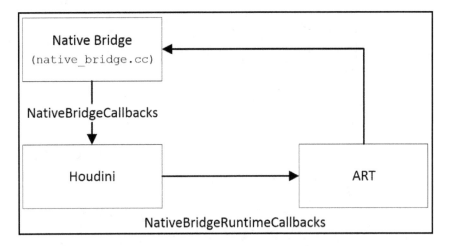

ART, Native Bridge, and Houdini

In the preceding figure, we can see that **ART** calls **Native Bridge** functions to load and initialize the **Native Bridge** module. The **Native Bridge** module invokes the callback functions registered by **Houdini** to handle all ARM native binary translations. During the initialization of **Native Bridge**, **NativeBridgeRuntimeCallbacks** are passed to the **Houdini** library so that the methods in the **Houdini** library can call JNI native functions.

Now let's take a look at the implementation of android::LoadNativeBridge:

```
bool LoadNativeBridge(const char* nb_library_filename,
        const NativeBridgeRuntimeCallbacks* runtime_cbs) {

  if (state != NativeBridgeState::kNotSetup) {
    // Setup has been called before. Ignore this call.
    if (nb_library_filename != nullptr) {
        ALOGW("Called LoadNativeBridge for an already set up native
            bridge. State is %s.", GetNativeBridgeStateString(state));
    }
    had_error = true;
    return false;
  }

  if (nb_library_filename == nullptr || *nb_library_filename == 0)
  {
    CloseNativeBridge(false);
    return false;
  } else {
    if (!NativeBridgeNameAcceptable(nb_library_filename)) {
      CloseNativeBridge(true);
    } else {
```

```
        // Try to open the library.
        void* handle = dlopen(nb_library_filename, RTLD_LAZY);
        if (handle != nullptr) {
          callbacks =
              reinterpret_cast<NativeBridgeCallbacks*>(dlsym(handle,
              kNativeBridgeInterfaceSymbol));
          if (callbacks != nullptr) {
            if (VersionCheck(callbacks)) {
              // Store the handle for later.
              native_bridge_handle = handle;
            } else {
              callbacks = nullptr;
              dlclose(handle);
              ALOGW("Unsupported native bridge interface.");
            }
          } else {
            dlclose(handle);
          }
        }

        if (callbacks == nullptr) {
          CloseNativeBridge(true);
        } else {
          runtime_callbacks = runtime_cbs;
          state = NativeBridgeState::kOpened;
        }
      }
      return state == NativeBridgeState::kOpened;
    }
  }
```

As we can see from the preceding code snippet, `android::LoadNativeBridge` checks the state first. It should be in a `kNotSetup` state. Otherwise, it will report an error and return.

To be convenient, we will refer to the function in the Android namespace as `LoadNativeBridge` instead of `android::LoadNativeBridge` in the next few paragraphs. The files that will be discussed can be found at:
`$AOSP/art/runtime/runtime.c`
`$AOSP/art/runtime/native_bridge_art_interface.c`
`$AOSP/system/core/libnativebridge/native_bridge.cc`

After that, it will check whether the first parameter is `NULL` and the filename is good to use or not. If everything is good, it will open the library through `dlopen` using the filename `nb_library_filename`.

So what is the content of the `nb_library_filename` filename? As we can see from the `Runtime::Init` function, the first parameter of `LoadNativeBridge` is initialized using a `Opt::NativeBridge` property:

```
std::string native_bridge_file_name =
runtime_options.ReleaseOrDefault(Opt::NativeBridge);
```

This property is initialized from the default property `ro.dalvik.vm.native.bridge`, which is defined in the `default.prop` file of the Android system. This is done in the `AndroidRuntime::startVm` function, as you can see in the following snippet. This function is defined in the `$AOSP/frameworks/base/core/jni/AndroidRuntime.cpp` file:

```
int AndroidRuntime::startVm(JavaVM** pJavaVM, JNIEnv** pEnv, bool zygote)
{
    ...
    // Native bridge library. "0" means that native bridge is disabled.
    property_get("ro.dalvik.vm.native.bridge", propBuf, "");
    if (propBuf[0] == '\0') {
        ALOGW("ro.dalvik.vm.native.bridge is not expected to be
            empty");
    } else if (strcmp(propBuf, "0") != 0) {
        snprintf(nativeBridgeLibrary, sizeof("-XX:NativeBridge=") +
        PROPERTY_VALUE_MAX, "-XX:NativeBridge=%s", propBuf);
        addOption(nativeBridgeLibrary);
    }
    ...
}
```

When Native Bridge is enabled, the `ro.dalvik.vm.native.bridge` property usually includes a shared library filename. In our case, it is `libhoudini.so` for Intel devices or `libnb.so` for Android-x86. If Native Bridge is disabled, its value is 0. Once the library is loaded successfully, it will use the `kNativeBridgeInterfaceSymbol` symbol to get the memory location and cast the location to a pointer of `NativeBridgeCallbacks`. This means that the Houdini library provides an implementation of `NativeBridgeCallbacks`. Let's look at what it is inside `NativeBridgeCallbacks`:

```
struct NativeBridgeCallbacks {
  uint32_t version;
  bool (*initialize)(const NativeBridgeRuntimeCallbacks*
        runtime_cbs, const char* private_dir, const char*
        instruction_set);
  void* (*loadLibrary)(const char* libpath, int flag);
  void* (*getTrampoline)(void* handle, const char* name, const
        char* shorty, uint32_t len);
  bool (*isSupported)(const char* libpath);
```

```
    const struct NativeBridgeRuntimeValues* (*getAppEnv)(const char*
        instruction_set);
    bool (*isCompatibleWith)(uint32_t bridge_version);
    NativeBridgeSignalHandlerFn (*getSignalHandler)(int signal);
};
```

From the preceding code snippet, we can see that `NativeBridgeCallbacks` includes a variable and seven callback functions:

- `version`: This is the version number of the interface. So far, there are two versions. Version 1 defines the first five callback functions and version 2 adds another two new functions, which we will see very shortly.
- `initialize`: This function initializes an instance of Native Bridge. Native Bridge's internal implementation must ensure multithread safety and Native Bridge is initialized only once.
- `loadLibrary` : This function loads a shared library that is supported by the Native Bridge.
- `getTrampoline` : This function gets a Native Bridge trampoline for the specified native method.
- `isSupported` : This function checks whether the instance of Native Bridge is valid and whether it is for an ABI that is supported by Native Bridge.

In version 2, the following two functions are added:

- `isCompatibleWith`: This function checks whether the bridge is compatible with the given version of library. A bridge may decide not to be forward- or backward-compatible, and `libnativebridge` will then stop using it.
- `getSignalHandler`: A callback function to retrieve a Native Bridge's signal handler for the specified signal. The runtime will ensure that the signal handler is being called after the runtime's own handler, but before all chained handlers. The native bridge should not try to install the handler by itself, as that will potentially lead to cycles.

Now we have concluded the first stage of the Native Bridge initialization. As we can see from the preceding lists, Native Bridge is loaded at the startup of ART. At this stage, the initialization is not process-specific. The library name is defined in the `ro.dalvik.vm.native.bridge` property. In our case, ART loads the `libhoudini.so` library through the `LoadNativeBridge` function defined in `libnativebridge.so`. After Native Bridge is loaded successfully, the state is set to `kOpened`.

Pre-initializing Native Bridge

In the second stage of Native Bridge initialization, it becomes process-specific. Native Bridge can be used by an Android application to load a native library in a different processor architecture than the current device. The other two states, kPreInitialized and kInitialized, are related to the creation of Android applications, as we know that all applications are forked from Zygote in Android. Let's look at the pre-initialization of Native Bridge first, as shown in the following diagram:

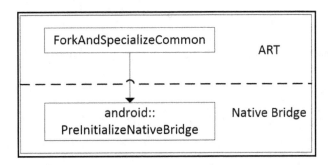

Pre-initialization of Native Bridge

During the creation of an application, the FadkAndSpecializeCommon function is called. The pre-initialization of Native Bridge is done in this function. This function is defined in the $AOSP/frameworks/base/core/jni/com_android_internal_os_Zygote.cpp file:

```
static pid_t ForkAndSpecializeCommon(JNIEnv* env, uid_t uid, gid_t
    gid, jintArray javaGids, jint debug_flags, jobjectArray
    javaRlimits, jlong permittedCapabilities, jlong
    effectiveCapabilities, jint mount_external, jstring
    java_se_info, jstring java_se_name, bool is_system_server,
    jintArray fdsToClose, jstring instructionSet, jstring dataDir) {
      SetSigChldHandler();

#ifdef ENABLE_SCHED_BOOST
  SetForkLoad(true);
#endif
...
  pid_t pid = fork();

  if (pid == 0) {
    // The child process.
...
    bool use_native_bridge = !is_system_server && (instructionSet !=
    NULL) && android::NativeBridgeAvailable();
    if (use_native_bridge) {
```

```
        ScopedUtfChars isa_string(env, instructionSet);
        use_native_bridge =
        android::NeedsNativeBridge(isa_string.c_str());
    }
    if (use_native_bridge && dataDir == NULL) {
      use_native_bridge = false;
      ALOGW("Native bridge will not be used because dataDir == NULL.");
    }

    if (!MountEmulatedStorage(uid, mount_external, use_native_bridge)) {
      ALOGW("Failed to mount emulated storage: %s", strerror(errno));
      if (errno == ENOTCONN || errno == EROFS) {
      } else {
        RuntimeAbort(env, __LINE__, "Cannot continue without emulated
        storage");
      }
    }

    if (!is_system_server) {
        int rc = createProcessGroup(uid, getpid());
        if (rc != 0) {
            if (rc == -EROFS) {
                ALOGW("createProcessGroup failed, kernel missing
                CONFIG_CGROUP_CPUACCT?");
            } else {
                ALOGE("createProcessGroup(%d, %d) failed: %s", uid,
                pid, strerror(-rc));
            }
        }
    }

    SetGids(env, javaGids);

    SetRLimits(env, javaRlimits);

    if (use_native_bridge) {
      ScopedUtfChars isa_string(env, instructionSet);
      ScopedUtfChars data_dir(env, dataDir);
      android::PreInitializeNativeBridge(data_dir.c_str(),
      isa_string.c_str());
    }
...
    env->CallStaticVoidMethod(gZygoteClass,
          gCallPostForkChildHooks,
          debug_flags, is_system_server ? NULL : instructionSet);
...
  } else if (pid > 0) {
    // the parent process
```

```
#ifdef ENABLE_SCHED_BOOST
    // unset scheduler knob
    SetForkLoad(false);
#endif

    }
    return pid;
}
```

In this `ForkAndSpecializeCommon` function, it checks whether the current process is not a SystemServer process and if the Native Bridge is ready to use. After that, it calls the `NeedsNativeBridge` function to check whether the current process needs to use Native Bridge or not:

```
bool NeedsNativeBridge(const char* instruction_set) {
    if (instruction_set == nullptr) {
        ALOGE("Null instruction set in NeedsNativeBridge.");
        return false;
    }
    return strncmp(instruction_set, kRuntimeISA,
                strlen(kRuntimeISA) + 1) != 0;
}
```

The `NeedsNativeBridge` function compares `instruction_set` with the current Android platform instruction set. If these two instruction sets are different, then we need to use Native Bridge; otherwise, we don't. The `NeedsNativeBridge` function is implemented in `native_bridge.cc`.

If Native Bridge is needed by the application, then `PreInitializeNativeBridge`, which is also implemented in `native_bridge.cc`, is going to be called with two parameters, `app_data_dir_in` and `instruction_set`:

```
bool PreInitializeNativeBridge(const char* app_data_dir_in,
        const char* instruction_set) {
    if (state != NativeBridgeState::kOpened) {
        ALOGE("Invalid state: native bridge is expected to be opened.");
        CloseNativeBridge(true);
        return false;
    }

    if (app_data_dir_in == nullptr) {
        ALOGE("Application private directory cannot be null.");
        CloseNativeBridge(true);
        return false;
    }

    const size_t len = strlen(app_data_dir_in) +
```

```
                      strlen(kCodeCacheDir) + 2; // '\0' + '/'
  app_code_cache_dir = new char[len];
  snprintf(app_code_cache_dir, len, "%s/%s", app_data_dir_in,
  kCodeCacheDir);

  state = NativeBridgeState::kPreInitialized;

#ifndef __APPLE__
  if (instruction_set == nullptr) {
    return true;
  }
  size_t isa_len = strlen(instruction_set);
  if (isa_len > 10) {
    ALOGW("Instruction set %s is malformed, must be less than or equal
    to 10 characters.", instruction_set);
    return true;
  }

  char cpuinfo_path[1024];

#if defined(__ANDROID__)
  snprintf(cpuinfo_path, sizeof(cpuinfo_path), "/system/lib"
#ifdef __LP64__
      "64"
#endif  // __LP64__
      "/%s/cpuinfo", instruction_set);
#else   // !__ANDROID__
  snprintf(cpuinfo_path, sizeof(cpuinfo_path), "./cpuinfo");
#endif

  // Bind-mount.
  if (TEMP_FAILURE_RETRY(mount(cpuinfo_path,
                              "/proc/cpuinfo",
                              nullptr,
                              MS_BIND,
                              nullptr)) == -1) {
    ALOGW("Failed to bind-mount %s as /proc/cpuinfo: %s", cpuinfo_path,
    strerror(errno));
  }
#else   // __APPLE__
  UNUSED(instruction_set);
  ALOGW("Mac OS does not support bind-mounting. Host simulation of
  native bridge impossible.");
#endif

  return true;
}
```

From the preceding code snippet, we can see that it will check whether the state is kOpened or not. Then PreInitializeNativeBridge will do two things. Firstly, it creates a code cache directory using the first parameter, app_data_dir_in, for Native Bridge in the data folder of the application. Next, it uses the second parameter, instruction_set, to find the /system/lib/<isa>/cpuinfo path and it does a bind-mount of it to /proc/cpuinfo. If Houdini is available in the device, you can find the /system/lib/arm/cpuinfo file in the system folder. Once the preceding two tasks are completed, the state of Native Bridge will be set to kPreInitialized.

Initializing Native Bridge

After the state is changed to kPreInitialized, the creation of the new Android application will continue in the ForkAndSpecializeCommon function. At the end of this function, it calls a callPostForkChildHooks registered function through a global variable, gCallPostForkChildHooks. The call stack will eventually go to a ZygoteHooks_nativePostForkChild function, which is the JNI implementation of the postForkChild Java method. The postForkChild function is called by Zygote in the child process after every fork. The following table is a summary of the call stack:

Function	Class	Language
ForkAndSpecializeCommon		C++
gCallPostForkChildHooks		C++
callPostForkChildHooks	Zygote	Java
postForkChild	ZygoteHooks	Java
ZygoteHooks_nativePostForkChild	JNI (postForkChild)	C++

The ZygoteHooks_nativePostForkChild function is implemented in the $AOSP/art/runtime/native/dalvik_system_ZygotHooks.cc file. The DidForkFromZygote function is implemented in the $AOSP/art/runtime/runtime.cc file.

The following diagram is a summary of functions involved in the second stage of the initialization of Native Bridge. Be aware that we are in the child process now. We can see that the **Runtime::DidForkFromZygote** function in **ART** will call the following Native Bridge interface functions: **InitializeNativeBridge** and **SetupEnvironment**. The Native Bridge interface functions will eventually call the registered callback functions in the Houdini library.

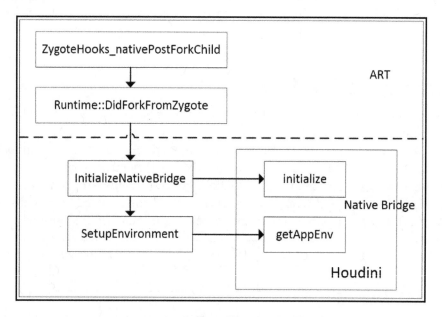

Initialization of Native Bridge

Let's look at the JNI implementation of `postForkChild`:

```
static void ZygoteHooks_nativePostForkChild(JNIEnv* env,
    jclass, jlong token, jint debug_flags,
    jstring instruction_set) {
...
  if (instruction_set != nullptr) {
    ScopedUtfChars isa_string(env, instruction_set);
    InstructionSet isa =
    GetInstructionSetFromString(isa_string.c_str());
    Runtime::NativeBridgeAction action =
    Runtime::NativeBridgeAction::kUnload;
    if (isa != kNone && isa != kRuntimeISA) {
      action = Runtime::NativeBridgeAction::kInitialize;
    }
    Runtime::Current()->DidForkFromZygote(env, action,
    isa_string.c_str());
```

```
  } else {
    Runtime::Current()->DidForkFromZygote(env,
    Runtime::NativeBridgeAction::kUnload, nullptr);
  }
}
```

Here, it checks the instruction set again to decide whether we need Native Bridge for the application. Then it calls the `Runtime::DidForkFromZygote` function to initialize Native Bridge in the new process:

```
void Runtime::DidForkFromZygote(JNIEnv* env,
    NativeBridgeAction action, const char* isa) {
  is_zygote_ = false;

  if (is_native_bridge_loaded_) {
    switch (action) {
      case NativeBridgeAction::kUnload:
        UnloadNativeBridge();
        is_native_bridge_loaded_ = false;
        break;

      case NativeBridgeAction::kInitialize:
        InitializeNativeBridge(env, isa);
        break;
    }
  }
...
}
```

As we can see, `Runtime::DidForkFromZygote` calls the `InitializeNativeBridge` based on the action. Now let's dive into the `InitializeNativeBridge` function, which is implemented in `native_bridge.cc`:

```
bool InitializeNativeBridge(JNIEnv* env,
    const char* instruction_set) {

  if (state == NativeBridgeState::kPreInitialized) {
    // Check for code cache: if it doesn't exist try to create it.
    struct stat st;
    if (stat(app_code_cache_dir, &st) == -1) {
      if (errno == ENOENT) {
        if (mkdir(app_code_cache_dir, S_IRWXU | S_IRWXG | S_IXOTH)
        == -1) {
          ALOGW("Cannot create code cache directory %s: %s.",
          app_code_cache_dir, strerror(errno));
          ReleaseAppCodeCacheDir();
        }
```

```
        } else {
          ALOGW("Cannot stat code cache directory %s: %s.",
          app_code_cache_dir, strerror(errno));
          ReleaseAppCodeCacheDir();
        }
      } else if (!S_ISDIR(st.st_mode)) {
        ALOGW("Code cache is not a directory %s.", app_code_cache_dir);
        ReleaseAppCodeCacheDir();
      }

      if (state == NativeBridgeState::kPreInitialized) {
        if (callbacks->initialize(runtime_callbacks, app_code_cache_dir,
        instruction_set)) {
          SetupEnvironment(callbacks, env, instruction_set);
          state = NativeBridgeState::kInitialized;
          ReleaseAppCodeCacheDir();
        } else {
          // Unload the library.
          dlclose(native_bridge_handle);
          CloseNativeBridge(true);
        }
      }
    } else {
      CloseNativeBridge(true);
    }

    return state == NativeBridgeState::kInitialized;
  }
```

In the `InitializeNativeBridge` function, it creates the folder for the code cache first. Then, it invokes the `initialize` function, implemented by the Houdini library in our case.

> The shared library is `libhoudini.so` in Intel devices. If you run Android-x86 on an Intel device, the shared library is `libnb.so`. We will discuss `libnb.so` later in this chapter.

After that, it calls another `SetupEnvironment` function in `native_bridge.cc` to set up the environment for the Native Bridge in the current application. Finally, it sets the state to `kInitialized`. Now Native Bridge is ready for the current application to use.

Loading a native library

Once Native Bridge is ready to use, we can have a look at what happens when an application loads a native library in a different processor architecture.

We know that, if we implement a native method in a shared library, we need to implement a `JNI_OnLoad` entry point, which is used to register native methods. The Java code needs to make a call to either `System.load` or `System.loadLibrary` to load this shared library. In the following table, it is the call stack from `System.loadLibrary` to `JNI_OnLoad`:

Function	Class	Language
`System.loadLibrary`	Runtime	Java
`doLoad`	Runtime	Java
`nativeLoad`	Runtime	JNI
`Runtime_nativeLoad`	Runtime	C++
`LoadNativeLibrary`	JavaVMExt	C++
`JNI_OnLoad`		C++

Let's look into the details of `JavaVMExt::LoadNativeLibrary`. This function is defined in `$AOSP/art/runtime/jni_internal.cc`. The following diagram is the part of `JavaVMExt::LoadNativeLibrary` related to Native Bridge:

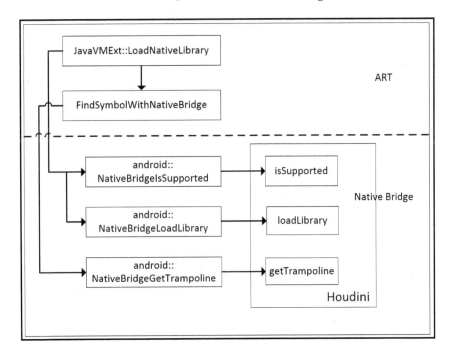

Loading native library

Android applications call to this function when they load native libraries. Usually, we refer to the native library in the same processor architecture here. With Native Bridge, we can load supported native libraries in a different processor architecture with this function as well:

```
bool JavaVMExt::LoadNativeLibrary(JNIEnv* env,
    const std::string& path, jobject class_loader,
    std::string* error_msg) {
...
  const char* path_str = path.empty() ? nullptr : path.c_str();
  void* handle = dlopen(path_str, RTLD_NOW);
  bool needs_native_bridge = false;
  if (handle == nullptr) {
    if (android::NativeBridgeIsSupported(path_str)) {
      handle = android::NativeBridgeLoadLibrary(path_str, RTLD_NOW);
      needs_native_bridge = true;
    }
  }
...
  bool was_successful = false;
  void* sym;
  if (needs_native_bridge) {
    library->SetNeedsNativeBridge();
    sym = library->FindSymbolWithNativeBridge("JNI_OnLoad", nullptr);
  } else {
    sym = dlsym(handle, "JNI_OnLoad");
  }
...
    typedef int (*JNI_OnLoadFn)(JavaVM*, void*);
    JNI_OnLoadFn jni_on_load = reinterpret_cast<JNI_OnLoadFn>(sym);
    int version = (*jni_on_load)(this, nullptr);
...
}
```

The `LoadNativeLibrary` function will call to `dlopen` to load the shared library first. If it is a shared library in a different processor architecture, such as an open ARM library on an Intel x86 platform, the `dlopen` call should fail. In this case, it will try to load the library again using Native Bridge instead of returning an error.

To use Native Bridge, it calls to the `NativeBridgeIsSupported` function first to check whether Native Bridge is supported or not. The `NativeBridgeIsSupported` function calls to the Houdini callback function, `isSupported`, to check whether the given shared library can be supported by Native Bridge or not:

```
bool NativeBridgeIsSupported(const char* libpath) {
  if (NativeBridgeInitialized()) {
```

```
    return callbacks->isSupported(libpath);
  }
  return false;
}
```

If the library can be supported by Native Bridge, `LoadNativeLibrary` will call another Native Bridge function, `android::NativeBridgeLoadLibrary`, to load the library:

```
void* NativeBridgeLoadLibrary(const char* libpath, int flag) {
  if (NativeBridgeInitialized()) {
    return callbacks->loadLibrary(libpath, flag);
  }
  return nullptr;
}
```

The Native Bridge `NativeBridgeLoadLibrary` function will make a call to the Houdini callback function `loadLibrary` to load the library. After the native library is loaded successfully, the `JNI_OnLoad` entry point will be found in the library and the system will call it to register the native methods registered by the native library. For a normal native library, the system function `dlsym` is used to get the `JNI_OnLoad` method, but the `FindSymbolWithNativeBridge` function is used to get `JNI_OnLoad` from the Houdini library:

```
void* FindSymbolWithNativeBridge(const std::string& symbol_name,
const char* shorty) {
    CHECK(NeedsNativeBridge());

    uint32_t len = 0;
    return android::NativeBridgeGetTrampoline(handle_,
    symbol_name.c_str(), shorty, len);
}
```

`FindSymbolWithNativeBridge` calls to the `NativeBridgeGetTrampoline` Native Bridge function, while `NativeBridgeGetTrampoline` calls to the `getTrampoline` Houdini callback function to do the actual work:

```
void* NativeBridgeGetTrampoline(void* handle, const char* name,
const char* shorty, uint32_t len) {
  if (NativeBridgeInitialized()) {
    return callbacks->getTrampoline(handle, name, shorty, len);
  }
  return nullptr;
}
```

From the preceding analysis, we can see that the ARM translator library Houdini uses the Native Bridge in Android to support ARM binary translation. The interfaces between the Houdini library and the system are two sets of callback functions. The callback functions defined in `NativeBridgeCallbacks` are used by the system to perform the function calls to the ARM native library, while the callback functions defined in `NativeBridgeRuntimeCallbacks` can be used by the functions in the Houdini library to call JNI functions in the system.

Integrating Houdini to the x86emu device

The goal of this chapter is to support Houdini ARM binary translation in Android emulator. After we have an overview of the internals of Native Bridge, which is the foundation of the Houdini library, we can work on Houdini support for our x86emu device.

Since the Houdini library is an Intel proprietary library, it is not available publicly. For those people who want to add Houdini to a new device, such as an Android emulator that is not supported by Intel, the only possible way is to copy the Houdini library from a supported device and add it to the unsupported device.

Fortunately, the open source project Android-x86 provides basic support for Houdini to any Intel devices, which we can use as a reference in this book. In this chapter, we will add Houdini to an Android emulator based on the Android-x86 project.

Changing the configuration of the x86emu build

The basic steps to support Houdini on a new device are:

- Change the device configurations according to what we have discussed in `Chapter 4`, *Customizing the Android Emulator*, in the *Why customize the Android emulator?* section
- Copy a suitable version of the Houdini library to the `system` folder

To work on the preceding two steps, let's start with the changes to the x86emu device configurations first. What we will do for this is that we will use the source code in `Chapter 4`, *Customizing the Android Emulator* as the baseline and make changes on top of it. This is also the approach that we will use in most of the chapters in this book. We will make independent changes based on the simplest code base for each topic. What I mean is that the source code for x86emu in `Chapter 4`, *Customizing the Android Emulator* is the simplest code base for the x86emu device.

Given that we already have a working copy of the AOSP source code for x86emu, we can make changes for this chapter in a new branch:

```
$ cd device/generic/x86emu
$ git checkout android-7.1.1_r4_x86emu_ch04_r1
$ git branch android-7.1.1_r4_ch05
$ git checkout android-7.1.1_r4_ch05
```

I created a tag for each chapter and we can use that as the start for the new development. The android-7.1.1_r4_x86emu_ch04_r1 tag is the baseline for Chapter 4, *Customizing the Android Emulator*. From the preceding commands, we create a new branch, android-7.1.1_r4_ch05, for the development work in this chapter. I didn't push the development branches to GitHub, but I pushed all the tags to GitHub. After we complete all the changes in this chapter, we will create a new tag, android-7.1.1_r4_x86emu_ch05_r1, for this chapter.

After we make all the changes, we also need to update the manifest file so that we can have a manifest to download the code for this chapter. Instead of using tags, I use branches to manage manifests. The branch for this chapter's manifests is android-7.1.1_r4_ch05_aosp. We can use the following command to download the source code of:

```
$ repo init -u https://github.com/shugaoye/manifests -b
android-7.1.1_r4_ch05_aosp
$ repo sync
```

If you set up the local mirror as we discussed in Chapter 2, *Setting Up the Development Environment*, you can check out the source code as follows:

```
$ repo init -u {your local mirror}/github/manifests.git -b
android-7.1.1_r4_ch05
$ repo sync
```

You need to create an android-7.1.1_r4_ch05 branch for your own local mirror referring to the android-7.1.1_r4_ch05_aosp branch.

After we create a working copy of the source code using the preceding manifest, we can look at the .repo/manifest.xml file:

```
<?xml version="1.0" encoding="UTF-8"?>
<manifest>

  <remote   name="github"
            fetch="." />

  <remote   name="aosp"
```

```
                       fetch="https://android.googlesource.com/" />
        <default revision="refs/tags/android-7.1.1_r4"
                 remote="aosp"
                 sync-c="true"
                 sync-j="1" />

        <!-- github/shugaoye -->
        <project path="kernel" name="goldfish" remote="github"
        revision="refs/tags/android-7.1.1_r4_x86emu_ch05_r1" />
        <project path="device/generic/common" name="device_generic_common"
         groups="pdk"
        remote="github" revision="refs/tags/android-7.1.1_r4_x86emu_ch05_r1" />
        <project path="device/generic/goldfish"
        name="device_generic_goldfish"
        remote="github" groups="pdk" revision="refs/tags/android-
        7.1.1_r4_x86emu_ch05_r1" />
        <project path="device/generic/x86emu" name="x86emu" remote="github"
        revision="refs/tags/android-7.1.1_r4_x86emu_ch05_r1" />

        <!-- aosp -->
        <project path="build" name="platform/build" groups="pdk,tradefed" >
          <copyfile src="core/root.mk" dest="Makefile" />
   ...
   </manifest>
```

In the preceding manifest file, we use the `android-7.1.1_r4_x86emu_ch05_r1` tag to tag all projects that are not in AOSP projects. The `device/generic/common` project is duplicated from Android-x86 and the `device/generic/goldfish` project is duplicated from AOSP. Besides `kernel` and `device/generic/x86emu`, these are the two projects that we need to change in this chapter.

Extending the x86emu device

Once we have done all the changes for the source code configuration, we can start to extend the x86emu device to support Houdini now. What are the changes that we have to make? Since I have done all the changes before I explained them here, let's use a tool to compare the difference between the source code in `Chapter 4`, *Customizing the Android Emulator* and this chapter's code.

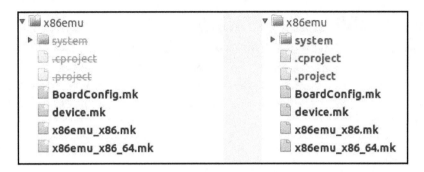

Changes to support Houdini

As we can see in the preceding screenshot, we added a `system` folder and we modified four Makefiles. We can ignore the `x86emu_x86_64.mk` Makefile, since we won't discuss 64-bit builds in this book. The changes to `x86emu_x86_64.mk` are similar to those for `x86emu_x86.mk`, so we save ourselves the effort of discussing similar things twice. It won't be a significant effort for you to enable a 64-bit build for x86emu by yourself. The other two files, `.cproject` and `.project`, are generated due to Eclipse integration and we can ignore them too. Let's look at `BoardConfig.mk`, `x86emu_x86.mk`, and `device.mk` one by one.

Changes to BoardConfig.mk

In the board configuration file, we need to add an ARM instruction set to the CPU ABI list so that the program can detect support for the ARM instruction set as follows:

```
...
# houdini
# Native Bridge ABI List
NATIVE_BRIDGE_ABI_LIST_32_BIT := armeabi-v7a armeabi
NATIVE_BRIDGE_ABI_LIST_64_BIT := arm64-v8a
TARGET_CPU_ABI_LIST_32_BIT := $(TARGET_CPU_ABI) $(TARGET_CPU_ABI2)
$(NATIVE_BRIDGE_ABI_LIST_32_BIT)
TARGET_CPU_ABI_LIST := $(TARGET_CPU_ABI_LIST_32_BIT)

BUILD_ARM_FOR_X86 := $(WITH_NATIVE_BRIDGE)
...
```

You may have noticed the `BUILD_ARM_FOR_X86` macro. This macro is used by Android-x86 Houdini support and we will discuss it later.

Changes to x86emu_x86.mk

In the product definition Makefile, `x86emu_x86.mk`, we set the `persist.sys.nativebridge` property to 1. Then we copy all files under the `$AOSP/device/generic/x86emu/system` folder to the `$OUT/system` image. All the files under the `$AOSP/device/generic/x86emu/system/lib/arm` folder are a copy of the Houdini libraries:

```
...
PRODUCT_PROPERTY_OVERRIDES := \
    persist.sys.nativebridge=1 \

NB_PATH := $(LOCAL_PATH)
NB_LIB_PATH := system/lib
NB_ARM_PATH := $(NB_LIB_PATH)/arm
NB_NBLIB_PATH := $(NB_ARM_PATH)/nb
NB_BIN_PATH := system/bin

PRODUCT_COPY_FILES += $(foreach LIB, $(filter-out nb liblog_legacy.so
libbinder_legacy.so,\
        $(notdir $(wildcard $(NB_PATH)/$(NB_ARM_PATH)/*))),
$(NB_PATH)/$(NB_ARM_PATH)/$(LIB):$(NB_ARM_PATH)/$(LIB):intel)
PRODUCT_COPY_FILES += $(foreach NB, $(filter-out libbinder_legacy.so,
$(notdir $(wildcard $(NB_PATH)/$(NB_NBLIB_PATH)/*))),\
        $(NB_PATH)/$(NB_NBLIB_PATH)/$(NB):$(NB_NBLIB_PATH)/$(NB):intel)
...
```

Changes to device.mk

In the device Makefile `device.mk`, we only added one line to include another Makefile, `nativebridge.mk`, in the `device/generic/common/nativebridge` directory. As we discussed in the section on source configuration, we use the one from Android-x86 to support Houdini integration. We will analyze the `nativebridge.mk` Makefile in the next section:

```
...
# Get native bridge settings
$(call inherit-product-if-
exists,device/generic/common/nativebridge/nativebridge.mk)
...
```

Using the Android-x86 implementation

Since we use Houdini support from the Android-x86 project, we can see that we only need to make very minor changes to the x86emu Makefiles.

Now let's look at `nativebridge.mk` in Android-x86:

```
# Enable native bridge
WITH_NATIVE_BRIDGE := true

# Native Bridge ABI List
NATIVE_BRIDGE_ABI_LIST_32_BIT := armeabi-v7a armeabi
NATIVE_BRIDGE_ABI_LIST_64_BIT := arm64-v8a

LOCAL_SRC_FILES := bin/enable_nativebridge

PRODUCT_COPY_FILES := $(foreach
f,$(LOCAL_SRC_FILES),$(LOCAL_PATH)/$(f):system/$(f))

PRODUCT_PROPERTY_OVERRIDES := \
    ro.dalvik.vm.isa.arm=x86 \
    ro.enable.native.bridge.exec=1 \

ifeq ($(TARGET_SUPPORTS_64_BIT_APPS),true)
PRODUCT_PROPERTY_OVERRIDES += \
    ro.dalvik.vm.isa.arm64=x86_64 \
    ro.enable.native.bridge.exec64=1
endif

PRODUCT_DEFAULT_PROPERTY_OVERRIDES := ro.dalvik.vm.native.bridge=libnb.so

PRODUCT_PACKAGES := libnb

$(call inherit-product-if-exists,vendor/intel/houdini/houdini.mk)
```

`nativebridge.mk` copies an `enable_nativebridge` script to the `system` folder first. After that, it sets the `ro.dalvik.vm.isa.arm` and `ro.enable.native.bridge.exec` properties. These two properties will be added to `system/build.prop` in the system image. It also sets the default property `ro.dalvik.vm.native.bridge` to `libnb.so`. This property is used by ART to find the Houdini library. Android-x86 uses the `libnb.so` library instead of `libhoudini.so`, which all supported Intel devices use. The `libnb.so` library is a wrapper of `libhoudini.so`. Since we use `libnb.so` as the ARM binary translation library, we need to add this package to the build.

Analyzing libnb.so

Since the `libnb.so` library is the key starting point for Native Bridge support in Android-x86, we will dive into the details of it now. The Makefile to build `libnb.so` can be found at `device/generic/common/nativebridge/Android.mk`. The source code for `libnb.so` includes only one file, `libnb.cpp`, as follows:

```cpp
#define LOG_TAG "libnb"

#include <dlfcn.h>
#include <cutils/log.h>
#include <cutils/properties.h>
#include "nativebridge/native_bridge.h"

namespace android {

static void *native_handle = nullptr;

static NativeBridgeCallbacks *get_callbacks()
{
    static NativeBridgeCallbacks *callbacks = nullptr;

    if (!callbacks) {
        const char *libnb = "/system/"
        #ifdef __LP64__
                "lib64/arm64/"
        #else
                "lib/arm/"
        #endif
                "libhoudini.so";
        if (!native_handle) {
            native_handle = dlopen(libnb, RTLD_LAZY);
            if (!native_handle) {
                ALOGE("Unable to open %s", libnb);
                return nullptr;
            }
        }
        callbacks = reinterpret_cast<NativeBridgeCallbacks *>
        (dlsym(native_handle, "NativeBridgeItf"));
    }
    return callbacks;
}

// NativeBridgeCallbacks implementations
static bool native_bridge2_initialize(const
  NativeBridgeRuntimeCallbacks *art_cbs, const char
  *app_code_cache_dir, const char *isa)
```

```
{
    ALOGV("enter native_bridge2_initialize %s %s",
    app_code_cache_dir, isa);
    if (property_get_bool("persist.sys.nativebridge", 0)) {
        if (NativeBridgeCallbacks *cb = get_callbacks()) {
return cb->initialize(art_cbs, app_code_cache_dir, isa);
        }
    } else {
        ALOGW("Native bridge is disabled");
    }
    return false;
}

static void *native_bridge2_loadLibrary(const char *libpath, int flag)
{
    ALOGV("enter native_bridge2_loadLibrary %s", libpath);
    NativeBridgeCallbacks *cb = get_callbacks();
    return cb ? cb->loadLibrary(libpath, flag) : nullptr;
}

static void *native_bridge2_getTrampoline(void *handle,
  const char *name, const char* shorty, uint32_t len)
{
    ALOGV("enter native_bridge2_getTrampoline %s", name);
    NativeBridgeCallbacks *cb = get_callbacks();
    return cb ? cb->getTrampoline(handle, name, shorty, len)
    : nullptr;
}

static bool native_bridge2_isSupported(const char *libpath)
{
    ALOGV("enter native_bridge2_isSupported %s", libpath);
    NativeBridgeCallbacks *cb = get_callbacks();
    return cb ? cb->isSupported(libpath) : false;
}

static const struct NativeBridgeRuntimeValues
*native_bridge2_getAppEnv(const char *abi)
{
    ALOGV("enter native_bridge2_getAppEnv %s", abi);
    NativeBridgeCallbacks *cb = get_callbacks();
    return cb ? cb->getAppEnv(abi) : nullptr;
}

static bool native_bridge2_is_compatible_compatible_with(uint32_t version)
{
    // For testing, allow 1 and 2, but disallow 3+.
    return version <= 2;
```

```
    }

    static NativeBridgeSignalHandlerFn native_bridge2_get_signal_handler(int
    signal)
    {
        ALOGV("enter native_bridge2_getAppEnv %d", signal);
        NativeBridgeCallbacks *cb = get_callbacks();
        return cb ? cb->getSignalHandler(signal) : nullptr;
    }

    static void __attribute__ ((destructor)) on_dlclose()
    {
        if (native_handle) {
            dlclose(native_handle);
            native_handle = nullptr;
        }
    }

    extern "C" {

    NativeBridgeCallbacks NativeBridgeItf = {
        version: 2,
        initialize: &native_bridge2_initialize,
        loadLibrary: &native_bridge2_loadLibrary,
        getTrampoline: &native_bridge2_getTrampoline,
        isSupported: &native_bridge2_isSupported,
        getAppEnv: &native_bridge2_getAppEnv,
        isCompatibleWith: &native_bridge2_is_compatible_compatible_with,
        getSignalHandler: &native_bridge2_get_signal_handler,
    };

    } // extern "C"
    } // namespace android
```

In `libnb.cpp`, we can see that it loads the `libhoudini.so` library, which is the original Houdini library from Intel, and it makes only two changes. It checks the `persist.sys.nativebridge` property before it does the initialization. The rest of the code provides a wrapper of `NativeBridgeCallbacks` and the wrapper functions call the one in the Houdini library directly.

Using binfmt_misc

Up to now, what we have discussed is how to load an ARM shared library in the Intel x86 architecture. Houdini can also support running standalone ARM applications on Intel devices as well. To do this, it uses a mechanism called binfmt_misc. binfmt_misc, which is a capability of the Linux kernel that allows arbitrary executable file formats to be recognized and passed to certain user space applications, such as emulators and virtual machines.

According to the Linux kernel documentation, this kernel feature allows you to invoke almost every program by simply typing its name in the shell. This includes, for example, compiled Java (TM), Python, or Emacs. To achieve this, you must tell binfmt_misc which interpreter should be invoked with which binary. binfmt_misc recognizes the binary-type by matching some bytes at the beginning of the file with a magic byte sequence (masking out specified bits) that you have supplied. binfmt_misc can also recognize a filename extension such as .com or .exe.

To use this method, first we must mount binfmt_misc:

```
$ mount binfmt_misc -t binfmt_misc /proc/sys/fs/binfmt_misc
```

To register a new binary type, we must set up a string that looks as follows:

```
:name:type:offset:magic:mask:interpreter:flags
```

Then we need to add it to /proc/sys/fs/binfmt_misc/register.

Here is what the fields mean:

- name is an identifier string. A new /proc file will be created with this name below the /proc/sys/fs/binfmt_misc directory.
- type is the type of recognition. It gives M for magic and E for extension.
- offset is the offset of the magic/mask in the file, counted in bytes. This defaults to 0 if you omit it (that is, you write :name:type::magic...).
- magic is the byte sequence that binfmt_misc is matching for. The magic string may contain hex-encoded characters such as \x0a or \xA4. In a shell environment, you should write \\x0a to prevent the shell from eating your \. If you chose the matching filename extension, this is the extension to be recognized (without the ., the \x0a specials are not allowed). Extension matching is case-sensitive.

- `mask` is a (optional, defaults to all `0xff`) mask. You can mask out some bits from matching by supplying a string like magic.
- `interpreter` is the program that should be invoked with the binary as the first argument (specify the full path).
- `flags` is an optional field that controls several aspects of the invocation of the interpreter. It is a string of capital letters and each controls a certain aspect.

In `nativebridge.mk`, it copies an `enable_nativebridge` script to the `system` folder. This file is used to enable Houdini in Android-x86. In Android-x86, Houdini is not enabled by default. This can be turned on at any time using an option in **Settings app** of Android-x86. Of course, this is not supported in the AOSP source code. When you turn on Houdini in Android-x86, it calls the `enable_nativebridge` script. This script does two things:

1. It downloads Houdini from the third-party project repository to the local repository and installs it in the `/system/lib/arm` system directory. It also sets the `persist.sys.nativebridge` property to 1.
2. In the second part of this script, it creates the `binfmt_misc` files in the `/proc` directory.

We won't use the `enable_nativebridge` script directly, but we want to run the second part of `enable_nativebridge` at the system start. With the second part, Houdini is enabled in the Android emulator by default. This can be done by adding the second part of `enable_nativebridge` to `device/generic/goldfish/init.goldfish.sh`. The following is the code snippet that we added to the end of `init.goldfish.sh`. This is the script that is used to set up the environment for the Android emulator during system startup:

```
...
#
# Houdini integration (Native Bridge)
#
houdini_bin=0
dest_dir=/system/lib$1/arm$1
binfmt_misc_dir=/proc/sys/fs/binfmt_misc

# if you don't see the files 'register' and 'status' in
/proc/sys/fs/binfmt_misc
# then run the following command:
# mount -t binfmt_misc none /proc/sys/fs/binfmt_misc

# this is to add the supported binary formats via binfmt_misc

if [ ! -e $binfmt_misc_dir/register ]; then
```

```
        mount -t binfmt_misc none $binfmt_misc_dir
fi

cd $binfmt_misc_dir
if [ -e register ]; then
    # register Houdini for arm binaries
    if [ -z "$1" ]; then
         echo
':arm_exe:M::\\x7f\\x45\\x4c\\x46\\x01\\x01\\x01\\x00\\x00\\x00\\x00\\x00\\
x00\\x00\\x00\\x00\\x02\\x00\\x28::'"$dest_dir/houdini:P" > register
         echo
':arm_dyn:M::\\x7f\\x45\\x4c\\x46\\x01\\x01\\x01\\x00\\x00\\x00\\x00\\x00\\
x00\\x00\\x00\\x00\\x03\\x00\\x28::'"$dest_dir/houdini:P" > register
    else
         echo
':arm64_exe:M::\\x7f\\x45\\x4c\\x46\\x02\\x01\\x01\\x00\\x00\\x00\\x00\\x00
\\x00\\x00\\x00\\x00\\x02\\x00\\xb7::'"$dest_dir/houdini64:P" > register
         echo
':arm64_dyn:M::\\x7f\\x45\\x4c\\x46\\x02\\x01\\x01\\x00\\x00\\x00\\x00\\x00
\\x00\\x00\\x00\\x00\\x03\\x00\\xb7::'"$dest_dir/houdini64:P" > register
    fi
    if [ -e arm${1}_exe ]; then
         houdini_bin=1
    fi
else
    log -pe -thoudini "No binfmt_misc support"
fi

if [ $houdini_bin -eq 0 ]; then
    log -pe -thoudini "houdini$1 enabling failed!"
else
    log -pi -thoudini "houdini$1 enabled"
fi

[ "$(getprop ro.zygote)" = "zygote64_32" -a -z "$1" ] && exec $0 64
```

After we rebuild the image and start the emulator, we can verify the changes using the following command:

```
$ adb shell
root@x86emu:/ # ls /proc/sys/fs/binfmt_misc/
arm_dyn
arm_exe
register
status
```

We can see that we registered two binfmt_misc types: arm_dyn and arm_exe. The /proc file arm_dyn is used to load the shared library and arm_exe is used to load the ARM executable:

```
root@x86emu:/ # cat /proc/sys/fs/binfmt_misc/arm_exe
enabled
interpreter /system/lib/arm/houdini
flags: P
offset 0
magic 7f454c4601010100000000000000000000020028
```

If we look at the content of arm_exe, from the preceding output we can see that the /system/lib/arm/houdini interpreter is used to interpret ARM binaries.

Building and testing

We have made all the code changes to enable Houdini now. We can build the system image using the following commands:

```
$ source build/envsetup.sh
$ lunch x86emu_x86-eng
$ m -j4
```

After we build the system image, we can test it. Of course, we can test the images using any Android application that can run on the ARM architecture. However, in order to get details about the test targets, we will use two unit test applications to verify our work in this chapter. The first one is a standalone ARM application that can be run from the command line. The second one is an Android application with a JNI shared library for ARM only. The Android emulator images and test binaries in this chapter can be downloaded from https ://sourceforge.net/projects/android-system-programming/files/android-7/ch05/c h05.zip/download.

The source code for these two test applications is hosted on GitHub. You can get the source code at https://github.com/shugaoye/asp-sample/tree/master/ch05.

To build the test applications, you need to have both Android SDK and NDK so that you can build both Android applications and native applications.

Testing the command-line application

After you clone the preceding Git repository for test applications, you can build and test them. Let's test the command-line application first. It is a very simple "hello world" application to print just one line message to standard output as follows:

```c
#include <stdio.h>

void main()
{
    printf("This is built using NDK r12.n");
}
```

You can build it and test it in the emulator as follows:

```
$ cd ch05/test1
$ ./build.sh
[armeabi-v7a] Install : ch05_test => libs/armeabi-v7a/ch05_test
$ file libs/armeabi-v7a/ch05_test
libs/armeabi-v7a/ch05_test: ELF 32-bit LSB  shared object, ARM, EABI5
version 1 (SYSV), dynamically linked (uses shared libs),
BuildID[sha1]=b3cf0ae12c0d5b192053dc40c31f665196145039, stripped
$ adb push libs/armeabi-v7a/ch05_test /data/local/tmp
[100%] /data/local/tmp/ch05_test
$ adb shell
root@x86emu:/ # cd /data/local/tmp
127|root@x86emu:/data/local/tmp # ./ch05_test
This is built using NDK r12.
```

After you build it, you can check the file format using the `file` command. You can see that the output is a 32-bit ARM ELF file. You can push this binary to the emulator using `adb` and run it. You will see that it can print the output message to standard output correctly.

Testing the Android JNI application

Next, let's test the Android application with the ARM JNI library.

The JNI library can be found at `ch05/test2/jni`. The processor architecture that can be supported is defined in `Application.mk` as follows:

```
# Build both ARMv5TE and ARMv7-A and x86 machine code.
# armeabi armeabi-v7a
APP_ABI := armeabi armeabi-v7a
APP_PLATFORM := android-23
```

We can see that we build the JNI library for `armeabi` and `armeabi-v7a`. Let's build the JNI library using NDK first:

```
$ cd ch05/test2/jni
$ ./build.sh
[armeabi] Install : libHelloJNI.so => libs/armeabi/libHelloJNI.so
[armeabi-v7a] Install: libHelloJNI.so => libs/armeabi-v7a/libHelloJNI.so
```

After we build the JNI library, we can import the Android source code to Eclipse or Android Studio to build the application itself. We won't explain the details of importing and building Android applications. You can read books on how to develop an Android application and how to develop a JNI library to find out more. What we want to investigate here is the test result. After we have the APK file, we can install it in the emulator and run it. At the same time, we can catch the debug log using logcat. Here is the log from my environment:

```
. . .
10-02 00:44:57.871: I/ActivityManager(1527): START u0
{act=android.intent.action.MAIN cat=[android.intent.category.LAUNCHER]
flg=0x10200000 cmp=fr.myrddin.hellojni/.HelloJNIActivity (has extras)} from
uid 10008 on display 0
10-02 00:44:57.900: I/ActivityManager(1527): Start proc
2652:fr.myrddin.hellojni/u0a53 for activity
fr.myrddin.hellojni/.HelloJNIActivity
10-02 00:44:57.902: I/art(2652): Late-enabling JIT
10-02 00:44:57.903: D/houdini(2652): [2652] Initialize library(version:
6.1.1a_x.48413 RELEASE)... successfully.
10-02 00:44:57.907: W/art(2652): Unexpected CPU variant for X86 using
defaults: x86
10-02 00:44:57.907: I/art(2652): JIT created with code_cache_capacity=2MB
compile_threshold=1000
10-02 00:44:58.546: W/art(1527): Long monitor contention event with owner
method=int
com.android.server.wm.WindowManagerService.relayoutWindow(com.android.serve
r.wm.Session, android.view.IWindow, int,
android.view.WindowManager$LayoutParams, int, int, int, int,
android.graphics.Rect, android.graphics.Rect, android.graphics.Rect,
android.graphics.Rect, android.graphics.Rect, android.graphics.Rect,
android.content.res.Configuration, android.view.Surface) from
WindowManagerService.java:3104 waiters=0 for 632ms
10-02 00:44:58.580: W/dex2oat(2667): Unexpected CPU variant for X86 using
defaults: x86
10-02 00:44:58.581: W/dex2oat(2667): Mismatch between dex2oat instruction
set features (ISA: X86 Feature string: smp,-ssse3,-sse4.1,-sse4.2,-avx,-
avx2) and those of dex2oat executable (ISA: X86 Feature string: smp,ssse3,-
sse4.1,-sse4.2,-avx,-avx2) for the command line:
10-02 00:44:58.581: W/dex2oat(2667): /system/bin/dex2oat --runtime-arg -
```

```
classpath --runtime-arg  --compiler-filter=interpret-only --instruction-
set=x86 --instruction-set-features=smp,ssse3,-sse4.1,-sse4.2,-avx,-avx2 --
runtime-arg -Xrelocate --boot-image=/system/framework/boot.art --runtime-
arg -Xms64m --runtime-arg -Xmx512m --compiler-filter=verify-at-runtime --
instruction-set-variant=x86 --instruction-set-features=default --dex-
file=/data/app/fr.myrddin.hellojni-1/base.apk --oat-file=/data/dalvik-
cache/x86/data@app@fr.myrddin.hellojni-1@base.apk@classes.dex
10-02 00:44:58.581: E/dex2oat(2667): Failed to create oat file:
/data/dalvik-cache/x86/data@app@fr.myrddin.hellojni-1@base.apk@classes.dex:
Permission denied
10-02 00:44:58.581: I/dex2oat(2667): dex2oat took 774.330us (threads: 2)
10-02 00:44:58.582: W/art(2652): Failed execv(/system/bin/dex2oat --
runtime-arg -classpath --runtime-arg  --compiler-filter=interpret-only --
instruction-set=x86 --instruction-set-features=smp,ssse3,-sse4.1,-sse4.2,-
avx,-avx2 --runtime-arg -Xrelocate --boot-image=/system/framework/boot.art
--runtime-arg -Xms64m --runtime-arg -Xmx512m --compiler-filter=verify-at-
runtime --instruction-set-variant=x86 --instruction-set-features=default --
dex-file=/data/app/fr.myrddin.hellojni-1/base.apk --oat-file=/data/dalvik-
cache/x86/data@app@fr.myrddin.hellojni-1@base.apk@classes.dex) because
non-0 exit status
10-02 00:44:58.603: D/houdini(2652): [2652] Added shared library
/data/app/fr.myrddin.hellojni-1/lib/arm/libHelloJNI.so for ClassLoader by
Native Bridge.
10-02 00:44:58.603: E/JNI(2652): Number : 4
...
10-02 00:44:59.906: I/ActivityManager(1527): Displayed
fr.myrddin.hellojni/.HelloJNIActivity: +2s9ms
...
```

We can see from the preceding log message that Houdini is initialized successfully and that the `libHelloJNI.so` JNI library is loaded by Native Bridge.

Summary

In this chapter, we introduced Native Bridge in Android architecture first so that we can understand how it works. Based on our understanding of Native Bridge, we extended the x86emu device with Houdini support. We changed the Makefiles of the x86emu device and we also utilized the open source project Android-x86 to save the effort of integration. After we integrated Houdini in x86emu, we tested two scenarios of Houdini use:

- A standalone command-line application
- An Android application with a native shared library built with JNI

In the next chapter, we will explore more about the x86emu start up process and we will learn how to debug the start up process using a customized ramdisk image.

6
Debugging the Boot Up Process Using a Customized ramdisk

In the last chapter, we learnt to enable Houdini in the Android emulator using our own x86emu device. With that, we can move on to more challenging tasks in the next few chapters. Most device- or system-level customization will involve changes to the Android system start up sequence. In this chapter, we will analyze the Android system start up sequence and learn the knowledge related to the customization and debugging of the start up sequence. In this chapter, we will cover the following topics:

- Android start up process analysis
- Starting up process for the Android-x86
- Creating a filesystem for the Android-x86 `initrd.img`

We will start with the analysis of a normal Android boot up process. After that, we will introduce the Android-x86 two-stage boot up. We will build a filesystem for the Android emulator that can work with Android-x86 `initrd.img`. This method provides a flexible way to help the debugging of start up process.

Analyzing the Android start up process

The Android system boot up sequence is similar to other embedded Linux systems that start from the Boot ROM inside the processor. The Boot ROM will find the bootloader. The bootloader will load the kernel and ramdisk image. The kernel uses the ramdisk as the root filesystem. In a desktop Linux environment, once the kernel initializes the essential devices, it will remount the root filesystem on physical storage such as a hard disk. In Android, the various partitions (system, data, cache, and so on) will be mounted to the root filesystem in memory instead of a storage device. The kernel will invoke the **init** process in the ramdisk to start the rest of the system, as shown in the following figure:

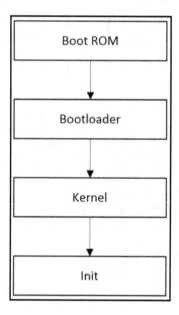

Bootloader and the kernel

As we can see, we won't be able to avoid the bootloader when we build our own devices. However, we won't spend too much time on this topic, since the bootloader is not our focus in this book. In the Android emulator, it is not necessary to have a bootloader, since there is a minimal bootloader built inside the emulator itself.

A very small bootloader in QEMU to boot Linux

If you are interested in the small bootloader in QEMU, you can refer to the AOSP source code at $AOSP/external/qemu/hw/arm/boot.c. Since the bootloader is hardware platform-specific, the bootloader implementation in QEMU is different for various hardware architectures, such as ARM, x86, or MIPS. The reason why I refer to the ARM implementation is because it is the cleanest and easiest to understand. You can refer to the book *Embedded Programming with Android* written by myself and published by Addison-Wesley Professional to find out more about bootloader for the Android emulator.

For VirtualBox, which we will use as the virtual hardware from Chapter 8, *Creating Your Own Device on VirtualBox* till Chapter 11, *Enabling VirtualBox-Specific Hardware Interfaces*, we will use the network boot to resolve the bootloader issue.

The Linux kernel is one of the key elements to support various hardware devices. We will discuss the customization and configuration of the Linux kernel throughout this book. In this chapter, we will focus on the init process and see how it works in the Android system.

Analyzing the init process and ramdisk

The implementation of the init process can be found in the $AOSP/system/core/init directory. If we look at the main function in init.cpp, it includes the code for ueventd and watchdogd, as shown in the following code snippet:

```
int main(int argc, char** argv) {
    if (!strcmp(basename(argv[0]), "ueventd")) {
        return ueventd_main(argc, argv);
    }

    if (!strcmp(basename(argv[0]), "watchdogd")) {
        return watchdogd_main(argc, argv);
    }
    ...
```

We won't discuss ueventd and watchdogd, since they are not related to our topics. We will focus on the mainline code of init.cpp. The mainline code of init implements the following logic:

1. Preparation for the environment, such as creating system folders, setting up the standard I/O, initialization of logging systems, and so on. The environment setup also includes the SELinux setup and loading the SELinux policy.

2. Parsing init scripts `init.rc`, `init.${ro.hardware}.rc`, and so on. Add items from the init scripts to the action or service in `action_list` and `service_list`.

3. Execute the `early-init` action in `action_list`.

4. Execute the `init` action in `action_list`.

5. Execute the `late-init` action in `action_list`.

6. Enter an infinite loop to perform the following tasks:

   1. Execute the action in `action_queue`.

   2. Restart the service marked as `SVC_RESTARTING` in `service_list`.

   3. Provide the property service, handling `/dev/keychord` events.

   4. Monitor system property changes, signals, and keyboard events.

The init scripts are stored in the ramdisk and are loaded in memory by the bootloader during boot up. If we look at the content of the x86emu `ramdisk.img`, we will see the following files:

The init scripts define two types of element: **actions** and **services**. The init process parses all the scripts and runs the tasks depending on the type of element.

Actions

The action syntax is as follows:

```
on <trigger>
    <command>
    <command>
    <command>
    . . .
```

Actions begin with the keyword `on`, followed by a trigger. Actions are left-aligned and the commands that follow are indented, as shown in the preceding snippet.

For example, we mount all partitions for the emulator using `fstab.goldfish` on trigger `fs`:

```
on fs
        mount_all /fstab.goldfish
```

Triggers are strings that can be used to match certain kinds of event and they are used to cause an action to occur. There are two types of action triggers: **predefined triggers** and **triggers activated on property-value changes**.

Predefined triggers could be `early-init`, `init`, `early-fs`, `fs`, `post-fs`, `early-boot`, or `boot` as defined in the init scripts.

Property-value triggers are in the following form:

```
<name>=<value>
```

Triggers of this form occur when the `<name>` property is set to a specific value `<value>`.

For example, when the `sys.init_log_level` property is changed, we need to reset the log level as follows:

```
on property:sys.init_log_level=*
    loglevel ${sys.init_log_level}
```

Commands in init scripts reassemble the shell commands and also add init-specific ones.

Services

Services are programs that init launches and (optionally) restarts when they exit. Services take the form of:

```
service <name> <pathname> [ <argument> ]*
    <option>
    <option>
    ...
```

The service will be known by init as <name>. The actual name of the binary that is pointed to by <pathname> will not be recognized.

Options are modifiers to services. They affect how and when init runs the service. We can use the following goldfish-specific service as an example:

```
service goldfish-setup /system/etc/init.goldfish.sh
    user root
    group root
    oneshot
```

The name of the service is goldfish-setup and it runs the init.goldfish.sh script as the root user. The oneshot option means that this service won't restart when it exits.

 A complete list of init commands and service options can be found in the following file:
$AOSP/system/core/init/readme.txt

Device-specific actions and services

The source code of system-generated init scripts is located in the $AOSP/system/core/rootdir folder. They are copied to $OUT/root in the build process.

The init process parses the init.rc script first. All other scripts are imported by init.rc and then parsed by the init process. If we look at the following code snippet of init.rc, we can see that there are a few scripts that are imported by init.rc:

```
# Copyright (C) 2012 The Android Open Source Project
#
# IMPORTANT: Do not create world writable files or directories.
# This is a common source of Android security bugs.
#

import /init.environ.rc
```

```
import /init.usb.rc
import /init.${ro.hardware}.rc
import /init.usb.configfs.rc
import /init.${ro.zygote}.rc
import /init.trace.rc

on early-init
...
```

The `init.${ro.hardware}.rc` script is the one that can be used to customize for device-specific changes. The `ro.hardware` property is passed to init at runtime so that init can load the right one for the device. We should try to avoid changes to other init scripts and keep the device-specific changes in `init.${ro.hardware}.rc` only.

If we look at the goldfish or ranchu device specifically, there are `init.goldfish.rc` and `init.ranchu.rc` scripts for them, respectively. Both scripts are part of the goldfish device, which can be found at `$AOSP/device/generic/goldfish`, as we can see in the following snippet. They are copied to `$OUT/root` in the build process:

```
$ ls device/generic/goldfish
audio              fstab.ranchu       libqemu    qemu-props
camera             gps                lights     sensors
data               init.goldfish.rc   opengl     ueventd.goldfish.rc
fingerprint        init.goldfish.sh   power      ueventd.ranchu.rc
fstab.goldfish     init.ranchu.rc     qemud      vibrator
```

Inside `init.goldfish.rc` or `init.ranchu.rc`, a `goldfish-setup` service is defined as follows:

```
service goldfish-setup /system/etc/init.goldfish.sh
    user root
    group root
    oneshot
```

In the last chapter, we added Houdini initialization to the `init.goldfish.sh` script and this is how Houdini can be initialized during boot up.

The hardware name in the Android emulator is passed by the kernel command line. When you start the emulator with `-verbose` and `-show-kernel`, you will see the following command-line parameters in the console:

```
. . .
emulator: argv[08] = "-append"
emulator: argv[09] = "qemu=1 clocksource=pit androidboot.console=ttyGF2
android.checkjni=1 console=ttyS0,38400 androidboot.hardware=ranchu
qemu.gles=1 android.qemud=1"
. . .
```

These parameters are passed to the kernel as kernel command-line parameters and then used by init to decide the hardware name. Since we cannot change the kernel parameters in the emulator, we cannot use our own script such as `init.x86emu.rc` in our device. If we want to customize the start up sequence, we should change the code in `$AOSP/device/generic/goldfish` and this is what we did in the last chapter.

The ideal approach to customizing the start up sequence is to keep all customizations under our own `device` folder, such as `$AOSP/device/generic/x86emu`. In that case, we can upgrade to the newer Android version very easily. The more general AOSP code we change, the more difficult it is to move to a new Android version.

If we can have control of the bootloader, we can pass our own kernel parameters through the bootloader. We will see this when we work on the x86vbox device in Chapter 8, *Creating Your Own Device on VirtualBox* till Chapter 11, *Enabling VirtualBox-Specific Hardware Interfaces*.

If you really need to change `init.rc` so that you can fully customize the boot up sequence, you can define the `TARGET_PROVIDES_INIT_RC := true` variable in your `BoardConfig.mk`. With this definition, you can copy `init.rc` to your `device` folder and change it for your device.

Source code and manifest changes

Now that we have been introduced to Android start up processes, we will now apply the two-stage boot up process from the Android-x86 project to the Android emulator. Before we talk about the two-stage boot up process, let's have a look at the changes for the AOSP source code and manifest file.

If we look at the following manifest file that we will use for this chapter, we can see that we only changed `kernel`, the `x86emu` device, and `newinstaller` from the Android-x86 project:

```xml
<?xml version="1.0" encoding="UTF-8"?>
<manifest>

  <remote   name="github"
            revision="refs/tags/android-7.1.1_r4_x86emu_ch06_r1"
            fetch="." />

  <remote   name="aosp"
            fetch="https://android.googlesource.com/" />
  <default  revision="refs/tags/android-7.1.1_r4"
            remote="aosp"
            sync-c="true"
            sync-j="1" />

  <!-- github/shugaoye -->
  <project path="kernel" name="goldfish" remote="github" />
  <project path="device/generic/x86emu" name="x86emu"
  remote="github" />
  <project path="bootable/newinstaller"
  name="platform_bootable_newinstaller" remote="github" />

  <!-- aosp -->
  <project path="build" name="platform/build" groups="pdk,tradefed" >
    <copyfile src="core/root.mk" dest="Makefile" />
  </project>
...
</manifest>
```

With the `newinstaller` project, we will build another ramdisk image, `initrd.img`, which will be used in the two stage boot up process.

A Git tag, `android-7.1.1_r4_x86emu_ch06_r1`, is used to baseline the source code changes in this chapter.

The Android-x86 start up process

In Chapter 1, *Introduction to Android System Programming*, we introduced the Android-x86 project, which is an open source project to provide the Android **Board Support Package** (**BSP**) for Intel devices. It uses an approach similar to Microsoft Windows or Linux distributions for desktops by using universal media to boot all kinds of Intel devices.

In order to achieve the goal of using one medium to boot all devices, it splits the boot sequence into two stages. The first stage is to boot a minimum embedded Linux environment to enable hardware devices. In the second stage, it switches to the Android system through chroot or switch_root. The second stage of the boot process is the same as we discussed previously. Let's look at the first stage of the Android-x86 boot process in detail. We will reuse it for the Android emulator in this chapter. This approach can help to simplify the start up process and it can also help us a lot with the debugging of start up processes.

The first-stage boot using initrd.img

The first stage of the start up process in Android-x86 uses a specific ramdisk initrd.img. The source code can be found at $AOSP/bootable/newinstaller. This project is duplicated from the Android-x86 project. As it is hosted in GitHub, I can make my own changes:

```
$ ls -1 -F
Android.mk
boot/
editdisklbl/
initrd/
install/
```

If we look at the contents in this `newinstaller` folder, we can see the preceding folders and files. The following is the explanation about the content of `newinstaller`:

- `boot`: This is the bootloader for the installation media. The images of Android-x86 can be built into different formats (ISO, UEFI, and so on)
- `editdisklbl`: A host tool used to edit system image partitions
- `initrd`: The ramdisk for the first-stage boot
- `install` : The installer for Android-x86
- `Android.mk` : Android Makefile for `newinstaller`

If we build `newinstaller`, it can generate a few different image formats, such as ISO, USB, or UEFI. To build a specified image, you can run the following command after you set up the environment and choose a build target:

```
$ make iso_img/usb_img/efi_img
```

Besides an installation image, it also produces another two images, `initrd.img` and `install.img`:

- `initrd.img` : The ramdisk image for the first stage boot up
- `install.img` : The image contains the Android-x86 installer

We will look at the details about both `initrd.img` and `install.img` to understand how the first stage boot works in Android-x86.

Inside initrd.img

If we look at the `initrd` folder, we can see the following contents:

```
$ cd bootable/newinstaller/initrd
$ ls -1F
bin/
init*
lib/
sbin/
scripts/
```

The content of `initrd.img` consists of a minimal Linux environment based on busybox. We can find busybox at `bin/busybox` and shared libraries required by busybox at `lib/`. There is an executable `init` file and a few folders inside the `initrd` folder. We know that the init process is the first process invoked by the kernel when the system starts. Android-x86 provides a separate init process to start the system inside `initrd.img`. This version of init is actually a shell script instead of a binary executable file:

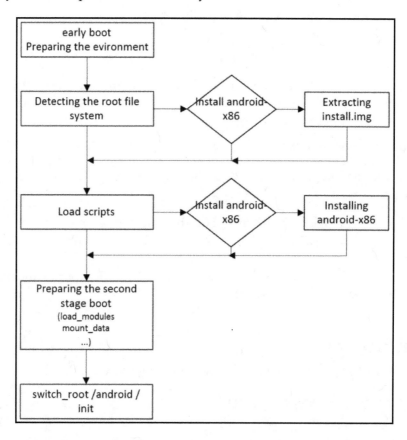

This shell script will perform the tasks shown in the preceding figure:

1. When the kernel invokes the script, it prepares the environment first. This includes the controlling tty setup, the initialization of debug logs, and the debug level.

2. After the environment is ready, it will try to find either an existing Android system or an installation media on the storage devices. In this step, `ramdisk.img` must be found, otherwise, it will return with an error.

3. Once an Android system or installation media is found; it will extract ramdisk.img to the working folder /android. If the INSTALL variable is set, it will extract install.img to the filesystem root as well. The working folder /android is used as the root of the Android system, while the current root is the image of initrd.img.

4. It now loads all additional scripts to prepare for the next steps. If the environment variable INSTALL is set to 1, it will invoke the installation script to install Android-x86 to a storage device such as a hard disk.

5. Before it switches to the Android system, it will load all the kernel modules for the devices, mount data and SD card partitions, set up the touch screen and display DPI, and so on.

6. Once everything is ready, it switches to the Android system using /android as the new root and invokes /init under the new root. The Android system will be started from this point onwards.

Let's look at a few important code snippets in the script to get a real feel for it:

```
#!/bin/busybox sh
#
# By Chih-Wei Huang <cwhuang@linux.org.tw>
# and Thorsten Glaser <tg@mirbsd.org>
#
# Last updated 2015/10/23
#
# License: GNU Public License
# We explicitely grant the right to use the scripts
# with Android-x86 project.
#

PATH=/sbin:/bin:/system/bin:/system/xbin; export PATH
...
echo -n Detecting Android-x86...
...
while :; do
    for device in ${ROOT:-/dev/[hmsv][dmr][0-9a-z]*}; do
        check_root $device && break 2
        mountpoint -q /mnt && umount /mnt
    done
    sleep 1
    echo -n .
done
...
```

In the preceding code snippet, we can see that it invokes the shell function check_root to find the root of the Android system in an infinite loop. If it could not find the root file system, it is stuck in this loop.

In the following check_root function, the environment variable SRC is passed from the kernel command line and specifies the path of the filesystem root. It will check whether a ramdisk.img can be found in this path or not. If a ramdisk.img can be found, it will be extracted to the /android path, which is the current directory, otherwise; it will return an error:

```
...
check_root()
{
...
    if [ -n "$iso" -a -e /mnt/$iso ]; then
        mount --move /mnt /iso
        mkdir /mnt/iso
        mount -o loop /iso/$iso /mnt/iso
        SRC=iso
    elif [ ! -e /mnt/$SRC/ramdisk.img ]; then
    return 1
    fi
    zcat /mnt/$SRC/ramdisk.img | cpio -id > /dev/null
...
```

After the root filesystem is detected, it will check the environment variable INSTALL. This INSTALL variable is also passed from the kernel command line. If INSTALL is set, it will extract install.img to the current root. This will overwrite some of the files in initrd.img and we will discuss this in more detail later:

```
...
if [ -n "$INSTALL" ]; then
    zcat /src/install.img | ( cd /; cpio -iud > /dev/null )
fi
...
```

Then it will load all other shell scripts from either the /scripts or /src/scripts folders:

```
...
# load scripts
for s in `ls /scripts/* /src/scripts/*`; do
    test -e "$s" && source $s
done
...
```

Once all the shell scripts are loaded in memory, it will check the INSTALL variable again to see whether it should execute the installation script:

```
...
[ -n "$INSTALL" ] && do_install

load_modules
mount_data
mount_sdcard
setup_tslib
setup_dpi
post_detect
...
exec ${SWITCH:-switch_root} /android /init

# avoid kernel panic
while :; do
    echo
    echo '        Android-x86 console shell. Use only in emergencies.'
    echo
    debug_shell fatal-err
done
```

No matter whether it executes the installation script or not, it will prepare the environment for the Android system to start. It will load kernel modules, mount data/sdcard partitions, and set up all other environment-related requirements. Lastly, it will execute switch_root or chroot to switch to the Android system. The Android system will be started from this point onwards.

The main difference between switch_root and chroot
switch_root is intended to switch the complete system over to a new root directory and remove dependencies on the old one, so that you can unmount the original root directory and proceed as if it had never been in use.
chroot is intended to be applied for the lifetime of a single process, with the rest of the system continuing to run in the old root directory, and the system being unchanged when the chrooted process exits.
In Android-x86, switch_root is used in release mode and chroot is used in debug mode.

Inside install.img

We have analyzed most of the first stage start up processes for Android-x86. One thing that we want to do more analysis on is how `install.img` works in the first stage start up process.

If the `INSTALL` environment variable is set, `install.img` will be extracted. This will overwrite some of the contents from `initrd.img`. Let's take a look at this now. If we list the contents of both directories `initrd` and `install`, we can see that `bin/`, `lib/`, `sbin/`, and `scripts/` are duplicated in both images in the following screenshot:

```
●●●  android-6 [x86emu]

roger@sz-lin-003:~/src/android-6/bootable/newinstaller$ ls -F
Android.mk  boot/  editdisklbl/  initrd/  install/
roger@sz-lin-003:~/src/android-6/bootable/newinstaller$ ls -F initrd/
bin/  init*  lib/  sbin/  scripts/
roger@sz-lin-003:~/src/android-6/bootable/newinstaller$ ls -F initrd/scripts/
0-auto-detect  1-install  2-mount  3-tslib  4-dpi
roger@sz-lin-003:~/src/android-6/bootable/newinstaller$ ls -F install/
bin/  grub/  grub2/  lib/  sbin/  scripts/
roger@sz-lin-003:~/src/android-6/bootable/newinstaller$ ls -F install/scripts/
1-install
roger@sz-lin-003:~/src/android-6/bootable/newinstaller$ █
```

In the `bin/`, `sbin/`, and `lib/` folders, there are tools such as `cfdisk`, `cgdisk`, `mkntfs`, `grub`, and so on. These are the tools used to partition hard disks, format extra filesystems, and so on.

The `scripts/` folder includes the installation script and we will look at `scripts/` to explore how the Android-x86 installation works.

If we look at the script files in both the `initrd` and `install` folders, we find that both include a `1-install` script. `initrd.img` is used as the root filesystem in the first stage boot. If the `INSTALL` variable is set, `install.img` will be extracted to the root as well. In that case, the one in the `install` folder will overwrite the one in the `initrd` folder. We can see from the following figure how `initrd.img`, `ramdisk.img`, and `install.img` are integrated to form the first stage and the second-stage filesystem:

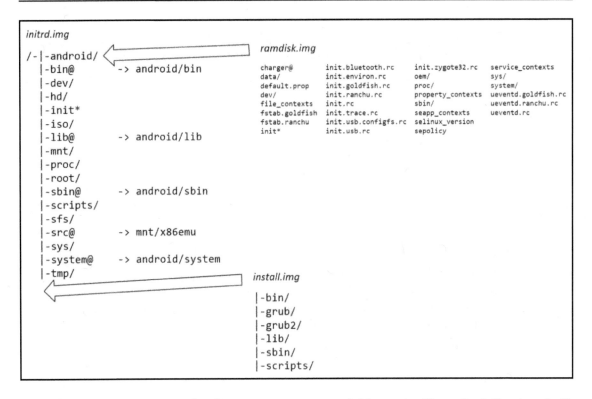

```
initrd.img
/-|-android/  <——————————————————
  |-bin@    -> android/bin
  |-dev/
  |-hd/
  |-init*
  |-iso/
  |-lib@    -> android/lib
  |-mnt/
  |-proc/
  |-root/
  |-sbin@   -> android/sbin
  |-scripts/
  |-sfs/
  |-src@    -> mnt/x86emu
  |-sys/
  |-system@ -> android/system
  |-tmp/
```

```
ramdisk.img

charger@          init.bluetooth.rc      init.zygote32.rc    service_contexts
data/             init.environ.rc        oem/                sys/
default.prop      init.goldfish.rc       proc/               system/
dev/              init.ranchu.rc         property_contexts   ueventd.goldfish.rc
file_contexts     init.rc                sbin/               ueventd.ranchu.rc
fstab.goldfish    init.trace.rc          seapp_contexts      ueventd.rc
fstab.ranchu      init.usb.configfs.rc   selinux_version
init*             init.usb.rc            sepolicy
```

```
install.img
|-bin/
|-grub/
|-grub2/
|-lib/
|-sbin/
|-scripts/
```

If we look at `1-install` under the `initrd/scripts` folder, we will see the following shell script function:

```
do_install()
{
    error -e 'n  Android-x86 installer is not available.\n
    Press RETURN to run live version.\n'
    read
    cd /android
}
```

It implements a `do_install` function, which will return an error message. If this script is not overwritten by the one from `install.img`, it means the installer is not available. If `install.img` is extracted, the real `do_install` function will be invoked to start the installation:

```
do_install()
{
  until install_hd; do
    if [ $retval -eq 255 ]; then
      dialog --title ' Error! ' --yes-label Retry --no-label Reboot
```

```
          --yesno 'nInstallation failed! Please check if you have enough
          free disk space to install Android-x86.' 8 51
            [ $? -eq 1 ] && rebooting
      fi
   done

   [ -n "$VESA" ] || runit="Run Android-x86"
  ...
  }
```

The `do_install` function will call another function, `install_hd`, and `install_hd` will call an `install_to` function to perform the actual installation. The `install_to` function takes a parameter that is the target device for the installation. It will perform the following installation tasks:

- It will format the target device first and then mount the device to the `/hd` folder.
- It will install GRUB as the bootloader.
- It will create a folder using the `android-$VER` naming convention in the `/hd` folder as the target installation folder. For example, as our device is x86emu, the installation target will be `/hd/android-x86emu`.
- It will use the `cpio` command to copy the files from the installation media to the installation target. These files include `kernel`, `initrd.img`, `ramdisk.img`, and everything under the `system` folder from the AOSP build. It depends on the configuration; it may either copy the `system.sfs` or `system.img` image file, or it may copy everything in the `system` folder directly to `/hd/android-$VER/system`.

In the following sections, we need to repeat the installation procedure to create a filesystem that can be used for the Android-x86 two-stage boot sequence.

Building x86emu with initrd.img

After we did all the analysis of `initrd.img` for Android-x86, we can build a similar one for the Android emulator now. Be aware that this can work only with ranchu, but not with goldfish. The goldfish emulator uses an older version of QEMU and it doesn't support the additional storage devices for the emulator. To support the boot from `initrd.img`, we have to change the layout of the filesystem. It is not good to change the original filesystem image in AOSP. We will create another file image to be used for the boot with `initrd.img`.

In the ranchu emulator, the images are emulated as virtio block devices. After we start the emulator, we can inspect the mount points, as shown in the following screenshot. We can see that `system.img` is mounted as `/dev/block/vda`, `userdata.img` as `/dev/block/vdb`, and `cache.img` as `/dev/block/vdc`:

```
set default SDK.
roger@sz-lin-003:~$ adb shell
root@x86emu:/ # mount
rootfs / rootfs ro,relatime 0 0
tmpfs /dev tmpfs rw,nosuid,relatime,mode=755 0 0
devpts /dev/pts devpts rw,relatime,mode=600 0 0
proc /proc proc rw,relatime 0 0
sysfs /sys sysfs rw,relatime 0 0
/sys/kernel/debug /sys/kernel/debug debugfs rw,relatime 0 0
none /acct cgroup rw,relatime,cpuacct 0 0
none /sys/fs/cgroup tmpfs rw,relatime,mode=750,gid=1000 0 0
tmpfs /mnt tmpfs rw,relatime,mode=755,gid=1000 0 0
none /dev/cpuctl cgroup rw,relatime,cpu 0 0
/dev/block/vda /system ext4 ro,relatime,data=ordered 0 0
/dev/block/vdb /cache ext4 rw,nosuid,nodev,noatime,errors=panic,data=ordered 0 0
/dev/block/vdc /data ext4 rw,nosuid,nodev,noatime,errors=panic,data=ordered 0 0
tmpfs /storage tmpfs rw,relatime,mode=755,gid=1000 0 0
none /proc/sys/fs/binfmt_misc binfmt_misc rw,relatime 0 0
root@x86emu:/ #
root@x86emu:/ #
root@x86emu:/ #
root@x86emu:/ #
root@x86emu:/ #
root@x86emu:/ #
```

ranchu images emulated as virtio block devices

All partitions in the ranchu emulator are mounted using the `fstab.ranchu` file, as we can see in the following snippet:

```
...
/dev/block/vda   /system   ext4        ro                      wait
/dev/block/vdb   /cache    ext4
noatime,nosuid,nodev,nomblk_io_submit,errors=panic      wait
/dev/block/vdc   /data     ext4
noatime,nosuid,nodev,nomblk_io_submit,errors=panic      wait
...
```

With the ranchu emulator, we can easily add another storage device with the `-hda` QEMU option. With this option, we can see that a new block device, `/dev/block/sda`, is available after the emulator starts. We will discuss this in more detail later. Before we can test this idea, we need to create the disk image first.

Creating a filesystem image

There are many ways that we can create disk images. QEMU can support many disk image formats. If you want to find details about the image formats that can be supported by QEMU, you can check using the following Linux command:

```
$ man qemu-img
```

The supported image formats are:

- **raw**: This plain disk image format has the advantage of being simple and easily exportable to all other emulators.
- **qcow2**: This is the QEMU image format, which is the most versatile format. It is a compressed image format, so it has a smaller image size and can support snapshots.
- **qcow**: This is the old QEMU image format.
- **cow**: This is the User Mode Linux Copy-On-Write image format.
- **vdi**: This is the VirtualBox 1.1-compatible image format.
- **vmdk**: This is the VMware 3- and 4-compatible image format.
- **vpc**: This is the VirtualPC-compatible image format (VHD).
- **cloop**: This is the Linux compressed loop image, useful only to reuse directly compressed CD-ROM images present, for example, in Knoppix CD-ROMs.

We will use the qcow2 file format to test our `initrd.img` for the Android emulator. In order to create a file image in qcow2 format, we need to add the following code in the `Android.mk` **Makefile** of `bootable/newinstaller`:

```
...
initrd:   $(BUILT_IMG)

X86EMU_EXTRA_SIZE := 100000000
X86EMU_DISK_SIZE := $(shell echo
${BOARD_SYSTEMIMAGE_PARTITION_SIZE}+${X86EMU_EXTRA_SIZE} | bc)
X86EMU_TMP := x86emu_tmp

qcow2_img: $(BUILT_IMG)
```

```
  mkdir -p $(PRODUCT_OUT)/${X86EMU_TMP}/${TARGET_PRODUCT}
  cd $(PRODUCT_OUT)/${X86EMU_TMP}/${TARGET_PRODUCT}; mkdir data
  mv $(PRODUCT_OUT)/initrd.img
$(PRODUCT_OUT)/${X86EMU_TMP}/${TARGET_PRODUCT}
  mv $(PRODUCT_OUT)/install.img
$(PRODUCT_OUT)/${X86EMU_TMP}/${TARGET_PRODUCT}
  mv $(PRODUCT_OUT)/ramdisk.img
$(PRODUCT_OUT)/${X86EMU_TMP}/${TARGET_PRODUCT}
  mv $(PRODUCT_OUT)/system.img
$(PRODUCT_OUT)/${X86EMU_TMP}/${TARGET_PRODUCT}
  make_ext4fs -T -1 -l $(X86EMU_DISK_SIZE)
$(PRODUCT_OUT)/${TARGET_PRODUCT}.img $(PRODUCT_OUT)/${X86EMU_TMP}
  mv $(PRODUCT_OUT)/${X86EMU_TMP}/${TARGET_PRODUCT}/*.img $(PRODUCT_OUT)/
  qemu-img convert -c -f raw -O qcow2 $(PRODUCT_OUT)/${TARGET_PRODUCT}.img
$(PRODUCT_OUT)/${TARGET_PRODUCT}-qcow2.img
  cd $(PRODUCT_OUT); qemu-img create -f qcow2 -b
  ./${TARGET_PRODUCT}-qcow2.img ./${TARGET_PRODUCT}.img
...
```

The first thing that we have to do in the preceding Makefile is to create a directory layout that can be used by initrd.img, as shown in the following snippet:

```
x86emu_x86.img

x86emu_x86/-|-data/
            |-kernel
            |-ramdisk.img
            |-initrd.img
            |-install.img
            |-system.img
```

Directory layout of x86emu_x86.img

We create a data folder to be used as data storage. Then, we move existing image files in the AOSP output folder to the $OUT/x86emu_tmp/x86emu_x86 directory in order to create the preceding directory structure. These file images will be moved back after the file image is generated.

Once we have the right directory structure, we can use the make_ext4fs command to create a raw filesystem image with the following options:

```
make_ext4fs -T {timestamp} -l {size of file system} {image file name}
{source directory} {target out directory}
```

The size of the filesystem is BOARD_SYSTEMIMAGE_PARTITION_SIZE; additionally, X86EMU_EXTRA_SIZE. BOARD_SYSTEMIMAGE_PARTITION_SIZE is defined in the board configuration file for the system image size. X86EMU_EXTRA_SIZE is for the space of ramdisk and kernel images.

The next step is to generate the qcow2 format from the raw file image using the qemu-img command. Both raw and qcow2 format images can be used by the emulator, but the raw file image is much larger than the qcow2 image.

Since the qcow2 image can support the snapshot feature, we can also generate a snapshot image (x86emu_x86.img) based on the qcow2 image (x86emu_x86-qcow2.img). If we use the snapshot image, we can restore to the original qcow2 image at any time. The snapshot image can be created using the following commands:

```
$ cd $OUT
$ qemu-img create -f qcow2 -b ./x86emu_x86-qcow2.img ./x86emu_x86.img
```

After the image is generated, we can inspect it using the qemu-img command as follows:

```
$ qemu-img info x86emu_x86.img
image: x86emu_x86.img
file format: qcow2
virtual size: 1.3G (1442177024 bytes)
disk size: 196K
cluster_size: 65536
backing file: ./x86emu_x86-qcow2.img
Format specific information:
    compat: 1.1
    lazy refcounts: false
```

We see that the x86emu_x86.img image is the snapshot image of x86emu_x86-qcow2.img.

In the image that we just created, there are no partitions created. When we mount it in the Android emulator, it will appear as a /dev/sda or /dev/block/sda device. If we want to create partitions for the image file, we need to use the edit_mbr tool to do so. You can explore this option on your own. With multiple partitions, we can put the system, data, and cache into different partitions, which is closer to the disk layout in most mobile devices.

Kernel changes

With effect from Android 4.4, SELinux is on by default. When we change the filesystem in Android, we have to take care of the SELinux settings as well. This will make the configuration more complicated than what we expect. If you are interested in this, you can do your homework to configure SELinux for this case.

In this book, we will disable SELinux by default so that we can concentrate on our topics. To disable SELinux, we have to make some changes the kernel configuration file. You can check the changes using the `git` command as follows:

```
$ cd $AOSP/kernel
$ git branch
* android-x86emu-3.10
$ gitk
```

We can see the changes in the `android-x86emu-3.10` branch using `gitk`, as shown in the following screenshot. We can see that we set the default security to DAC and removed the SELinux setting, `CONFIG_SECURITY_SELINUX=y`:

```
------------------- arch/x86/configs/i386_ranchu_defconfig -------------------
index 7540dbb..563ad21 100644
@@ -362,8 +362,9 @@ CONFIG_PROVIDE_OHCI1394_DMA_INIT=y
 CONFIG_KEYS=y
 CONFIG_KEYS_DEBUG_PROC_KEYS=y
 CONFIG_SECURITY=y
+CONFIG_DEFAULT_SECURITY_DAC=y
+CONFIG_DEFAULT_SECURITY=""
 CONFIG_SECURITY_NETWORK=y
-CONFIG_SECURITY_SELINUX=y
 CONFIG_CRYPTO_SHA256=y
 CONFIG_CRYPTO_AES_586=y
 CONFIG_CRYPTO_TWOFISH=y
------------------- arch/x86/configs/x86_64_ranchu_defconfig -------------------
index dc6a094..79aef97 100644
@@ -357,8 +357,9 @@ CONFIG_PROVIDE_OHCI1394_DMA_INIT=y
 CONFIG_KEYS=y
 CONFIG_KEYS_DEBUG_PROC_KEYS=y
 CONFIG_SECURITY=y
+CONFIG_DEFAULT_SECURITY_DAC=y
+CONFIG_DEFAULT_SECURITY=""
 CONFIG_SECURITY_NETWORK=y
-CONFIG_SECURITY_SELINUX=y
 CONFIG_CRYPTO_SHA256=y
 CONFIG_CRYPTO_TWOFISH=y
 # CONFIG_CRYPTO_ANSI_CPRNG is not set
```

Disabling SELinux in the ranchu kernel

Booting a disk image on the Android emulator

Once we have done all the changes, we can build the qcow2 image using the following command:

```
$ make qcow2_img USE_SQUASHFS=0
...
make_ext4fs -T -1 -S out/target/product/x86emu/root/file_contexts -L
system -l 1342177280 -a system
out/target/product/x86emu/obj/PACKAGING/systemimage_intermediates/system.im
g out/target/product/x86emu/system out/target/product/x86emu/system
Creating filesystem with parameters:
    Size: 1342177280
    Block size: 4096
    Blocks per group: 32768
    Inodes per group: 8192
    Inode size: 256
    Journal blocks: 5120
    Label: system
    Blocks: 327680
    Block groups: 10
    Reserved block group size: 79
Created filesystem with 2122/81920 inodes and 178910/327680 blocks
Install system fs image: out/target/product/x86emu/system.img
```

As we can see from the preceding command-line output, `system.img` will be built as usual. After that, the ramdisk image, `initrd.img`, will be created as follows. Pay attention to the VER environment variable. We changed the script to set it as x86emu. The original one in Android-x86 is the current date, such as 2016-11-11:

```
VER ?= $(shell date +"%F")
```

This variable is used as part of the installation folder name. Let's continue reviewing the build log:

```
out/target/product/x86emu/system.img+ maxsize=1370278272 blocksize=2112
total=1342177280 reserve=13842048
rm -rf out/target/product/x86emu/installer
out/host/linux-x86/bin/acp -pr bootable/newinstaller/initrd
out/target/product/x86emu/installer
ln -s /bin/ld-linux.so.2 out/target/product/x86emu/installer/lib
mkdir -p out/target/product/x86emu/installer/android
out/target/product/x86emu/installer/iso
out/target/product/x86emu/installer/mnt
out/target/product/x86emu/installer/proc
```

```
out/target/product/x86emu/installer/sys
out/target/product/x86emu/installer/tmp
out/target/product/x86emu/installer/sfs
out/target/product/x86emu/installer/hd
echo "VER=x86emu" > out/target/product/x86emu/installer/scripts/00-ver
out/host/linux-x86/bin/mkbootfs out/target/product/x86emu/installer | gzip
-9 > out/target/product/x86emu/initrd.img
```

After ramdisk `initrd.img` is created, the raw and qcow2 file images will be created as we have added in the `Android.mk` file for `bootable/newinstaller`:

```
mkdir -p out/target/product/x86emu/x86emu_tmp/x86emu_x86
cd out/target/product/x86emu/x86emu_tmp/x86emu_x86; mkdir data
mv out/target/product/x86emu/initrd.img
out/target/product/x86emu/x86emu_tmp/x86emu_x86
mv out/target/product/x86emu/install.img
out/target/product/x86emu/x86emu_tmp/x86emu_x86
mv out/target/product/x86emu/ramdisk.img
out/target/product/x86emu/x86emu_tmp/x86emu_x86
mv out/target/product/x86emu/system.img
out/target/product/x86emu/x86emu_tmp/x86emu_x86
make_ext4fs -T -1 -l 1442177280 out/target/product/x86emu/x86emu_x86.img
out/target/product/x86emu/x86emu_tmp out/target/product/x86emu/x86emu_tmp
Creating filesystem with parameters:
    Size: 1442177024
    Block size: 4096
    Blocks per group: 32768
    Inodes per group: 8016
    Inode size: 256
    Journal blocks: 5501
    Label:
    Blocks: 352094
    Block groups: 11
    Reserved block group size: 87
Created filesystem with 17/88176 inodes and 340722/352094 blocks
mv out/target/product/x86emu/x86emu_tmp/x86emu_x86/*.img
out/target/product/x86emu/
qemu-img convert -c -f raw -O qcow2
out/target/product/x86emu/x86emu_x86.img
out/target/product/x86emu/x86emu_x86-qcow2.img
cd out/target/product/x86emu; qemu-img create -f qcow2 -b ./x86emu_x86-
qcow2.img ./x86emu_x86.img
Formatting './x86emu_x86.img', fmt=qcow2 size=1442177024
backing_file='./x86emu_x86-qcow2.img' encryption=off cluster_size=65536
lazy_refcounts=off
```

We have the `x86emu_x86-qcow2.img` qcow2 image and the `x86emu_x86.img` snapshot image now. In order to test the images, we can use a shell script to help us. The shell script can be downloaded from GitHub at the following URL:

`https://github.com/shugaoye/asp-sample/blob/master/scripts/test-initrd.sh`

To run this script, you should set up your SDK environment first so that we can find the emulator in the `$PATH` environment variable:

```
#!/bin/sh

if [ -z "$1" ]; then
   EMULATOR1=emulator
else
   EMULATOR1="/opt/VirtualGL/bin/vglrun emulator"
fi

if [ -z "$OUT" ]; then
   IMG_ROOT=.
else
   IMG_ROOT=$OUT
fi

$EMULATOR1 @a23x86 -verbose -show-kernel -shell -system
$IMG_ROOT/system.img -ramdisk $IMG_ROOT/initrd.img -initdata
$IMG_ROOT/userdata.img -kernel $IMG_ROOT/kernel -qemu -append "qemu=1
clocksource=pit android.checkjni=1 DEBUG=2 console=ttyS0,11520
androidboot.hardware=ranchu qemu.gles=1 android.qemud=1 root=/dev/sda
SRC=x86emu_x86" -hda $IMG_ROOT/x86emu_x86.img
```

To launch this script, you can use the AOSP build result directly or you can download the images from SourceForge at the following URL:

`https://sourceforge.net/projects/android-system-programming/files/android-7/ch06/ch06.zip/download`

If you use the AOSP build result, the script will use the `$OUT` environment variable to look for the images. If the `$OUT` environment variable is not set, it will assume that the images are stored in the current directory.

To run the Android emulator in a remote *X* window session, we need to use VirtualGL for OpenGL ES support. With any command-line parameter, the script will launch the emulator using VirtualGL. If you use a Linux machine with a local *X* window session, you don't have to do this.

To use `initrd.img` as the ramdisk, we can see that we specify `initrd.img` in the -`ramdisk` option in the emulator command line. The next thing that we need to pay attention to is the QEMU options. We can specify QEMU options after the `-qemu` Android emulator option. We use two QEMU options, `-append` and `-hda`. With the `-hda` option, we can add the `x86emu_x86-qcow2.img` image or the `x86emu_x86.img` snapshot image as another hard disk for the emulator. With the `-append` option, we can provide kernel parameters that we want to pass to the ranchu kernel. All other kernel parameters are the same as the one provided by the emulator except for the following parameters:

- `DEBUG=2`: This option sets the debug level to 2 so that we can get the debug console during boot up
- `root=/dev/sda`: This option specifies the root device as `/dev/sda`, which is the `x86emu_x86-qcow2.img` image or the `x86emu_x86.img` snapshot image that we provide as a QEMU option
- `SRC=x86emu_x86`: This option defines the folder name on the root device that init can use to find all images

You can launch the script from the command line and you will see the following screen output:

```
$ test-initrd.sh
...
(debug-found)@android:/android # mount
rootfs on / type rootfs (rw)
proc on /proc type proc (rw,relatime)
sys on /sys type sysfs (rw,relatime)
tmpfs on /android type tmpfs (rw,relatime)
/dev/block/sda on /mnt type ext4 (rw,relatime,data=ordered)
/dev/loop0 on /android/system type ext4 (rw,relatime,data=ordered)
(debug-found)@android:/android # losetup -a
/dev/loop0: 0 /mnt/x86emu_x86/system.img
```

In the command-line log and the following screenshot, you can see that the `/dev/sda` root device is found and mounted at `/mnt`. The Android system image is mounted as a loop device to `/dev/loop0`:

```
android-6 [x86emu]
File Edit View Search Terminal Help
[    1.095411] EXT4-fs (sda): recovery complete
[    1.106603] EXT4-fs (sda): mounted filesystem with ordered data mode. Opts: (
null)
[    1.163998] EXT4-fs (sda): re-mounted. Opts: (null)
[    1.166441] EXT4-fs (loop0): couldn't mount as ext3 due to feature incompatib
ilities
[    1.167264] EXT4-fs (loop0): couldn't mount as ext2 due to feature incompatib
ilities
[    1.232814] EXT4-fs (loop0): recovery complete
[    1.266343] EXT4-fs (loop0): mounted filesystem with ordered data mode. Opts:
 (null)
 found at /dev/sda

Type 'exit' to continue booting...

Running MirBSD Korn Shell...
(debug-found)@android:/android # [    1.600220] tsc: Refined TSC clocksource cal
ibration: 3392.295 MHz
[    1.601641] Switching to clocksource tsc

(debug-found)@android:/android # ls /
android   dev     init     lib      proc    sbin     sfs     sys      tmp
bin       hd      iso      mnt      root    scripts  src     system
(debug-found)@android:/android # █
```

Debug console of initrd.img

After you exit the shell console, the Android system will start up as usual. With this approach, you can get a debug console at the point when you want to troubleshoot any issues. You can also change any Android startup scripts on-the-fly without rebuilding a new image to test. All the flexibilities in this setup will help debugging of the boot up process a lot.

Summary

In this chapter, we learnt about the startup process for the Android system. After that, we dived deep into the startup process for Android-x86. We found a new way to boot up the system to a minimum Linux environment first and then use that environment to boot the Android system. In this process, we can gain control by obtaining a shell console so that we can examine the system at a given point. To support this kind of boot, we learnt how to build a system image that can be used together with `initrd.img`.

In the next chapter, we will continue exploring how to customize the Android emulator by adding a Wi-Fi connection to it.

7
Enabling Wi-Fi on the Android Emulator

In the last three chapters, we have explored ways to customize and extend the Android emulator. In this chapter, we will pursue this topic to add Wi-Fi support in the Android emulator. If you are a developer using the Android emulator, you may notice that there is only data connection in the Android emulator. Some applications may be aware of the connection type and exhibit different behaviors according to the connection type. In this case, you cannot use an emulator to test your applications. In this chapter, we will cover the following topics:

- Introducing Wi-Fi architecture in Android
- Extending the x86emu device to support Wi-Fi connections
- Testing a Wi-Fi connection on the x86emu device

The topics in this chapter are at an advanced level. We will analyze the Wi-Fi source code at the beginning of the chapter to help understand the Wi-Fi architecture. I recommend that you open a source code editor and locate the functions under discussion. This is a very efficient way to understand the source code analysis part in this chapter.

Wi-Fi on Android

In `Chapter 3`, *Discovering Kernel, HAL, and Virtual Hardware*, we discussed the porting layers related to the Android system, we used goldfish lights as an example to depict the calling sequence from an application to HAL to access the hardware. We will use a similar approach in this chapter to explore the Wi-Fi architecture of Android. Based on what we understand about Wi-Fi architecture, we will add Wi-Fi to the emulator later in this chapter.

The Wi-Fi architecture

As we know from previous chapters, Android applications use managers to access system services. The managers will use various system services to access **Hardware Abstraction Layer** (**HAL**). The Wi-Fi architecture also follows the same approach for applications to access Wi-Fi hardware.

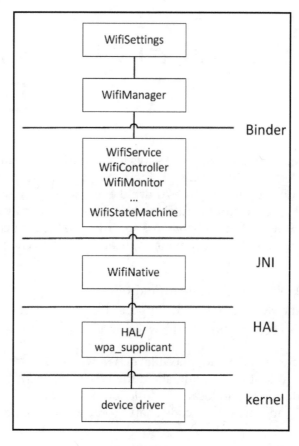

Android Wi-Fi architecture

As we can see from the preceding diagram showing Wi-Fi layers in the Android system, **WifiSettings** is the application in the default AOSP build used to control Wi-Fi connections. **WifiSettings** uses **WifiManager** to get access to Wi-Fi services.

WifiManager provides the following functionalities:

- Providing a list of configured networks--the attributes of individual entries can be modified.
- Monitoring the current active Wi-Fi network, if any. Connectivity can be established or torn down, and dynamic information about the state of the network can be queried.
- Providing the results of access point scans, containing enough information to make decisions about what access point to connect to.
- Defining the names of various intent actions that are broadcast upon any sort of change in the Wi-Fi state.

When `WifiManager` is created, it gets an interface of `IWifiManager`, as shown in the following code snippet. This interface is implemented by `WifiService` through the binder mechanism:

```
public WifiManager(Context context, IWifiManager service, Looper looper) {
    mContext = context;
    mService = service;
    mLooper = looper;
    mTargetSdkVersion = context.getApplicationInfo().targetSdkVersion;
}
```

`WifiManager` is defined in the `$AOSP/frameworks/base/wifi/java/android/net/wifi/WifiManager.java` file.

In the `WifiService` implementation, it uses `WifiStateMachine` to manage Wi-Fi states:

```
public final class WifiServiceImpl extends IWifiManager.Stub {
    private static final String TAG = "WifiService";
    private static final boolean DBG = true;
    private static final boolean VDBG = false;

    final WifiStateMachine mWifiStateMachine;
      private final Context mContext;
...
```

`WifiServiceImpl` is defined in the `$AOSP/frameworks/opt/net/wifi/service/java/com/android/server/wifi/WifiServiceImpl.java` file.

We can see how the Wi-Fi HAL is initialized through `WifiStateMachine` in the following sequence diagram:

There is a very good Android source code cross-reference tool at `http://x ref.opersys.com/`.
You can search the definition of functions and locate the location of source code using this cross reference tool.

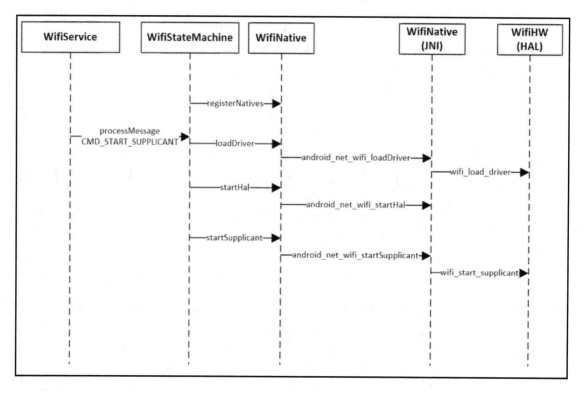

Sequence diagram of Android Wi-Fi initialization

`WifiStateMachine` processes requests from `WifiManager`. When the system initializes Wi-Fi by sending a `CMD_START_SUPPLICANT` command, `WifiStateMachine` will call its `processMessage` method to handle this request as shown in the following code snippet:

```java
public boolean processMessage(Message message) {
    logStateAndMessage(message, getClass().getSimpleName());
    switch (message.what) {
        case CMD_START_SUPPLICANT:
            if (mWifiNative.loadDriver()) {
                try {
                    mNwService.wifiFirmwareReload(mInterfaceName, "STA");
                } catch (Exception e) {
                    loge("Failed to reload STA firmware " + e);
                    // Continue
                }

                try {
                    // A runtime crash can leave the interface up and
                    // IP addresses configured, and this affects
                    // connectivity when supplicant starts up.
                    // Ensure interface is down and we have no IP
                    // addresses before a supplicant start.
                    mNwService.setInterfaceDown(mInterfaceName);
                    mNwService.clearInterfaceAddresses(mInterfaceName);

                    // Set privacy extensions
                    mNwService.setInterfaceIpv6PrivacyExtensions(mInterfaceName, true);

                    // IPv6 is enabled only as long as access point is connected since:
                    // - IPv6 addresses and routes stick around after disconnection
                    // - kernel is unaware when connected and fails to start IPv6 negotiation
                    // - kernel can start autoconfiguration when 802.1x is not complete
                    mNwService.disableIpv6(mInterfaceName);
                } catch (RemoteException re) {
                    loge("Unable to change interface settings: " + re);
                } catch (IllegalStateException ie) {
                    loge("Unable to change interface settings: " + ie);
                }

                /* Stop a running supplicant after a runtime restart
                 * Avoids issues with drivers that do not handle interface down
                 * on a running supplicant properly.
                 */
                mWifiMonitor.killSupplicant(mP2pSupported);

                if (WifiNative.startHal() == false) {
                    /* starting HAL is optional */
                    loge("Failed to start HAL");
```

The `processMessage` method calls to native methods through `WifiNative` to load the Wi-Fi driver (`loadDriver`) and start the Wi-Fi HAL (`startHAL`).

Pay attention to the function calls `mWifiNative.loadDriver`, and `WifiNative.startHal`, as shown in the following flow diagram:

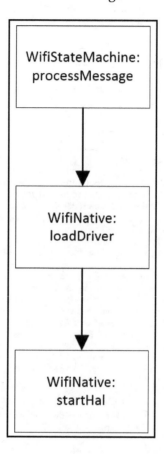

The **WifiNative** implementation includes the Java part and the native part. The Java implementation can be found at `$AOSP/frameworks/opt/net/wifi/service/java/com/android/server/wifi/WifiNative.java`.

The native implementation can be found at `$AOSP/frameworks/opt/net/wifi/service/jni/com_android_server_wifi_WifiNative.cpp`.

When the instance of the `WifiNative` class is created, it loads the Wi-Fi service shared library first and calls to a `registerNatives` function to register all native functions as follows:

```
public class WifiNative {
...
    static {
        /* Native functions are defined in libwifi-service.so */
        System.loadLibrary("wifi-service");
        registerNatives();
    }

    private static native int registerNatives();

    public native static boolean loadDriver();
...
```

The native implementation of `registerNatives` is shown in the following snippet. It registers the native functions through a `gWifiMethods` global variable:

```
/* User to register native functions */
extern "C"
jint Java_com_android_server_wifi_WifiNative_registerNatives(JNIEnv* env,
jclass clazz) {
    return AndroidRuntime::registerNativeMethods(env,
            "com/android/server/wifi/WifiNative", gWifiMethods,
            NELEM(gWifiMethods));
}
```

In this function, it calls to another framework function, `registerNativeMethods`, to register native methods at the Java layer so that the Java layer can call the functions implemented in `WifiNative`. You might know the function `registerNativeMethods`, if you have worked on Android NDK programming. We can look at the `gWifiMethods` global variable in the following snippet. The `gWifiMethods` global variable includes a list of native functions that are implemented in `WifiNative`, which should be exported as Java native methods of the `WifiNative` class. We can see that `loadDriver` and `startHalNative` are in the list:

```
/*
 * JNI registration.
 */
static JNINativeMethod gWifiMethods[] = {
    /* name, signature, funcPtr */

    { "loadDriver", "()Z", (void *)android_net_wifi_loadDriver },
    { "isDriverLoaded", "()Z", (void *)android_net_wifi_isDriverLoaded },
    { "unloadDriver", "()Z", (void *)android_net_wifi_unloadDriver },
    { "startSupplicant", "(Z)Z", (void *)android_net_wifi_startSupplicant },
    { "killSupplicant", "(Z)Z", (void *)android_net_wifi_killSupplicant },
    { "connectToSupplicantNative", "()Z", (void *)android_net_wifi_connectToSupplicant },
    { "closeSupplicantConnectionNative", "()V",
            (void *)android_net_wifi_closeSupplicantConnection },
    { "waitForEventNative", "()Ljava/lang/String;", (void*)android_net_wifi_waitForEvent },
    { "doBooleanCommandNative", "(Ljava/lang/String;)Z", (void*)android_net_wifi_doBooleanCommand },
    { "doIntCommandNative", "(Ljava/lang/String;)I", (void*)android_net_wifi_doIntCommand },
    { "doStringCommandNative", "(Ljava/lang/String;)Ljava/lang/String;",
            (void*) android_net_wifi_doStringCommand },
    { "startHalNative", "()Z", (void*) android_net_wifi_startHal },
    { "stopHalNative", "()V", (void*) android_net_wifi_stopHal },
```

The `loadDriver` method is implemented in the `android_net_wifi_loadDriver` function as follows:

```
static jboolean android_net_wifi_loadDriver(JNIEnv* env, jobject)
{
    return (::wifi_load_driver() == 0);
}
```

It calls to a `wifi_load_driver` function, which is a part of Wi-Fi HAL at `$AOSP/hardware/libhardware_legacy/wifi/wifi.c`.

```
int wifi_load_driver()
{
    char driver_status[PROPERTY_VALUE_MAX];
    #ifdef WIFI_DRIVER_MODULE_PATH
    FILE *proc;
    char line[sizeof(DRIVER_MODULE_TAG)+10];
    #endif
```

```
    if (!property_get(DRIVER_PROP_NAME, driver_status, NULL)
    || strcmp(driver_status, "ok") != 0) {
        return 0;   /* driver not loaded */
    }
    #ifdef WIFI_DRIVER_MODULE_PATH
    /*
     * If the property says the driver is loaded, check to
     * make sure that the property setting isn't just left
     * over from a previous manual shutdown or a runtime
     * crash.
     */
    if ((proc = fopen(MODULE_FILE, "r")) == NULL) {
        ALOGW("Could not open %s: %s", MODULE_FILE, strerror(errno));
        property_set(DRIVER_PROP_NAME, "unloaded");
        return 0;
    }
    while ((fgets(line, sizeof(line), proc)) != NULL) {
        if (strncmp(line, DRIVER_MODULE_TAG, strlen(DRIVER_MODULE_TAG))
        == 0)
        {
            fclose(proc);
            return 1;
        }
    }
    fclose(proc);
    property_set(DRIVER_PROP_NAME, "unloaded");
    return 0;
    #else
    return 1;
    #endif
}
```

The `WIFI_DRIVER_MODULE_PATH` macro needs to be defined to specify the path of the driver module, if there is a specific Wi-Fi driver that needs to be used. After the driver has loaded successfully, a `wlan.driver.status` property is set to the value `ok`.

Now we will look at another method, `startHalNative`. It is implemented in the `android_net_wifi_startHal` function:

```
static jboolean android_net_wifi_startHal(JNIEnv* env, jclass cls) {
    JNIHelper helper(env);
    wifi_handle halHandle = getWifiHandle(helper, cls);
    if (halHandle == NULL) {
        if(init_wifi_hal_func_table(&hal_fn) != 0 ) {
            ALOGD("Can not initialize the basic function pointer
            table");
            return false;
```

```
        }

        wifi_error res = init_wifi_vendor_hal_func_table(&hal_fn);
        if (res != WIFI_SUCCESS) {
            ALOGD("Can not initialize the vendor function pointer
            table");
            return false;
        }

        int ret = set_iface_flags("wlan0", 1);
        if(ret != 0) {
            return false;
        }

        res = hal_fn.wifi_initialize(&halHandle);
        if (res == WIFI_SUCCESS) {
            helper.setStaticLongField(cls, WifiHandleVarName,
            (jlong)halHandle);
            ALOGD("Did set static halHandle = %p", halHandle);
        }
        env->GetJavaVM(&mVM);
        mCls = (jclass) env->NewGlobalRef(cls);
        ALOGD("halHandle = %p, mVM = %p, mCls = %p", halHandle, mVM,
        mCls);
        return res == WIFI_SUCCESS;
    } else {
        return (set_iface_flags("wlan0", 1) == 0);
    }
}
```

Wi-Fi chip vendors usually provide two components the Wi-Fi implementations. The first one is a kernel driver as we discussed in the loadDriver and the second one is a vendor HAL library. The startHalNative function is used to hook vendor-implemented functions to a pre-defined list of functions. As we can see in the preceding code snippet, the init_wifi_hal_func_table function is called to initialize the list of functions in hal_fn. After that, the init_wifi_vendor_hal_func_table function is called to initialize the function pointers in hal_fn. If this operation is successful, it will call to the vendor initialization function, hal_fn.wifi_initialize.

QEMU networking and wpa_supplicant in Android

At HAL, `wpa_supplicant` is used to support the authentication between the device and access point. It starts as a native daemon in the Android system. Control requests from the upper layer are sent to `wpa_supplicant` and `wpa_supplicant` deals with device drivers and kernel networking systems to provide the network connections.

Since the Android emulator uses QEMU, the networking system is provided by the QEMU networking system. QEMU provides multiple network backends including TAP, VDE, socket, and SLIRP. The Android emulator uses user networking (SLIRP), which is the default networking backend of QEMU. Since SLIRP is a software implementation of TCP/IP networking stacks, it does not require root privileges to support networking functionalities. As a software implementation, it has the following limitations:

- Lot of overhead so the performance is poor
- In general, ICMP traffic does not work so you cannot use ping within a guest
- On Linux hosts, ping can work within the guest if the initial setup is done by root
- The guest is not directly accessible from the host or the external network

The following is a typical diagram of what SLIRP networking looks like in the Android emulator:

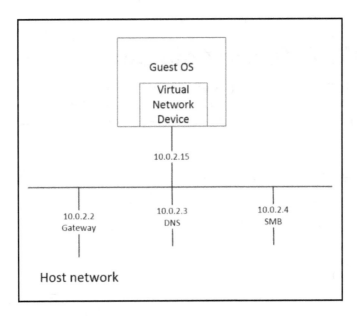

A QEMU SLIRP network

In the preceding diagram, the client has an IP address of **10.0.2.15** and the gateway has an IP address of **10.0.2.2**. The default DNS IP address is **10.0.2.3**. It may support SMB, which is optional. If you start an Android emulator, the default network interface is eth0 with an IP address of **10.0.2.15**. This is usually used to simulate a cellular data connection. To simulate a Wi-Fi connection, we can add one more network interface, eth1, using the following QEMU options:

```
-netdev user,id=mynet1,net=10.0.2.0/24,dhcpstart=10.0.2.50 -device virtio-
net,netdev=mynet1
```

With the -device QEMU option, we add a new network device, mynet1, which uses virtio network hardware. QEMU can simulate many existing network hardware types and we choose virtio network hardware in this chapter. You may choose others if you like.

With the -netdev QEMU option, we specify the attributes of this network device by providing an IP address range and the starting address for DHCP protocol.

Be aware that the previous option can only work with ranchu not goldfish. To start the Android emulator with the preceding QEMU option, we can run the following command:

```
$ emulator @a25x86 -qemu -netdev
user,id=mynet1,net=10.0.2.0/24,dhcpstart=10.0.2.50 -device virtio-
net,netdev=mynet1
```

Adding Wi-Fi to the emulator

With the introduction of Wi-Fi architecture in Android, we can now extend the emulator to support Wi-Fi. To add Wi-Fi in the emulator, we need to build wpa_supplicant for the emulator and choose the right device driver for the eth1 network interface.

Enabling wpa_supplicant in BoardConfig.mk

In the default emulator build, wpa_supplicant is not built. To enable building wpa_supplicant for the emulator, we can add the following lines in our BoardConfig.mk:

```
BOARD_WPA_SUPPLICANT_DRIVER := WIRED
WPA_SUPPLICANT_VERSION      := VER_0_8_X VER_2_1_DEVEL
BOARD_WLAN_DEVICE           := eth1
```

When `BOARD_WPA_SUPPLICANT_DRIVER` is defined, the following configuration in `external/wpa_supplicant_8/wpa_supplicant/Android.mk` will be changed to true:

```
ifneq ($(BOARD_WPA_SUPPLICANT_DRIVER),)
  CONFIG_DRIVER_$(BOARD_WPA_SUPPLICANT_DRIVER) := y
endif
```

The value of `BOARD_WPA_SUPPLICANT_DRIVER` tells which driver should be built. Since we use a wired Ethernet connection to simulate Wi-Fi, we will choose the *wired* driver, which can be found at `external/wpa_supplicant_8/src/drivers/driver_wired.c`.

We also define the `wpa_supplicant` version to use and the wired Ethernet interface.

Providing a proper wpa_supplicant configuration

To make `wpa_supplicant` work correctly, we need to prepare a `wpa_supplicant.conf` configuration file with the right permission. Wi-Fi-related configuration files are stored in the `/data/misc/wifi/` directory. This directory is owned by the `wifi` user, which is also the user that the `wpa_supplicant` runs as.

The `wpa_supplicant.conf` configuration file for the `eth1` wired connection can be found in the following snippet:

```
ctrl_interface=eth1
ap_scan=2
update_config=1
device_name=x86emu
manufacturer=unknown
serial_number=
device_type=10-0050F204-5
config_methods=physical_display virtual_push_button
external_sim=1

network={
    ssid="WiredSSID"
    key_mgmt=NONE
    engine=1
    priority=1
}
```

In this configuration file, we defined the network SSID to be used and the authentication method to establish the connection. Since this is a predefined wired connection, we set the authentication method as `key_mgmt=NONE`, which means we don't need to use any authentication method for this case.

To copy `wpa_supplicant.conf` to the `/data/misc/wifi/` directory with the right permission, we need to change `device.mk` as follows:

```
# Wi-Fi support
PRODUCT_PROPERTY_OVERRIDES := \
    wifi.interface=eth1

PRODUCT_PACKAGES += \
    libwpa_client \
    hostapd \
    dhcpcd.conf \
    wlutil \
    wpa_supplicant \
    wpa_supplicant.conf

# These are the hardware-specific features
PRODUCT_COPY_FILES += \
frameworks/native/data/etc/android.hardware.wifi.xml:system/etc/
permissions/android.hardware.wifi.xml

# For android_filesystem_config.h
PRODUCT_PACKAGES += \
    fs_config_files

PRODUCT_COPY_FILES += \
device/generic/x86emu/wpa_supplicant.conf:data/misc/wifi/
wpa_supplicant.conf \
```

In `device.mk`, we define the `wifi.interface` to `eth1` as we discussed previously. After that, we add all Wi-Fi-related modules to `PRODUCT_PACKAGES` so that they can be added to the system image. We copy the `wpa_supplicant.conf` configuration file to the `/data/misc/wifi` directory so that it can be accessed with read and write permissions by `wpa_supplicant`. This file is owned by the `wifi` user with permission `0555`.

From the Android 6 release, the system permission for files from the vendor is defined in an `android_filesystem_config.h` file under the `device` folder. `PRODUCT_PACKAGES` must include `fs_config_dirs` and/or `fs_config_files` in order to install them to `/system/etc/fs_config_dirs` and `/system/etc/fs_config_files`, respectively. The generated `fs_config_dirs` and `fs_config_files` files are used to set the runtime permission. We can see the owner and permission defined in `android_filesystem_config.h` in the following snippet:

```
#include <private/android_filesystem_config.h>

#define NO_ANDROID_FILESYSTEM_CONFIG_DEVICE_DIRS
/* static const struct fs_path_config android_device_dirs[] = { }; */
```

```
/* Rules for files.
** These rules are applied based on "first match", so they
** should start with the most specific path and work their
** way up to the root. Prefixes ending in * denotes wildcard
** and will allow partial matches.
*/
static const struct fs_path_config android_device_files[] = {
    { 00555, AID_WIFI, AID_WIFI, 0, "data/misc/wifi/wpa_supplicant.conf" },
#ifdef NO_ANDROID_FILESYSTEM_CONFIG_DEVICE_DIRS
    { 00000, AID_ROOT, AID_ROOT, 0, "system/etc/fs_config_dirs" },
#endif
};
```

The last change in `device.mk` is related to the settings user interface. The Wi-Fi settings user interface is not available in the emulator build. To enable the Wi-Fi settings, we need to add `android.hardware.wifi.xml` to the `system/etc/permissions` folder.

Creating services in init scripts

To initialize network interface eth1 and start `wpa_supplicant`, we need to define related services in init scripts.

Initializing network interface eth1

To initialize `eth1`, we can refer to the initialization of `eth0` in the emulator. The network interface `eth0` is initialized in the `system/etc/init.goldfish.sh` shell script as follows:

```
#!/system/bin/sh

# Setup networking when boot starts
ifconfig eth0 10.0.2.15 netmask 255.255.255.0 up
route add default gw 10.0.2.2 dev eth0
...
```

As we can see, a fixed IP address `10.0.2.15` is assigned to the `eth0` interface. We can add the following commands to initialize the interface `eth1`:

```
ifconfig eth1 up
dhcpcd -d eth1
```

In the preceding commands, we enable the interface `eth1` first using the `ifconfig` command. Then, instead of using a fixed IP address, we use the DHCP client to get the IP address for `eth1`.

As we discussed when covering the init process of Android in Chapter 6, *Debugging the Boot Up Process Using a Customized ramdisk*, the init process will process the init.rc script during the system startup. The init.rc script will include a hardware-specific init script, init.${ro.hardware}.rc. In our case, the ro.hardware is ranchu, so the hardware-specific init script is init.ranchu.rc.

In the init.ranchu.rc init script, a service, as shown in the following snippet, is defined to run the init.goldfish.sh shell script:

```
...
service goldfish-setup /system/etc/init.goldfish.sh
    user root
    group root
    oneshot
...
```

That's how the goldfish- or ranchu- related setup process is done in an emulator.

Starting up wpa_supplicant

We can add a service in the init.ranchu.rc script to start wpa_supplicant. The following are the services that we added to the init.ranchu.rc script:

```
service wpa_supplicant /system/bin/wpa_supplicant -ieth1 -Dwired -
c/data/misc/wifi/wpa_supplicant.conf -e/data/misc/wifi/entropy.bin -
g@android:wpa_eth1
    class main
    socket wpa_eth1 dgram 660 wifi wifi
    disabled
    oneshot
```

This service is used to start or restart the eth1 interface using the DHCP client. For the service of wpa_supplicant, we start it with the following options:

- -i: Use the network interface eth1 for Wi-Fi
- -D: Use the wired driver for Wi-Fi on the interface eth1
- -c: Use the configuration file at /data/misc/wifi/wpa_supplicant.conf
- -e: Define the path of the entropy file
- -g: Define the global ctrl_interface as @android:wpa_eth1

If we refer to the sequence diagram of Wi-Fi initialization earlier in this chapter, the wpa_supplicant start sequence can be explained using the following steps:

1. WifiStateMachine processes the CMD_START_SUPPLICANT command.
2. WifiStateMachine calls the startSupplicant method of WifiNative.
3. The startSupplicant method is a native method implemented as the android_net_wifi_startSupplicant native function. This native function calls the wifi_start_supplicant function defined in Wi-Fi HAL wifi.c.

The wifi_start_supplicant function starts the wpa_supplicant through setting the ctl.start system property. ctl.start and ctl.stop are two system properties implemented by the property service that can be used to start or stop a service defined in the init scripts:

```c
int wifi_start_supplicant(int p2p_supported)
{
    char supp_status[PROPERTY_VALUE_MAX] = {'\0'};
    ...
    property_get("wlan.interface", primary_iface, WIFI_TEST_INTERFACE);

    property_set("ctl.start", supplicant_name);
    sched_yield();
    ...
}
```

Building the source code

We have made all the changes required to support Wi-Fi in emulators now. Let's build the AOSP source code for this chapter so that we can test the Wi-Fi connection.

Getting the source code

As we have done in previous chapters, we will have a look at the projects that we have changed in this chapter. We can check this from the manifest file for this chapter:

```xml
<?xml version="1.0" encoding="UTF-8"?>
<manifest>

  <remote  name="github"
           revision="refs/tags/android-7.1.1_r4_x86emu_ch07_r2"
           fetch="." />
```

```xml
<remote   name="aosp"
          fetch="https://android.googlesource.com/" />
<default  revision="refs/tags/android-7.1.1_r4"
          remote="aosp"
          sync-c="true"
          sync-j="1" />

<!-- github/shugaoye -->
<project path="kernel" name="goldfish" remote="github" />
<project path="device/generic/x86emu" name="x86emu" remote="github" />
<project path="bootable/newinstaller"
name="platform_bootable_newinstaller"
 remote="github" />
<project path="device/generic/goldfish"
name="device_generic_goldfish"
 remote="github" groups="pdk" />

<!-- aosp -->
<project path="build" name="platform/build" groups="pdk,tradefed" >
  <copyfile src="core/root.mk" dest="Makefile" />
</project>


...
</manifest>
```

The preceding code is the `default.xml` file at
`https://github.com/shugaoye/manifests/blob/android-7.1.1_r4_ch07_aosp/d`
`efault.xml`.

We can see that we have an `android-7.1.1_r4_x86emu_ch07_r2` tag for this chapter. In this chapter, we have our own projects, `kernel`, `x86emu`, `newinstaller`, and `goldfish`. We will use this manifest to download or update the source code for this chapter:

```
$ repo init https://github.com/shugaoye/manifests -b
android-7.1.1_r4_x86emu_ch07_r2
$ repo sync
```

After we have the source code for this chapter, we can set the environment and build the system as follows:

```
$ . build/envsetup.sh
$ lunch x86emu_x86-eng
$ make -j4
```

Enabling boot with initrd.img

As we learnt in Chapter 6, *Debugging the Boot Up Process Using a Customized ramdisk*, we can boot the emulator in two stages. This is very helpful to debug the init process and troubleshoot issues at system level. in Chapter 6, *Debugging the Boot Up Process Using a Customized ramdisk*, we create a separate disk image, x86emu_x86.img, to store all the necessary file images to support a first-stage boot up similar to Android-x86. The x86emu_x86.img image appears in the system as /dev/sda and includes all images: system.img, install.img, initrd.img, ramdisk.img, kernel, and so on.

In this chapter, we will change the Android-x86 newinstaller further to support two-stages boot up just using system.img instead of creating a separate image. We will use the first stage boot to help our debugging of Wi-Fi initialization later in this chapter.

In the first stage of boot-up, the init script in initrd.img will mount the system image and extract ramdisk.img to a filesystem in memory. Since we will use system.img directly, we need to put ramdisk.img inside the system.img. We do this using the Makefile in the x86emu device instead of changing the AOSP source code. The following is the build target that we add to device/generic/x86emu/Makefile:

```
qcow2_img:
    mkdir -p ${OUT}/system/x86emu_ch07
    cp ${OUT}/ramdisk.img ${OUT}/system/x86emu_ch07
    cd ../../..;make qcow2_img USE_SQUASHFS=0
```

In the qcow2_img build target, we create an x86emu_ch07 folder in the system image and we copy ramdisk.img to this folder. After that, we build a system image in QCOW2 format.

To build the system image in QCOW2 format, we need to change `Android.mk` in the `bootable/newinstaller` folder:

```
---------------------------------- Android.mk ----------------------------------
index 3120ff0..dc5a900 100644
@@ -23,7 +23,7 @@ LOCAL_STATIC_LIBRARIES := libdiskconfig_host libcutils liblog
 edit_mbr := $(HOST_OUT_EXECUTABLES)/$(LOCAL_MODULE)
 include $(BUILD_HOST_EXECUTABLE)

-VER ?= $(shell date +"%F")
+VER ?= x86emu_ch07

 # use squashfs for iso, unless explictly disabled
 ifneq ($(USE_SQUASHFS),0)
@@ -99,5 +99,7 @@ $(EFI_IMAGE): $(wildcard $(LOCAL_PATH)/boot/boot/*/*) $(BUILT_IMG) $(ESP_LAYOUT)
 iso_img: $(ISO_IMAGE)
 usb_img: $(ISO_IMAGE)
 efi_img: $(EFI_IMAGE)
+qcow2_img: $(BUILT_IMG)
+        qemu-img convert -c -f raw -O qcow2 $(PRODUCT_OUT)/system.img $(PRODUCT_OUT)/system-qcow2.img

 endif
```

diff in bootable/newinstaller/Android.mk

From the preceding diff tool output, we can see that we changed the VER variable to x86emu_ch07. The init script of `initrd.img` uses this variable to find the folder of images. The second change is to add a build target to generate the QCOW2 image using the `qemu-img` tool.

Finally, we need to change the init script in `initrd.img` as follows to extract `ramdisk.img` inside `system.img`:

```
...
check_root()
{
    if [ "`dirname $1`" = "/dev" ]; then
        [ -e $1 ] || return 1
        blk=`basename $1`
        [ ! -e /dev/block/$blk ] && ln $1 /dev/block
        dev=/dev/block/$blk
    else
        dev=$1
    fi
    try_mount ro $dev /mnt || return 1
    if [ -n "$iso" -a -e /mnt/$iso ]; then
        mount --move /mnt /iso
        mkdir /mnt/iso
        mount -o loop /iso/$iso /mnt/iso
        SRC=iso
```

```
    elif [ ! -e /mnt/$SRC/ramdisk.img ]; then
        return 1
    fi
    zcat /mnt/$SRC/ramdisk.img | cpio -id > /dev/null
    if [ -e /mnt/$SRC/system.sfs ]; then
        mount -o loop /mnt/$SRC/system.sfs /sfs
        mount -o loop /sfs/system.img system
    elif [ -e /mnt/$SRC/system.img ]; then
        remount_rw
        mount -o loop /mnt/$SRC/system.img system
    elif [ -d /mnt/$SRC/system ]; then
        remount_rw
        mount --bind /mnt/$SRC/system system
    else
        echo Moving mount point to /android/system
        mount --move /mnt /android/system
    fi
    mkdir mnt
    echo " found at $1"
    rm /sbin/mke2fs
    hash -r
}
...
echo -n Detecting x86emu...
export DEBUG=2
export SRC=x86emu_ch07
...
```

The original script will try to find the system image in SQUASH format (system.sfs) or a plain image (system.img). If none of the system images can be found, it will try to find a system/ folder as the system image. After that, it will mount the image file or the folder to /android/system. In our case, the system image is already mounted at /mnt, so we just move the mount point from /mnt to /android/system.

The second change to the init script is to define the DEBUG and SRC environment variables. These two variables are passed from the kernel command line in *Chapter 6, Debugging the Boot Up Process Using a Customized ramdisk*. Here, we define them inside the script, so we don't need to worry about the kernel command line in our test script.

Once we have done all these changes, we can build the initrd.img and system image as follows:

```
$ cd device/generic/x86emu
$ make qcow2_img
...
Created filesystem with 1976/81920 inodes and 158476/327680 blocks
```

```
Install system fs image: out/target/product/x86emu/system.img
out/target/product/x86emu/system.img+ maxsize=1370278272 blocksize=2112
total=1342177280 reserve=13842048
rm -rf out/target/product/x86emu/installer
out/host/linux-x86/bin/acp -pr bootable/newinstaller/initrd
out/target/product/x86emu/installer
ln -s /bin/ld-linux.so.2 out/target/product/x86emu/installer/lib
mkdir -p out/target/product/x86emu/installer/android
out/target/product/x86emu/installer/iso
out/target/product/x86emu/installer/mnt
out/target/product/x86emu/installer/proc
out/target/product/x86emu/installer/sys
out/target/product/x86emu/installer/tmp
out/target/product/x86emu/installer/sfs
out/target/product/x86emu/installer/hd
echo "VER=x86emu_ch07" > out/target/product/x86emu/installer/scripts/00-ver
out/host/linux-x86/bin/mkbootfs out/target/product/x86emu/installer | gzip
-9 > out/target/product/x86emu/initrd.img
qemu-img convert -c -f raw -O qcow2 out/target/product/x86emu/system.img
out/target/product/x86emu/system-qcow2.img
make[1]: Leaving directory `/home/roger/src/android-6'

#### make completed successfully (03:30 (mm:ss)) ####
```

We can see from the preceding output that `initrd.img` is created and `system-qcow2.img` is generated from `system.img`.

Testing Wi-Fi on an emulator

We have now prepared all the images that we need for the testing process. The prebuilt test images for this chapter can be downloaded from the following URL:

```
https://sourceforge.net/projects/android-system-programming/files/android-7/ch0
7/ch07.zip/download
```

Booting an Android emulator using initrd.img

We can execute the following command to boot the system using `initrd.img` first:

```
$ cd $OUT
$ emulator @a25x86 -ranchu -verbose -show-kernel -system ./system-qcow2.img
-ramdisk ./initrd.img -initdata ./userdata-qcow2.img -kernel ./kernel -qemu
-netdev user,id=mynet1,net=10.0.2.0/24,dhcpstart=10.0.2.50 -device virtio-
net,netdev=mynet1
```

In the preceding command, we use QCOW2-format images for both system and user data, since they are much smaller than the plain file images. We use `initrd.img` as the ramdisk so that we can debug the configuration in the first stage of boot up. We can also change this script to use `ramdisk.img` directly. In this case, it is the normal start up process of the emulator.

Once we start the emulator using `initrd.img`, we can enter the debug console, in which we can check the configuration and make necessary changes before we move forward.

```
● ● ◉    sgye@sz-linux-atd-E7440: ~/vol1/test/ch07
[     1.100423] scsi 1:0:0:0: CD-ROM              QEMU       QEMU DVD-ROM      2.2. PQ
: 0 ANSI: 5
[     1.103496] sr0: scsi3-mmc drive: 4x/4x cd/rw xa/form2 tray
[     1.104549] cdrom: Uniform CD-ROM driver Revision: 3.20
[     1.107287] sr 1:0:0:0: Attached scsi generic sg0 type 5
[     1.108800] Freeing unused kernel memory: 488k freed
[     1.110086] Write protecting the kernel text: 4936k
[     1.111053] Write protecting the kernel read-only data: 1776k
Detecting x86emu...
Type 'exit' to continue booting...

Moving mount point to /android/system
 found at /dev/vda

Type 'exit' to continue booting...

Running MirBSD Korn Shell...
(debug-found)@android:/android # mount
rootfs on / type rootfs (rw)
proc on /proc type proc (rw,relatime)
sys on /sys type sysfs (rw,relatime)
tmpfs on /android type tmpfs (rw,relatime)
/dev/block/vda on /android/system type ext4 (ro,relatime,data=ordered)
(debug-found)@android:/android # █
```

From the output, we can see that the system image on the device, `/dev/block/vda`, is mounted to `/android/system`. At this point, we have an opportunity to check and change any start up scripts before we launch them. For example, we can edit `init.ranchu.rc` to increase the debug level of `wpa_supplicant` with the `–dd` option before we start the Android system.

Booting an Android emulator using ramdisk.img

To boot the system using `ramdisk.img`, we can execute the following command:

```
$ cd $OUT
$ emulator @a25x86 -ranchu -verbose -show-kernel -system ./system-qcow2.img
-ramdisk ./ramdisk.img -initdata ./userdata-qcow2.img -kernel ./kernel -
qemu -netdev user,id=mynet1,net=10.0.2.0/24,dhcpstart=10.0.2.50 -device
virtio-net,netdev=mynet1
```

Debugging Wi-Fi start up processes

Once the system starts, we can check the `wpa_supplicant` debug message using logcat as follows:

```
$ adb logcat -s "wpa_supplicant"
```

```
-------- beginning of main
-------- beginning of system
10-26 14:27:14.081  1478  1478 D wpa_supplicant: wpa_supplicant v2.5-devel-6.0.1
10-26 14:27:14.082  1478  1478 D wpa_supplicant: random: Added entropy from /data/misc/wifi/entropy.bin
(own_pool_ready=2)
10-26 14:27:14.082  1478  1478 D wpa_supplicant: random: Trying to read entropy from /dev/random
10-26 14:27:14.082  1478  1478 D wpa_supplicant: Get randomness: len=20 entropy=1
10-26 14:27:14.082  1478  1478 D wpa_supplicant: random: Updated entropy file /data/misc/wifi/entropy.bin
(own_pool_ready=2)
10-26 14:27:14.082  1478  1478 D wpa_supplicant: Global control interface '@android:wpa_eth1'
10-26 14:27:14.082  1478  1478 D wpa_supplicant: Using Android control socket 'wpa_eth1'
10-26 14:27:14.083  1478  1478 I wpa_supplicant: Successfully initialized wpa_supplicant
10-26 14:27:14.083  1478  1478 D wpa_supplicant: Initializing interface 'eth1' conf '/data/misc/wifi/
wpa_supplicant.conf' driver 'wired' ctrl_interface 'N/A' bridge 'N/A'
10-26 14:27:14.083  1478  1478 D wpa_supplicant: Configuration file '/data/misc/wifi/wpa_supplicant.conf' -> '/data/misc/
wifi/wpa_supplicant.conf'
10-26 14:27:14.083  1478  1478 D wpa_supplicant: Reading configuration file '/data/misc/wifi/wpa_supplicant.conf'
10-26 14:27:14.084  1478  1478 D wpa_supplicant: ctrl_interface='eth1'
10-26 14:27:14.084  1478  1478 D wpa_supplicant: ap_scan=0
10-26 14:27:14.084  1478  1478 D wpa_supplicant: update_config=1
10-26 14:27:14.084  1478  1478 D wpa_supplicant: device_name='x86emu_x86'
10-26 14:27:14.084  1478  1478 D wpa_supplicant: manufacturer='unknown'
10-26 14:27:14.084  1478  1478 D wpa_supplicant: model_name='x86emu_x86_ch7'
10-26 14:27:14.084  1478  1478 D wpa_supplicant: model_number='x86emu_x86_ch7'
10-26 14:27:14.084  1478  1478 D wpa_supplicant: serial_number=''
10-26 14:27:14.084  1478  1478 D wpa_supplicant: config_methods='physical_display virtual_push_button'
10-26 14:27:14.084  1478  1478 D wpa_supplicant: external_sim=1
10-26 14:27:14.084  1478  1478 D wpa_supplicant: Line: 13 - start of a new network block
10-26 14:27:14.084  1478  1478 D wpa_supplicant: ssid - hexdump(len=9): 57 69 72 65 64 53 53 49 44
10-26 14:27:14.084  1478  1478 D wpa_supplicant: key_mgmt: 0x4
10-26 14:27:14.084  1478  1478 D wpa_supplicant: engine=1 (0x1)
10-26 14:27:14.084  1478  1478 D wpa_supplicant: priority=1 (0x1)
10-26 14:27:14.084  1478  1478 D wpa_supplicant: Priority group 1
10-26 14:27:14.084  1478  1478 D wpa_supplicant:    id=0 ssid='WiredSSID'
10-26 14:27:14.084  1478  1478 D wpa_supplicant: wpa_driver_wired_init: Added multicast membership with packet socket
```

We can see that `wpa_supplicant` started successfully using Ethernet `eth1` and global control socket `wpa_eth1`. This global control socket is specified in `init.ranchu.rc` as part of the `wpa_supplicant` service as follows:

```
service wpa_supplicant /system/bin/wpa_supplicant -ieth1 -Dwired -
c/data/misc/wifi/wpa_supplicant.conf -e/data/misc/wifi/entropy.bin -
g@android:wpa_eth1 -dd
    class main
    socket wpa_eth1 dgram 660 wifi wifi
    disabled
    oneshot
```

We can also check the network status using the `ifconfig` command in the following snippet. We can see that `eth0` is assigned a fixed IP address, `10.0.2.15`, and `eth1` is assigned the IP address `10.0.2.50` through DHCP:

```
sgye@sz-linux-atd-E7440: ~/vol1/test/ch07
          RX packets:0 errors:0 dropped:0 overruns:0 frame:0
          TX packets:0 errors:0 dropped:0 overruns:0 carrier:0
          collisions:0 txqueuelen:0
          RX bytes:0 TX bytes:0

eth0      Link encap:Ethernet  HWaddr 52:54:00:12:34:56
          inet addr:10.0.2.15  Bcast:10.0.2.255  Mask:255.255.255.0
          inet6 addr: fe80::5054:ff:fe12:3456/64 Scope: Link
          UP BROADCAST RUNNING MULTICAST  MTU:1500  Metric:1
          RX packets:0 errors:0 dropped:0 overruns:0 frame:0
          TX packets:9 errors:0 dropped:0 overruns:0 carrier:0
          collisions:0 txqueuelen:1000
          RX bytes:0 TX bytes:1518

eth1      Link encap:Ethernet  HWaddr 52:54:00:12:34:57
          inet addr:10.0.2.50  Bcast:10.0.2.255  Mask:255.255.255.0
          inet6 addr: fe80::5054:ff:fe12:3457/64 Scope: Link
          UP BROADCAST RUNNING MULTICAST  MTU:1500  Metric:1
          RX packets:45 errors:0 dropped:0 overruns:0 frame:0
          TX packets:84 errors:0 dropped:0 overruns:0 carrier:0
          collisions:0 txqueuelen:1000
          RX bytes:7204 TX bytes:6318

root@x86emu:/ # 
```

Once the system starts up, we can go to **Settings** | **Wi-Fi** and we will see the following screen. The access point SSID is **WiredSSID** and we can turn Wi-Fi on or off as we expect:

Summary

In this chapter, we introduced the Wi-Fi architecture in Android and we also did an analysis of the Wi-Fi initialization process. Based on that, we modified our x86emu device to support simulated Wi-Fi through a wired Ethernet interface `eth1`. We used the advanced features in QEMU to add the second network interface to the ranchu emulator. With all these changes to x86emu, we built and tested the image. In order to help with debugging, we reused the technique that we learnt from `Chapter 6`, *Debugging the Boot Up Process Using a Customized ramdisk*, to boot the system using `initrd.img` so that we can get a debug console before the Android system is started.

With all the knowledge from `Chapter 4`, *Customizing the Android Emulator* to `Chapter 7`, *Enabling Wi-Fi on the Android Emulator*, we learnt how to create a new device based on an existing one. We also learnt how to customize and extend the device to support new features. From the next chapter to `Chapter 11`, *Enabling VirtualBox-Specific Hardware Interfaces*, we will take on a new challenge to support a new platform that is not supported by AOSP. We will create and build a new x86vbox device to explore more advanced topics in the Android system programming world.

8
Creating Your Own Device on VirtualBox

We have learned how to customize and enhance an existing device to support new features using x86emu. The x86emu device is a device created on top of the following Android emulators: goldfish and ranchu. From this chapter to Chapter 11, *Enabling VirtualBox-Specific Hardware Interfaces*, we will move to an advanced topic: porting Android systems. What can we do with a hardware platform that is not supported by AOSP?

In this chapter, we will move to a new device, x86vbox. We will create this new x86vbox device to run it on VirtualBox. Since VirtualBox is virtual hardware that is not supported by AOSP directly, we have to create the HAL layer by ourselves. Creating the HAL layer by ourselves doesn't mean we have to create everything from scratch. As I mentioned earlier, porting and customization are the art of integration. We can integrate device drivers for the devices that we need from other open source projects. In this chapter, we will cover the following topics:

- Analyzing the HAL of the Android-x86 project and using the Android-x86 HAL for the x86vbox device
- Creating the x86vbox device based on the analysis of Android-x86 HAL
- Analyzing the start-up process for x86vbox

HAL of x86vbox

Before we create the new x86vbox device, we need to resolve a key issue: creating the HAL for x86vbox. What this means is that we need to support the hardware devices that appear on VirtualBox. As we said previously, the Android-x86 project is a project that aims to provide **Board Support Package (BSP)** for any x86-based computing devices. Even though VirtualBox is a virtualized x86 hardware environment, we can still use part of Android-x86 projects to support it. In the following table, we can see a list of projects that we reused from Android-x86. There are three project categories that we need to include in our build from Android-x86:

- **Linux kernel**: Android-x86 provides a kernel that can work with Android for Intel x86 architecture.
- **HAL for Intel x86 architecture**: Android-x86 includes HAL support on most devices that you can find on your PC.
- **Android system projects and framework projects**: Android-x86 changed some projects under the `system/` and `frameworks/` directories to meet x86 architecture-specific requirements. For example, `init` and `init.rc` under `system/core` have been changed to work with the two-stage start up of Android-x86.

In the following table, we can also look at the projects in another dimension:

- AOSP projects changed by Android-x86.
- Android-x86 only projects.
- x86vbox--only projects.

In this chapter and the following chapters, we will create the x86vbox device and make changes to some of the following projects to run x86vbox on VirtualBox.

In the following table, all kernel- and HAL-related projects from AOSP, Android-x86, and x86vbox are listed. The projects that are created or changed by them are marked with **X**:

Project	AOSP	Android-x86	x86vbox	HAL module
`kernel`	X	X	X	
`device/generic/x86vbox`			X	
`bionic`	X	X		
`bootable/newinstaller`		X	X	
`device/generic/common`	X	X	X	

device/generic/firmware		X		
external/alsa-lib		X		
external/alsa-utils		X		
external/bluetooth/bluez		X		bluetooth.default audio.a2dp.default
external/bluetooth/glib		X		
external/bluetooth/sbc		X		
external/busybox		X		
external/drm_gralloc	X	X		gralloc.drm
external/drm_hwcomposer	X	X		hwcomposer.drm
external/e2fsprogs	X	X		
external/ffmpeg		X		
external/libdrm	X	X		
external/libpciaccess		X		
external/libtruezip		X		
external/llvm	X	X		
external/mesa		X		
external/s2tc		X		
external/stagefright-plugins		X		
external/v86d		X		
frameworks/av	X	X		
frameworks/base	X	X	X	
frameworks/native	X	X		
hardware/broadcom/wlan	X	X		
hardware/gps		X		gps.default gps.huawei
hardware/intel/audio_media	X	X		audio.primary.hdmi
hardware/intel/libsensors		X		sensors.hsb
hardware/libaudio		X		audio.primary.x86

hardware/libcamera		X		camera.x86
hardware/libhardware	X	X		libhardware
hardware/libhardware_legacy	X	X		audio_policy.default
hardware/liblights		X		lights.default
hardware/libsensors		X		sensors.hdaps sensors.iio sensors.kbd sensors.s103t sensors.w500
hardware/ril	X	X		
hardware/x86power		X		power.x86
system/core	X	X		

The manifest for x86vbox

Based on an analysis of the preceding table, we can create the manifest file for x86vbox. From the preceding table, we can see that we reuse 39 projects from Android-x86 to form the HAL of VirtualBox. Out of these 39 projects, 16 of them are from AOSP and changed by Android-x86. To run our x86vbox device on VirtualBox, we need to create the device x86vbox at device/generic/x86vbox. We also need to change four projects: kernel, bootable/newinstaller, device/generic/common, and frameworks/base.

In the manifest of the x86vbox, we will include the preceding projects for the x86 kernel, HAL, and have modified system/ as well as frameworks/:

```
<?xml version="1.0" encoding="UTF-8"?>
<manifest>

  <remote  name="github"
           revision="refs/tags/android-7.1.1_r4_x86vbox_ch08_r1"
           fetch="." />

  <remote  name="aosp"
           fetch="https://android.googlesource.com/" />
  <default revision="refs/tags/android-7.1.1_r4"
           remote="aosp"
           sync-c="true"
           sync-j="1" />

  <!-- github/android-7.1.1_r4_ch08 -->
```

```
<project path="kernel" name="goldfish" remote="github" />
<project path="bootable/newinstaller"
name="platform_bootable_newinstaller"
remote="github" />
<project path="device/generic/common" name="device_generic_common"
groups="pdk"
remote="github" />
<project path="device/generic/x86vbox" name="x86vbox"
remote="github" />
<project path="bootable/recovery" name="android_bootable_recovery"
remote="github" groups="pdk" />

<project path="frameworks/base" name="platform_frameworks_base"
groups="pdk-cw-fs,pdk-fs" remote="github" />

<project path="bionic" name="platform_bionic" groups="pdk"
remote="github" />
<project path="device/generic/firmware"
name="device_generic_firmware"
remote="github" />
<project path="external/alsa-lib" name="platform_external_alsa-lib"
remote="github" />
<project path="external/alsa-utils"
name="platform_external_alsa-utils"
remote="github" />
<project path="external/bluetooth/bluez"
name="platform_external_bluetooth_bluez" remote="github" />
<project path="external/bluetooth/glib"
name="platform_external_bluetooth_glib"
remote="github" />
<project path="external/bluetooth/sbc"
name="platform_external_bluetooth_sbc"
remote="github" />
<project path="external/busybox" name="platform_external_busybox"
remote="github" />
<project path="external/drm_gralloc"
name="platform_external_drm_gralloc"
groups="drm_gralloc" remote="github" />
<project path="external/drm_hwcomposer"
name="platform_external_drm_hwcomposer"
groups="drm_hwcomposer" remote="github" />
<project path="external/e2fsprogs" name="platform_external_e2fsprogs"
groups="pdk" remote="github" />
<project path="external/ffmpeg" name="platform_external_ffmpeg"
remote="github" />
<project path="external/libdrm" name="platform_external_libdrm"
groups="pdk"
remote="github" />
```

```
<project path="external/libtruezip"
name="platform_external_libtruezip"
remote="github" />
<project path="external/llvm" name="platform_external_llvm"
groups="pdk"
remote="github" />
<project path="external/mesa" name="platform_external_mesa"
remote="github" />
<project path="external/s2tc" name="platform_external_s2tc"
remote="github" />
<project path="external/stagefright-plugins"
name="platform_external_stagefright-plugins" remote="github" />
<project path="external/v86d" name="platform_external_v86d"
remote="github" />
<project path="frameworks/av" name="platform_frameworks_av"
groups="pdk"
remote="github" />
<project path="frameworks/native" name="platform_frameworks_native"
groups="pdk" remote="github" />
<project path="hardware/broadcom/wlan"
name="platform_hardware_broadcom_wlan"
groups="pdk,broadcom_wlan" remote="github" />
<project path="hardware/gps" name="platform_hardware_gps"
remote="github" />
<project path="hardware/intel/audio_media"
name="platform_hardware_intel_audio_media" groups="intel"
remote="github" />
<project path="hardware/intel/libsensors"
name="platform_hardware_intel_libsensors" remote="github" />
<project path="hardware/libaudio" name="platform_hardware_libaudio"
remote="github" />
<project path="hardware/libcamera" name="platform_hardware_libcamera"
remote="github" />
<project path="hardware/libhardware"
name="platform_hardware_libhardware"
groups="pdk" remote="github" />
<project path="hardware/libhardware_legacy"
name="platform_hardware_libhardware_legacy" groups="pdk"
remote="github" />
<project path="hardware/liblights" name="platform_hardware_liblights"
remote="github" />
<project path="hardware/libsensors"
name="platform_hardware_libsensors"
remote="github" />
<project path="hardware/ril" name="platform_hardware_ril"
groups="pdk"
remote="github" />
<project path="hardware/x86power" name="platform_hardware_x86power"
```

```
remote="github" />
<project path="system/core" name="platform_system_core" groups="pdk"
remote="github" />

<!-- aosp -->
<project path="build" name="platform/build" groups="pdk,tradefed" >
  <copyfile src="core/root.mk" dest="Makefile" />
</project>

...
</manifest>
```

We can see that the manifest of x86vbox includes two parts. The first part includes the x86 kernel, x86vbox HAL, and modified AOSP projects that are all in GitHub. The second part includes the original AOSP projects. All the projects in the second part are not touched by either Android-x86 or x86vbox. The majority of projects in the first part are changed by Android-x86 only so we don't have to do anything for these projects as well.

In the first part of manifest, all the projects in the external/ or hardware/ directory are x86 HAL-related projects. The only AOSP project that you may have questions is **bionic**. You may be wondering why it is changed by Android-x86, since it is the C library of Android. You may know that system calls are implemented in the C library in the Linux system. There are two system calls ioperm and iopl missing from the original bionic and they are needed by the external/v86d project, which is the user space daemon for the vesafb frame buffer driver.

All the preceding analysis helps us to clarify the scope of work. As we can see, the scope of work is not as big as we thought at the beginning. There are many open source projects available nowadays. If we can reuse them as much as possible, the amount of work usually can be reduced dramatically.

All Android-x86 projects in GitHub are forked from the Android-x86 mirror so that we can change them.

Creating a new x86vbox device

Once we have the HAL for VirtualBox, we can create a new device named x86vbox now. If we review how we created the x86emu device in Chapter 4, *Customizing the Android Emulator*, we know that we need to have a board/device configuration Makefile and a product definition Makefile for a new device. We can also create a new device by inheriting it from an existing device. If we look at the preceding table of x86 HAL, we can see that there is a common x86 device project, device/common, which can be found in Android-x86. We will create our new device x86vbox by inheriting from this common device for x86. The x86vbox that we create in this chapter is a 32-bit x86 device. You can follow the same instructions to create an x86_64 device by yourself.

As we did in Chapter 4, *Customizing the Android Emulator*, we create an AndroidProducts.mk Makefile to include the product definition Makefile for x86vbox as follows:

```
PRODUCT_MAKEFILES := \
    $(LOCAL_DIR)/x86vbox.mk
```

Product definition Makefile of x86vbox

As we know, the AOSP build system will look for AndroidProducts.mk to find the product definition Makefile for a particular device. Let's review the product definition Makefile x86vbox.mk as follows:

```
# includes the base of Android-x86 platform
$(call inherit-product,device/generic/common/x86.mk)

# Overrides
PRODUCT_NAME := x86vbox
PRODUCT_BRAND := Android-x86
PRODUCT_DEVICE := x86vbox
PRODUCT_MODEL := x86vbox_ch8

TARGET_KERNEL_SOURCE := kernel
TARGET_KERNEL_CONFIG := android-x86_defconfig
TARGET_ARCH := x86

PRODUCT_OUT ?= out/target/product/$(PRODUCT_DEVICE)

include $(TARGET_KERNEL_SOURCE)/AndroidKernel.mk

# define build targets for kernel
.PHONY: $(TARGET_PREBUILT_KERNEL)
```

```
LOCAL_KERNEL := $(TARGET_PREBUILT_KERNEL)

PRODUCT_COPY_FILES += \
    $(LOCAL_KERNEL):kernel \
```

As we can see, the product definition Makefile is very simple. It does the following things:

- It includes the general x86 product definition Makefile, `device/generic/common/x86.mk`
- It defines product definition variables such as `PRODUCT_NAME`, `PRODUCT_BRAND`, `PRODUCT_DEVICE`, `PRODUCT_MODEL`, and so on
- It specifies how to build the kernel for x86vbox

It looks even simpler than the one we created in `Chapter 4`, *Customizing the Android Emulator* for x86emu. The inherited `x86.mk` Makefile did most actual work and we will analyze it in greater depth later.

Board configuration of x86vbox

Another Makefile that we will create for x86vbox is the board configuration Makefile `BoardConfig.mk` as follows:

```
TARGET_NO_BOOTLOADER := true

TARGET_ARCH := x86
TARGET_CPU_ABI := x86

TARGET_CPU_ABI_LIST_32_BIT := $(TARGET_CPU_ABI) $(TARGET_CPU_ABI2)
$(NATIVE_BRIDGE_ABI_LIST_32_BIT)
TARGET_CPU_ABI_LIST := $(TARGET_CPU_ABI_LIST_32_BIT)

TARGET_USERIMAGES_USE_EXT4 := true
BOARD_SYSTEMIMAGE_PARTITION_SIZE := 1153433600
BOARD_USERDATAIMAGE_PARTITION_SIZE := 419430400
BOARD_CACHEIMAGE_PARTITION_SIZE := 69206016
BOARD_CACHEIMAGE_FILE_SYSTEM_TYPE := ext4
BOARD_FLASH_BLOCK_SIZE := 512
TARGET_USERIMAGES_SPARSE_EXT_DISABLED := true

BOARD_SEPOLICY_DIRS += build/target/board/generic/sepolicy
BOARD_SEPOLICY_DIRS += build/target/board/generic_x86/sepolicy

include device/generic/common/BoardConfig.mk
```

This looks very simple as well. It defines the target architecture--specific variables `TARGET_ARCH`, `TARGET_CPU_ABI`, `TARGET_CPU_ABI_LIST_32_BIT`, and `TARGET_CPU_ABI_LIST`. Then it defines the parameters for the system image file. Finally, it includes the common board configuration the Makefile `device/generic/common/BoardConfig.mk` and we will look at this in a moment.

Common x86 devices

In the Android-x86 project, it defines a common x86 device so that everybody can create a specific x86 device based on it. The inherited device can be either a 32-bit or a 64-bit x86 device.

We can have a look at the content of `device/generic/common` first as follows:

```
sgye@ubuntu14: ~/vol1/android-6
sgye@ubuntu14:~/vol1/android-6$ ls -F device/generic/common
alsa/                       init.sh               ppp/
Android.mk                  init.x86.rc           system.prop
app/                        io_switch/            tablet-mode/
bluetooth/                  keylayout/            tp_smapi/
BoardConfig.mk              media_codecs.xml      ueventd.x86.rc
device.mk                   media_profiles.xml    wacom/
excluded-input-devices.xml  modules.blacklist     wpa_supplicant.conf
fstab.x86                   nativebridge/         x86_64.mk
gpu/                        overlay/              x86.mk
idc/                        packages.mk
sgye@ubuntu14:~/vol1/android-6$
```

We can see that there are a lot of files and directories. We will start the analysis from the `BoardConfig.mk` and `x86.mk` Makefiles first.

In `BoardConfig.mk`, the variables needed by the build system are defined as follows:

```
TARGET_BOARD_PLATFORM := android-x86

# Some framework code requires this to enable BT
BOARD_HAVE_BLUETOOTH := true
```

```
BOARD_USE_LEGACY_UI := true

# BOARD_SYSTEMIMAGE_PARTITION_SIZE = $(if $(MKSQUASHFS),0,1610612736)

# customize the malloced address to be 16-byte aligned
BOARD_MALLOC_ALIGNMENT := 16

# Enable dex-preoptimization to speed up the first boot sequence
# of an SDK AVD. Note that this operation only works on Linux for now
ifeq ($(HOST_OS),linux)
WITH_DEXPREOPT := true
WITH_DEXPREOPT_PIC := true
endif

# the following variables could be overridden
TARGET_PRELINK_MODULE := false
TARGET_NO_KERNEL ?= false
TARGET_NO_RECOVERY ?= true
TARGET_EXTRA_KERNEL_MODULES := tp_smapi
ifneq ($(filter efi_img,$(MAKECMDGOALS)),)
TARGET_KERNEL_ARCH ?= x86_64
endif
TARGET_USES_64_BIT_BINDER := $(if $(filter x86_64,$(TARGET_ARCH)
$(TARGET_KERNEL_ARCH).),true)

BOARD_USES_GENERIC_AUDIO ?= false
BOARD_USES_ALSA_AUDIO ?= true
...
```

It is a long list. It defines audio, Wi-Fi, GPU, and Bluetooth-related features. It is also a disabled emulator-related build.

Now, let's have a look at x86.mk:

```
PRODUCT_PROPERTY_OVERRIDES := \
    ro.com.android.dateformat=MM-dd-yyyy \

$(call inherit-product,$(LOCAL_PATH)/device.mk)
$(call inherit-product,$(LOCAL_PATH)/packages.mk)

# Get a list of languages.
$(call inherit-product,$(SRC_TARGET_DIR)/product/locales_full.mk)

# Get everything else from the parent package
$(call inherit-product,$(SRC_TARGET_DIR)/product/full.mk)
```

In x86.mk, it includes two generic Makefiles, full.mk and locales_full.mk, from the AOSP build system. If we recall the device definition Makefile for x86emu, it also includes these two Makefiles from the build system.

There are another two local Makefiles, device.mk and packages.mk, imported by x86.mk. In packages.mk, the HAL module packages are defined as follows:

```
PRODUCT_PACKAGES := \
    camera.x86 \
    com.android.future.usb.accessory \
    drmserver \
    gps.default \
    gps.huawei \
    hwcomposer.x86 \
    io_switch \
    libGLES_android \
    libhuaweigeneric-ril \
    lights.default \
    power.x86 \
    powerbtnd \
    sensors.hsb \
    tablet-mode \
    v86d \
    wacom-input \

PRODUCT_PACKAGES += \
    libwpa_client \
    hostapd \
    wpa_supplicant \
    wpa_supplicant.conf \
```

This is not an exhaustive list of packages. There are more components added to PRODUCT_PACKAGES in device.mk as follows:

```
PRODUCT_DIR := $(dir $(lastword $(filter-out device/common/%,$(filter device/%,$(ALL_PRODUCTS))))))

PRODUCT_PROPERTY_OVERRIDES := \
    ro.ril.hsxpa=1 \
    ro.ril.gprsclass=10 \
    keyguard.no_require_sim=true \
    ro.com.android.dataroaming=true

PRODUCT_DEFAULT_PROPERTY_OVERRIDES := \
    ro.arch=x86 \
    persist.rtc_local_time=1 \
```

```
PRODUCT_COPY_FILES := \...
PRODUCT_TAGS += dalvik.gc.type-precise

PRODUCT_CHARACTERISTICS := tablet

PRODUCT_AAPT_CONFIG := normal large xlarge mdpi hdpi
PRODUCT_AAPT_PREF_CONFIG := mdpi

DEVICE_PACKAGE_OVERLAYS := $(LOCAL_PATH)/overlay

# Get the firmwares
$(call inherit-product,device/generic/firmware/firmware.mk)

# Get the touchscreen calibration tool
$(call inherit-product-if-exists,external/tslib/tslib.mk)

# Get the alsa files
$(call inherit-product-if-exists,hardware/libaudio/alsa.mk)

# Get GPS configuration
$(call inherit-product-if-exists,device/common/gps/gps_as.mk)

# Get the hardware acceleration libraries
$(call inherit-product-if-exists,$(LOCAL_PATH)/gpu/gpu_mesa.mk)

# Get the sensors hals
$(call inherit-product-if-exists,hardware/libsensors/sensors.mk)

# Get tablet dalvik parameters
$(call inherit-product,frameworks/native/build/tablet-10in-xhdpi-2048-
dalvik-heap.mk)

# Get GMS
$(call inherit-product-if-exists,vendor/google/products/gms.mk)

# Get native bridge settings
$(call inherit-product-if-
exists,$(LOCAL_PATH)/nativebridge/nativebridge.mk)
```

In device.mk, it defines the properties for x86 devices and it is followed by a long list of files to be copied. At the end, it includes individual Makefiles for various components, such as firmware, touchscreen a calibration tool, audio, GPS, a sensor and native bridge, and so on. You can find and investigate each of them in the respective folders by yourself. In this chapter, we just give an overview about how we can create the x86vbox device. We will delve into the details of some hardware interfaces in later chapters.

Getting the source code and building the x86vbox device

To build the x86vbox device, we can get the source code from GitHub and AOSP using the following command:

```
$ repo init https://github.com/shugaoye/manifests -b
android-7.1.1_r4_ch08_aosp
$ repo sync
```

The `android-7.1.1_r4_ch08_aosp` tag is used to baseline the changes in this chapter.

After we get the source code for this chapter, we can set the environment and build the system as follows:

```
$ source build/envsetup.sh
$ lunch x86vbox-eng
$ make -j4
```

Boot up process and device initialization

Since we use the Android-x86 kernel and HAL for x86vbox, we will further analyze about the start-up process of x86vbox in this section. From the analysis, we can understand how Android-x86 supports multiple devices using one codebase. You can review the two-stage start-up process that we discussed in Chapter 6, *Debugging the Boot Up Process using a Customized ramdisk*. We will work on a more detailed analysis on top of that introduction now.

The kernel of Android-x86 is different from the kernel that we used in Chapter 6, *Debugging the Boot Up Process using a Customized ramdisk* for emulators. The Android-x86 kernel does not have any idea about what hardware interfaces it needs to support, so it builds as many device drivers as possible with it. On the other hand, the goldfish kernel does know what hardware it needs to support. This difference means they are built in two different ways. The goldfish kernel includes all devices supported inside the kernel, so it does not use kernel modules at all. However, it is impossible for Android-x86 kernel to do this, since it would make the size of the kernel too big. The kernel of Android-x86 uses kernel modules extensively.

We will focus on an analysis about how device nodes are created and how the kernel modules are loaded during the start-up process in this chapter. Since Android-x86 boots up in two stages, the device initialization is also split into two stages.

Device initialization before Android start-up

The boot-up process will start with an embedded Linux environment as the first stage. Most devices will be initialized during this stage. The good thing is that Android-x86 can enter a shell environment with a debug console using a defined environment variable. In this console, we can check the system status to find out whether we have the right configuration that we want to create. The default init script comes with two debug checkpoints. The first checkpoint is after the root device is mounted. The second checkpoint is entered after all the drivers are loaded. Of course, you can set up as many checkpoints as you want by changing the init script.

The following is the part of the init script that we want to look at before we enter the first checkpoint:

```
PATH=/sbin:/bin:/system/bin:/system/xbin; export PATH
...
# early boot
if test x"$HAS_CTTY" != x"Yes"; then
    # initialise /proc and /sys
    busybox mount -t proc proc /proc
    busybox mount -t sysfs sys /sys
    # let busybox install all applets as symlinks
    busybox --install -s
    # spawn shells on tty 2 and 3 if debug or installer
    if test -n "$DEBUG" || test -n "$INSTALL"; then
        # ensure they can open a controlling tty
        mknod /dev/tty c 5 0
        # create device nodes then spawn on them
        mknod /dev/tty2 c 4 2 && openvt
        mknod /dev/tty3 c 4 3 && openvt
    fi
    if test -z "$DEBUG" || test -n "$INSTALL"; then
        echo 0 0 0 0 > /proc/sys/kernel/printk
    fi
    # initialise /dev (first time)
    mkdir -p /dev/block
    echo /sbin/mdev > /proc/sys/kernel/hotplug
    mdev -s
    # re-run this script with a controlling tty
    exec env HAS_CTTY=Yes setsid cttyhack /bin/sh "$0" "$@"
fi
...
```

In the early boot stage, the init script mounts the /proc and /sys filesystems using by kernels. After that, it sets up the symbolic links of busybox so that we can use all the commands of busybox. Then, it will set /sbin/mdev as the handler for hotplug. The mdev command is a minimal implementation of udev. mdev can dynamically manage the device nodes under /dev, when a new device is detected by the kernel. mdev is part of busybox so we need to create all busybox symbolic links first. It also requires the /proc and /sys filesystem. After the hotplug is set, the script runs the command mdev −s to find all existing devices currently found by the kernel. At this point, all device nodes under /dev are created.

udev and mdev

udev is a device manager for the Linux kernel. As the successor to devfsd and hotplug, udev primarily manages device nodes in the /dev directory. At the same time, udev also handles all user space events raised while hardware devices are added into the system or removed from it, including firmware loading as required by certain **devices.**

mdev is a minimum implementation of udev in busybox. It is used in embedded systems to replace udev. mdev lacks some features in udev, such as completed implementation of device driver loading, and so on. We can see that Android-x86 uses mdev in the first start up stage.

Let's look at the kernel modules and device nodes at this stage:

```
⊗ ⊖ ⊜  sgye@sz-ubuntu-14: ~
[   13.377125] usb 2-1: Manufacturer: VirtualBox
[   13.392715] input: VirtualBox USB Tablet as /devices/pci0000:00/0000:00:06.03
[   13.394836] hid-generic 0003:80EE:0021.0001: input,hidraw0: USB HID v1.10 Mo0
[   13.576822] random: nonblocking pool is initialized
[   13.735542] clocksource: Switched to clocksource tsc
[   13.739254] input: AT Translated Set 2 keyboard as /devices/platform/i8042/s4

Type 'exit' to continue booting...

Running MirBSD Korn Shell...
(debug-found)@android:/android # lsmod
Module                  Size  Used by     Not tainted
atkbd                  15064  0
(debug-found)@android:/android # ls /dev
ashmem          ptyq3           tty19           tty8
binder          ptyq4           tty2            tty9
block           ptyq5           tty20           ttyS0
console         ptyq6           tty21           ttyS1
cpu             ptyq7           tty22           ttyS2
cpu_dma_latency ptyq8           tty23           ttyS3
full            ptyq9           tty24           ttyp0
fuse            ptyqa           tty25           ttyp1
hpet            ptyqb           tty26           ttyp2
input           ptyqc           tty27           ttyp3
```

Kernel modules and device nodes

As we can see from the preceding screenshot, all device nodes are created under /dev. However, there is only one kernel module loaded at this time. We are in the first checkpoint now.

Let's move on and see what happens in the script before we hit another checkpoint in the following code snippet. To exit from the first checkpoint, we need to run the exit command to continue executing the script.

```
(debug-found)@android:/android # exit
```

After exit from the first checkpoint, it will continue to execute the following script:

```
...
[ -n "$INSTALL" ] && do_install

load_modules
mount_data
mount_sdcard
setup_tslib
setup_dpi
post_detect

if [ 0$DEBUG -gt 1 ]; then
    echo -e "\nUse Alt-F1/F2/F3 to switch between virtual consoles"
    echo -e "Type 'exit' to enter Android...\n"

    debug_shell debug-late
fi

...
```

We can see that the init script performs the following tasks before it enters the next checkpoint:

1. Loads kernel modules.
2. Mounts the data partition.
3. Mounts the SD card.
4. Sets up the touch screen calibration tool.
5. Sets up the screen DPI.
6. Performs any other post-boot detection.

You can study the script for tasks 2 to 6 by yourself, since they are very straightforward and easy to understand. We want to look at the first task in more detail here:

```
auto_detect()
{
    tmp=/tmp/dev2mod
    echo 'dev2mod() { while read dev; do case $dev in' > $tmp
    sort -r /lib/modules/`uname -r`/modules.alias | \
        sed -n 's/^alias  *\([^ ]*\)  *\(.*\)/\1)busybox modprobe
        \2;;/p' >> $tmp
    echo 'esac; done; }' >> $tmp
    sed -i '/brcmfmac/d' $tmp
    source $tmp
    cat /sys/bus/*/devices/*/uevent | grep MODALIAS | sed
    's/^MODALIAS=//'
    | sort -u | dev2mod
    cat /sys/devices/virtual/wmi/*/modalias | dev2mod
}

load_modules()
{
    if [ -z "$FOUND" ]; then
        auto_detect
    fi

    # 3G modules
    for m in $EXTMOD; do
        busybox modprobe $m
    done
}
```

The `load_modules` script function is implemented in the script file `0-auto-detect`, as shown in the preceding snippet. It calls another function, `auto-detect`, to do the actual work. This function is not that easy to understand. Let's explain what it does now. The purpose of this function is to create a shell command called `dev2mod` on-the-fly. What this `dev2mod` function does is take the module alias as a parameter and load the respective driver module according to the module alias. After the `dev2mod` command is created, `auto_detect` will call this function using the devices found by the kernel under the `/sys/bus` folder.

All the kernel modules of the Android-x86 kernel can be found in the `/lib/modules/4.x.x-android-x86/modules.alias` file. This file is processed to add the `modprobe` command at the end of each line so that the kernel module can be loaded with the module alias as a parameter. The temporary script file can be found at `/tmp/dev2mod` and it looks like the following code snippet:

```
# cat /tmp/dev2mod
dev2mod() { while read dev; do case $dev in
xts)busybox modprobe xts;;
xtea)busybox modprobe tea;;
xeta)busybox modprobe tea;;
xcbc)busybox modprobe xcbc;;
wp512)busybox modprobe wp512;;
wp384)busybox modprobe wp512;;
wp256)busybox modprobe wp512;;
...
acpi*:80860ABC:*)busybox modprobe intel_lpss_acpi;;
acpi*:80860AAC:*)busybox modprobe intel_lpss_acpi;;
acpi*:193C9890:*)busybox modprobe snd_soc_max98090;;
acpi*:10EC5670:*)busybox modprobe snd_soc_rt5670;;
acpi*:10EC5650:*)busybox modprobe snd_soc_rt5645;;
acpi*:10EC5645:*)busybox modprobe snd_soc_rt5645;;
acpi*:10EC5642:*)busybox modprobe snd_soc_rt5640;;
acpi*:10EC5640:*)busybox modprobe snd_soc_rt5640;;
acpi)busybox modprobe acpi_cpufreq;;
esac; done; }
```

Before the devices in the `/sys` filesystem are passed to the `dev2mod` function, we can take a look at how the output looks like on my system as follows:

```
# cat /sys/bus/*/devices/*/uevent | grep MODALIAS | sed 's/^MODALIAS=//'
| sort -u
acpi:ACPI0003:
acpi:APP0001:SMC-NAPA:
acpi:LNXCPU:
acpi:LNXPWRBN:
acpi:LNXSLPBN:
acpi:LNXSYBUS:
acpi:LNXSYSTM:
acpi:LNXVIDEO:
acpi:PNP0000:
acpi:PNP0100:
acpi:PNP0103:PNP0C01:
acpi:PNP0200:
acpi:PNP0303:
acpi:PNP0400:
acpi:PNP0501:
```

```
acpi:PNP0700:
acpi:PNP0A03:
acpi:PNP0B00:
acpi:PNP0C02:
acpi:PNP0C0A:
acpi:PNP0C0F:
acpi:PNP0F03:
acpi:PNP8390:
cpu:type:x86,ven0000fam0006mod003A:feature:,0000,0001,0002,0003,0004,0005,0
006,0
hdaudio:v83847680r00103401a01
hid:b0003g0001v000080EEp00000021
pci:v0000106Bd0000003Fsv00000000sd00000000bc0Csc03i10
pci:v00001AF4d00001000sv00001AF4sd00000001bc02sc00i00
pci:v00008086d00001237sv00000000sd00000000bc06sc00i00
pci:v00008086d0000265Csv00000000sd00000000bc0Csc03i20
pci:v00008086d00002668sv00008384sd00007680bc04sc03i00
pci:v00008086d00007000sv00000000sd00000000bc06sc01i00
pci:v00008086d00007111sv00000000sd00000000bc01sc01i8A
pci:v00008086d00007113sv00000000sd00000000bc06sc80i00
pci:v000080EEd0000BEEFsv00000000sd00000000bc03sc00i00
pci:v000080EEd0000CAFEsv00000000sd00000000bc08sc80i00
platform:alarmtimer
platform:goldfish_pdev_bus
platform:i8042
platform:microcode
platform:pcspkr
platform:platform-framebuffer
platform:reg-dummy
platform:rtc_cmos
platform:serial8250
scsi:t-0x00
scsi:t-0x05
serio:ty01pr00id00ex00
serio:ty06pr00id00ex00
usb:v1D6Bp0001d0404dc09dsc00dp00ic09isc00ip00in00
usb:v1D6Bp0002d0404dc09dsc00dp00ic09isc00ip00in00
usb:v80EEp0021d0100dc00dsc00dp00ic03isc00ip00in00
virtio:d00000001v00001AF4
```

As we can see from the preceding output, it includes all module aliases found by the kernel. The preceding output of module aliases will be passed to the shell script function `dev2mod` through a pipe. The `dev2mod` function will load all respective kernel modules found by the kernel.

After the `load_modules` are executed, we enter the second checkpoint and we can take a look at the system status now:

```
sgye@sz-ubuntu-14: ~
(debug-late)@android:/android # lsmod
Module                    Size  Used by      Not tainted
psmouse                  100557  0
pcspkr                     1558  0
snd_hda_codec_idt         40526  1
snd_hda_codec_generic     47705  1 snd_hda_codec_idt
i2c_piix4                  9562  0
snd_hda_intel             23673  0
snd_hda_codec             91625  3 snd_hda_codec_idt,snd_hda_codec_generic,snd_hdal
snd_hda_core              45841  4 snd_hda_codec_idt,snd_hda_codec_generic,snd_hdac
snd_hwdep                  4547  1 snd_hda_codec
snd_pcm                   71431  3 snd_hda_intel,snd_hda_codec,snd_hda_core
snd_timer                 16182  1 snd_pcm
snd                       50625  7 snd_hda_codec_idt,snd_hda_codec_generic,snd_hdar
soundcore                  5263  1 snd
8250_fintek                2371  0
parport_pc                14555  0
parport                   21789  1 parport_pc
atkbd                     15064  0
(debug-late)@android:/android # 
```

Kernel modules are loaded

We can see from the preceding screenshot that there are many kernel modules loaded in the system now. From the kernel module name, we can see that the audio, mouse, and keyboard drivers are loaded. This is how the device drivers are loaded automatically by the Android-x86 init script in `initrd.img`. At the end of the init script, it will invoke `chroot` or `switch_root` according to the setting of the environment variable `DEBUG`. In either case, the root filesystem will be changed to the Android `ramdisk.img` and will start the Android init process as follows:

```
...
[ -n "$DEBUG" ] && SWITCH=${SWITCH:-chroot}

# We must disable mdev before switching to Android
# since it conflicts with Android's init
echo > /proc/sys/kernel/hotplug

exec ${SWITCH:-switch_root} /android /init
...
```

The Android init process will perform the hardware initialization for these devices that cannot be detected by the kernel automatically. The init process will also initialize the HAL of Android-x86.

HAL initialization during the Android start-up

Let's look in greater detail into the hardware initialization of devices that cannot be detected by the kernel automatically, and the initialization of Android-x86 HAL, in this section. One of the peripherals that haven't been initialized is the frame buffer for the graphic user interface in Android. We will use it as an example to explain how hardware is initialized by the init process in Android's `ramdisk.img`.

If we recall the analysis of the init process in Chapter 6, *Debugging the Boot Up Process Using a Customized ramdisk*, the init process will execute the `init.rc` script, which is general for all Android devices. In the `init.rc` script, it will import a device-specific script `init.${ro.hardware}.rc`. In our case, this script is `init.x86vbox.rc` on the target device. The `ro.hardware` property is set according to the kernel command-line parameter, `androidboot.hardware`, which we set it to `x86vbox`. The source code of `init.x86vbox.rc` can be found at `device/generic/common/init.x86.rc`. It is copied to the target output using the following line in `device.mk`. Be aware that the script name is changed after the copy:

```
...
PRODUCT_COPY_FILES := \
    $(if $(wildcard
$(PRODUCT_DIR)init.rc),$(PRODUCT_DIR)init.rc:root/init.rc) \
    $(if $(wildcard
$(PRODUCT_DIR)init.sh),$(PRODUCT_DIR),$(LOCAL_PATH)/)init.sh:system/etc/ini
t.sh \
    ...
    $(if $(wildcard
$(PRODUCT_DIR)init.$(TARGET_PRODUCT).rc),$(PRODUCT_DIR)init.$(TARGET_PRODUC
T).rc,$(LOCAL_PATH)/init.x86.rc):root/init.$(TARGET_PRODUCT).rc \
    $(if $(wildcard
$(PRODUCT_DIR)ueventd.$(TARGET_PRODUCT).rc),$(PRODUCT_DIR)ueventd.$(TARGET_
PRODUCT).rc,$(LOCAL_PATH)/ueventd.x86.rc):root/ueventd.$(TARGET_PRODUCT).rc
\
    ...
```

Another thing that we can see from the preceding code snippet is that a shell script, `init.sh`, is also copied to the system image at `/system/etc/init.sh`. This is the script used to load device drivers and initialize HAL in `init.x86vbox.rc`.

In `init.x86vbox.rc`, an action trigger is defined as follows:

```
on post-fs
    exec -- /system/bin/logwrapper /system/bin/sh /system/etc/init.sh
```

In the predefined trigger, `post-fs`, the `init.sh` script will be executed as part of the initialization process. The following is the code snippet of `init.sh`:

```
...
PATH=/sbin:/system/bin:/system/xbin

DMIPATH=/sys/class/dmi/id
BOARD=$(cat $DMIPATH/board_name)
PRODUCT=$(cat $DMIPATH/product_name)

# import cmdline variables
for c in `cat /proc/cmdline`; do
    case $c in
        BOOT_IMAGE=*|iso-scan/*|*.*=*)
            ;;
        *=*)
            eval $c
            if [ -z "$1" ]; then
                case $c in
                    HWACCEL=*)
                        set_property debug.egl.hw $HWACCEL
                        ;;
                    DEBUG=*)
                        [ -n "$DEBUG" ] && set_property debug.logcat 1
                        ;;
                esac
            fi
            ;;
    esac
done

[ -n "$DEBUG" ] && set -x || exec &> /dev/null

# import the vendor specific script
hw_sh=/vendor/etc/init.sh
[ -e $hw_sh ] && source $hw_sh

case "$1" in
    netconsole)
        [ -n "$DEBUG" ] && do_netconsole
        ;;
    bootcomplete)
        do_bootcomplete
```

```
            ;;
    hci)
          do_hci
          ;;
    init|"")
          do_init
          ;;
  esac

  return 0
```

As we can see from the preceding code snippet, the `init.sh` script processes the kernel command line first. After that, it runs into a multi-selection statement. It executes a function according to the first parameter passed to it. This parameter is used to let the `do_init` function initialize a particular HAL module. In the case of the first parameter, it's `init` or without parameter, it will execute the `do_init` function. In this case, all HAL modules will be initialized and this is the case that we want to investigate now. We can see what the `do_init` function does as follows:

```
function do_init()
{
    init_misc
    init_hal_audio
    init_hal_bluetooth
    init_hal_camera
    init_hal_gps
    init_hal_gralloc
    init_hal_hwcomposer
    init_hal_lights
    init_hal_power
    init_hal_sensors
    init_tscal
    init_ril
    post_init
}
```

The `do_init` function will call individual HAL module initialization functions one by one. We won't look at all of them here. We will take a look at how the frame buffer device is initialized in the `init_hal_gralloc` function. This is the one that we will investigate more in Chapter 10, *Enabling Graphics*, since graphic support is one of the most important tasks when it comes to porting:

```
function init_uvesafb()
{
    case "$PRODUCT" in
        ET2002*)
```

```
            UVESA_MODE=${UVESA_MODE:-1600x900}
            ;;
    *)
            ;;
    esac

    [ "$HWACCEL" = "0" ] && bpp=16 || bpp=32
    modprobe uvesafb mode_option=${UVESA_MODE:-1024x768}-$bpp
    ${UVESA_OPTION:-mtrr=3 scroll=redraw}
}

function init_hal_gralloc()
{
    case "$(cat /proc/fb | head -1)" in
        *virtiodrmfb)
        # set_property ro.hardware.hwcomposer drm
            ;&
        0*inteldrmfb|0*radeondrmfb|0*nouveaufb|0*svgadrmfb)
            set_property ro.hardware.gralloc drm
            set_drm_mode
            ;;
        "")
            init_uvesafb
            ;&
        0*)
            ;;
    esac

    [ -n "$DEBUG" ] && set_property debug.egl.trace error
}
```

In the `init_hal_gralloc` function, it will perform the respective tasks according to the content of /proc/fb. From /proc/fb, it can detect the type of graphic hardware on the device. If the type of graphic hardware cannot be detected, it will use a general VESA frame buffer (uvesafb), which is used in our case for VirtualBox. It will call another shell function, `init_uvesafb`, to load the VESA frame buffer driver. The uvesafb driver will start a user space daemon v86d to execute the x86 BIOS code. The code is executed in a controlled environment and the results are passed back to the kernel via the netlink interface. This is how the graphic driver is initialized in our environment.

Summary

In this chapter, we analyzed the Android-x86 HAL and integrated it to x86vbox so that we are able to boot x86vbox over the next few chapters. We also analyzed the start-up process of Android-x86. We used the debug console in the first stage of the start-up process to analyze the kernel module loading process. Before we can actually boot the x86vbox on VirtualBox, one issue that we haven't resolved is which bootloader we should use. Unlike the emulator, it does not need a bootloader, since the emulator uses a built-in mini bootloader to load the kernel and ramdisk. VirtualBox is very similar to real hardware. We won't be able to boot up an operating system without a proper bootloader.

In the next chapter, we will discuss this issue and we will explain how we can resolve it using PXE boot supported by VirtualBox.

9
Booting Up x86vbox Using PXE/NFS

In the last chapter, we created the x86vbox device and we were able to build it in our environment. In this chapter, we will start to debug the boot up process for x86vbox. The first thing that we meet in the boot up process is the bootloader issue. We could use the same GRUB bootloader as Android-x86. With GRUB, we still have issues about how to configure and install it on the storage media. If we go this way, we need to spend some time talking about the topics related to bootloader.

Using VirtualBox as a virtual hardware platform, we have a much simpler solution. We can use the built-in PXE boot mechanism to avoid bootloader issues. From a debugging point of view, PXE boot can make the entire boot up process more transparent to us. With PXE boot, we can move the installation of bootloader out of the picture so we can concentrate on debugging the Android system itself. In this chapter, we will cover the following topics:

- Setting up a PXE boot environment
- Configuring VirtualBox to boot from PXE
- Setting up the root filesystem using NFS

Setting up a PXE boot environment

What is PXE? **PXE** means **Preboot Execution Environment**. To build a Linux environment, what we need is to find a way to load the kernel and ramdisk to the system memory. This is one of the major tasks performed by most Linux bootloaders. The bootloader usually fetches the kernel and ramdisk from some kind of storage device, such as flash storage, hard disk, USB, and so on. It can also be retrieved from a network connection. PXE is a method that can boot a device with LAN connection and a PXE-capable **network interface controller** (**NIC**).

As shown in the following diagram, PXE uses the DHCP and TFTP protocols to complete the boot process. In the simplest environment, a PXE server is set up as both a DHCP and TFTP server. The NIC client obtains the IP address from the DHCP server and uses the TFTP protocol to get the kernel and ramdisk images to start the boot process:

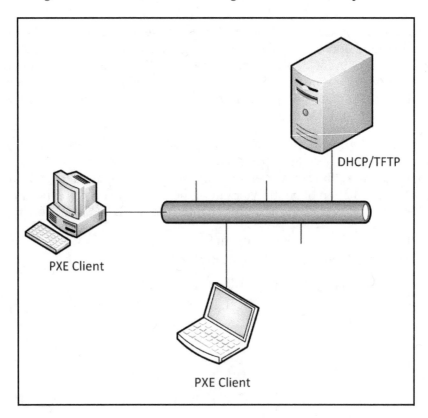

PXE boot environment

In this section, we will learn how to prepare a PXE-capable ROM for a VirtualBox virtio network adapter so that we can use this ROM and boot the system via PXE. We will also learn how to set up a PXE server, which is the key element in the PXE setup. In VirtualBox, it includes a built-in PXE server. We will use this built-in PXE server to boot the Android system.

Preparing PXE Boot ROM

Even though PXE boot is supported by VirtualBox, the setup is not consistent on a different NIC. You may get error messages such as `PXE-E3C - TFTP Error - Access Violation` during the boot. This is because PXE boot depends on LAN Boot ROM. When you choose different network adapters, you may get different test results. To get a consistent test result, you can use the LAN Boot ROM from the Etherboot/gPXE project. gPXE is an open source (GPL) network bootloader. It provides a direct replacement for proprietary PXE ROMs, with many extra features such as DNS, HTTP, iSCSI, and so on. There is a page at the gPXE project website about how to set up LAN Boot ROM for VirtualBox:

`http://www.etherboot.org/wiki/romburning/vbox`

The following table lists network adapters supported by VirtualBox:

VirtualBox adapters	PCI vendor ID	PCI device ID	Mfr name	Device name
Am79C970A	1022h	2000h	AMD	PCnet-PCI II (AM79C970A)
Am79C973	1022h	2000h	AMD	PCnet-PCI III (AM79C973)
82540EM	8086h	100Eh	Intel	Intel PRO/1000 MT Desktop (82540EM)
82543GC	8086h	1004h	Intel	Intel PRO/1000 T Server (82543GC)
82545EM	8086h	100Fh	Intel	Intel PRO/1000 MT Server (82545EM)
virtio	1AF4h	1000h		Paravirtualized Network (virtio-net)

Since paravirtualized networks have better performance in most situations, we will explore how to support PXE boot using the virtio-net network adapter.

Downloading and building the LAN Boot ROM

There may be LAN Boot ROM binary images available on the Internet, but they are not provided at the gPXE project. We have to build from source code according to the instructions from the gPXE project website.

Let's download and build the source code using the following commands:

```
$ git clone git://git.etherboot.org/scm/gpxe.git
$ cd gpxe/src
$ make bin/1af41000.rom   # for virtio 1af4:1000
```

Fixing up the ROM image

Before the ROM image can be used, the ROM image has to be updated due to VirtualBox having the following requirements on ROM image size:

- Size must be 4K aligned (that is, a multiple of 4,096)
- Size must not be greater than 64K

Let's check the image size first and make sure that it is not larger than 65,536 bytes (64K):

```
$ ls -l bin/1af41000.rom | awk '{print $5}'
62464
```

We can see that it is less than 64K. Now we have to pad the image file to a 4K boundary. We can do this using the following commands:

```
$ python
>>> 65536 - 62464             # Calculate padding size
3072
>>> f = open('bin/1af41000.rom', 'a')
>>> f.write('\0' * 3072)      # Pad with zeroes
>>> f.close()
```

We check the image file size again:

```
$ ls -l bin/1af41000.rom | awk '{print $5}'
65536
```

As we can see, the file size is 64K now. To be convenient, I will upload this file at the following link and you can download it:

```
https://sourceforge.net/projects/android-system-programming/files/android-7/ch1
4/1af41000.rom/download
```

Configuring the virtual machine to use the LAN Boot ROM

The user-based VirtualBox configuration can be stored in the $HOME/.VirtualBox folder and we need to use this folder for the built-in PXE server.

This folder is not created by default, so we need to create it first:

```
$ mkdir .VirtualBox
```

After we create this folder, we can launch VirtualBox and quit. Then, let's look at the content of the $HOME/.VirtualBox folder again, as shown in the following screenshot:

```
🅧 🅐 🅞   roger@x86vbox: ~
roger@x86vbox:~$ mkdir .VirtualBox
roger@x86vbox:~$ ls .VirtualBox/
roger@x86vbox:~$ virtualbox
roger@x86vbox:~$ ls -F .VirtualBox/
compreg.dat          vbox-ssl-cacertificate.crt   VirtualBox.xml        xpti.dat
selectorwindow.log   VBoxSVC.log                  VirtualBox.xml-prev
roger@x86vbox:~$
```

From the preceding screenshot, we can see that the content of this folder is empty before we run VirtualBox. After we execute VirtualBox and quit, there are a list of files that are created by VirtualBox in this folder.

Now, we can change the configuration to use the LAN Boot ROM we just created. To use this LAN Boot ROM, we can use the VBoxManage command to update VirtualBox settings. We use the following command to set the LanBootRom path:

```
$ VBoxManage setextradata global
VBoxInternal/Devices/pcbios/0/Config/LanBootRom
$HOME/.VirtualBox/1af41000.rom
```

We copied the LAN Boot ROM to $HOME/.VirtualBox/1af41000.rom. We use global here, then all VMs will use the gPXE LAN Boot ROM. We can change global to a specific virtual machine name. In that case, the gPXE LAN Boot ROM will only be used by that virtual machine.

Having set up the configuration, let's look at the `$HOME/.VirtualBox/VirtualBox.xml`
configuration file:

```xml
<?xml version="1.0"?>
<!--
** DO NOT EDIT THIS FILE.
** If you make changes to this file while any VirtualBox related
application
** is running, your changes will be overwritten later, without taking
effect.
** Use VBoxManage or the VirtualBox Manager GUI to make changes.
-->
<VirtualBox xmlns="http://www.virtualbox.org/" version="1.12-linux">
  <Global>
    <ExtraData>
      <ExtraDataItem name="GUI/DetailsPageBoxes"
      value="general,system,preview,display,storage,audio,
      network,usb,sharedFolders,description"/>
      <ExtraDataItem name="GUI/LastWindowPosition"
      value="475,240,770,550"/>
      <ExtraDataItem name="GUI/SplitterSizes" value="255,511"/>
      <ExtraDataItem name="GUI/UpdateCheckCount" value="2"/>
      <ExtraDataItem name="GUI/UpdateDate" value="1 d, 2017-05-15,
      stable, 5.1.2"/>
<ExtraDataItem
    name="VBoxInternal/Deices/pcbios/o/Config/LanBootRom"
    value="/home/roger/.VirtualBox/1af41000.rom"/>
    </ExtraData>
...
```

As we can see, the `VBoxInternal/Deices/pcbios/o/Config/LanBootRom`
configuration is set in this configuration file.

To remove the preceding configuration, we just have to reset the path value as follows. The
`$VM_NAME` argument can be `global` or a virtual machine name:

```
$ VBoxManage setextradata $VM_NAME
VBoxInternal/Devices/pcbios/0/Config/LanBootRom
```

You can also check the current configuration using the following command:

```
$ VBoxManage getextradata $VM_NAME
VBoxInternal/Devices/pcbios/0/Config/LanBootRom
Value: /home/roger/.VirtualBox/1af41000.rom
```

Setting up the PXE boot environment

With a proper PXE ROM installed, we can set up the PXE server now. Before we set up a PXE server, we need to think about the network connections. There are three ways a virtual machine in VirtualBox can connect to the network:

- **Bridged network**: This connects to the same physical network as the host. It looks like the virtual machine connects to the same LAN connection as the host.
- **Host-only network**: This connects to a virtual network that is only visible by the virtual machine and the host. In this configuration, the virtual machine cannot connect to an outside network, such as the Internet.
- **NAT network**: This one connects to the host network through NAT. This is the most common choice. In this configuration, the virtual machine can access the external network, but the external network cannot connect to the virtual machine directly. For example, if you set up a FTP service on the virtual machine, the computers on the LAN of the host cannot access this FTP service. If you want to publish this service, you have to use port forwarding settings to do this.

With these concepts in mind, if you want to use a dedicated machine as the PXE server, you can use a bridged network in your environment. However, you must be very careful using this setup. This is usually done by the IT group in your organization, since you cannot set up a DHCP server on the LAN without affecting others. We won't use this option here.

The host-only network is actually a good choice for this case, because this kind of network is an isolated network configuration. The network connection only exists between the host and the virtual machine. It is possible to use the host-only network to set up the PXE server, but we won't use this option in our setup.

In VirtualBox, PXE booting in the NAT network is supported. With this option, we don't need to set up a separate PXE server by ourselves. We will use this built-in PXE server in this book. The test environment from this chapter to Chapter 14, *Customizing and Debugging Recovery* will use this setup.

Configuring and testing the PXE boot

We can create a virtual machine instance to test the environment. We will demonstrate this in the Ubuntu 14.04 environment. The same setup can be duplicated to the Windows or OS X environment as well.

Setting up the virtual machine

Let's create a virtual machine called **pxeAndroid** in VirtualBox first. After starting the VirtualBox, we can click the **New** button to create a new virtual machine, as shown in the following screenshot:

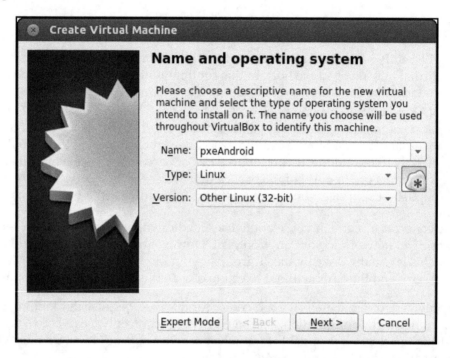

We call it **pxeAndroid** and choose **Linux** as the type of virtual machine. We can just follow the wizard to create this virtual machine with a suitable configuration. After the virtual machine is created, we need to make a few changes to the settings.

The first thing that needs to be changed is the network configuration. We need to set the network adapter as a NAT network. We can click the name of the virtual machine, **pxeAndroid,** first and then click on the **Settings** button to change the settings. Select the **Network** option on the left-hand side, as we can see in the following screenshot:

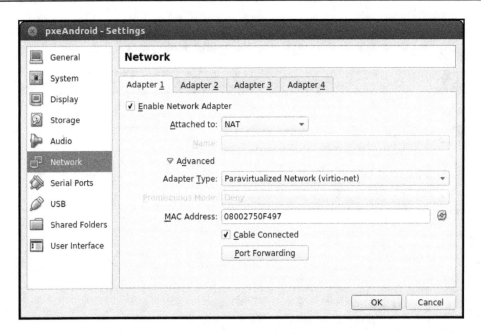

We select **Adapter 1**, the default for the NAT network. We need to change the **Adapter Type** to **Paravirtualized Network (virtio-net)** since we will use the PXE ROM that we just built. The NAT network can connect to the outside network. It supports port forwarding so that we can access certain services in the virtual machine. The one that we need to set up here is the ADB service. We need to use ADB to debug the x86vbox device later. We can set up the port forwarding for ADB as follows:

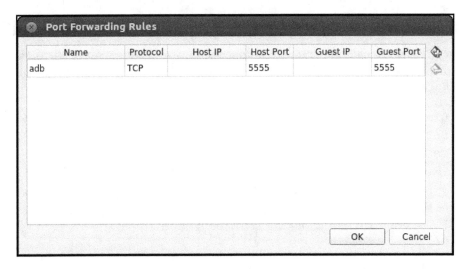

Next, we can click on the **System** option to specify that the default boot order is to boot from the network interface, as shown in the following screenshot:

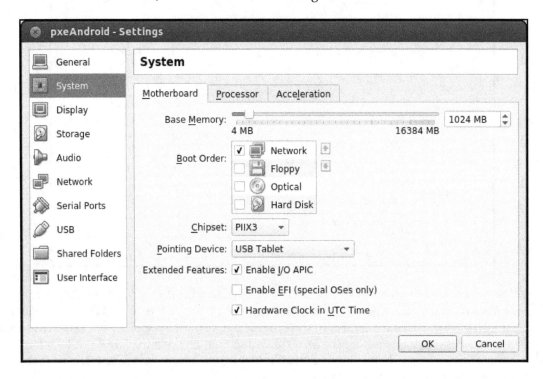

Using VirtualBox internal PXE booting with NAT

Once we set up the virtual machine, we can use the built-in PXE server of VirtualBox for PXE boot using the NAT network. To use the built-in PXE server, we need to set it up using the following steps:

1. Create a $HOME/.VirtualBox/TFTP folder. The built-in TFTP root is at $HOME/.VirtualBox/TFTP on Linux or %USERPROFILE%\.VirtualBox\TFTP on Windows.

2. Usually, the default boot image name is pxelinux.0 for PXE boot, but it is vmname.pxe for the VirtualBox built-in PXE. For example, if we use pxeAndroid as the virtual machine name, we have to make a copy of pxelinux.0 and name it pxeAndroid.pxe under the TFTP root folder.

Configuring pxelinux.cfg

Before we can test the virtual machine that we just set up, we need to specify it in the configuration file to let the PXE boot know where to find the kernel and ramdisk images.

The PXE boot process is something like this:

1. When the **pxeAndroid** virtual machine powers on, the client will get the IP address through DHCP.
2. After the DHCP configuration is found, the configuration includes the standard information such as IP address, subnet mask, gateway and DNS, and so on. In addition, it also provides the location of the TFTP server and the filename of a boot image. The name of the boot image is usually `pxelinux.0`. The name of the boot image is `vmname.pxe` for the built-in PXE boot environment where the vmname should be the name of virtual machine. For example, it is `pxeAndroid.pxe` for our virtual machine.
3. The client contacts the TFTP server to obtain the boot image. The boot image should be put under `TFTP` root, which is `$HOME/.VirtualBox/TFTP` in our case.
4. The TFTP server sends the boot image (`pxelinux.0` or `vmname.pxe`), and the client executes it.
5. By default, the boot image searches the `pxelinux.cfg` directory on the TFTP server for boot configuration files.
6. The client downloads all the files it needs (kernel, ramdisk, root filesystem, and so on) and then loads them.
7. The `pxeAndroid` target machine reboots.

In step 5, the boot image searches the boot configuration files in the following steps:

1. First, it searches for the boot configuration file that is named according to the MAC address represented in lower case hexadecimal digits with dash separators. For example, for the MAC address 08:00:27:90:99:7B, it searches for the file `08-00-27-90-99-7b`.
2. Then, it searches for the configuration file using the IP address (of the machine that is being booted) in upper-case hexadecimal digits. For example, for the IP address 192.168.56.100, it searches for the `C0A83864` file.
3. If that file is not found, it removes one hexadecimal digit from the end and tries again. However, if the search is still not successful, it finally looks for a file named `default` (in lower case).

For example, if the boot filename is $HOME/.VirtualBox/TFTP/pxeAndroid.pxe, the Ethernet MAC address is 08:00:27:90:99:7B, and the IP address is 192.168.56.100, the boot image looks for filenames in the following order:

```
$HOME/.VirtualBox/TFTP/pxelinux.cfg/08-00-27-90-99-7b
$HOME/.VirtualBox/TFTP/pxelinux.cfg/C0A83864
$HOME/.VirtualBox/TFTP/pxelinux.cfg/C0A8386
$HOME/.VirtualBox/TFTP/pxelinux.cfg/C0A838
$HOME/.VirtualBox/TFTP/pxelinux.cfg/C0A83
$HOME/.VirtualBox/TFTP/pxelinux.cfg/C0A8
$HOME/.VirtualBox/TFTP/pxelinux.cfg/C0A
$HOME/.VirtualBox/TFTP/pxelinux.cfg/C0
$HOME/.VirtualBox/TFTP/pxelinux.cfg/C
$HOME/.VirtualBox/TFTP/pxelinux.cfg/default
```

The pxelinux.0 boot image is part of an open source project the Syslinux. We can get the boot image and the menu user interface from the Syslinux project using the following command:

```
$ sudo apt-get install syslinux
```

After Syslinux is installed, pxelinux.0 can be copied to the TFTP root folder as follows:

```
$ cp /usr/lib/syslinux/pxelinux.0 $HOME/.VirtualBox/TFTP/pxelinux.0
```

To have a better user interface, we can copy menu.c32 to the TFTP folder as well:

```
$ cp /usr/lib/syslinux/menu.c32 $HOME/.VirtualBox/TFTP/menu.c32
```

pxelinux.cfg/default

Now, we will look at how to configure the boot configuration file $HOME/.VirtualBox/TFTP/pxelinux.cfg/default. In our setup, it looks like the following code snippet:

```
prompt 1
default menu.c32
timeout 100

label 1. NFS Installation (serial port) - x86vbox
menu x86vbox_install_serial
kernel x86vbox/kernel
append ip=dhcp console=ttyS3,115200 initrd=x86vbox/initrd.img root=/dev/nfs
rw androidboot.hardware=x86vbox INSTALL=1 DEBUG=2 SRC=/x86vbox
ROOT=10.0.2.2:/home/sgye/vol1/android-x86vbox/out/target/product qemu=1
qemu.gles=0
```

```
label 2. x86vbox (ROOT=/dev/sda1, serial port)
menu x86vbox_sda1
kernel x86vbox/kernel
append ip=dhcp console=ttyS3,115200 initrd=x86vbox/initrd.img
androidboot.hardware=x86vbox DEBUG=2 SRC=/android-x86vbox ROOT=/dev/sda1
...
```

The preceding file can be download from `https://github.com/shugaoye/asp-sample/blo b/master/ch09/pxelinux.cfg/default`.

You can copy it from the above mentioned GitHub URL and you need to change the NFS shared folder to your own `ROOT=10.0.2.2:/{your NFS shared folder}`.

The syntax in the boot configuration file can be found at the following URL from the Syslinux project:

`http://www.syslinux.org/wiki/index.php?title=SYSLINUX`

In the preceding configuration file that we use in this chapter, we can see the following commands and options:

- `prompt`: It will let the bootloader know if it will show a LILO-style *boot:* prompt. With this command-line prompt, you can input the option directly. All the boot options are defined by the command `label`.
- `default`: It defines the default boot option.
- `timeout`: If more than one `label` entry is available, this directive indicates how long to pause at the boot: prompt until booting automatically, in units of 1/10 s. The timeout is cancelled when any key is pressed, the assumption being that the user will complete the command line. A timeout of zero will disable the timeout completely. The default is 0.
- `label`: A human-readable string that describes a kernel and options. The default label is `linux`, but you can change this with the `DEFAULT` keyword.
- `kernel`: The kernel file that the boot image will boot.
- `append`: The kernel command line that can be passed to the kernel during the boot.

In the preceding configuration file, we show two boot options. In the first option, we can boot to a minimum Linux environment using the NFS root filesystem. We can install the x86vbox images from that environment to the hard disk. In the second option, we can boot x86vbox from the `/dev/sda1` disk partition. We will explore these options in detail later.

Setting up a serial port for debugging

The reason why we want to boot Android using PXE and NFS is because we want to use a very simple bootloader and find an easier way to debug the system. In order to see the debug log, we want to redirect the debug output from the video console to a serial port so that we can separate the graphic user interface from the debug output. We need to do two things in order to meet our goals.

The Linux kernel debug message can be redirected to a specific channel using kernel command-line arguments. We specify this in PXE boot configuration with the `console=ttyS3,115200` option. This is defined in `pxelinux.cfg/default` as follows:

```
label 1. NFS Installation (serial port) - x86vbox
menu x86vbox_install_serial
kernel x86vbox/kernel
append ip=dhcp console=ttyS3,115200 initrd=x86vbox/initrd.img root=/dev/nfs
rw androidboot.hardware=x86vbox INSTALL=1 DEBUG=2 SRC=/x86vbox
ROOT=10.0.2.2:/home/sgye/vol1/android-x86vbox/out/target/product qemu=1
qemu.gles=0
```

We will explain the details about kernel parameters in the `append` option later in this chapter. The next thing is that we need to create a virtual serial port that we can connect to. We configure this in the virtual machine settings page, as shown in the following screenshot:

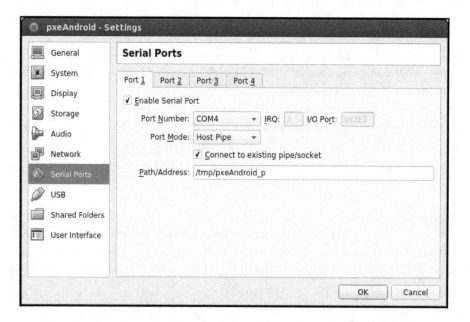

We use a host pipe to simulate the virtual serial port. We can set the path as something like `/tmp/pxeAndroid_p`.

The mapping between `COMx` to `/dev/ttySx` is as follows:

```
/dev/ttyS0  -  COM1
/dev/ttyS1  -  COM2
/dev/ttyS2  -  COM3
/dev/ttyS3  -  COM4
```

To connect to the host pipe, we can use a tool such as `minicom`. If you don't have `minicom` installed, you can install and configure `minicom` as follows:

$ sudo apt-get install minicom

To set up `minicom`, we can use the following command:

$ sudo minicom -s

After `minicom` starts, select **Serial port setup**, and set **Serial Device** as **unix#/tmp/pxeAndroid_p**. Once this is done, select **Save setup as dfl** and **Exit from Minicom** as shown in the following screenshot. Now we can connect to the virtual serial port using `minicom`.

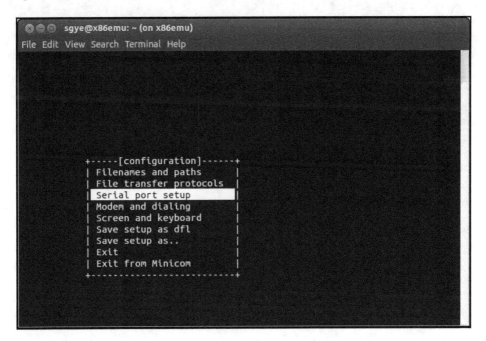

After we have made all the changes for the x86vbox configuration, we can power on the virtual machine and test it. We should be able to see the following boot up screen:

```
⊗ ⊜ ⊡   pxeAndroid [Running] - Oracle VM VirtualBox
 File  Machine  View  Input  Devices  Help
iPXE initialising devices...ok



iPXE 1.0.0+ -- Open Source Network Boot Firmware -- http://ipxe.org
Features: DNS TFTP HTTP PXE PXEXT Menu

net0: 08:00:27:50:f4:97 using virtio-net on PCI00:03.0 (open)
  [Link:up, TX:0 TXE:0 RX:0 RXE:0]
DHCP (net0 08:00:27:50:f4:97)...... ok
net0: 10.0.2.15/255.255.255.0 gw 10.0.2.2
Next server: 10.0.2.4
Filename: pxeAndroid.pxe
tftp://10.0.2.4/pxeAndroid.pxe... ok
!PXE entry point found (we hope) at 9CF9:03F0 via plan A
UNDI code segment at 9CF9 len 0694
UNDI data segment at 9D63 len 25C8
Getting cached packet  01 02 03
My IP address seems to be 0A00020F 10.0.2.15
ip=10.0.2.15:10.0.2.4:10.0.2.2:255.255.255.0
BOOTIF=01-08-00-27-50-f4-97
SYSUUID=5b8ed689-bc6c-4068-8e27-0f971c90b961
TFTP prefix:
Trying to load: pxelinux.cfg/default                          ok
boot:

                                  🔲 ⊙ 🖧 ⁄ ▭ 🖴 🖳 🖵 ⊘ ⏏ Right Ctrl
```

We can see from the preceding screenshot that the virtual machine loads the `pxelinux.cfg/default` file and waits on the boot prompt. We are ready to boot from PXE ROM now.

NFS filesystem

We created the x86vbox device in Chapter 8, *Creating Your Own Device on VirtualBox,* and we were able to build it. However, we did not discuss how to boot images. The issue here is the output from the build is the standard AOSP images. They are not able to be used by VirtualBox directly. For example, `system.img` can be used by the emulator, but not VirtualBox. VirtualBox can use standard virtual disk images in VDI, VHD, or VMDK formats, but not a raw disk image such as `system.img`.

In the Android-x86 build, the output is an installation image, such as ISO or USB disk image formats. With an installation image, it can be burnt to a CDROM and USB drive. Then, we can boot VirtualBox from CDROM or USB to install the system just as we install Windows on our PC. It is quite tedious and not efficient to use this method when we are debugging a system. As a developer, we want a simple and quick way so that we can start the debugging immediately after we build the system.

The method that we will use here is to boot the system using the NFS filesystem. The key point is that we will treat the output folder of the AOSP build as the root filesystem directly so that we can boot the system using it without any additional work.

If you are an embedded system developer, you may have used this method in your work already. When we work on the initial debugging phase of an embedded Linux system, we often use the NFS filesystem as the root filesystem. With this method, we can avoid flashing the images to the flash storage every time after the build.

Preparing the kernel

To support NFS boot, we need a Linux kernel with NFS filesystem support. The default Linux kernel for Android doesn't have NFS boot support. In order to boot Android and mount the NFS directory as the root filesystem, we have to recompile the Linux kernel with the following options enabled:

```
CONFIG_IP_PNP=y
CONFIG_IP_PNP_DHCP=y
CONFIG_IP_PNP_BOOTP=y
CONFIG_IP_PNP_RARP=y
CONFIG_USB_USBNET=y
CONFIG_USB_NET_SMSC95XX=y
CONFIG_USB=y
CONFIG_USB_SUPPORT=y
CONFIG_USB_ARCH_HAS_EHCI=y
CONFIG_NETWORK_FILESYSTEMS=y
CONFIG_NFS_FS=y
CONFIG_NFS_V3=y
CONFIG_NFS_V3_ACL=y
CONFIG_ROOT_NFS=y
```

We can use `menuconfig` to change the kernel configuration or copy a configuration file with NFS support.

To configure the kernel build using `menuconfig`, we can use the following commands:

```
$ source build/envsetup.sh
$ lunch x86vbox-eng
$ make -C kernel O=$OUT/obj/kernel ARCH=x86 menuconfig
```

We can also use the configuration file with NFS enabled in my GitHub. We can observe the difference between this configuration file and the default kernel configuration file from Android-x86 as follows:

```
$ diff kernel/arch/x86/configs/android-x86_defconfig ~/src/android-
x86_nfs_defconfig
216a217
> # CONFIG_SYSTEM_TRUSTED_KEYRING is not set
1083a1085
> CONFIG_DNS_RESOLVER=y
1836c1838
< CONFIG_VIRTIO_NET=m
---
> CONFIG_VIRTIO_NET=y
1959c1961
< CONFIG_E1000=m
---
> CONFIG_E1000=y
5816a5819
> # CONFIG_ECRYPT_FS is not set
5854,5856c5857,5859
< CONFIG_NFS_FS=m
< CONFIG_NFS_V2=m
< CONFIG_NFS_V3=m
---
> CONFIG_NFS_FS=y
> CONFIG_NFS_V2=y
> CONFIG_NFS_V3=y
5858c5861
< # CONFIG_NFS_V4 is not set
---
> CONFIG_NFS_V4=y
5859a5863,5872
> CONFIG_NFS_V4_1=y
> CONFIG_NFS_V4_2=y
> CONFIG_PNFS_FILE_LAYOUT=y
> CONFIG_PNFS_BLOCK=y
> CONFIG_NFS_V4_1_IMPLEMENTATION_ID_DOMAIN="kernel.org"
> # CONFIG_NFS_V4_1_MIGRATION is not set
> CONFIG_NFS_V4_SECURITY_LABEL=y
> CONFIG_ROOT_NFS=y
> # CONFIG_NFS_USE_LEGACY_DNS is not set
```

```
> CONFIG_NFS_USE_KERNEL_DNS=y
5861,5862c5874,5875
< CONFIG_GRACE_PERIOD=m
< CONFIG_LOCKD=m
---
> CONFIG_GRACE_PERIOD=y
> CONFIG_LOCKD=y
5865c5878,5880
< CONFIG_SUNRPC=m
---
> CONFIG_SUNRPC=y
> CONFIG_SUNRPC_GSS=y
> CONFIG_SUNRPC_BACKCHANNEL=y
5870a5886
> # CONFIG_CIFS_UPCALL is not set
5873a5890
> # CONFIG_CIFS_DFS_UPCALL is not set
6132c6149,6153
< # CONFIG_KEYS is not set
---
> CONFIG_KEYS=y
> # CONFIG_PERSISTENT_KEYRINGS is not set
> # CONFIG_BIG_KEYS is not set
> # CONFIG_ENCRYPTED_KEYS is not set
> # CONFIG_KEYS_DEBUG_PROC_KEYS is not set
6142a6164
> # CONFIG_INTEGRITY_SIGNATURE is not set
6270a6293
> # CONFIG_ASYMMETRIC_KEY_TYPE is not set
6339a6363
> CONFIG_ASSOCIATIVE_ARRAY=y
6352a6377
> CONFIG_OID_REGISTRY=y
```

We can copy this configuration file and use it to build the Linux kernel. The following commands just show how to build the kernel separately. You don't have to do this if you build x86vbox by checking out the source code of this chapter. This is included in the x86vbox device Makefiles:

```
$ repo init https://github.com/shugaoye/manifests -b
android-7.1.1_r4_x86vbox_ch08_r1
$ repo sync
$ source build/envsetup.sh
$ lunch x86vbox-eng
$ make -C kernel O=$OUT/obj/kernel ARCH=x86
```

After the build, we can copy the kernel and ramdisk files to the TFTP root at
`$HOME/.VirtualBox/TFTP/x86vbox`.

Setting up the NFS server

When we have a NFS-capable kernel, we need to set up the NFS server on our development host so that we can mount to the NFS folders exported by our NFS server. We can check whether the NFS server is already installed or not using the following command:

```
$ dpkg -l | grep nfs
```

If the NFS server is not installed, we can install it using the following command:

```
$ sudo apt-get install nfs-kernel-server
```

Once we have a NFS server ready, we need to export our root filesystem through NFS. We will use the AOSP build output folder as we mentioned previously. We can add the following line to the `/etc/exports` configuration file:

```
$AOSP/out/target/product/ *(rw,sync,insecure,no_subtree_check,async)
```

After that, we execute the following command to export the `$AOSP/out/target/product` folder. You need to replace `$AOSP` with the absolute path in your setup:

```
$ sudo exportfs -a
```

Configuring the PXE boot menu

When we have a real bootloader such as PXE Boot ROM, we have a way to support the boot path like a real Android device. As we know, Android devices can boot to three different modes--bootloader mode, recovery mode, and the normal start-up.

With PXE Boot ROM, we can easily support the same and more. By configuring the `pxelinux.cfg/default` file, we can allow x86vbox to boot in different paths. We will configure multiple boot paths here.

Booting to NFS installation

Since we cannot use AOSP image files to boot x86vbox directly, we need to install AOSP images to the VirtualBox hard disk. This is very similar to Android-x86. In Android-x86, we need to use a CDROM or USB stick to install the system so that we can boot Android after the installation. Instead of using a CDROM or USB image for the installation, we can install the system from the NFS path directly. If we set the NFS path to the $AOSP/out/target/product path, we can install the system right after the completion of the build.

We can boot the system to an installation mode so that we can use the Android-x86 installation script that we discussed to install x86vbox images to the virtual hard disk:

```
label 1. NFS Installation (serial port) - x86vbox
menu x86vbox_install_serial
kernel x86vbox/kernel
append ip=dhcp console=ttyS3,115200 initrd=x86vbox/initrd.img root=/dev/nfs
rw androidboot.hardware=x86vbox INSTALL=1 DEBUG=2 SRC=/x86vbox
ROOT=10.0.2.2:$AOSP/out/target/product
```

In the preceding configuration, we use the NFS-capable kernel from the TFTP folder such as $HOME/.VirtualBox/TFTP/x86vbox/kernel. The initrd.img ramdisk image is also stored in the same folder. Both files under the TFTP folder can actually be symbolic links to the AOSP output. In this case, we don't have to copy them after the build, as we can see from the following screenshot:

```
sgye@x86vbox: ~/.VirtualBox/TFTP/x86vbox
sgye@x86vbox:~/.VirtualBox/TFTP/x86vbox$ ls -al
total 24
drwxrwxr-x 2 sgye aosp 4096 May 14 22:15 .
drwxr-xr-x 6 sgye aosp 4096 Jan  5 20:32 ..
lrwxrwxrwx 1 sgye aosp   69 May 14 22:13 initrd.img -> /home/sgye/vol1/android-x
86vbox/out/target/product/x86vbox/initrd.img
lrwxrwxrwx 1 sgye aosp   65 May 14 22:14 kernel -> /home/sgye/vol1/android-x86vb
ox/out/target/product/x86vbox/kernel
lrwxrwxrwx 1 sgye aosp   70 May 14 22:14 ramdisk.img -> /home/sgye/vol1/android-
x86vbox/out/target/product/x86vbox/ramdisk.img
lrwxrwxrwx 1 sgye aosp   79 May 14 22:14 ramdisk-recovery.img -> /home/sgye/vol1
/android-x86vbox/out/target/product/x86vbox/ramdisk-recovery.img
sgye@x86vbox:~/.VirtualBox/TFTP/x86vbox$
```

We use the following three options to configure the NFS boot:

- `ip=dhcp`: Use DHCP to get the IP address from the DHCP server. The DHCP server can be the built-in DHCP server of VirtualBox or an external DHCP server.
- `root=/dev/nfs`: Use the NFS boot.
- `ROOT=10.0.2.2:$AOSP/out/target/product`: The root is the AOSP output folder in the development host. If we use the built-in PXE, the IP address `10.0.2.2` is the default host IP address in the NAT network. It could be changed using the VirtualBox configuration. In your configuration, you need to replace `$AOSP` with an absolute path.

We want to monitor the debug output so we set the console to the virtual serial port that we configured previously as `console=ttyS3,115200`. We can use a host pipe to connect to it using `minicom`.

We set three kernel parameters by using the Android-x86 init script and installation script:

- `INSTALL=1`: Tells the init script that we want to install the system
- `DEBUG=2`: This will bring us to the debug console during the boot process
- `SRC=/x86vbox` : This is the directory for the root filesystem

Finally, the `androidboot.hardware=x86vbox` option is passed to the Android init process to tell it which init script to run. In this case, the device init script `init.x86vbox.rc` will be executed as we discussed in the previous chapter.

In our PXE boot menu, we can add another configuration for the installation without the `console=ttyS3,115200` option. In this case, all debug output will print on the screen, which is the default standard output.

To find out what is installed on the harddisk, you can refer to `Chapter 6`, *Debugging the Boot Up Process Using a Customized ramdisk*. The filesystem layout on the hard disk is similar to the directory layout for `x86emu_x86.img`.

Booting from a hard disk

We can have another option, as follows, to boot the system from the hard disk after we install the system using the previous configuration:

```
label 2. x86vbox (ROOT=/dev/sda1, serial port)
menu x86vbox_sda1_S3
kernel x86vbox/kernel
append ip=dhcp console=ttyS3,115200 initrd=x86vbox/initrd.img
androidboot.hardware=x86vbox DEBUG=2 SRC=/android-x86vbox ROOT=/dev/sda1
```

In the preceding configuration, we use the /dev/sda1 device as the root and we don't have the INSTALL=1 option. With this configuration, the virtual machine will boot to the Android system from the hard disk /dev/sda1 and the debug output will print to the virtual serial port.

We can use another similar configuration that prints the debug output to the screen.

Booting to recovery

With the PXE boot menu, we can configure the system to boot to recovery as well. We can use the following configuration:

```
label 5. x86vbox recovery (ROOT=/dev/sda2)
menu x86vbox_recovery
kernel x86vbox/kernel
append ip=dhcp console=ttyS3,115200 initrd=x86vbox/ramdisk-recovery.img
androidboot.hardware=x86vbox DEBUG=2 SRC=/android-x86vbox ROOT=/dev/sda2
```

We will use a configuration similar to this in Chapter 12, *Introducing Recovery* to Chapter 14, *Customizing and Debugging Recovery*, when we explore recovery programming. The difference here is that we use a recovery ramdisk instead of initrd.img. Since recovery is a self-contained environment, we can set the ROOT variable to other partitions as well.

 Be aware that the x86vbox recovery configuration cannot be tested in this chapter. We will test this in Chapter 12, *Introducing Recovery* to Chapter 14, *Customizing and Debugging Recovery*.

With all the preceding setup, we can boot to the PXE boot menu, as shown in the following screenshot:

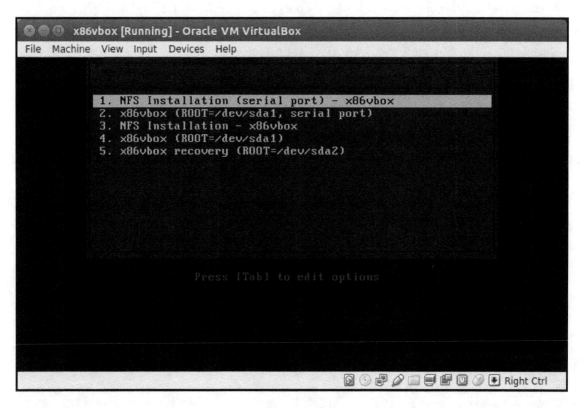

We can select the first option from the preceding PXE boot menu to boot to a debug console as follows:

```
  ⊗⊖⊕   sgye@x86vbox: ~/.VirtualBox/TFTP/x86vbox
[     9.181975]    Magic number: 1:662:687
[     9.182402] rtc_cmos rtc_cmos: setting system clock to 2017-05-14 14:41:15 U)
[     9.191484]    sda: sda1 sda2 sda3 sda4 < sda5 sda6 sda7 sda8 >
[     9.192536] sd 0:0:0:0: [sda] Attached SCSI disk
[     9.195437] Sending DHCP requests ., OK
[     9.209124] IP-Config: Got DHCP answer from 10.0.2.2, my adrs   10.15
                                                                 [     9.6:
[     9.677204]        device=eth0, hwaddr=08:00:27:c1:d8:7a, ipaddr=10.0.2.15, ma2
[     9.742640]        host=10.0.2.15, domain=, nis-domain=(none)
[     9.769548]        bootserver=10.0.2.4, rootserver=10.0.2.4, rootpath=
[     9.796563]        nameserver0=10.0.2.3
[     9.827065] Freeing unused kernel memory: 692K (c18e2000 - c198f000)
[     9.912004] Write protecting the kernel text: 5672k
[     9.912395] Write protecting the kernel read-only data: 2828k
+ exec
+ exec
Detecting Android-x86...boot using /mnt//x86vbox/ramdisk.img ...
Found system.img
 found at 10.0.2.2:/home/sgye/vol1/android-x86vbox/out/target/product

Type 'exit' to continue booting...

Running MirBSD Korn Shell...
(debug-found)@android:/android # █
CTRL-A Z for help | unix-socket | NOR | Minicom 2.7 | VT102 | Online 0:0 | id_p
```

From the preceding debug output, we can see that the virtual machine obtains the IP address 10.0.2.15 from DHCP server 10.0.2.2. The NFS root is found at IP address 10.0.2.2, which is the development host. In the default VirtualBox NAT network setup, the IP address of the DHCP server or the host is 10.0.2.2. The IP address of the built-in TFTP server is 10.0.2.4. The DNS server IP address is 10.0.2.3.

It is possible to boot the Android system from the $OUT/system directory using the NFS filesystem. However, we need to make changes to netd to disable flushing the routing rules. The changes can be done in the following file in the flushRules function:
$AOSP/system/netd/server/RouteController.cpp
Without this change, the network connection will be reset after the routing rules are flushed. However, we can still use NFS boot to perform the first stage-boot or install the system to hard disk.

Summary

In this chapter, we learnt a debugging method using a combination of PXE boot and the NFS root filesystem. This is a common practice in the embedded Linux development world. We try to use a similar setup for Android system development. As we can see, this setup can make the development and debugging process more efficient. We can use this setup to remove the bootloader dependency. We can also reduce the time to flash or provision build images to the device.

I wrote an article to discuss a more advanced case about the PXE/NFS setup using an external DHCP/TFTP server running in the host-only network environment. If you are interested in this topic, you can read it at the following URL:
`https://www.packtpub.com/books/content/booting-android-system-using-pxenfs`

In the next chapter, we will continue our journey on the boot up process of x86vbox. We will explore and learn how to enable the graphic system on VirtualBox so that we can bring up the Android system eventually for the x86vbox device.

10
Enabling Graphics

In the last chapter, we learnt how to boot the x86vbox device using PXE and NFS. We can boot the device to an embedded Linux environment, which is the first stage of the Android-x86 boot. In this stage, we can use a debug console to verify the status of the system so that we can make sure everything is right before we start the real Android system. In this chapter, we will talk about the first issue we meet during Android system boot up. This is about how to enable the Android graphics system for the x86vbox device. We will cover the following topics in this chapter:

- Overview of Android graphics architecture
- Delving into graphics HAL
- Analyzing the Android emulator graphics HAL for comparison

The graphics system probably is the most complicated software stack in the Android system architecture.
As you will see, the content in this chapter is much longer than the rest. Reading and understanding the content in this chapter may be harder. What I suggest is that you can open a source code editor and load the relevant source code while you read this chapter. This will help you a lot to understand the source code and the points that I want to address in this chapter.

Introduction to the Android graphics architecture

The graphics system in Android is similar to the architecture that we discussed in `Chapter 3`, *Discovering Kernel, HAL, and Virtual Hardware*. There we used goldfish lights HAL as an example to do a detailed analysis from the application level to the HAL and device driver layer. This analysis helps us to understand the Android architecture vertically.

However, the graphics system could be the most complicated system in the Android architecture. It would require another book to give a detailed introduction to the Android graphics system. The focus of this book is on how we can port Android systems to a new hardware platform. To focus on this goal, we will address the graphics HAL in this chapter instead of discussing the entire graphics system. The graphics system will work if we can choose the right graphics HAL and configure it right.

According to Google documents about the implementation of graphics, Android graphics support requires the following components:

- EGL driver
- OpenGL ES 1.x driver
- OpenGL ES 2.0 driver
- OpenGL ES 3.x driver (optional)
- Vulkan (optional)
- Gralloc HAL implementation
- Hardware Composer HAL implementation

In the preceding list, OpenGL ES implementation is the most complicated component in the graphics system. We will discuss how it is chosen and integrated in an Android emulator and Android-x86. We won't go into the details of how to analyze the OpenGL ES implementation, but we will have an overview about the underlying OpenGL ES libraries. OpenGL ES 1.x and 2.0 must be supported in an Android system. OpenGL ES 3.x is an optional component at the moment. EGL driver is usually implemented as part of the OpenGL ES implementation and we will see this when we discuss the Android emulator and Android-x86 (x86vbox) graphics system.

Vulkan is a new generation of GPU API from Khronos Group. Vulkan is new and optional and was only introduced in Android 7. Covering Vulkan is beyond the scope of this book, so we won't discuss it. Gralloc HAL is the one that handles the graphics hardware and it is our focus for a deep analysis. In most of the porting work of the graphics system, Gralloc HAL is the key to enabling graphics.

Hardware composer is part of the graphics HAL. However, it is not a component that we must have for Android emulator or Android-x86. The **Hardware Composer** (**HWC**) HAL is used to composite surfaces to the screen. The HWC abstracts objects such as overlays and helps offload some work that would normally be done with OpenGL.

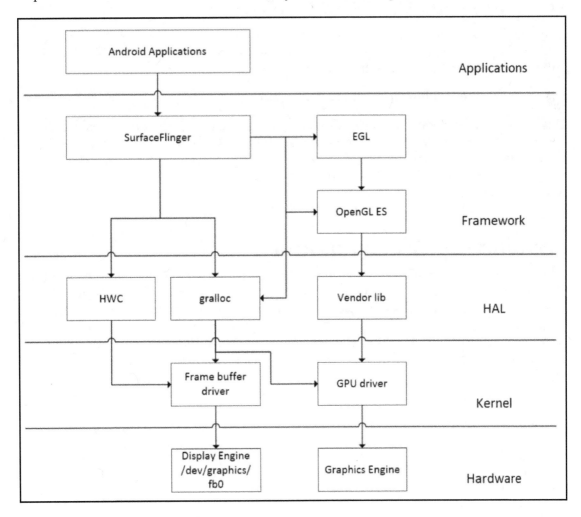

Android graphics architecture

As we can see from the preceding Android graphics architecture diagram, we can also divide related components into different layers in the Android architecture as we did in previous chapters. This architecture diagram is a simplified view of a graphics system. **SurfaceFlinger** is the system service to the application layer for graphics-related system support. **SurfaceFlinger** will connect to the **OpenGL ES** library and **HAL** layer components to perform the actual work. In the **HAL**, we have **HWC**, **gralloc**, and a vender-specific GPU library that will talk to the drivers in the kernel space.

Delving into graphics HAL

After we have an overview of graphics system architecture, we will analyze the Gralloc module, which is the graphics HAL. In the AOSP source code, the skeleton of Gralloc HAL implementation can be found at the following folder:

$AOSP/hardware/libhardware/modules/gralloc

This is a general implementation that provides a reference for developers to create their own Gralloc module. Gralloc will access framebuffer and GPU to provide services to the upper layer. In this section, we will analyze this general implementation first. After the analysis of this general Gralloc HAL module, we will introduce the Gralloc HAL of the Android emulator.

Loading the Gralloc module

When application developers draw images to the screen, there are two ways to do it. They can use Canvas or OpenGL. Beginning in Android 4.0, both methods use hardware acceleration by default. To use hardware acceleration, we need to use Open GL libraries and eventually the Gralloc module will be loaded as part of the graphics system initialization. As we saw in Chapter 3, *Discovering Kernel, HAL, and Virtual Hardware*, each HAL module has a reference ID that can be used by the hw_get_module function to load it to memory. The hw_get_module function is defined in the $AOSP/hardware/libhardware/hardware.c file:

```
int hw_get_module(const char *id, const struct hw_module_t **module)
{
    return hw_get_module_by_class(id, NULL, module);
}
```

In `hw_get_module`, it actually calls another function, `hw_get_module_by_class`, to do the work:

```
int hw_get_module_by_class(const char *class_id, const char *inst,
                           const struct hw_module_t **module)
{
    int i = 0;
    char prop[PATH_MAX] = {0};
    char path[PATH_MAX] = {0};
    char name[PATH_MAX] = {0};
    char prop_name[PATH_MAX] = {0};


    if (inst)
        snprintf(name, PATH_MAX, "%s.%s", class_id, inst);
    else
        strlcpy(name, class_id, PATH_MAX);

    snprintf(prop_name, sizeof(prop_name), "ro.hardware.%s", name);
    if (property_get(prop_name, prop, NULL) > 0) {
        if (hw_module_exists(path, sizeof(path), name, prop) == 0) {
            goto found;
        }
    }

    for (i=0 ; i<HAL_VARIANT_KEYS_COUNT; i++) {
        if (property_get(variant_keys[i], prop, NULL) == 0) {
            continue;
        }
        if (hw_module_exists(path, sizeof(path), name, prop) == 0) {
            goto found;
        }
    }

    /* Nothing found, try the default */
    if (hw_module_exists(path, sizeof(path), name, "default") == 0) {
        goto found;
    }

    return -ENOENT;

found:
    return load(class_id, path, module);
}
```

In the preceding function, it tries to find the Gralloc module shared library using the following names in `/system/lib/hw` or `/vendor/lib/hw`:

```
gralloc.<ro.hardware>.so
gralloc.<ro.product.board>.so
gralloc.<ro.board.platform>.so
gralloc.<ro.arch>.so
```

If any of the preceding files exist, they will call the `load` function to load the shared library. If none of them exist, a default shared library, `gralloc.default.so`, will be used. The hardware module ID for Gralloc is defined in the `gralloc.h` file as follows:

```
#define GRALLOC_HARDWARE_MODULE_ID "gralloc"
```

The `load` function will call `dlopen` to load the library and will call `dlsym` to get the address of the data structure `hw_module_t`:

```
static int load(const char *id,
        const char *path,
        const struct hw_module_t **pHmi)
{
    int status = -EINVAL;
    void *handle = NULL;
    struct hw_module_t *hmi = NULL;

    handle = dlopen(path, RTLD_NOW);
    if (handle == NULL) {
        char const *err_str = dlerror();
        ALOGE("load: module=%s\n%s", path, err_str?err_str:"unknown");
        status = -EINVAL;
        goto done;
    }

    const char *sym = HAL_MODULE_INFO_SYM_AS_STR;
    hmi = (struct hw_module_t *)dlsym(handle, sym);
    if (hmi == NULL) {
        ALOGE("load: couldn't find symbol %s", sym);
        status = -EINVAL;
        goto done;
    }

    if (strcmp(id, hmi->id) != 0) {
        ALOGE("load: id=%s != hmi->id=%s", id, hmi->id);
        status = -EINVAL;
        goto done;
    }
```

```
    hmi->dso = handle;

    status = 0;

done:
    if (status != 0) {
        hmi = NULL;
        if (handle != NULL) {
            dlclose(handle);
            handle = NULL;
        }
    } else {
        ALOGV("loaded HAL id=%s path=%s hmi=%p handle=%p",
                id, path, *pHmi, handle);
    }

    *pHmi = hmi;

    return status;
}
```

After we get the address of the data structure `hw_module_t`, we can call the `open` method defined in Gralloc HAL to initialize the framebuffer and GPU.

As we discussed in `Chapter 3`, *Discovering Kernel, HAL, and Virtual Hardware*, the hardware vendor needs to implement three HAL data structures as follows:

```
struct hw_module_t;
struct hw_module_methods_t;
struct hw_device_t;
```

After the HAL shared library is loaded, the data structure `hw_module_t` is used to discover the HAL module, as we can see in the preceding code snippet. Each HAL module should implement an `open` method in the data structure `hw_module_methods_t`, which is responsible for the initialization of hardware. We can see that the `gralloc_device_open` function is defined as the `open` method in the following code snippet for the Gralloc module:

```
static struct hw_module_methods_t gralloc_module_methods = {
        .open = gralloc_device_open
};

struct private_module_t HAL_MODULE_INFO_SYM = {
    .base = {
        .common = {
            .tag = HARDWARE_MODULE_TAG,
            .version_major = 1,
```

```
                    .version_minor = 0,
                    .id = GRALLOC_HARDWARE_MODULE_ID,
                    .name = "Graphics Memory Allocator Module",
                    .author = "The Android Open Source Project",
                    .methods = &gralloc_module_methods
              },
              .registerBuffer = gralloc_register_buffer,
              .unregisterBuffer = gralloc_unregister_buffer,
              .lock = gralloc_lock,
              .unlock = gralloc_unlock,
        },
        .framebuffer = 0,
        .flags = 0,
        .numBuffers = 0,
        .bufferMask = 0,
        .lock = PTHREAD_MUTEX_INITIALIZER,
        .currentBuffer = 0,
    };
```

In the data structure `hw_module_methods_t`, the `open` method is assigned as a static function, `gralloc_device_open`. The `HAL_MODULE_INFO_SYM` symbol is defined as `struct private_module_t`.

You may notice that we actually cast the `HAL_MODULE_INFO_SYM_AS_STR` symbol to `hw_module_t`, while we loaded the Gralloc module. In this default Gralloc module, the data structure `hw_module_t` is implemented using another two inherited data structures, `private_module_t` and `gralloc_module_t`. Let's look at the relationship between `private_module_t`, `gralloc_module_t`, and `hw_module_t`.

 If you feel a little lost with the analysis, I suggest you look at the source code while you read this section. If you don't have the AOSP source code available, there is a very good cross-reference site for AOSP code at `http://xref.opersys.com/`.
You can visit this site and search for the data structures that we are discussing.

The data structure `private_module_t` is defined in the following file:

`$AOSP/hardware/libhardware/modules/gralloc/gralloc_priv.h`

```
    struct private_module_t {
        gralloc_module_t base;

        private_handle_t* framebuffer;
        uint32_t flags;
        uint32_t numBuffers;
```

```
        uint32_t bufferMask;
        pthread_mutex_t lock;
        buffer_handle_t currentBuffer;
        int pmem_master;
        void* pmem_master_base;

        struct fb_var_screeninfo info;
        struct fb_fix_screeninfo finfo;
        float xdpi;
        float ydpi;
        float fps;
    };
```

As we can see, the first base field, or member variable in C++ terms, is the data structure `gralloc_module_t`. The second member variable framebuffer is a pointer of data type `private_handle_t`. It is a handle pointing to the framebuffer and we will explore it later.

The member variable `flags` is used to indicate whether the system can support double buffering. If it is supported the `PAGE_FLIP` bit is set to 1; otherwise, it is set to 0.

The `numBuffers` member variable indicates the number of buffers in the framebuffer. It is related to the visible resolution and virtual resolution. For example, if the visible resolution of the display is 800 x 600, the virtual resolution can be 1600 x 600. In this case, the framebuffer can have two buffers for the display and the system can support double buffers for the display.

The `bufferMask` member variable is used to mark the use of buffers in a framebuffer device. If we assume there are two buffers in the framebuffer, the `bufferMask` variable can have four values in binary 00, 01, 10, and 11. The value 00 indicates both buffers are empty. The value 01 means the first buffer is in use and the second buffer is empty. The value 10 means the first buffer is empty and the second buffer is in use. The value 11 means both buffers are busy.

The `lock` member variable is used to protect access to `private_module_t`.

The `currentBuffer` member variable is used to track the current buffer for rendering.

The `info` and `finfo` member variables are data types `fb_var_screeninfo` and `fb_fix_screeninfo`. They are used to store the properties of the display device. The properties in `fb_var_screeninfo` are programmable while the properties in `fb_fix_screeninfo` are read-only.

The `xdpi` and `ydpi` member variables are used to describe the pixel density in terms of horizontal and vertical.

The `fps` member variable is the refresh rate of the display in frames per second.

The `gralloc_module_t` data structure is defined in the following file:

`$AOSP/hardware/libhardware/include/hardware/gralloc.h`

```
typedef struct gralloc_module_t {
    struct hw_module_t common;
    int (*registerBuffer)(struct gralloc_module_t const* module,
            buffer_handle_t handle);
    int (*unregisterBuffer)(struct gralloc_module_t const* module,
            buffer_handle_t handle);
    int (*lock)(struct gralloc_module_t const* module,
            buffer_handle_t handle, int usage,
            int l, int t, int w, int h,
            void** vaddr);
    int (*unlock)(struct gralloc_module_t const* module,
            buffer_handle_t handle);
    ...
}
```

As we expect, the first field in `gralloc_module_t` is `hw_module_t` from the preceding code snippet. The relationship among these three data structures is similar to the following UML class diagram in object-oriented notation:

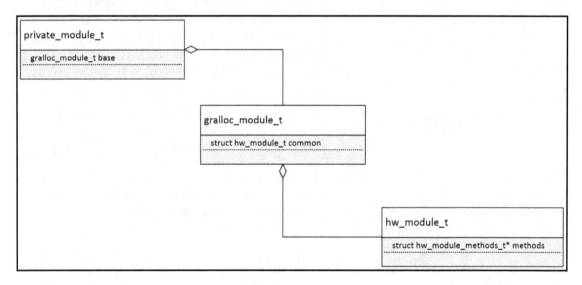

Relationship between Gralloc data structures

This is the way to simulate inheritance relationships in the C language. In this way, we can cast data types of `private_module_t` to `gralloc_module_t` or `hw_module_t`.

A set of member functions is defined in `gralloc_module_t`. We will look at four of them in this chapter.

The `registerBuffer` and `unregisterBuffer` member functions are used to register or unregister a buffer. To register a buffer, we map a buffer to the process space of the application.

The `lock` and `unlock` member functions are used to lock or unlock a buffer. The buffer is described using `buffer_handle_t` as a parameter of the function. We can use the l, t, w, and h parameters to provide the position and the size of the buffer. After the buffer is locked, we can get the address of the buffer in the `vaddr` output parameter. We should unlock the buffer after use.

Initializing GPU

We have talked about HAL data structures `hw_module_t` and `hw_module_methods_t` for the Gralloc module. The last one, `hw_device_t`, is initialized in the `open` method of the Gralloc HAL module. Now we can look at the `open` method of the Gralloc module as follows:

```
int gralloc_device_open(const hw_module_t* module, const char* name,
      hw_device_t** device)
{
    int status = -EINVAL;
    if (!strcmp(name, GRALLOC_HARDWARE_GPU0)) {
        gralloc_context_t *dev;
        dev = (gralloc_context_t*)malloc(sizeof(*dev));

        memset(dev, 0, sizeof(*dev));

        dev->device.common.tag = HARDWARE_DEVICE_TAG;
        dev->device.common.version = 0;
        dev->device.common.module = const_cast<hw_module_t*>(module);
        dev->device.common.close = gralloc_close;

        dev->device.alloc   = gralloc_alloc;
        dev->device.free    = gralloc_free;

        *device = &dev->device.common;
        status = 0;
    } else {
```

```
            status = fb_device_open(module, name, device);
      }
      return status;
  }
```

As we can see here, the `gralloc_device_open` function can be used to initialize two kinds of device, `GRALLOC_HARDWARE_GPU0` and `GRALLOC_HARDWARE_FB0`, according to the `name` input parameter.

Let's look at the initialization of the GPU0 device first. The output parameter of the `open` method is the address of the `hw_device_t` data structure. After the calling applications get an instance of `hw_device_t`, they can use the hardware device to do their work. In the `open` method of Gralloc HAL, it allocates the memory for the `gralloc_context_t` data structure first. After that, it populates its `device` member variable and assigns the output parameter to the address of the `dev->device.common` member variable. As we expect, the output is the address of an `hw_device_t` instance. Let's look at the relationship between `gralloc_context_t`, `alloc_device_t`, and `hw_device_t`:

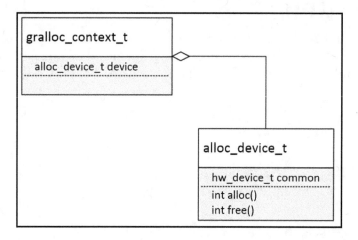

As we can see from the preceding diagram, the first field or member variable of `gralloc_context_t` is `device`, which is data type `alloc_device_t`:

```
struct gralloc_context_t {
    alloc_device_t   device;
    /* our private data here */
};
```

The following is the definition of the `alloc_device_t` data structure. It is defined in the `gralloc.h` file:

```
typedef struct alloc_device_t {
    struct hw_device_t common;

    int (*alloc)(struct alloc_device_t* dev,
            int w, int h, int format, int usage,
            buffer_handle_t* handle, int* stride);

    int (*free)(struct alloc_device_t* dev,
            buffer_handle_t handle);

    void (*dump)(struct alloc_device_t *dev, char *buff, int buff_len);

    void* reserved_proc[7];
} alloc_device_t;
```

We can see that the data type of the first field of `alloc_device_t` is `hw_device_t`. This is the technique for simulating inheritance relationships in the C language that we mentioned when we discussed the relationship between `private_module_t`, `gralloc_module_t` and `hw_module_t`.

The `alloc` and `free` methods of the Gralloc device are implemented in the `gralloc_alloc` and `gralloc_free` functions in the `gralloc.cpp` file.

Initializing framebuffer

If we call the `open` method of the Gralloc module with the `name` value as `GRALLOC_HARDWARE_FB0`, it will initialize the framebuffer device. The `fb_device_open` function is called to open the framebuffer device:

```
status = fb_device_open(module, name, device);
```

The `fb_device_open` function is implemented in the `framebuffer.cpp` file as follows:

```
int fb_device_open(hw_module_t const* module, const char* name,
        hw_device_t** device)
{
    int status = -EINVAL;
    if (!strcmp(name, GRALLOC_HARDWARE_FB0)) {
        /* initialize our state here */
        fb_context_t *dev = (fb_context_t*)malloc(sizeof(*dev));
        memset(dev, 0, sizeof(*dev));
```

```
        /* initialize the procs */
        dev->device.common.tag = HARDWARE_DEVICE_TAG;
        dev->device.common.version = 0;
        dev->device.common.module = const_cast<hw_module_t*>(module);
        dev->device.common.close = fb_close;
        dev->device.setSwapInterval = fb_setSwapInterval;
        dev->device.post          = fb_post;
        dev->device.setUpdateRect = 0;

        private_module_t* m = (private_module_t*)module;
        status = mapFrameBuffer(m);
        if (status >= 0) {
            int stride = m->finfo.line_length /
            (m->info.bits_per_pixel >> 3);
            /*
             * Auto detect current depth and select mode
             */
            int format;
            if (m->info.bits_per_pixel == 32) {
                format = (m->info.red.offset == 16) ?
                HAL_PIXEL_FORMAT_BGRA_8888
                : (m->info.red.offset == 24) ?
                HAL_PIXEL_FORMAT_RGBA_8888 :
                HAL_PIXEL_FORMAT_RGBX_8888;
            } else if (m->info.bits_per_pixel == 16) {
                format = HAL_PIXEL_FORMAT_RGB_565;
            } else {
                ALOGE("Unsupported format %d", m->info.bits_per_pixel);
                return -EINVAL;
            }
            const_cast<uint32_t&>(dev->device.flags) = 0;
            const_cast<uint32_t&>(dev->device.width) = m->info.xres;
            const_cast<uint32_t&>(dev->device.height) = m->info.yres;
            const_cast<int&>(dev->device.stride) = stride;
            const_cast<int&>(dev->device.format) = format;
            const_cast<float&>(dev->device.xdpi) = m->xdpi;
            const_cast<float&>(dev->device.ydpi) = m->ydpi;
            const_cast<float&>(dev->device.fps) = m->fps;
            const_cast<int&>(dev->device.minSwapInterval) = 1;
            const_cast<int&>(dev->device.maxSwapInterval) = 1;
            *device = &dev->device.common;
        }
    }
    return status;
}
```

In the `fb_device_open` function, it allocates memory for the `fb_context_t` data structure. After that, it populates the fields in the data structure. As we discussed in the GPU0 initialization, we expect the output as an instance of the `hw_device_t` data structure so that the caller can use the framebuffer device through the `hw_device_t` HAL data structure. We have a similar inheritance relationship between these three data structures, `fb_context_t`, `framebuffer_device_t`, and `hw_device_t`, as shown in the following diagram:

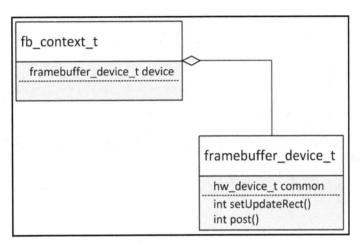

Relationship between fb_context_t, framebuffer_device_t, and hw_device_t

The `fb_context_t` data structure includes `framebuffer_device_t` as the first field as follows:

```
struct fb_context_t {
    framebuffer_device_t   device;
};
```

In turn, the `framebuffer_device_t` data structure includes `hw_device_t` as the first field, so `fb_context_t` can be used as either `framebuffer_device_t` or `hw_device_t`:

```
typedef struct framebuffer_device_t {
    struct hw_device_t common;

    const uint32_t   flags;

    const uint32_t   width;
    const uint32_t   height;

    const int        stride;
```

```
const int        format;

const float      xdpi;
const float      ydpi;

const float      fps;

const int        minSwapInterval;

const int        maxSwapInterval;

const int        numFramebuffers;

int reserved[7];
int (*setSwapInterval)(struct framebuffer_device_t* window,
        int interval);
int (*setUpdateRect)(struct framebuffer_device_t* window,
        int left, int top, int width, int height);
int (*post)(struct framebuffer_device_t* dev, buffer_handle_t
buffer);
int (*compositionComplete)(struct framebuffer_device_t* dev);
void (*dump)(struct framebuffer_device_t* dev, char *buff, int
buff_len);
int (*enableScreen)(struct framebuffer_device_t* dev, int enable);
void* reserved_proc[6];

} framebuffer_device_t;
```

As for the rest of the fields in `framebuffer_device_t`, they are:

- `flags`: Used to describe some attributes of the framebuffer.
- `width` and `height`: Dimensions of the framebuffer in pixels.
- `stride`: Framebuffer stride in pixels or the number of pixels per line.
- `format`: Framebuffer pixel format. It can be `HAL_PIXEL_FORMAT_RGBX_8888`, `HAL_PIXEL_FORMAT_565`, and so on.
- `xdpi` and `ydpi`: Resolution of the framebuffer's display panel in pixels per inch.
- `fps`: Display panel refresh rate in frames per second.
- `minSwapInterval`: Minimum swap interval supported by this framebuffer.
- `maxSwapInterval`: Maximum swap interval supported by this framebuffer.
- `numFramebuffers`: Number of framebuffers supported.

Before it can fill in all the fields of `framebuffer_device_t`, the `fb_device_open` function calls a `mapFrameBuffer` function to get the information about the framebuffer. Besides getting framebuffer information, this `mapFrameBuffer` function also maps the framebuffer to the current process space so that the current process can use it. In Android, the Gralloc module is owned and managed by SurfaceFlinger.

Let's have a look at the `mapFrameBuffer` function now:

```
static int mapFrameBuffer(struct private_module_t* module)
{
    pthread_mutex_lock(&module->lock);
    int err = mapFrameBufferLocked(module);
    pthread_mutex_unlock(&module->lock);
    return err;
}
```

As we can see, `mapFrameBuffer` acquires a mutex first and calls another function, `mapFrameBufferLocked`, to do the rest of the work:

```
int mapFrameBufferLocked(struct private_module_t* module)
{
    // already initialized...
    if (module->framebuffer) {
        return 0;
    }

    char const * const device_template[] = {
            "/dev/graphics/fb%u",
            "/dev/fb%u",
            0 };

    int fd = -1;
    int i=0;
    char name[64];

    while ((fd==-1) && device_template[i]) {
        snprintf(name, 64, device_template[i], 0);
        fd = open(name, O_RDWR, 0);
        i++;
    }
    if (fd < 0)
        return -errno;
    ...
```

In the `mapFrameBufferLocked` function, it checks whether there is a `/dev/graphics/fb0` or `/dev/fb0` device node. If the device node exists, it tries to open it and stores the file descriptor in the `fd` variable:

```
...
struct fb_fix_screeninfo finfo;
if (ioctl(fd, FBIOGET_FSCREENINFO, &finfo) == -1)
    return -errno;

struct fb_var_screeninfo info;
if (ioctl(fd, FBIOGET_VSCREENINFO, &info) == -1)
    return -errno;
...
```

Next, it will use `ioctl` commands to get framebuffer information. There are two framebuffer data structures, `fb_fix_screeninfo` and `fb_var_screeninfo`, which can be used to communicate with framebuffer. The `fb_fix_screeninfo` data structure stores fixed framebuffer information and the `fb_var_screeninfo` data structure stores programmable framebuffer information:

```
...
info.reserved[0] = 0;
info.reserved[1] = 0;
info.reserved[2] = 0;
info.xoffset = 0;
info.yoffset = 0;
info.activate = FB_ACTIVATE_NOW;

/*
 * Request NUM_BUFFERS screens (at lest 2 for page flipping)
 */
info.yres_virtual = info.yres * NUM_BUFFERS;


uint32_t flags = PAGE_FLIP;
#if USE_PAN_DISPLAY
    if (ioctl(fd, FBIOPAN_DISPLAY, &info) == -1) {
        ALOGW("FBIOPAN_DISPLAY failed, page flipping not supported");
#else
    if (ioctl(fd, FBIOPUT_VSCREENINFO, &info) == -1) {
        ALOGW("FBIOPUT_VSCREENINFO failed, page flipping not supported");
#endif
        info.yres_virtual = info.yres;
        flags &= ~PAGE_FLIP;
    }

    if (ioctl(fd, FBIOGET_FSCREENINFO, &finfo) == -1)
```

```
            return -errno;

    if (finfo.smem_len <= 0)
            return -errno;

    if (finfo.smem_len / finfo.line_length < info.yres_virtual)
            info.yres_virtual = finfo.smem_len / finfo.line_length;

    if (info.yres_virtual < info.yres * 2) {
            // we need at least 2 for page-flipping
            info.yres_virtual = info.yres;
            flags &= ~PAGE_FLIP;
            ALOGW("page flipping not supported (yres_virtual=%d,
            requested=%d)",
                    info.yres_virtual, info.yres*2);
    }
    ...
```

After it gets the framebuffer information, it tries to set the virtual resolution of the framebuffer device. The xres and yres fields are used to store the visible resolution of the framebuffer device while the xres_virtual and yres_virtual fields are used to store the virtual resolution of the framebuffer device.

To set the virtual resolution, it tries to increase the virtual vertical resolution as the info.yres * NUM_BUFFERS value. NUM_BUFFERS is a macro for the number of buffers that can be used in the framebuffer devices. In our case, the NUM_BUFFERS value is 2, so we can use the double buffer technology for the display. It sets the virtual resolution using the ioctl command FBIOPUT_VSCREENINFO. If it can set the virtual resolution successfully, it will set the PAGE_FLIP bit in flags; otherwise, it will clear the PAGE_FLIP bit:

```
    ...
    if (ioctl(fd, FBIOGET_VSCREENINFO, &info) == -1)
            return -errno;

    if (finfo.smem_len / finfo.line_length < info.yres_virtual)
            info.yres_virtual = finfo.smem_len / finfo.line_length;

    uint64_t  refreshQuotient =
    (
            uint64_t( info.upper_margin + info.lower_margin + info.yres ) *
            ( info.left_margin  + info.right_margin + info.xres ) *
            info.pixclock
    );

    /* Beware, info.pixclock might be 0 under emulation, so avoid
     * a division-by-0 here (SIGFPE on ARM) */
    int refreshRate = refreshQuotient > 0 ? (int)(1000000000000000LLU /
```

```
        refreshQuotient) : 0;

    if (refreshRate == 0) {
        // bleagh, bad info from the driver
        refreshRate = 60*1000;   // 60 Hz
    }
    ...
```

After it sets the virtual resolution, it will calculate the refresh rate. To understand the calculation of the refresh rate, you can refer to the document in the Linux kernel source code at `Documentation/fb/framebuffer.txt`:

```
    ...
    if (int(info.width) <= 0 || int(info.height) <= 0) {
        // the driver doesn't return that information
        // default to 160 dpi
        info.width  = ((info.xres * 25.4f)/160.0f + 0.5f);
        info.height = ((info.yres * 25.4f)/160.0f + 0.5f);
    }

    float xdpi = (info.xres * 25.4f) / info.width;
    float ydpi = (info.yres * 25.4f) / info.height;
    float fps  = refreshRate / 1000.0f;

    module->finfo = finfo;
    module->xdpi = xdpi;
    module->ydpi = ydpi;
    module->fps = fps;
    ...
```

Next, it will calculate the pixel density for both horizontal and vertical. It also converts the refresh rate to frames per second and stores this to `fps`. After it has all the information, it will store them to the fields of the data structure, `private_module_t`.

Finally, it will map the framebuffer to the process address space:

```
    ...
    while (info.yres_virtual > 0) {
        size_t fbSize = roundUpToPageSize(finfo.line_length *
        info.yres_virtual);
        module->numBuffers = info.yres_virtual / info.yres;
        void* vaddr = mmap(0, fbSize, PROT_READ|PROT_WRITE, MAP_SHARED,
        fd, 0);
        if (vaddr != MAP_FAILED) {
            module->info = info;
            module->flags = flags;
            module->bufferMask = 0;
            module->framebuffer = new private_handle_t(dup(fd),
```

```
        fbSize, 0);
        module->framebuffer->base = intptr_t(vaddr);
        memset(vaddr, 0, fbSize);
        return 0;
    }

    ALOGE("Error mapping the framebuffer (%s)", strerror(errno));

    info.yres_virtual -= info.yres;
    ALOGW("Fallback to use fewer buffer: %d", info.yres_virtual /
    info.yres);
    if (ioctl(fd, FBIOPUT_VSCREENINFO, &info) == -1)
        break;

    if (info.yres_virtual <= info.yres)
        flags &= ~PAGE_FLIP;
    }

    return -errno;
}
```

The size of the framebuffer by virtual resolution is `finfo.line_length *
info.yres_virtual`. The value of `finfo.line_length` is equal to the number of bytes
per line and the value of `info.yres_virtual` is the number of lines per frame. In order to
do memory mapping, we have to round the size to the page boundary using the
`roundUpToPageSize` function.

The actual number of buffers that can be used in the framebuffer device is
`info.yres_virtual` divided by `info.yres` and it is stored in the `numBuffers` field. The
`bufferMask` field is set to 0 and this means all buffers are empty and can be used.

It calls the `mmap` system call to map the framebuffer to the current process address space.
The starting address of the framebuffer in the current process address space is `vaddr`,
which is returned from the `mmap` system call. It is stored to the `framebuffer->base` field,
so that the Gralloc module can use it to allocate buffers for the applications later.

Up to now, we have completed the analysis of the `mapFrameBuffer` function. This function
is the one that is responsible for most of the work in initializing framebuffer devices in the
Gralloc HAL module.

Allocating and releasing the graphic buffer

So far in this chapter, we have discussed loading the Gralloc module and the `open` method provided by the Gralloc module. Let's now review the points when the upper layer loads, initializes, and uses the Gralloc module:

- For example, the Gralloc module is used mostly by `SurfaceFlinger`. `SurfaceFlinger` uses Gralloc; when it creates an instance of `FramebufferNativeWindow`, in the `FramebufferNativeWindow` constructor, it will call `hw_get_module` to get an instance of `hw_module_t`.
- In the `hw_module_t` data structure, it has a field called `methods` with data type `hw_module_methods_t`. In `hw_module_methods_t`, it has an `open` method that returns a `hw_device_t` data structure.
- With `hw_device_t`, `SurfaceFlinger` can use the `alloc` and `free` methods inside `hw_device_t` to allocate or release graphic buffers.

Let's look at how the Gralloc module allocates and releases graphic buffers in this section. We will look at the source code of `gralloc_alloc` first:

```
static int gralloc_alloc(alloc_device_t* dev,
        int w, int h, int format, int usage,
        buffer_handle_t* pHandle, int* pStride)
{
    if (!pHandle || !pStride)
        return -EINVAL;

    size_t size, stride;

    int align = 4;
    int bpp = 0;
    switch (format) {
        case HAL_PIXEL_FORMAT_RGBA_8888:
        case HAL_PIXEL_FORMAT_RGBX_8888:
        case HAL_PIXEL_FORMAT_BGRA_8888:
            bpp = 4;
            break;
        case HAL_PIXEL_FORMAT_RGB_888:
            bpp = 3;
            break;
        case HAL_PIXEL_FORMAT_RGB_565:
        case HAL_PIXEL_FORMAT_RAW16:
            bpp = 2;
            break;
        default:
            return -EINVAL;
```

```
        }

        private_module_t* m = reinterpret_cast<private_module_t*>(
                            dev->common.module);

        size_t bpr = usage & GRALLOC_USAGE_HW_FB ? m->finfo.line_length :
        (w*bpp + (align-1)) & ~(align-1);
        size = bpr * h;
        stride = bpr / bpp;

        int err;
        if (usage & GRALLOC_USAGE_HW_FB) {
            err = gralloc_alloc_framebuffer(dev, size, usage, pHandle);
        } else {
            err = gralloc_alloc_buffer(dev, size, usage, pHandle);
        }

        if (err < 0) {
            return err;
        }

        *pStride = stride;
        return 0;
    }
```

As we can see in the preceding code snippet, the `alloc` method is implemented in the `gralloc_alloc` function. `gralloc_alloc` has the following parameters:

- `dev`: It has an `alloc_device` data type that inherits from `hw_device_t`.
- `w` : It is the width of the graphic buffer.
- `h`: It is the height of graphic buffer.
- `format` : It defines the color format of pixels. For example, the format can be `HAL_PIXEL_FORMAT_RGBA_8888`, `HAL_PIXEL_FORMAT_RGB_888`, `HAL_PIXEL_FORMAT_RGB_565`, and so on.
- `usage` : It defines the use of graphic buffer. For example, if the `GRALLOC_USAGE_HW_FB` bit is set, the buffer will be allocated from the framebuffer.
- `pHandle` : It has a `buffer_handle_t` data type. We will discuss the details of this data structure. It is used to store the allocated buffer.
- `pStride` : The number of pixels per line.

In `gralloc_alloc`, it checks the format of pixels to decide the size of pixels. It can be 32 bits, 24 bits, 16 bits, and so on. The size of the pixel is stored in the `bpp` variable. The `bpr` variable is the number of bytes per line and it is calculated using `w` multiplied by `bpp`. The `bpr` variable needs to be aligned to four bytes boundary for memory allocation. The size of the buffer can be calculated using `h` multiplied by `bpr`.

After the size of the buffer is calculated, it will call the `gralloc_alloc_framebuffer` or `gralloc_alloc_buffer` functions according to the `GRALLOC_USAGE_HW_FB` bit.

The graphic buffer that is allocated by `gralloc_alloc` is stored in the `buffer_handle_t` data type. `buffer_handle_t` is defined as a pointer of `native_handle`. `native_handle` is used as a parent class of `private_handle_t`. `private_handle_t` is the actual data type used to manage the graphic buffer and it is a hardware-dependent data structure.

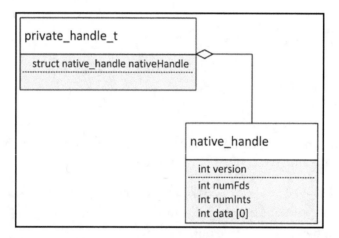

Relationship between private_handle_t and native_handle

The preceding diagram shows the relationship between `private_handle_t` and `native_handle`. The following is the definition of `native_handle`:

```
typedef struct native_handle
{
    int version;      /* sizeof(native_handle_t) */
    int numFds;       /* number of file-descriptors at &data[0] */
    int numInts;      /* number of ints at &data[numFds] */
    int data[0];      /* numFds + numInts ints */
} native_handle_t;
```

The `version` field is set to the size of `native_handle`. The `numFds` and `numInts` fields describe the number of file descriptors and integers in the `data` array. The `data` array is used to store hardware-specific information, which we can see in the following definition of `private_handle_t`:

```
#ifdef __cplusplus
struct private_handle_t : public native_handle {
#else
struct private_handle_t {
    struct native_handle nativeHandle;
#endif

    enum {
        PRIV_FLAGS_FRAMEBUFFER = 0x00000001
    };

    // file-descriptors
    int     fd;
    // ints
    int     magic;
    int     flags;
    int     size;
    int     offset;

    // FIXME: the attributes below should be out-of-line
    uint64_t base __attribute__((aligned(8)));
    int     pid;

#ifdef __cplusplus
    static inline int sNumInts() {
        return (((sizeof(private_handle_t) -
        sizeof(native_handle_t))/sizeof(int)) - sNumFds);
    }
    static const int sNumFds = 1;
    static const int sMagic = 0x3141592;

    private_handle_t(int fd, int size, int flags) :
        fd(fd), magic(sMagic), flags(flags), size(size), offset(0),
        base(0), pid(getpid())
    {
        version = sizeof(native_handle);
        numInts = sNumInts();
        numFds = sNumFds;
    }
    ~private_handle_t() {
        magic = 0;
    }
```

```
        static int validate(const native_handle* h) {
            const private_handle_t* hnd = (const private_handle_t*)h;
            if (!h || h->version != sizeof(native_handle) ||
                    h->numInts != sNumInts() || h->numFds != sNumFds ||
                    hnd->magic != sMagic)
            {
                ALOGE("invalid gralloc handle (at %p)", h);
                return -EINVAL;
            }
            return 0;
        }
    #endif
    };
```

The `fd` member variable is a file descriptor that is used to describe a framebuffer or shared memory region. The `magic` member variable is stored as a magic number defined in the `sMagic` static variable. The `flags` member variable is used to describe the type of graphic buffer. For example, if it is equal to `PRIV_FLAGS_FRAMEBUFFER`, this buffer is allocated from framebuffer. The `size` member variable is the size of the graphic buffer. The `offset` member variable is the offset from the starting address in memory. The `base` member variable is the address allocated for the buffer. The `pid` member variable is the process ID of the creator of the graphic buffer.

The constructor fills in the member variables of `native_handle`. The `validate` member function is used to validate whether the graphic buffer is an instance of `private_handle_t` or not.

As we mentioned previously, the Gralloc module that we are analyzing is the default implementation in AOSP, and is built as `galloc.default.so`. In this implementation, GPU is not used and the buffer will be allocated either in the framebuffer or shared memory. Even though this is not the ideal case for performance, it has the least hardware dependency, which is good as a reference to understand a more complicated Gralloc module implementation.

Allocating from framebuffer

As we can see from the `gralloc_alloc` function, when the `usage` bit is set to `GRALLOC_USAGE_HW_FB`, the `gralloc_alloc_framebuffer` function is called. The `gralloc_alloc_framebuffer` function will allocate the buffer from the framebuffer device:

```
static int gralloc_alloc_framebuffer_locked(alloc_device_t* dev,
        size_t size, int usage, buffer_handle_t* pHandle)
{
    private_module_t* m = reinterpret_cast<private_module_t*>(
            dev->common.module);

    // allocate the framebuffer
    if (m->framebuffer == NULL) {
        // initialize the framebuffer, the framebuffer is mapped once
        // and forever.
        int err = mapFrameBufferLocked(m);
        if (err < 0) {
            return err;
        }
    }

    const uint32_t bufferMask = m->bufferMask;
    const uint32_t numBuffers = m->numBuffers;
    const size_t bufferSize = m->finfo.line_length * m->info.yres;
    if (numBuffers == 1) {
        // If we have only one buffer, we never use page-flipping.
        // Instead we return a regular buffer which will be
        // memcpy'ed to the main screen when post is called.
        int newUsage = (usage & ~GRALLOC_USAGE_HW_FB) |
        GRALLOC_USAGE_HW_2D;
        return gralloc_alloc_buffer(dev, bufferSize, newUsage,
        pHandle);
    }

    if (bufferMask >= ((1LU<<numBuffers)-1)) {
        // We ran out of buffers.
        return -ENOMEM;
    }

    // create a "fake" handles for it
    intptr_t vaddr = intptr_t(m->framebuffer->base);
    private_handle_t* hnd = new private_handle_t(dup(m->framebuffer->fd),
    size, private_handle_t::PRIV_FLAGS_FRAMEBUFFER);
```

```
        // find a free slot
        for (uint32_t i=0 ; i<numBuffers ; i++) {
            if ((bufferMask & (1LU<<i)) == 0) {
                m->bufferMask |= (1LU<<i);
                break;
            }
            vaddr += bufferSize;
        }

        hnd->base = vaddr;
        hnd->offset = vaddr - intptr_t(m->framebuffer->base);
        *pHandle = hnd;

        return 0;
    }

    static int gralloc_alloc_framebuffer(alloc_device_t* dev,
            size_t size, int usage, buffer_handle_t* pHandle)
    {
        private_module_t* m = reinterpret_cast<private_module_t*>(
                dev->common.module);
        pthread_mutex_lock(&m->lock);
        int err = gralloc_alloc_framebuffer_locked(dev, size, usage,
        pHandle);
        pthread_mutex_unlock(&m->lock);
        return err;
    }
```

gralloc_alloc_framebuffer acquires a mutex first and calls to another function, gralloc_alloc_framebuffer_locked. In the locked version, it calls to a mapFrameBufferLocked function, which we analyzed before to get the framebuffer information and map it to the current process address space.

It will check whether the framebuffer device can support double buffering or not. If it can support double buffering, it creates a new private_handle_t instance and fills in the information in this instance and returns to the caller. If the buffer is allocated from the framebuffer device, it will mark the flags member variable of private_handle_t to PRIV_FLAGS_FRAMEBUFFER. It will also set the framebuffer usage status in bufferMask, which is a member variable of private_module_t.

If it cannot support double buffering, it calls to gralloc_alloc_buffer to allocate a buffer from the system memory and returns to the caller.

Allocating from system memory

When the usage bit is not set to GRALLOC_USAGE_HW_FB or the system cannot support double buffering, we have to allocate the buffer from system memory using gralloc_alloc_buffer. Let's look at the implementation of gralloc_alloc_buffer:

```
static int gralloc_alloc_buffer(alloc_device_t* dev,
        size_t size, int /*usage*/, buffer_handle_t* pHandle)
{
    int err = 0;
    int fd = -1;

    size = roundUpToPageSize(size);

    fd = ashmem_create_region("gralloc-buffer", size);
    if (fd < 0) {
        ALOGE("couldn't create ashmem (%s)", strerror(-errno));
        err = -errno;
    }

    if (err == 0) {
        private_handle_t* hnd = new private_handle_t(fd, size, 0);
        gralloc_module_t* module = reinterpret_cast<gralloc_module_t*>(
                dev->common.module);
        err = mapBuffer(module, hnd);
        if (err == 0) {
            *pHandle = hnd;
        }
    }

    ALOGE_IF(err, "gralloc failed err=%s", strerror(-err));

    return err;
}
```

In gralloc_alloc_buffer, it rounds up the buffer size to the page size first. Then it creates an anonymous shared memory region using ashmem_create_region. It creates a new private_handle_t instance to represent this shared memory region.

This shared memory region is described as a file descriptor. To use it, we need to map it to the current process address space. This is done with the `mapBuffer` function:

```
int mapBuffer(gralloc_module_t const* module,
        private_handle_t* hnd)
{
    void* vaddr;
    return gralloc_map(module, hnd, &vaddr);
}
```

`mapBuffer` calls to another function, `gralloc_map`, to do the memory mapping:

```
static int gralloc_map(gralloc_module_t const* /*module*/,
        buffer_handle_t handle,
        void** vaddr)
{
    private_handle_t* hnd = (private_handle_t*)handle;
    if (!(hnd->flags & private_handle_t::PRIV_FLAGS_FRAMEBUFFER)) {
        size_t size = hnd->size;
        void* mappedAddress = mmap(0, size,
                PROT_READ|PROT_WRITE, MAP_SHARED, hnd->fd, 0);
        if (mappedAddress == MAP_FAILED) {
            ALOGE("Could not mmap %s", strerror(errno));
            return -errno;
        }
        hnd->base = uintptr_t(mappedAddress) + hnd->offset;
        //ALOGD("gralloc_map() succeeded fd=%d, off=%d, size=%d, vaddr=%p",
        //          hnd->fd, hnd->offset, hnd->size, mappedAddress);
    }
    *vaddr = (void*)hnd->base;
    return 0;
}
```

In `grallo_map`, if the file descriptor in `private_handle_t` is a framebuffer device, we don't have to do the mapping again, since the framebuffer is initialized and mapped to the `SurfaceFlinger` address space in `fb_device_open`, as we analyzed before.

If it is a shared memory region, it needs to be mapped to the current process address space using the `mmap` system function.

Releasing graphic buffers

As we mentioned previously, the Gralloc module can be used to allocate and release graphic buffers. Now that we have learnt how to allocate buffers from framebuffer devices or system memory, let's have a look at how to release graphic buffers.

To release graphic buffers, the `gralloc_free` function is used:

```
static int gralloc_free(alloc_device_t* dev,
        buffer_handle_t handle)
{
    if (private_handle_t::validate(handle) < 0)
        return -EINVAL;

    private_handle_t const* hnd = reinterpret_cast<private_handle_t const*>
    (handle);
    if (hnd->flags & private_handle_t::PRIV_FLAGS_FRAMEBUFFER) {
        // free this buffer
        private_module_t* m = reinterpret_cast<private_module_t*>(
                dev->common.module);
        const size_t bufferSize = m->finfo.line_length * m->info.yres;
        int index = (hnd->base - m->framebuffer->base) / bufferSize;
        m->bufferMask &= ~(1<<index);
    } else {
        gralloc_module_t* module = reinterpret_cast<gralloc_module_t*>(
                dev->common.module);
        terminateBuffer(module, const_cast<private_handle_t*>(hnd));
    }

    close(hnd->fd);
    delete hnd;
    return 0;
}
```

To release a graphic buffer, the buffer is described using `buffer_handle_t`. `gralloc_free` will validate the buffer first using the `private_handle_t::validate` static function.

The `handle` parameter can be cast to a pointer of `private_handle_t` as we recall from the discussion on `private_handle_t` and `native_handle` previously. If the `flags` field of `hnd` is `PRIV_FLAGS_FRAMEBUFFER`, it means the buffer is allocated from the framebuffer device. It will update `bufferMask` to release it from the framebuffer.

If the buffer is allocated from system memory, it will call the `terminateBuffer` function to release the memory:

```
int terminateBuffer(gralloc_module_t const* module,
        private_handle_t* hnd)
{
    if (hnd->base) {
        // this buffer was mapped, unmap it now
        gralloc_unmap(module, hnd);
    }

    return 0;
}
```

The `terminateBuffer` function calls to another function, `gralloc_unmap`, to release the memory:

```
static int gralloc_unmap(gralloc_module_t const* /*module*/,
        buffer_handle_t handle)
{
    private_handle_t* hnd = (private_handle_t*)handle;
    if (!(hnd->flags & private_handle_t::PRIV_FLAGS_FRAMEBUFFER))
    {
        void* base = (void*)hnd->base;
        size_t size = hnd->size;
        //ALOGD("unmapping from %p, size=%d", base, size);
        if (munmap(base, size) < 0) {
            ALOGE("Could not unmap %s", strerror(errno));
        }
    }
    hnd->base = 0;
    return 0;
}
```

In `gralloc_unmap`, again, it checks that this buffer is not from the framebuffer and it calls the `munmap` system function to release it.

Rendering framebuffer

As we discussed previously in this chapter, the Gralloc module can support two kinds of device: Gralloc devices and framebuffer devices. In the `open` method of the Gralloc device, it creates a device named `GRALLOC_HARDWARE_GPU0` and supports two methods, `alloc` and `free`, as we can see in the following snippet. We have discussed both methods in detail earlier in this chapter:

```
...
if (!strcmp(name, GRALLOC_HARDWARE_GPU0)) {
    gralloc_context_t *dev;
    dev = (gralloc_context_t*)malloc(sizeof(*dev));

    /* initialize our state here */
    memset(dev, 0, sizeof(*dev));

    /* initialize the procs */
    dev->device.common.tag = HARDWARE_DEVICE_TAG;
    dev->device.common.version = 0;
    dev->device.common.module = const_cast<hw_module_t*>(module);
    dev->device.common.close = gralloc_close;

    dev->device.alloc    = gralloc_alloc;
    dev->device.free     = gralloc_free;

    *device = &dev->device.common;
...
```

In the `open` method of the framebuffer device, it creates a device named `GRALLOC_HARDWARE_FB0` and supports four methods `close`, `setSwapInterval`, `post`, and `setUpdateRect`:

```
...
if (!strcmp(name, GRALLOC_HARDWARE_FB0)) {
    /* initialize our state here */
    fb_context_t *dev = (fb_context_t*)malloc(sizeof(*dev));
    memset(dev, 0, sizeof(*dev));

    /* initialize the procs */
    dev->device.common.tag = HARDWARE_DEVICE_TAG;
    dev->device.common.version = 0;
    dev->device.common.module = const_cast<hw_module_t*>(module);
    dev->device.common.close = fb_close;
    dev->device.setSwapInterval = fb_setSwapInterval;
    dev->device.post             = fb_post;
    dev->device.setUpdateRect = 0;
```

```
        private_module_t* m = (private_module_t*)module;
    ...
```

You can refer to the AOSP source code or the following URL for information about the implementation of these methods:

`http://xref.opersys.com/android-7.0.0_r1/xref/hardware/libhardware/modules/gral loc/framebuffer.cpp`

Let's look at the `post` method, which is implemented in `fb_post`:

```
    static int fb_post(struct framebuffer_device_t* dev, buffer_handle_t
    buffer)
    {
        if (private_handle_t::validate(buffer) < 0)
            return -EINVAL;

        fb_context_t* ctx = (fb_context_t*)dev;

        private_handle_t const* hnd = reinterpret_cast<private_handle_t const*>
        (buffer);
        private_module_t* m = reinterpret_cast<private_module_t*>(
                dev->common.module);

        if (hnd->flags & private_handle_t::PRIV_FLAGS_FRAMEBUFFER) {
            const size_t offset = hnd->base - m->framebuffer->base;
            m->info.activate = FB_ACTIVATE_VBL;
            m->info.yoffset = offset / m->finfo.line_length;
            if (ioctl(m->framebuffer->fd, FBIOPUT_VSCREENINFO, &m->info) == -1)
    {

                ALOGE("FBIOPUT_VSCREENINFO failed");
                m->base.unlock(&m->base, buffer);
                return -errno;
            }
            m->currentBuffer = buffer;

        } else {
            // If we can't do the page_flip, just copy the buffer to the front
            // FIXME: use copybit HAL instead of memcpy

            void* fb_vaddr;
            void* buffer_vaddr;

            m->base.lock(&m->base, m->framebuffer,
                    GRALLOC_USAGE_SW_WRITE_RARELY,
                    0, 0, m->info.xres, m->info.yres, &fb_vaddr);

            m->base.lock(&m->base, buffer,
```

```
                    GRALLOC_USAGE_SW_READ_RARELY,
                    0, 0, m->info.xres, m->info.yres, &buffer_vaddr);

        memcpy(fb_vaddr, buffer_vaddr, m->finfo.line_length * m-
        >info.yres);

        m->base.unlock(&m->base, buffer);
        m->base.unlock(&m->base, m->framebuffer);
    }

    return 0;
}
```

After an application has prepared the graphic buffer, it needs to post the buffer to the display so that users can see it on the screen. This `fb_post` function is used to display the graphic buffer to the screen. It takes two parameters, `dev` and `buffer`. The `dev` parameter is the pointer of an instance of the data structure of `framebuffer_device_t`, which was discussed previously (refer to the diagram about the relationship between `fb_context_t` and `framebuffer_device_t`). As per the previous discussion, `dev` can be cast to `ctx`, which is a pointer of `fb_context_t`.

After we have an instance of the device, we can get the instance of the Gralloc module from it as follows:

```
private_module_t* m = reinterpret_cast<private_module_t*>(
dev->common.module);
```

Another parameter is `buffer` and it has a `buffer_handle_t` data type. It includes the buffer to be posted. As we discussed previously, it can be cast as a point of `private_handle_t` and it is stored in the `hnd` variable. This buffer can be a graphic buffer in system memory or it can be part of the framebuffer. Based on the value of the `hnd->flags` member variable, we can find out what kind of buffer it is.

If it is a buffer as part of the framebuffer, we need to activate it as the buffer for the display. This can be done using the framebuffer's `ioctl` function. To call the `ioctl` function, we need a data structure of `fb_var_screeninfo` and this can be found in `m->info`. To swap the buffer in double buffering, we just need to set the vertical offset and activate it as follows:

```
    ...
        m->info.activate = FB_ACTIVATE_VBL;
        m->info.yoffset = offset / m->finfo.line_length;
        if (ioctl(m->framebuffer->fd, FBIOPUT_VSCREENINFO, &m->info) == -1)
  {
    ...
```

If it is a buffer allocated in system memory, we need to copy it to the framebuffer. In this case, it tries to lock both the graphic buffer and framebuffer first, and then it copies the graphic buffer using `memcpy`:

```
memcpy(fb_vaddr, buffer_vaddr, m->finfo.line_length * m->info.yres);
```

Graphics HAL of the Android emulator

After we have analyzed the default Gralloc module implementation, we want to briefly look at another Gralloc module implementation so that we can compare how a Gralloc module should be implemented on varying Graphic hardware.

The Gralloc module we will analyze in this section is the Gralloc module used by the Android emulator. The default Gralloc module `gralloc.default.so` only uses framebuffer devices and it doesn't use GPU. If the default Gralloc module is used, OpenGL support has to be implemented in the software layer. This is the case with VirtualBox for the time being, since there is no Mesa/DRM-compliant implementation in the VirtualBox host side for OpenGL. This doesn't mean VirtualBox doesn't support OpenGL. It does support OpenGL and 3D hardware acceleration, but the implementation is not compliant with the open source Mesa/DRM architecture.

If you are interested in this topic about OpenGL support on VirtualBox, you may read the following threads in the Android-x86 discussion group: `https://groups.google.com/forum/?hl=en#!starred/android-x86/gZYx 6oWx4LI`

Overview of hardware GLES emulation

3D graphics support on Andriod emulator is implemented in different ways as follows:

- `host`: This is the default mode. This is also called hardware GLES emulation. It uses specific translator libraries to convert guest EGL/GLES commands into host GL ones. This requires valid OpenGL drivers installed on the host machine.
- `swiftshader`: This is a software library for high-performance graphics rendering on the CPU. It takes advantage of SIMD on modern CPUs to perform graphics rendering.
- `mesa`: This is deprecated. It is a software library using the Mesa3D library. It is slower than swiftshader mode, and slower than the `host` mode by a large margin.
- `guest`: This is a pure software implementation on the guest side.

To choose a graphic mode in the emulator, you can either specify it on the command line with the `-gpu` option or define it in the `config.ini` configuration file as follows:

```
hw.gps=yes
hw.gpu.enabled=yes
hw.gpu.mode=swiftshader
```

We will look at the Gralloc module implementation in the `host` mode here. In the hardware GLES emulation, there are several host "translator" libraries implemented: EGL, GLES 1.1, and GLES 2.0 ABIs (Application Binary Interface) defined by Khronos. These libraries translate the corresponding function calls into calls to the appropriate host OpenGL APIs.

There are the same set of system libraries implemented inside the emulated guest system for EGL, GLES 1.1, and GLES 2.0 ABIs. They collect the sequence of EGL/GLES function calls and translate them into a custom wire protocol stream that is sent to the emulator program through a high-speed communication channel called a "QEMU pipe." The pipe is implemented with a custom kernel driver and it can provide a very fast channel for communication between the host and the guest system. I have given a brief introduction about the QEMU pipe in Chapter 3, *Discovering Kernel, HAL, and Virtual Hardware* and you can refer to it for more information.

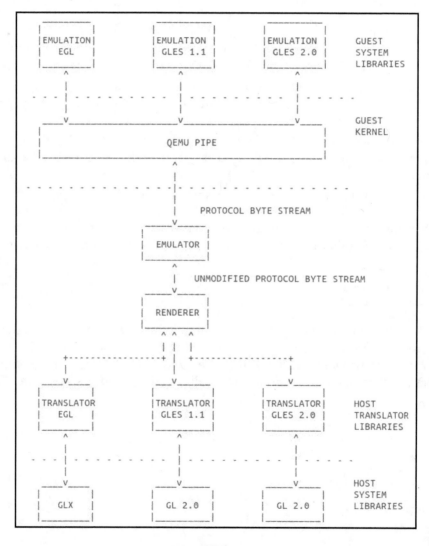

Hardware GLES emulation

You can find the preceding diagram in the emulator source code at
`$AOSP/external/qemu/distrib/android-emugl/DESIGN`.

The emulator source code is not downloaded using the manifest file in this chapter. You can
refer to the following URL:

```
https://android.googlesource.com/platform/external/qemu/+/master/distrib/androi
d-emugl/DESIGN
```

Or you can get the entire repository using the following command:

```
$ git clone https://android.googlesource.com/platform/external/qemu
```

The preceding diagram shows components on both the host (emulator) side and the guest
side for the GLES emulation. We may treat the host side implementation as GPU, and
QEMU PIPE is the connection between GPU and CPU. There are two things that need to
access GPU for 3D graphics acceleration: the Gralloc module and the vendor library. The
vendor library here refers to the hardware GLES emulation library for Android emulator.
The Gralloc module is the one that we want to explore in this section.

The GLES hardware emulation Gralloc module is very similar to the default Gralloc module
that we have discussed in this chapter. It needs to implement the following three HAL data
structures:

```
struct hw_module_t;
struct hw_module_methods_t;
struct hw_device_t;
```

For the first data structure, `hw_module_t`, both Gralloc modules have their own
implementation called `private_module_t`, which is inherited from `hw_module_t`, but the
definitions are different, as we can see in the following snippet.

The `private_module_t` in the default Gralloc module is as follows:

```
struct private_module_t {
    gralloc_module_t base;

    private_handle_t* framebuffer;
    uint32_t flags;
    uint32_t numBuffers;
    uint32_t bufferMask;
    pthread_mutex_t lock;
    buffer_handle_t currentBuffer;
    int pmem_master;
    void* pmem_master_base;
```

```
        struct fb_var_screeninfo info;
        struct fb_fix_screeninfo finfo;
        float xdpi;
        float ydpi;
        float fps;
    };
```

The `private_module_t` in the GLES emulation Gralloc module is as follows:

```
    struct private_module_t {
        gralloc_module_t base;
    };
```

For the `hw_device_t` data structure implementation, we can get the details from the following table. We can create two kinds of devices, GPU0 and FB0, using the `open` method in the `hw_module_methods_t` data structure. In both implementations, data structures inherited from `hw_device_t` are used:

hw_device_t in Gralloc module	GPU0	FB0
Android emulator	`gralloc_device_t`	`fb_device_t`
Default Gralloc	`gralloc_context_t`	`fb_context_t`

We have analyzed both `gralloc_context_t` and `fb_context_t` in the *Initializing GPU* section. We can look at the definitions of `gralloc_device_t` and `fb_device_t` in the following GLES emulation implementation:

```
    struct gralloc_device_t {
        alloc_device_t  device;

        AllocListNode *allocListHead;      // double linked list of allocated
    buffers
        pthread_mutex_t lock;
    };

    struct fb_device_t {
        framebuffer_device_t  device;
    };
```

Initializing GPU0 and FB0 in GLES emulation

As we know, device initialization is done in the `open` method defined in the `hw_module_methods_t` data structure. Let's look at the implementation of the `open` method in GLES emulation. It is implemented in the `gralloc_device_open` function, as we can see in the following snippet:

```
static int gralloc_device_open(const hw_module_t* module,
                               const char* name,
                               hw_device_t** device)
{
    int status = -EINVAL;

    D("gralloc_device_open %s\n", name);

    pthread_once( &sFallbackOnce, fallback_init );
    if (sFallback != NULL) {
        return sFallback->common.methods->open(&sFallback->common,
        name, device);
    }

    if (!strcmp(name, GRALLOC_HARDWARE_GPU0)) {

        // Create host connection and keep it in the TLS.
        // return error if connection with host can not be established
        HostConnection *hostCon = HostConnection::get();
        if (!hostCon) {
            ALOGE("gralloc: failed to get host connection
            while opening %s\n",
            name);
            return -EIO;
        }

        //
        // Allocate memory for the gralloc device (alloc interface)
        //
        gralloc_device_t *dev;
        dev = (gralloc_device_t*)malloc(sizeof(gralloc_device_t));
        if (NULL == dev) {
            return -ENOMEM;
        }

        // Initialize our device structure
        //
        dev->device.common.tag = HARDWARE_DEVICE_TAG;
        dev->device.common.version = 0;
        dev->device.common.module = const_cast<hw_module_t*>(module);
```

```
                    dev->device.common.close = gralloc_device_close;

                    dev->device.alloc    = gralloc_alloc;
                    dev->device.free     = gralloc_free;
                    dev->allocListHead   = NULL;
                    pthread_mutex_init(&dev->lock, NULL);

                    *device = &dev->device.common;
                    status = 0;
            }
            else if (!strcmp(name, GRALLOC_HARDWARE_FB0)) {
            ...
            }

            return status;
    }
```

The preceding code snippet is part of the GPU0 initialization. Before it creates the devices for GPU0 or FB0, it will call a `fallback_init` function to check the system settings for hardware emulation. In `fallback_init`, it will check a `ro.kernel.qemu.gles` system property. If this property is set to 0, the GPU emulation will be disabled. The default Gralloc module will be used. In this case, the `open` method defined in the default Gralloc module, sFallback, will be called.

For the GPU0 initialization, it will check whether the device name is equal to GRALLOC_HARDWARE_GPU0 or not. If it is GPU0, it will get the host connection first. The host connection is the QEMU pipe link between the host and the guest system as we discussed before.

After that, it initializes the GPU0 device as the initialization process that we discussed for the default Gralloc module.

Next, let's have a look at the FB0 initialization as follows:

```
    static int gralloc_device_open(const hw_module_t* module,
                                   const char* name,
                                   hw_device_t** device)
    {
        int status = -EINVAL;

        D("gralloc_device_open %s\n", name);

        pthread_once( &sFallbackOnce, fallback_init );
        if (sFallback != NULL) {
            return sFallback->common.methods->open(&sFallback->common,
            name, device);
```

```
}

if (!strcmp(name, GRALLOC_HARDWARE_GPU0)) {
   ...
}
else if (!strcmp(name, GRALLOC_HARDWARE_FB0)) {

    // return error if connection with host can not be established
    DEFINE_AND_VALIDATE_HOST_CONNECTION;

    //
    // Query the host for Framebuffer attributes
    //
    D("gralloc: query Frabuffer attribs\n");
    EGLint width = rcEnc->rcGetFBParam(rcEnc, FB_WIDTH);
    D("gralloc: width=%d\n", width);
    EGLint height = rcEnc->rcGetFBParam(rcEnc, FB_HEIGHT);
    D("gralloc: height=%d\n", height);
    EGLint xdpi = rcEnc->rcGetFBParam(rcEnc, FB_XDPI);
    D("gralloc: xdpi=%d\n", xdpi);
    EGLint ydpi = rcEnc->rcGetFBParam(rcEnc, FB_YDPI);
    D("gralloc: ydpi=%d\n", ydpi);
    EGLint fps = rcEnc->rcGetFBParam(rcEnc, FB_FPS);
    D("gralloc: fps=%d\n", fps);
    EGLint min_si = rcEnc->rcGetFBParam(rcEnc,
    FB_MIN_SWAP_INTERVAL);
    D("gralloc: min_swap=%d\n", min_si);
    EGLint max_si = rcEnc->rcGetFBParam(rcEnc,
    FB_MAX_SWAP_INTERVAL);
    D("gralloc: max_swap=%d\n", max_si);

    //
    // Allocate memory for the framebuffer device
    //
    fb_device_t *dev;
    dev = (fb_device_t*)malloc(sizeof(fb_device_t));
    if (NULL == dev) {
        return -ENOMEM;
    }
    memset(dev, 0, sizeof(fb_device_t));

    // Initialize our device structure
    //
    dev->device.common.tag = HARDWARE_DEVICE_TAG;
    dev->device.common.version = 0;
    dev->device.common.module = const_cast<hw_module_t*>(module);
    dev->device.common.close = fb_close;
    dev->device.setSwapInterval = fb_setSwapInterval;
```

```
dev->device.post                = fb_post;
dev->device.setUpdateRect       = 0; //fb_setUpdateRect;
dev->device.compositionComplete = fb_compositionComplete;

const_cast<uint32_t&>(dev->device.flags) = 0;
const_cast<uint32_t&>(dev->device.width) = width;
const_cast<uint32_t&>(dev->device.height) = height;
const_cast<int&>(dev->device.stride) = width;
const_cast<int&>(dev->device.format) =
HAL_PIXEL_FORMAT_RGBA_8888;
const_cast<float&>(dev->device.xdpi) = xdpi;
const_cast<float&>(dev->device.ydpi) = ydpi;
const_cast<float&>(dev->device.fps) = fps;
const_cast<int&>(dev->device.minSwapInterval) = min_si;
const_cast<int&>(dev->device.maxSwapInterval) = max_si;
*device = &dev->device.common;

status = 0;
}
```

In the FB0 initialization, it tries to get the host connection and an rcEnc pointer, which is an instance of the renderControl_encoder_context_t data structure, using the DEFINE_AND_VALIDATE_HOST_CONNECTION macro. With rcEnc, it can get the framebuffer attributes (width, height, xdpi, ydpi, fps, min_si, and max_si) from the host connection. After that, it creates an instance of the fb_device_t data structure and fills in the framebuffer attributes in this instance of fb_device_t.

GPU0 device implementation

As we did for the default Gralloc module, we will analyze the alloc and free methods in the GPU0 device. The alloc method is implemented in the gralloc_alloc function. The gralloc_alloc function is much longer than the one in the default Gralloc module, but it basically does three things:

- Checks the usage parameter and decides the pixel format to decide the size of the pixel.
- According to the information provided by the usage parameter, w, h, format, and usage create a shared memory region and allocate buffers in the host side (GPU).
- Stores both the shared memory region and host side (GPU) buffer information in the Gralloc device data structure grdev.

Now let's take a look at the code for `gralloc_alloc`:

```
static int gralloc_alloc(alloc_device_t* dev,
                         int w, int h, int format, int usage,
                         buffer_handle_t* pHandle, int* pStride)
{
    D("gralloc_alloc w=%d h=%d usage=0x%x\n", w, h, usage);

    gralloc_device_t *grdev = (gralloc_device_t *)dev;
    if (!grdev || !pHandle || !pStride) {
        ALOGE("gralloc_alloc: Bad inputs (grdev: %p, pHandle: %p,
        pStride: %p",
        grdev, pHandle, pStride);
        return -EINVAL;
    }

    //
    // Note: in screen capture mode, both sw_write
    // and hw_write will be on
    // and this is a valid usage
    //
    bool sw_write = (0 != (usage & GRALLOC_USAGE_SW_WRITE_MASK));
    bool hw_write = (usage & GRALLOC_USAGE_HW_RENDER);
    bool sw_read = (0 != (usage & GRALLOC_USAGE_SW_READ_MASK));
    bool hw_cam_write = usage & GRALLOC_USAGE_HW_CAMERA_WRITE;
    bool hw_cam_read = usage & GRALLOC_USAGE_HW_CAMERA_READ;
    bool hw_vid_enc_read = usage & GRALLOC_USAGE_HW_VIDEO_ENCODER;

    // Keep around original requested format for later validation
    int frameworkFormat = format;
    // Pick the right concrete pixel format given the endpoints as
    // encoded in the usage bits.
    // Every end-point pair needs explicit listing here.
    if (format == HAL_PIXEL_FORMAT_IMPLEMENTATION_DEFINED) {
        // Camera as producer
        ...
    if (usage & GRALLOC_USAGE_HW_FB) {
        // keep space for postCounter
        ashmem_size += sizeof(uint32_t);
    }

    if (sw_read || sw_write || hw_cam_write || hw_vid_enc_read) {
        // keep space for image on guest memory if SW access is needed
        // or if the camera is doing writing
        if (yuv_format) {
            size_t yStride = (w*bpp + (align - 1)) & ~(align-1);
            size_t uvStride = (yStride / 2 + (align - 1)) & ~(align-1);
            size_t uvHeight = h / 2;
```

```
            ashmem_size += yStride * h + 2 * (uvHeight * uvStride);
            stride = yStride / bpp;
        } else {
            size_t bpr = (w*bpp + (align-1)) & ~(align-1);
            ashmem_size += (bpr * h);
            stride = bpr / bpp;
        }
    }

    D("gralloc_alloc format=%d, ashmem_size=%d, stride=%d,
    tid %d\n", format,
            ashmem_size, stride, gettid());
```

In the preceding code of `gralloc_alloc`, it creates an instance of data structure `gralloc_device_t` first. After that, it checks the `usage` and `format` parameters to decide the size of the pixels and the corresponding GLES color format and pixel type to store in the `bpp`, `glFormat`, and `glType` variables. With the necessary information, it can calculate the size of the shared memory that needs to be allocated for the graphic buffer and stores it in the `ashmem_size` variable:

```
    //
    // Allocate space in ashmem if needed
    //
    int fd = -1;
    if (ashmem_size > 0) {
        // round to page size;
        ashmem_size = (ashmem_size + (PAGE_SIZE-1)) & ~(PAGE_SIZE-1);

        fd = ashmem_create_region("gralloc-buffer", ashmem_size);
        if (fd < 0) {
            ALOGE("gralloc_alloc failed to create ashmem region: %s\n",
                    strerror(errno));
            return -errno;
        }
    }

    cb_handle_t *cb = new cb_handle_t(fd, ashmem_size, usage,
                                    w, h, frameworkFormat, format,
                                    glFormat, glType);

    if (ashmem_size > 0) {
        //
        // map ashmem region if exist
        //
        void *vaddr;
        int err = map_buffer(cb, &vaddr);
        if (err) {
```

```
            close(fd);
            delete cb;
            return err;
        }

        cb->setFd(fd);
    }

    //
    // Allocate ColorBuffer handle on the host (only if h/w access is
    //allowed) only do this for some h/w usages, not all.
    //
    if (usage & (GRALLOC_USAGE_HW_TEXTURE | GRALLOC_USAGE_HW_RENDER |
                 GRALLOC_USAGE_HW_2D | GRALLOC_USAGE_HW_COMPOSER |
                 GRALLOC_USAGE_HW_FB) ) {
        DEFINE_HOST_CONNECTION;
        if (hostCon && rcEnc) {
            cb->hostHandle = rcEnc->rcCreateColorBuffer(rcEnc, w, h,
            glFormat);
            D("Created host ColorBuffer 0x%x\n", cb->hostHandle);
        }

        if (!cb->hostHandle) {
            // Could not create colorbuffer on host !!!
            close(fd);
            delete cb;
            return -EIO;
        }
    }
```

As for the shared memory size `ashmem_size`, it allocates a shared memory region using the `ashmem_create_region` function and it obtains the shared memory region as an `fd` file descriptor. To store the shared memory region and the GPU buffer (the host side buffer), which we will discuss now, it creates an instance of the `cb_handle_t` data structure. If we recall, we used the `private_handle_t` data structure in the default Gralloc module to represent an allocated graphic buffer. Here, `cb_handle_t` is an equivalent of `private_handle_t`:

```
    struct cb_handle_t : public native_handle {

        cb_handle_t(int p_fd, int p_ashmemSize, int p_usage,
                int p_width, int p_height, int p_frameworkFormat,
                int p_format, int p_glFormat, int p_glType) :
        ...
        // file-descriptors
        int fd;
```

```
    // ints
    int magic;
    int usage;
    int width;
    int height;
    int frameworkFormat;
    int format;
    int glFormat;
    int glType;
    int ashmemSize;

    union {
        intptr_t ashmemBase;
        uint64_t padding;
    } __attribute__((aligned(8)));

    int ashmemBasePid;
    int mappedPid;
    int lockedLeft;
    int lockedTop;
    int lockedWidth;
    int lockedHeight;
    uint32_t hostHandle;
};
```

Because `cb_handle_t` is a large data structure, in the preceding code snippet we did not show all the member functions of `cb_handle_t`. From the member variables, we can see that they are similar to `private_handle_t`. You can refer to the section on `private_handle_t` for an explanation of most member variables. Pay attention to the last member variable, `hostHandle`, which is used to store the buffer allocated on GPU (the host side in GLES emulation). If you are interested in host side GLES emulation, you can refer to the QEMU source code.

Let's look at the last piece of code for `gralloc_alloc`:

```
//
// alloc succeeded - insert the allocated handle to the allocated
// list
//
AllocListNode *node = new AllocListNode();
pthread_mutex_lock(&grdev->lock);
node->handle = cb;
node->next =  grdev->allocListHead;
node->prev =  NULL;
if (grdev->allocListHead) {
    grdev->allocListHead->prev = node;
}
```

```
    grdev->allocListHead = node;
    pthread_mutex_unlock(&grdev->lock);

    *pHandle = cb;
    if (frameworkFormat == HAL_PIXEL_FORMAT_YCbCr_420_888) {
        *pStride = 0;
    } else {
        *pStride = stride;
    }
    return 0;
}
```

After the buffer is allocated on GPU and the shared memory region is acquired from the system memory, they are stored in the `grdev` variable and added to a linked list node to the double linked list in `gralloc_device_t`.

For the `free` method of `gralloc_device_t`, it is much simpler than `alloc`. To save space, I won't list the source code here. The `free` method is implemented in the `gralloc_free` function. What it does is:

1. Validate the `buffer_handle_t` point to a valid `cb_handle_t` data structure.
2. Release the buffer on the host side (GPU), calling the `rcCloseColorBuffer` function.
3. Un-map the buffer in the shared memory region and release the shared memory.
4. Remove the node from the linked list.
5. Free the memory used by the `cb_handle_t` data structure.

FB0 device implementation

For the implementation of the `FB0` device, we will look at the `post` method as we did for the default Gralloc module analysis. This is implemented in the `fb_post` function and we can look at the implementation as follows:

```
static int fb_post(struct framebuffer_device_t* dev, buffer_handle_t
buffer)
{
    fb_device_t *fbdev = (fb_device_t *)dev;
    cb_handle_t *cb = (cb_handle_t *)buffer;

    if (!fbdev || !cb_handle_t::validate(cb) || !cb->canBePosted()) {
        return -EINVAL;
    }
```

```
    // Make sure we have host connection
    DEFINE_AND_VALIDATE_HOST_CONNECTION;

    // increment the post count of the buffer
    intptr_t *postCountPtr = (intptr_t *)cb->ashmemBase;
    if (!postCountPtr) {
        // This should not happen
        return -EINVAL;
    }
    (*postCountPtr)++;

    // send post request to host
    rcEnc->rcFBPost(rcEnc, cb->hostHandle);
    hostCon->flush();

    return 0;
}
```

What it does is very simple; it increases the post count of the buffer and calls to the rcFBpost function to update the buffer in GPU.

We have completed our analysis of Android emulator graphics HAL now. I hope the analysis of the generic graphics HAL and Android emulator graphics HAL has helped you understand the graphics HAL in your system.

Summary

In this chapter, we explored and reviewed two Gralloc HAL module implementations, the default Gralloc module and the one used by Android emulator. The default Gralloc HAL uses framebuffer devices only and the OpenGLES support uses a software implementation. The one used by Android emulator is a hardware emulation on the host side. The implementation is similar to the GPU-based Gralloc module.

Since graphics systems are so complex, we will continue exploring this topic a little more when looking at VirtualBox-specific implementation in the next chapter. We will explain the loading process of Gralloc HAL and OpenGL ES libraries. We will build a VirtualBox extension pack for Android so that we can utilize the capability provided by VirtualBox.

11
Enabling VirtualBox-Specific Hardware Interfaces

In the last chapter, we did a deep analysis of Android Gralloc HAL modules. We analyzed the default Gralloc module and the hardware GPU emulation Gralloc HAL for the Android emulator. We don't have time to walk through the boot up process related to the graphics system yet. In this chapter, we will walk through the boot up process of the graphics system and explore the VirtualBox-specific hardware drivers. At the end of this chapter, we will have a relatively complete system on VirtualBox. We will cover the following topics in this chapter:

- OpenGL ES and graphics hardware initialization
- Integration of VirtualBox Guest Additions

OpenGL ES and graphics hardware initialization

In Android systems, the initialization of the graphics system is done by SurfaceFlinger. Besides the Gralloc HAL that we discussed in `Chapter 10`, *Enabling Graphics*, another important part of graphics system initialization is the loading of OpenGL ES libraries. In our VirtualBox implementation, we use most of the HAL modules from Android-x86. The graphics system support includes the following components:

- Gralloc HAL
- Mesa lib for OpenGL ES
- uvesafb framebuffer driver or VirtualBox video driver

We have discussed Gralloc HAL in the last chapter. We will explore the loading of the OpenGL ES library and uvesafb framebuffer driver in this chapter. We will use the default uvesafb framebuffer driver in the introduction of graphics system initialization. We will also introduce how to use the native graphic driver from VirtualBox when we talk about the integration of VirtualBox Guest Additions later in this chapter.

Loading OpenGL ES libraries

OpenGL ES stands for **Open GL Embedded System**, which is a subset of OpenGL from Khronos. EGL is an interface between OpenGL ES and the underlying native platform. The API of EGL is supposed to be platform-agnostic, but the implementation of the EGL API is not.

The implementation of OpenGL ES in Android includes the Java API and native implementation. These two parts can be found at:

- Java API: `$AOSP/frameworks/base/opengl`
- OpenGL ES native: `$AOSP/frameworks/native/opengl`

These two parts of the OpenGL implementation depend on a vendor implementation to provide the full function of the OpenGL ES API. During the system start-up, the system will search for paths `/system/lib/egl` or `/vendor/lib/egl` to find the vendor OpenGL libraries.

The OpenGL ES vendor libraries should follow the following naming conventions. If the vendor library is a single library, it should use the name as `libGLES_*.so`. In our case, the OpenGL ES library for VirtualBox is `libGLES_mesa.so`, which is provided as a single library.

If the vendor libraries are provided as separate libraries, they must be something like the following:

- `/system/lib/egl/libEGL_*.so`
- `/system/lib/egl/libGLESv1_CM_*.so`
- `/system/lib/egl/libGLESv2_*.so`

This is the case for the Android emulator hardware emulation libraries. We can find the following ones for the Android emulator:

- `/system/lib/egl/libEGL_emulation.so`
- `/system/lib/egl/libGLESv1_CM_emulation.so`
- `/system/lib/egl/libGLESv2_emulation.so`

The vendor libraries are loaded during the `SurfaceFlinger` initialization. Before we go to the details about the start up process, let's have a look at the message from the debug log first.

I removed the timestamp from the following log so that we can have a better format:

```
I SurfaceFlinger: SurfaceFlinger is starting
I SurfaceFlinger: SurfaceFlinger's main thread ready to run. Initializing
graphics H/W...
D libEGL  : loaded /system/lib/egl/libGLES_mesa.so
W linker  : /system/lib/libglapi.so has text relocations. This is wasting
memory and prevents security hardening. Please fix.
I HAL     : loaded HAL id=gralloc path=/system/lib/hw/gralloc.default.so
hmi=0x5 handle=0xb7145664
I EGL-DRI2: found extension DRI_Core version 1
I EGL-DRI2: found extension DRI_SWRast version 5
I EGL-DRI2: found extension DRI_TexBuffer version 2
I EGL-DRI2: found extension DRI_IMAGE version 11
I HAL     : loaded HAL id=gralloc path=/system/lib/hw/gralloc.default.so
hmi=0x0 handle=0xb7145664
I powerbtn: open event0(Power Button) ok fd=4
W gralloc : page flipping not supported (yres_virtual=768, requested=1536)
I gralloc : using (fd=12)
I gralloc : id            = VESA VGA
I gralloc : xres          = 1024 px
I gralloc : yres          = 768 px
I gralloc : xres_virtual  = 1024 px
I gralloc : yres_virtual  = 768 px
I gralloc : bpp           = 32
I gralloc : r             = 16:8
I gralloc : g             =  8:8
I gralloc : b             =  0:8
I gralloc : a             = 24:8
I gralloc : stride        = 4096
I gralloc : fbSize        = 12582912
I gralloc : width         = 163 mm (159.568100 dpi)
I gralloc : height        = 122 mm (159.895081 dpi)
I gralloc : refresh rate  = 65.46 Hz
E SurfaceFlinger: hwcomposer module not found
```

As we can see, when the main thread of `SurfaceFlinger` is ready to run, it loads the `/system/lib/egl/libGLES_mesa.so` library during the x86vbox device boot up. After that, it loads and initializes the `gralloc.default.so` Gralloc module:

```
I SurfaceFlinger: EGL information:
I SurfaceFlinger: vendor    : Android
I SurfaceFlinger: version   : 1.4 Android META-EGL
I SurfaceFlinger: extensions: EGL_KHR_get_all_proc_addresses
EGL_ANDROID_presentation_time EGL_KHR_swap_buffers_with_damage
EGL_KHR_image_base EGL_KHR_gl_texture_2D_image EGL_KHR_gl_texture_3D_image
EGL_KHR_gl_texture_cubemap_image EGL_KHR_gl_renderbuffer_image
EGL_KHR_reusable_sync EGL_KHR_fence_sync EGL_KHR_create_context
EGL_KHR_surfaceless_context EGL_ANDROID_image_native_buffer
EGL_KHR_wait_sync EGL_ANDROID_recordable
I SurfaceFlinger: Client API: OpenGL_ES
I SurfaceFlinger: EGLSurface: 8-8-8-8, config=0xb46a3800
```

Next, `SurfaceFlinger` initializes the EGL library as the preceding log message. The EGL version in our environment is 1.4:

```
I SurfaceFlinger: OpenGL ES informations:
I SurfaceFlinger: vendor    : VMware, Inc.
I SurfaceFlinger: renderer  : Gallium 0.4 on llvmpipe (LLVM 3.7, 256 bits)
I SurfaceFlinger: version   : OpenGL ES 3.0 Mesa 12.0.1 (git-c3bb2e3)
I SurfaceFlinger: extensions: GL_EXT_blend_minmax GL_EXT_multi_draw_arrays
GL_EXT_texture_compression_dxt1 GL_EXT_texture_format_BGRA8888
GL_OES_compressed_ETC1_RGB8_texture GL_OES_depth24
GL_OES_element_index_uint GL_OES_fbo_render_mipmap GL_OES_mapbuffer
GL_OES_rgb8_rgba8 GL_OES_standard_derivatives GL_OES_stencil8
GL_OES_texture_3D GL_OES_texture_float GL_OES_texture_float_linear
GL_OES_texture_half_float GL_OES_texture_half_float_linear
GL_OES_texture_npot GL_EXT_texture_sRGB_decode GL_OES_EGL_image
GL_OES_depth_texture GL_OES_packed_depth_stencil
GL_EXT_texture_type_2_10_10_10_REV GL_OES_get_program_binary
GL_APPLE_texture_max_level GL_EXT_discard_framebuffer
GL_EXT_read_format_bgra GL_NV_fbo_color_attachments
GL_OES_EGL_image_external GL_OES_EGL_sync GL_OES_vertex_array_object
GL_ANGLE_texture_compression_dxt3 GL_ANGLE_texture_compression_dxt5
GL_EXT_texture_rg GL_EXT_unpack_subimage GL_NV_draw_buffers
GL_NV_read_buffer GL_NV_read_depth GL_NV_read_depth_stencil
GL_NV_read_stencil GL_EXT_draw_buffers GL_EXT_map_buffer_ra
I SurfaceFlinger: GL_MAX_TEXTURE_SIZE = 8192
I SurfaceFlinger: GL_MAX_VIEWPORT_DIMS = 8192
D SurfaceFlinger: Open /dev/tty0 OK
I HAL      : loaded HAL id=gralloc path=/system/lib/hw/gralloc.default.so
hmi=0xb769a108 handle=0xb7145664
I HAL      : loaded HAL id=gralloc path=/system/lib/hw/gralloc.default.so
```

```
hmi=0xb769a108 handle=0xb7145664
D SurfaceFlinger: Set power mode=2, type=0 flinger=0xb70e2000
D SurfaceFlinger: shader cache generated - 24 shaders in 25.081509 ms
```

After EGL initialization, the OpenGL ES library is initialized, as we can see from the preceding log message. We can see that OpenGL ES 3.0 is supported by the Mesa library. The rendering engine is a software implementation using Gallium with `llvmpipe`.

 Each graphics hardware vendor usually has their own implementation of OpenGL. Mesa is an open source implementation of OpenGL. Mesa has multiple backends for OpenGL support. It can support both hardware and software implementation according to the hardware GPU. If you don't have a hardware GPU, Mesa has three CPU-based implementations: swrast, softpipe, and llvmpipe. The one that we used in x86vbox is llvmpipe. There are two architectures for Mesa driver implementation. Gallium is the new architecture for the Mesa driver implementation.

Analyzing the loading process

After we have a general introduction about OpenGL ES implementation in x86vbox (reuse from Android-x86), we will analyze the source code to have another level of understanding. Since the detail implementation of graphics systems and OpenGL ES is huge, we won't be able to cover them in a chapter. We will focus on the loading process of graphics systems and the OpenGL ES library in our analysis.

 Again, you may feel frustrated while we walk through the source code. The best way to help with this is to open your source code editor while you read this chapter. If you don't have AOSP source code at hand, you can always refer to the following website:
http://xref.opersys.com/
You can just search for the function name that we discuss in this chapter to locate the source code.

From the preceding debug log, we will start from the point where we see the first debug message related to the graphics system and `SurfaceFlinger`, as follows:

```
I SurfaceFlinger: SurfaceFlinger is starting
I SurfaceFlinger: SurfaceFlinger's main thread ready to run. Initializing
graphics H/W...
```

The first message is printed by the constructor of `SurfaceFlinger` and the second message is printed out from the `init` method of `SurfaceFlinger`.

The source code of `SurfaceFlinger` can be found at:
`$AOSP/frameworks/native/services/surfaceflinger/SurfaceFlinger.cpp`.

We will start our analysis from **SurfaceFlinger:init**, according to the flow shown in the following diagram:

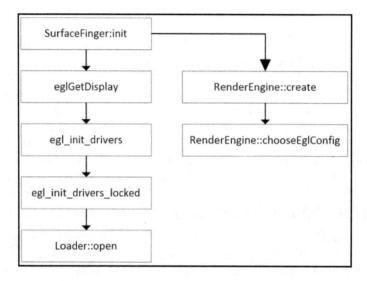

Loading of OpenGL ES libraries

In `SurfaceFlinger:init`, as shown in the following code snippet, it calls the EGL function `eglGetDisplay` first. After that, it tries to create a hardware composer instance. With the instances of display `mEGLDisplay` and hardware composer `mHwc`, it creates a rendering engine using the underlying OpenGL ES implementation:

```
void SurfaceFlinger::init() {
    ALOGI( "SurfaceFlinger's main thread ready to run. "
           "Initializing graphics H/W...");

    Mutex::Autolock _l(mStateLock);

    // initialize EGL for the default display
    mEGLDisplay = eglGetDisplay(EGL_DEFAULT_DISPLAY);
    eglInitialize(mEGLDisplay, NULL, NULL);

    ...

    // Initialize the H/W composer object.  There may or may not
    // be an actual hardware composer underneath.
    mHwc = new HWComposer(this,
```

```
        *static_cast<HWComposer::EventHandler *>(this));

    // get a RenderEngine for the given display / config
    mRenderEngine = RenderEngine::create(mEGLDisplay, mHwc-
    >getVisualID());

    // retrieve the EGL context that was selected/created
    mEGLContext = mRenderEngine->getEGLContext();
```

Let's analyze the EGL function `eglGetDisplay` first. The `eglGetDisplay` function is implemented in the `frameworks/native/opengl/libs/EGL/eglApi.cpp` file, as shown in the following code snippet:

```
EGLDisplay eglGetDisplay(EGLNativeDisplayType display)
{
    clearError();

    uintptr_t index = reinterpret_cast<uintptr_t>(display);
    if (index >= NUM_DISPLAYS) {
        return setError(EGL_BAD_PARAMETER, EGL_NO_DISPLAY);
    }

    if (egl_init_drivers() == EGL_FALSE) {
        return setError(EGL_BAD_PARAMETER, EGL_NO_DISPLAY);
    }

    EGLDisplay dpy = egl_display_t::getFromNativeDisplay(display);
    return dpy;
}
```

In `eglGetDisplay`, it checks the index of display to be initialized first. In the current Android code, the `EGL_DEFAULT_DISPLAY` parameter is zero and the definition of `NUM_DISPLAYS` is 1. This means it can only support one display in the current Android implementation. What does this mean here? For example, if you have a laptop, you can connect it to a projector. In this case, you can have two displays at the same time. Some new computers can even connect to three displays at the same time nowadays. After checking the number of displays, it calls the `egl_init_drivers` function to load the OpenGL ES libraries:

```
static EGLBoolean egl_init_drivers_locked() {
    if (sEarlyInitState) {
        // initialized by static ctor. should be set here.
        return EGL_FALSE;
    }

    // get our driver loader
    Loader& loader(Loader::getInstance());
```

```
        // dynamically load our EGL implementation
        egl_connection_t* cnx = &gEGLImpl;
        if (cnx->dso == 0) {
            cnx->hooks[egl_connection_t::GLESv1_INDEX] =
                    &gHooks[egl_connection_t::GLESv1_INDEX];
            cnx->hooks[egl_connection_t::GLESv2_INDEX] =
                    &gHooks[egl_connection_t::GLESv2_INDEX];
            cnx->dso = loader.open(cnx);
        }

        return cnx->dso ? EGL_TRUE : EGL_FALSE;
    }

    static pthread_mutex_t sInitDriverMutex = PTHREAD_MUTEX_INITIALIZER;

    EGLBoolean egl_init_drivers() {
        EGLBoolean res;
        pthread_mutex_lock(&sInitDriverMutex);
        res = egl_init_drivers_locked();
        pthread_mutex_unlock(&sInitDriverMutex);
        return res;
    }
```

The `egl_init_drivers` function acquires a mutex and calls to another function, `egl_init_drivers_locked`, to load the OpenGL ES libraries. In the `egl_init_drivers_locked` function, it gets an instance of a `Loader` class, which is defined using the **singleton pattern**. After that, it initializes the global variable `gEGLImpl`, which is defined as the data structure `egl_connection_t`:

```
    struct egl_connection_t {
        enum {
            GLESv1_INDEX = 0,
            GLESv2_INDEX = 1
        };

        inline egl_connection_t() : dso(0) { }
        void *              dso;
        gl_hooks_t *        hooks[2];
        EGLint              major;
        EGLint              minor;
        egl_t               egl;

        void*               libEgl;
        void*               libGles1;
        void*               libGles2;
    };
```

In the `egl_connection_t` data structure, it defines the following fields:

- `dso`: This is a pointer that points to a `driver_t` data structure defined inside the `Loader` class. This `driver_t` data structure stores the handle of OpenGL ES libraries after they are loaded by the `Loader` class.

- `hooks`: This is an array of the pointers of the `gl_hooks_t` data structure. The `gl_hooks_t` data structure is used to define all the function pointers of the OpenGL ES API. After the OpenGL ES libraries are loaded, the OpenGL ES functions inside the libraries will be initialized and assigned to the `hooks` field. There are two OpenGL ES versions that are defined in enum { GLESv1_INDEX , GLESv2_INDEX }. The `hooks[GLESv1_INDEX]` is used to store OpenGL ES version 1 APIs and it points to the `gHooks[GLESv1_INDEX]` global variable. The same is for GLESv2_INDEX. The list of OpenGL ES APIs can be found in the following file: `$AOSP/frameworks/native/opengl/libs/entries.in`

- `major` and `minor`: These two are used to store the EGL version.

- `egl`: This is defined as `egl_t`, which is used to store the EGL APIs. The list of EGL APIs can be found in the following file: `$AOSP/frameworks/native/opengl/libs/EGL/egl_entries.in`

- `libEgl`, `libGles1`, and `libGles2`: These are the handles of OpenGL ES wrapper libraries. We will see the initialization of these libraries in a moment.

After the `cnx` data structure is initialized, it calls the `loader.open` function to load the libraries. Let's look at the `loader.open` function:

```
void* Loader::open(egl_connection_t* cnx)
{
    void* dso;
    driver_t* hnd = 0;

    dso = load_driver("GLES", cnx, EGL | GLESv1_CM | GLESv2);
    if (dso) {
        hnd = new driver_t(dso);
    } else {
        // Always load EGL first
        dso = load_driver("EGL", cnx, EGL);
        if (dso) {
            hnd = new driver_t(dso);
            hnd->set( load_driver("GLESv1_CM", cnx, GLESv1_CM),
            GLESv1_CM );
            hnd->set( load_driver("GLESv2",    cnx, GLESv2),    GLESv2 );
        }
    }
```

```
        LOG_ALWAYS_FATAL_IF(!hnd, "couldn't find an OpenGL ES
        implementation");

#if defined(__LP64__)
    cnx->libEgl   = load_wrapper("/system/lib64/libEGL.so");
    cnx->libGles2 = load_wrapper("/system/lib64/libGLESv2.so");
    cnx->libGles1 = load_wrapper("/system/lib64/libGLESv1_CM.so");
#else
    cnx->libEgl   = load_wrapper("/system/lib/libEGL.so");
    cnx->libGles2 = load_wrapper("/system/lib/libGLESv2.so");
    cnx->libGles1 = load_wrapper("/system/lib/libGLESv1_CM.so");
#endif
    LOG_ALWAYS_FATAL_IF(!cnx->libEgl,
            "couldn't load system EGL wrapper libraries");

    LOG_ALWAYS_FATAL_IF(!cnx->libGles2 || !cnx->libGles1,
            "couldn't load system OpenGL ES wrapper libraries");

    return (void*)hnd;
}
```

In `Loader::open`, it tries to load a single OpenGL ES library first. If it fails, it tries to load the separated libraries one by one. If the libraries are loaded successfully, it stores the handles to the `driver_t` data structure. We explained about `driver_t` previously when we talked about the `dso` field in the `egl_connection_t` data structure. The actual loading process is done in the `load_driver` function and we will look at it soon. After the OpenGL ES libraries are loaded, it also tries to load the wrapper libraries using the `load_wrapper` function. The `load_wrapper` function just calls the `dlopen` system call and returns the handle so we don't need to investigate it.

Loading the driver

Let's analyze the `load_driver` function, which is the one that finds and loads the OpenGL ES user space driver:

```
    void *Loader::load_driver(const char* kind,
            egl_connection_t* cnx, uint32_t mask)
    {
        class MatchFile {
        public:
            static String8 find(const char* kind) {
        ...
        };
```

```
String8 absolutePath = MatchFile::find(kind);
if (absolutePath.isEmpty()) {
    // this happens often, we don't want to log an error
    return 0;
}
const char* const driver_absolute_path = absolutePath.string();

void* dso = dlopen(driver_absolute_path, RTLD_NOW | RTLD_LOCAL);
if (dso == 0) {
    const char* err = dlerror();
    ALOGE("load_driver(%s): %s", driver_absolute_path, err?
    err:"unknown");
    return 0;
}

ALOGD("loaded %s", driver_absolute_path);

if (mask & EGL) {
    getProcAddress = (getProcAddressType)dlsym(dso,
    "eglGetProcAddress");

    ALOGE_IF(!getProcAddress,
            "can't find eglGetProcAddress() in %s",
            driver_absolute_path);

    egl_t* egl = &cnx->egl;
    __eglMustCastToProperFunctionPointerType* curr =
        (__eglMustCastToProperFunctionPointerType*)egl;
    char const * const * api = egl_names;
    while (*api) {
        char const * name = *api;
        __eglMustCastToProperFunctionPointerType f =
            (__eglMustCastToProperFunctionPointerType)dlsym(dso,
            name);
        if (f == NULL) {
            // couldn't find the entry-point, use
            // eglGetProcAddress()

            f = getProcAddress(name);
            if (f == NULL) {
                f = (__eglMustCastToProperFunctionPointerType)0;
            }
        }
        *curr++ = f;
        api++;
    }
}
```

```
    if (mask & GLESv1_CM) {
        init_api(dso, gl_names,
            (__eglMustCastToProperFunctionPointerType*)
                &cnx->hooks[egl_connection_t::GLESv1_INDEX]->gl,
            getProcAddress);
    }

    if (mask & GLESv2) {
      init_api(dso, gl_names,
            (__eglMustCastToProperFunctionPointerType*)
                &cnx->hooks[egl_connection_t::GLESv2_INDEX]->gl,
            getProcAddress);
    }

    return dso;
  }
```

In the `load_driver` function, it defines a `MatchFile` inner class. It uses the
`MatchFile::find` method to find the path of the libraries. The `load_driver` function has
three parameters: `kind`, `cnx`, and `mask`. According to the kind of libraries, the parameter
kind could be `GLES`, `EGL`, `GLESv1_CM`, or `GLESv2`. Once it gets the absolute path of a library,
it calls the `dlopen` system function to open the shared library. The `mask` parameter is a bit
map of the `kind` parameter. Using the `mask` parameter, it can initialize the `cnx` parameter
according to the kind of library. As we mentioned before, the `cnx` parameter, which is an
instance of `egl_connection_t`, has an `egl` field to store all the EGL function pointers. It
has another field, `hooks[GLESv1_INDEX]/ hooks[GLESv2_INDEX]`, to store all OpenGL
ES functions.

If the library type is EGL, it gets the address of the `eglGetProcAddress` function by first
calling the `dlsym` system function. After that, it will loop through all the function names
defined in the `egl_names` global variable to find out the addresses and store them in
`cnx->egl`. During the process, it tries to get the address using the `dlsym` system function
first. If the call to `dlsym` fails, it will try it again using the `eglGetProcAddress` function.

If the library type is either `GLESv1_CM` or `GLESv2`, it calls another function, `init_api`, to
initialize all OpenGL ES function pointers. In the `init_api` function, it will loop through
all the function names defined in the `gl_names` global variable to find out the addresses
and store them in `cnx->hooks[egl_connection_t::GLESv?_INDEX]->gl`.

Now we have done all the initialization of the OpenGL ES user space drivers and we can
use the `egl_connection_t` data structure to access all OpenGL ES vendor APIs.

Creating the rendering engine

After the OpenGL ES vendor libraries are loaded, `SurfaceFlinger:init` will create the rendering engine:

```
mRenderEngine = RenderEngine::create(mEGLDisplay, mHwc->getVisualID());
```

Inside `RenderEngine::create`, it will call `RenderEngine::chooseEglConfig`, which will print out the debug message for EGL:

```
EGLConfig RenderEngine::chooseEglConfig(EGLDisplay display, int format) {
    status_t err;
    EGLConfig config;

    // First try to get an ES2 config
    err = selectEGLConfig(display, format, EGL_OPENGL_ES2_BIT,
    &config);
    ...
    eglGetConfigAttrib(display, config, EGL_ALPHA_SIZE, &a);
    ALOGI("EGL information:");
    ALOGI("vendor    : %s", eglQueryString(display, EGL_VENDOR));
    ALOGI("version   : %s", eglQueryString(display, EGL_VERSION));
    ALOGI("extensions: %s", eglQueryString(display, EGL_EXTENSIONS));
    ALOGI("Client API: %s", eglQueryString(display,
    EGL_CLIENT_APIS)?:"Not
    Supported");
    ALOGI("EGLSurface: %d-%d-%d-%d, config=%p", r, g, b, a, config);

    return config;
}
```

At the end of `RenderEngine::create`, it will print out the OpenGL ES initialization information as follows:

```
RenderEngine* RenderEngine::create(EGLDisplay display, int hwcFormat) {
    EGLConfig config = EGL_NO_CONFIG;
    if (!findExtension(
            eglQueryStringImplementationANDROID(display,
            EGL_EXTENSIONS),
            "EGL_ANDROIDX_no_config_context")) {
        config = chooseEglConfig(display, hwcFormat);
    }

    ...

    engine->setEGLHandles(config, ctxt);

    ALOGI("OpenGL ES informations:");
```

```
        ALOGI("vendor    : %s", extensions.getVendor());
        ALOGI("renderer  : %s", extensions.getRenderer());
        ALOGI("version   : %s", extensions.getVersion());
        ALOGI("extensions: %s", extensions.getExtension());
        ALOGI("GL_MAX_TEXTURE_SIZE = %zu", engine->getMaxTextureSize());
        ALOGI("GL_MAX_VIEWPORT_DIMS = %zu", engine->getMaxViewportDims());

        eglMakeCurrent(display, EGL_NO_SURFACE, EGL_NO_SURFACE,
        EGL_NO_CONTEXT);
        eglDestroySurface(display, dummy);

        return engine;
}
```

The uvesafb framebuffer driver

Th framebuffer driver is the third component that we need to support the graphics system for x86vbox. Since you may run VirtualBox on different Intel devices, they may use different graphics hardware, such as Nvidia, AMD, or Intel. To get the best performance in a virtualization environment, you may want to explore various GPU virtualization technologies, such as GPU passthrough, GPU sharing, GPU software emulation, and so on. To have a simple solution, we use the default solution from Android-x86, which is the uvesafb framebuffer driver.

What is uvesafb?

The uvesafb is a user space VESA framebuffer driver that works with VESA 2.0-compliant graphic cards. VESA BIOS extensions provide the primary functionality of VESA standard through the BIOS interface. On Linux, uvesafb needs a user space daemon called `v86d` as a backend for kernel drivers that need to execute x86 BIOS code. Since BIOS code can only be executed in a controlled environment, the code executed by `v86d` can be run either in a fully software-emulated environment or a virtualized environment supported by the CPU. The `v86d` has been ported to Android by the Android-x86 project. It can be found at `$AOSP/external/v86d`. Since the `v86d` project needs additional system calls such as `ioperm` and `iopl`, the Android-x86 project changed the bionic library to support these system calls.

You can refer to the following kernel document to find out more about uvesafb:

`https://www.kernel.org/doc/Documentation/fb/uvesafb.txt`

Testing the uvesafb framebuffer driver

Before we try to understand how uvesafb is loaded in our environment, we can test it using two framebuffer testing tools, `fbset` and `fbtest`.

As we know, we can boot to a debug console using two stages boot of Android-x86 from `Chapter 9`, *Booting Up x86vbox Using PXE/NFS*. We can test uvesafb in the debug console with `fbset` and `fbtest`.

`fbset` is a system tool to show or change the settings of the framebuffer device. You can refer to the help page of Linux commands to find out how to use `fbset`. In our environment, we use `busybox` in the first stage boot and we use `toybox` or `toolbox` in the Android environment. `fbset` is supported by `busybox`, so we can use it in the first stage or the second stage boot through `busybox`.

`fbtest` is a framebuffer test program that can be found at `https://git.kernel.org/pub/s cm/linux/kernel/git/geert/fbtest.git`.

I cloned it from the kernel Git repository and ported it to the Android environment. The source code for Android can be found at GitHub via the following link:

`https://github.com/shugaoye/fbtest`

To build `fbtest`, we can get it from GitHub and build it in the AOSP build environment:

```
$ cd {your AOSP root folder}
$ source build/envsetup.sh
$ lunch x86vbox-eng
```

After we set up the AOSP build environment, we can check out and build the `fbtest` source code using the following commands:

```
$ cd $HOME
$ git clone https://github.com/shugaoye/fbtest
$ cd fbtest
$ git checkout -b android-x86 remotes/origin/android-x86
$ make
```

Be aware that I changed the Makefile and that it depends on the AOSP environment variable $OUT, as follows:

```
# Paths and settings
TARGET_PRODUCT = x86vbox
ANDROID_ROOT   = $(OUT)/../../../..
BIONIC_LIBC    = $(ANDROID_ROOT)/bionic/libc
PRODUCT_OUT    = $(ANDROID_ROOT)/out/target/product/$(TARGET_PRODUCT)
CROSS_COMPILE  = \
    $(ANDROID_ROOT)/prebuilts/gcc/linux-x86/x86/x86_64-linux-android-
    4.9/bin/x86_64-linux-android-

ARCH_NAME = x86

# Tool names
AS             = $(CROSS_COMPILE)as
AR             = $(CROSS_COMPILE)ar
...
```

If we look at the preceding `fbtest/Rules.make` Makefile, we use the $OUT environment variable to find the right AOSP build environment. After that, we can use prebuilt toolchains and the `bionic` library to build `fbtest`.

After we build `fbtest`, we can copy it to the `$OUT/system/bin` folder so that we can use it in the test environment later. As we remember from Chapter 9, *Booting Up x86vbox Using PXE/NFS*, we can boot to a debug console in the first stage boot using PXE/NFS. In this case, we can change and test `fbtest` without rebooting the x86vbox, since we can access the build result through NFS from x86vbox.

Let's boot x86vbox to the debug console in the first stage boot and perform the tests. As we recall, we have a minimal embedded Linux environment in the debug console of the first stage boot. We have a built-in `busybox` available in this environment. Before we test the framebuffer device, we must load the `uvesafb` module manually, as shown in the following screenshot:

```
●●●   android [x86vbox-eng]
[    19.231321] input: PC Speaker as /devices/platform/pcspkr/input/input6
[    19.274185] EXT4-fs (sda1): re-mounted. Opts: (null)

Use Alt-F1/F2/F3 to switch between virtual consoles
Type 'exit' to enter Android...

Running MirBSD Korn Shell...
(debug-late)@android:/android # [    19.467963] input: ImExPS/2 Generic Explorer7
[    20.637084] random: nonblocking pool is initialized

(debug-late)@android:/android # system/xbin/modprobe uvesafb
[    26.077421] uvesafb: Unknown symbol cn_netlink_send (err 0)
[    26.081162] uvesafb: Unknown symbol cn_del_callback (err 0)
[    26.084093] uvesafb: Unknown symbol cn_add_callback (err 0)
[    26.107968] uvesafb: Oracle Corporation, Oracle VM VirtualBox VBE Adapter, 00
[    26.145120] uvesafb: protected mode interface info at c000:4400
[  . 26.146246] uvesafb: pmi: set display start = c00c444f, set palette = c00c450
[    26.148204] uvesafb: pmi: ports = 1ce 1cf 1cf 1d0 3b6 3b7
[    26.149397] uvesafb: no monitor limits have been set, default refresh rate wd
[    26.152209] uvesafb: scrolling: ypan using protected mode interface, yres_vi0
[    26.159437] Console: switching to colour frame buffer device 80x30
[    26.164749] uvesafb: framebuffer at 0xe0000000, mapped to 0xf8c00000, using k
[    26.166195] fb0: VESA VGA frame buffer device
(debug-late)@android:/android # █
```

We use the following command to load the uvesafb module:

```
(debug-late)@android: /android # system/xbin/modprobe uvesafb
```

From the debug output, we can see that the underlying graphic hardware is Oracle VM VirtualBox VBE Adapter.

After the uvesafb module is loaded, we can find the /dev/fb0 device. We can use fbset to change the settings of the framebuffer device. For example, we can switch to different supported resolutions as we want. Let's just run the fbset command and see what happens. If we run fbset without any parameters, we can see the following output:

```
(debug-late)@android:/android # fbset

mode "640x480-60"
        # D: 23.845 MHz, H: 29.844 kHz, V: 60.048 Hz
        geometry 640 480 640 9830 16
        timings 41937 80 16 13 1 63 3
        accel false
        rgba 5/11,6/5,5/0,0/0
endmode
```

If `fbset` is run without any parameters, it just prints out the current settings of the framebuffer device. As we can see from the output, if we load `uvesafb` without any parameters, the default resolution is 640 x 480 in 16-bit colors.

We can try to change the resolution with the name of the resolution as follows:

```
(debug-late)@android:/android # fbset vga
fbset: /etc/fb.modes: No such file or directory
fbset: unknown video mode 'vga'
```

We got an error message that tells us that the resolution is not defined in the `/etc/fb.modes` file. We need to create this file to change resolutions. We can add the following resolutions in `/etc/fb.modes` as follows:

```
mode "640x480-60"
        # D: 23.845 MHz, H: 29.844 kHz, V: 60.048 Hz
        geometry 640 480 640 9830 16
        timings 41937 80 16 13 1 63 3
        accel false
        rgba 5/11,6/5,5/0,0/0
endmode

mode "1024x768-60"
        # D: 64.033 MHz, H: 47.714 kHz, V: 60.018 Hz
        geometry 1024 768 1024 768 32
        timings 15617 159 52 23 1 107 3
        accel false
        rgba 8/16,8/8,8/0,8/24
endmode
```

Now we can test the resolution change. If we run the following command, we can change to a higher resolution with true color:

```
(debug-late)@android:/android # fbset 1024x768-60
```

After we load the framebuffer driver and test the configuration changes, we can test the framebuffer by drawing something on the screen. Using the `fbtest` command that we built in this section, we can run a set of framebuffer test cases. First, let's find out how many test cases `fbtest` can run:

```
(debug-late)@android:/android # fbtest -f /dev/fb0 -l
Listing all tests
test001: Draw a 16x12 checkerboard pattern
test002: Draw a grid and some circles
test003: Draw the 16 Linux console colors
test004: Show the penguins
test005: Draw the default color palette
```

```
test006: Draw grayscale bands
test007: DirectColor test
test008: Draw the UV color space
test009: Show the penguins using copy_rect
test010: Hello world
test011: Panning test
test012: Filling squares
```

If we run `fbtest` with the `-l` option, it prints out the list of test cases available. We can see that we have 12 test cases:

```
(debug-late)@android:/android # fbtest -f /dev/fb0 test002
```

As an example, we can run test case 002 and we will see the following screen. Feel free to test any of the preceding test cases yourself.

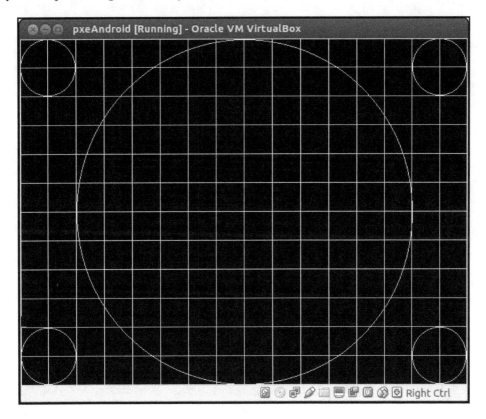

Initializing uvesafb in x86vbox

The initialization of uvesafb in x86vbox is done in the start up script init.sh. If we recall the discussion on HAL initialization in Chapter 8, *Creating Your Own Device on VirtualBox*, we can see the following code in init.sh. We discussed the initialization of graphics HAL in Chapter 8, *Creating Your Own Device on VirtualBox* briefly, and we can look into the details now:

```
function init_uvesafb()
{
    case "$PRODUCT" in
        ET2002*)
            UVESA_MODE=${UVESA_MODE:-1600x900}
            ;;
        *)
            ;;
    esac

    [ "$HWACCEL" = "0" ] && bpp=16 || bpp=32
    modprobe uvesafb mode_option=${UVESA_MODE:-1024x768}-$bpp
${UVESA_OPTION:-
    mtrr=3 scroll=redraw}
}

function init_hal_gralloc()
{
    case "$(cat /proc/fb | head -1)" in
        *virtiodrmfb)
#            set_property ro.hardware.hwcomposer drm
            ;&
        0*inteldrmfb|0*radeondrmfb|0*nouveaufb|0*svgadrmfb)
            set_property ro.hardware.gralloc drm
            set_drm_mode
            ;;
        "")
            init_uvesafb
            ;&
        0*)
            ;;
    esac

    [ -n "$DEBUG" ] && set_property debug.egl.trace error
}
```

In our current setup, let's see what the content of /proc/fb is. We can check this from either the debug console or the adb console. Before a framebuffer device is initialized, the content of /proc/fb is empty. In our case, it is empty, since there is no framebuffer device available until the init.sh script is executed. If the output is empty, the init.sh script will call the init_uvesafb function to initialize uvesafb. After the framebuffer device is initialized, we can see the content of /proc/fb as follows:

```
root@x86vbox:/ # cat /proc/fb
0 VESA VGA
```

If there is a framebuffer device available before init.sh is called, init_hal_gralloc will set the ro.hardware.gralloc system property for DRM drivers. For the devices that init_hal_gralloc cannot handle, it will do nothing.

In init_uvesafb, the actual command to load uvesafb can be extended to the following one:

```
# modprobe uvesafb mode_option=1024x768-32 mtrr=3 scroll=redraw
```

The options of uvesafb are:

- mtrr:n: Set up memory type range registers for the framebuffer, where n can be:
  - 0: Disabled (equivalent to the nomtrr option)
  - 3: Write-combining (default)

  The memory type range registers are a set of processor supplementary capabilities control registers in Intel processors. Write-combining allows bus write transfers to be combined into a larger transfer before bursting them over the bus. This can help to improve the graphics performance.

- redraw: Scroll by redrawing the affected part of the screen.
- mode_option: Set the resolution to a supported one.

After `uvesafb` is loaded, we can find all the supported resolutions using the following command:

```
# cat /sys/bus/platform/drivers/uvesafb/uvesafb.0/vbe_modes
640x400-8, 0x0100
640x480-8, 0x0101
800x600-8, 0x0103
1024x768-8, 0x0105
1280x1024-8, 0x0107
320x200-15, 0x010d
320x200-16, 0x010e
320x200-24, 0x010f
640x480-15, 0x0110
640x480-16, 0x0111
640x480-24, 0x0112
800x600-15, 0x0113
800x600-16, 0x0114
800x600-24, 0x0115
1024x768-15, 0x0116
1024x768-16, 0x0117
1024x768-24, 0x0118
1280x1024-15, 0x0119
1280x1024-16, 0x011a
1280x1024-24, 0x011b
320x200-32, 0x0140
640x400-32, 0x0141
640x480-32, 0x0142
800x600-32, 0x0143
1024x768-32, 0x0144
1280x1024-32, 0x0145
320x200-8, 0x0146
1600x1200-32, 0x0147
1152x864-8, 0x0148
1152x864-15, 0x0149
1152x864-16, 0x014a
1152x864-24, 0x014b
1152x864-32, 0x014c
```

Integrating VirtualBox Guest Additions

Up to now, we can boot x86vbox to Android. What we can do further is integrate VirtualBox Guest Additions to x86vbox.

VirtualBox is a virtualization environment. We can install a guest operating system as it is in VirtualBox. However, there are some limitations to working in this way. To run a guest operating system in a host environment, you may expect more things than just hardware virtualization. For example, you may find the mouse cursor to behave badly when you move between the host and guest system. You may want to share data between the hosts and guests easily, such as shared clipboard, shared folder, and so on. To meet these requirements, the host and guest need to know each other and have a way to talk to each other. In VirtualBox architecture, there is a component called **Host-Guest Communication Manager** (**HGCM**). On the host side, VirtualBox implements a service called HGCM service that can serve the requests from the guest. On the guest side, there are a few kernel drivers from VirtualBox that can be used to communicate to the host.

The additional features that VirtualBox provides for the host and guest integration are usually included in a package called **VirtualBox Extension Pack**. In the VirtualBox Extension Pack, it includes the necessary files for both the host side and the guest side. The VirtualBox Extension Pack can be download at `https://www.virtualbox.org/wiki/Downloads`.

For the guest side, there are binary tools and source code for device drivers, which are included in a separate distribution package called VirtualBox Guest Additions. There are separate VirtualBox Guest Additions for Windows, Linux, and OS X. There are no Guest Additions for Android. However, since Android uses the Linux kernel, we can build the kernel drivers for Android using the source code for Linux. After we install the VirtualBox Extension Pack, we can find an image file `VBoxGuestAdditions.iso`, as follows:

```
$ cd /usr/share/virtualbox
$ ls
nls                     src                     VBoxSysInfo.sh
rdesktop-vrdp-keymaps   VBoxCreateUSBNode.sh
rdesktop-vrdp.tar.gz    VBoxGuestAdditions.iso
```

We can extract this image file and can find the following files inside VirtualBox Guest Additions:

```
$ ls
deffiles     routines.sh     vboxadd-x11                              x86
installer    vboxadd         VBoxGuestAdditions-amd64.tar.bz2
install.sh   vboxadd-service VBoxGuestAdditions-x86.tar.bz2
```

There are two compressed files: VBoxGuestAdditions-amd64.tar.bz2 and VBoxGuestAdditions-x86.tar.bz2. As we can see its content from the following screenshot, this is a list of folders and files of the Guest Additions for Intel x86 Linux guest:

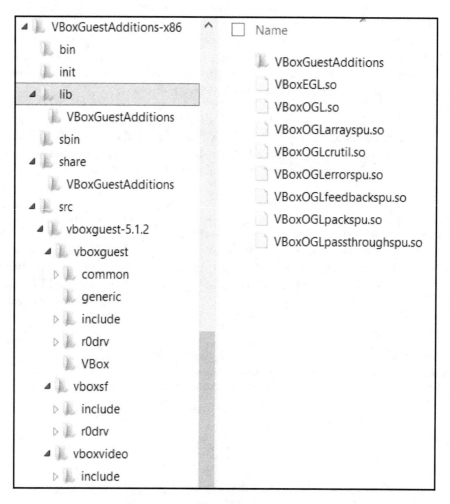

VirtualBox Guest Additions

There are source codes for three drivers available in the Guest Additions: `vboxguest`, `vboxsf`, and `vboxvideo`:

- `vboxguest`: This module provides the basic services in the guest operating system to communicate to the host.
- `vboxsf`: This module is a kernel driver to provide the capability to share files between host and guest.
- `vboxvideo`: This module is a video driver for the guest. With this driver, we can use graphics hardware acceleration through the host.

We will build and integrate these three drivers to x86vbox.

Building VirtualBox Guest Additions

The only dependency of the drivers in Guest Additions is the kernel source code. It is very easy to build the drivers for Android. To build the Guest Additions, you can get the source code from your VirtualBox installation, or you can get a version from my GitHub as follows:

```
$ source build/envsetup.sh
$ lunch x86vbox-eng
$ cd $HOME
$ git clone https://github.com/shugaoye/vboxguest-linux-modules
$ cd vboxguest-linux-modules
$ make BUILD_TARGET_ARCH=x86 KERN_DIR=$OUT/obj/KERNEL_OBJ
```

After we have built the drivers successfully, we can find the driver modules as follows:

```
$ ls
build_in_tmp  Makefile     vboxguest.ko  vboxsf.ko   vboxvideo.ko
LICENSE       vboxguest    vboxsf        vboxvideo
```

We can store the kernel modules in a `vbox` folder under our `x86vbox` device folder, so we can copy them to the filesystem in the build process:

```
$ croot
$ cd device/generic/x86vbox
$ ls vbox
vboxguest.ko   vboxsf.ko   vboxvideo.ko
```

After we have the loadable modules of Guest Additions, we can add them to our x86vbox device Makefile x86vbox.mk, as follows:

```
...
PRODUCT_COPY_FILES += \
device/generic/x86vbox/vbox/vboxguest.ko:system/vendor/vbox/vboxguest.ko \
    device/generic/x86vbox/vbox/vboxsf.ko:system/vendor/vbox/vboxsf.ko \
device/generic/x86vbox/vbox/vboxvideo.ko:system/vendor/vbox/vboxvideo.ko \
...
```

These three modules will be copied to the /system/vendor/vbox folder in the system image.

Integrating vboxsf

With the loadable module vboxsf.ko, we have the capability to exchange files between the host and the guest at the runtime of the Android system. To create a shared folder between the host and guest, we need to load the vboxsf.ko module first.

To use vboxsf.ko, we need a tool called mount.vboxsf, which can be used to mount a shared folder on the host filesystem to the Android filesystem. This mount.vboxsf tool is part of the utilities provided by VirtualBox Guest Additions. We put it under our x86vbox device folder as follows:

```
$ ls mount.vboxsf/
Android.mk   mount.vboxsf.c   vbsfmount.h
```

It includes a C file and a header file. We created the following Android Makefile to build it:

```
LOCAL_PATH:= $(call my-dir)
include $(CLEAR_VARS)

LOCAL_SRC_FILES:= mount.vboxsf.c

LOCAL_CFLAGS:=-O2 -g
#LOCAL_CFLAGS+=-DLINUX

LOCAL_MODULE:=mount.vboxsf
LOCAL_MODULE_TAGS := optional

include $(BUILD_EXECUTABLE)
```

To include it in the system image, we also need to add it to the `x86vbox.mk` Makefile as follows:

```
...
PRODUCT_PACKAGES += \
    mount.vboxsf \
...
```

In order to load `vboxsf.ko` during the system boot up, we need to add the loading of `vboxsf.ko` to the start up script in `initrd.img`. If we recall from `Chapter 6`, *Debugging the Boot Up Process Using a Customized Ramdisk*, we discussed the init script in the `initrd.img`. The shell script function `load_modules` is called to load most of the device drivers in the first stage boot up. We can change this script to load VirtualBox device drivers as follows:

```
load_modules()
{
    if [ -z "$FOUND" ]; then
        auto_detect
    fi

    # 3G modules
    for m in $EXTMOD; do
        busybox modprobe $m
    done

    if [ -n "$VBOX_GUEST_ADDITIONS" ]; then
        echo "Loading VBOX_GUEST_ADDITIONS ..."
        insmod /android/system/vendor/vbox/vboxguest.ko
        insmod /android/system/vendor/vbox/vboxsf.ko
        if [ ! -e /android$SDCARD ]; then
            mkdir /android$SDCARD
            /android/system/bin/mount.vboxsf sdcard /android$SDCARD
        fi
    fi
}
```

We defined a `VBOX_GUEST_ADDITIONS` kernel parameter, which can be used to enable the loading of VirtualBox-specific device drivers. If this kernel parameter is defined, we will load both loadable modules, `vboxguest.ko` and `vboxsf.ko`. Another kernel parameter, `SDCARD`, is also defined so that we can mount the shared folder to be an external SD card storage. The `SDCARD` kernel parameter is used by the shell script function `mount_sdcard` as well.

To define these two kernel parameters on the kernel command line, we need to change the PXE boot script at `$HOME/.VirtualBox/TFTP/pxelinux.cfg/default` as follows:

```
label 1. x86vbox (2 stages boot)
menu x86vbox_initrd
kernel x86vbox/kernel
append ip=dhcp console=ttyS3,115200 androidboot.selinux=permissive
buildvariant=eng initrd=x86vbox/initrd.img androidboot.hardware=x86vbox
DEBUG=2 SRC=/android-x86vbox ROOT=/dev/sda1 VBOX_GUEST_ADDITIONS=1
SDCARD=vendor DATA=sda2 X86VBOX=1
```

Pay attention to the two variables `SDCARD` and `VBOX_GUEST_ADDITIONS`. They are the two new kernel parameters that we added to support the loading of VirtualBox device drivers. To mount the shared folder, we add the following command in the script:

```
/android/system/bin/mount.vboxsf sdcard /android$SDCARD
```

The first parameter to `mount.vboxsf` is the shared folder that we defined in the VirtualBox settings, as shown in the following screenshot:

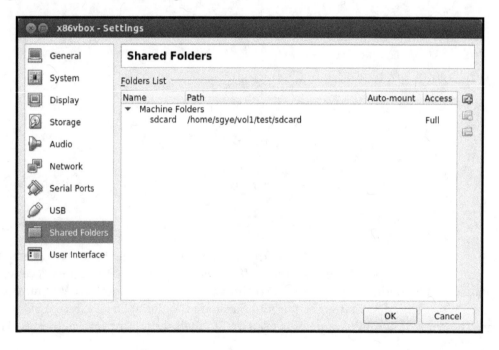

With all the changes related to the shared folder, we can have a method that can be used to share data between the host and the guest very easily.

Integrating vboxvideo

In the VirtualBox Guest Additions, there is another device driver that can be used in Android, which is `vboxvideo.ko`. This is a device driver for video hardware. It provides a much more powerful video driver compared to the uvesafb that we just discussed in this chapter.

The uvesafb is a standard framebuffer driver based on VESA 2.0 standard and it does not support hardware acceleration on VirtualBox. The `vboxvideo.ko` is a DRM/DRI-based video driver with hardware acceleration support.

 Direct Rendering Infrastructure (**DRI**) is a new architecture of the X Window system on the Linux platform to allow X clients to talk to the graphics hardware directly. **Direct Rendering Manager** (**DRM**) is the kernel side of the DRI architecture.

The Android-x86 project is the first open source project that brought Mesa/DRM to the Android platform. This is an open source OpenGL ES implementation for the supported graphics hardware. With the following components, we should be able to support hardware acceleration for OpenGL ES on Android:

- `external_libdrm`
- `external_mesa`
- `external_drm_gralloc`

We have the DRM driver with `vboxvideo` on VirtualBox, but the related implementation still needs to add to `external_mesa` and `external_drm_gralloc` to support OpenGL ES using the host GPU.

Without the VirtualBox-specific implementation in `external_mesa` and `external_drm_gralloc`, we can only use the same software-based implementation in Mesa for OpenGL ES and the default Gralloc module, `gralloc.default.so`. This is why most VirtualBox-based emulator solutions such as Genymotion, Andy, or AMI DuOS are still using hardware GPU emulation, which is similar to the one we discussed in the *Overview of hardware GLES emulation* section in `Chapter 10`, *Enabling Graphics*.

To load `vboxvideo.ko`, we need to add these additional three lines in `load_modules`:

```
if [ -n "$VBOX_VIDEO_DRIVER" ]; then
    modprobe ttm
    modprobe drm_kms_helper
    insmod /android/system/vendor/vbox/vboxvideo.ko
fi
```

The `ttm` and `drm_kms_helper` kernel modules are two kernel modules needed by `vboxvideo.ko`. We also use a `VBOX_VIDEO_DRIVER` kernel parameter to configure the loading of `vboxvideo.ko`. With this kernel parameter, we can switch between the uvesafb framebuffer and the VirtualBox framebuffer. After the system boot up, we can see the following log message. We can see that `vboxvideo` is loaded successfully:

```
[   25.240357] vboxguest: misc device minor 53, IRQ 20, I/O port d040, MMIO
at)
[   25.261044] [drm] Initialized drm 1.1.0 20060810
[   25.290777] [drm] VRAM 08000000
[   25.309754] [TTM] Zone  kernel: Available graphics memory: 440884 kiB
[   25.337733] [TTM] Zone highmem: Available graphics memory: 1034776 kiB
[   25.349078] [TTM] Initializing pool allocator
[   25.349735] fbcon: vboxdrmfb (fb0) is primary device
[   25.360984] Console: switching to colour frame buffer device 100x37
[   25.380299] vboxvideo 0000:00:02.0: fb0: vboxdrmfb frame buffer device
[   25.388745] [drm] Initialized vboxvideo 1.0.0 20130823 for 0000:00:02.0
on m0
```

From the log message, we can see that a `vboxdrmfb` framebuffer device is created by `vboxvideo`. We can check the framebuffer settings using `fbset` as we did before. We can see that the hardware acceleration is set to true for `vboxdrmfb`:

```
(debug-late)@android:/android # fbset

mode "800x600-0"
        # D: 0.000 MHz, H: 0.000 kHz, V: 0.000 Hz
        geometry 800 600 800 600 32
        timings 0 0 0 0 0 0
        accel true
        rgba 8/16,8/8,8/0,0/0
endmode
```

We can also check the output from /proc/fb. Since the output is 0 vboxdrmfb, the init_hal_gralloc shell function in init.sh won't load uvesafb:

```
(debug-late)@android:/android # cat /proc/fb
0 vboxdrmfb
```

With this setup, we can launch x86vbox using the vboxvideo driver instead of uvesafb. As I mentioned, there is still a lot of work that needs to be done before we can fully utilize all the potential capabilities from vboxvideo.

Building and testing images with VirtualBox Guest Additions

To build and test the image in this chapter, we can use the repo tool to retrieve the source code in this chapter as follows:

We can get the source code from GitHub and AOSP using the following command:

```
$ repo init https://github.com/shugaoye/manifests -b
android-7.1.1_r4_ch11_aosp
$ repo sync
```

After we get the source code for this chapter, we can set the environment and build the system as follows:

```
$ source build/envsetup.sh
$ lunch x86vbox-eng
$ make -j4
```

To build initrd.img, we can run the following command:

```
$ make initrd USE_SQUASHFS=0
```

Summary

In this chapter, we learned the start up process of graphics systems. This includes the OpenGL ES libraries, Gralloc module, and device driver. We discussed the Gralloc module in the last chapter. In this chapter, we analyzed another two components, OpenGL ES libraries and the framebuffer driver. With all this knowledge in mind, we integrated the drivers from VirtualBox Guest Additions to the x86vbox device. In the next chapter, we will start to work on another project to explore how recovery works in Android systems.

12
Introducing Recovery

In this book, we have completed two projects so far. With the first x86emu project, we learnt how to extend an existing device to support additional features. After that, we learnt how to create a new device using the second project, x86vbox. There is another important topic at the system-level programming of Android, which is how to patch or update a released system.

In Android systems, the way to patch or update a released system is using a tool called **recovery**. In the next three chapters, we will learn how to build recovery on an x86vbox device. Since x86vbox is a built for VirtualBox, we will use VirtualBox as virtual hardware for this chapter to `Chapter 14`, *Creating OTA Update Packages*. We will also prepare and test a few update packages using the recovery that we build. In this chapter, we will cover the following topics:

- Recovery introduction
- Analyzing recovery source code
- Building recovery for x86vbox

Recovery introduction

In Android, recovery is a minimal Linux environment including a kernel and a dedicated ramdisk. When this minimal Linux environment boots up, it runs a binary tool, recovery, to enter the so-called recovery mode. The Linux kernel and ramdisk of recovery mode are usually stored in a dedicated bootable partition. In recovery mode, both the kernel and the root filesystem are in memory so it can manage other partitions without any dependencies.

There are two ways to update devices in the field. The first method is to use fastboot protocol through bootloader. The devices can be reflashed using bootloader. In this case, you can boot your device in fastboot mode and flash your device using the fastboot tool from Android SDK. The second way to flash a device is to use the recovery mode. If you boot the devices into recovery mode, you can flash the device using an image file on the storage or providing an image through USB in sideload mode.

The image files that can be used by bootloader and recovery are different. The image files from the AOSP build output can be used by bootloader directly. We can flash image files `system.img`, `userdata.img`, `boot.img` or `recovery.img` directly using the `fastboot` tool in bootloader. We cannot use these image files for recovery. We have to build image files for recovery specially using tools provided in AOSP. We will cover this topic in the next chapter.

The key advantage of recovery mode over the fastboot protocol is the **over-the-air** (**OTA**) update support. If an update is available from the OTA servers, the users will receive a notification. The users can download the update to a cache or data partition. After the update package is verified using its signature, the users can respond to the update notification. After that, the device will reboot into recovery mode. In recovery mode, the recovery binary is started and it will use the command-line arguments stored in the `/cache/recovery/command` file to find the update package to update the system image.

Android device partitions

To enable recovery on a device, we need to look at the device partitions again. In Android SDK, we have the following image files that can be used by the emulator:

```
$ ls system-images/android-25/default/x86
build.prop     kernel-ranchu   ramdisk.img          system.img
kernel-qemu    NOTICE.txt      source.properties    userdata.img
```

After we boot up the emulator, we can see that the following partitions are mounted:

```
root@x86emu:/ # mount
rootfs / rootfs ro,seclabel,relatime 0 0
tmpfs /dev tmpfs rw,seclabel,nosuid,relatime,mode=755 0 0
devpts /dev/pts devpts rw,seclabel,relatime,mode=600 0 0
proc /proc proc rw,relatime 0 0
sysfs /sys sysfs rw,seclabel,relatime 0 0
selinuxfs /sys/fs/selinux selinuxfs rw,relatime 0 0
debugfs /sys/kernel/debug debugfs rw,seclabel,relatime 0 0
none /acct cgroup rw,relatime,cpuacct 0 0
none /sys/fs/cgroup tmpfs rw,seclabel,relatime,mode=750,gid=1000 0 0
tmpfs /mnt tmpfs rw,seclabel,relatime,mode=755,gid=1000 0 0
```

```
none /dev/cpuctl cgroup rw,relatime,cpu 0 0
/dev/block/vda /system ext4 ro,seclabel,relatime,data=ordered 0 0
/dev/block/vdb /cache ext4
rw,seclabel,nosuid,nodev,noatime,errors=panic,data=ordered 0 0
/dev/block/vdc /data ext4
rw,seclabel,nosuid,nodev,noatime,errors=panic,data=ordered 0 0
. . .
```

We can see that `system`, `data`, and `cache` partitions are mounted as virtio block devices.
Since virtio is a virtualization standard for network and disk device drivers, the
performance should be better than physical device drivers. With only these partitions, we
won't be able to create a system that can use the recovery tool. In the following figure, these
are the minimum partitions that we need to have on the storage device to support both
fastboot and recovery:

Android device partitions

- **boot**: This is the partition that contains the kernel and ramdisk image.
- **system**: This is the partition that contains the Android system. It is usually
  mounted as read-only and can only be changed during an OTA update.
- **vendor**: This is the partition that contains the private system files from the
  vendor. It is similar to the system partition, which is mounted as read-only and
  can only be changed during an OTA update.

- **userdata**: This partition contains the data saved by applications installed by the user. This partition is usually not touched by the OTA update process.
- **cache**: This partition holds temporary data. The OTA package installations can use it as a workspace.
- **recovery**: This partition contains a Linux kernel and a ramdisk for recovery. It is similar to the boot partition except the ramdisk image is the one used by recovery mode only.
- **misc**: This partition is used by recovery to store information across different boot sessions.

In this chapter, we will build recovery for the x86vbox device. As we learnt from `Chapter 8`, *Creating Your Own Device on VirtualBox*, to `Chapter 11`, *Enabling VirtualBox-Specific Hardware Interfaces*, we use only one partition to store everything for the x86vbox device. We will extend the x86vbox device to use multiple partitions according to the preceding explanation in this chapter later.

Analyzing recovery

Before we start to build recovery for our x86vbox device, we will analyze the code flow of recovery to understand how it works. There are two ways to enter recovery mode from the end user perspective. When users want to perform a factory reset or an OTA update is available, the main system can write a recovery command to the **bootloader control block (BCB)** and cache partition before resetting the system.

The second way to enter recovery mode is to use a key combination manually. After turning off the phone, press a key combination at the same time to enter the recovery mode manually. The key combination is defined by the device manufacturing, for example, it can be a combination of volume down and power buttons.

In both cases, entering the recovery mode is closely related to the implementation of bootloader. The Android system, recovery, and bootloader communicate with each other using two interfaces: the partitions /cache and /misc. We can depict the communication interfaces using the following diagram:

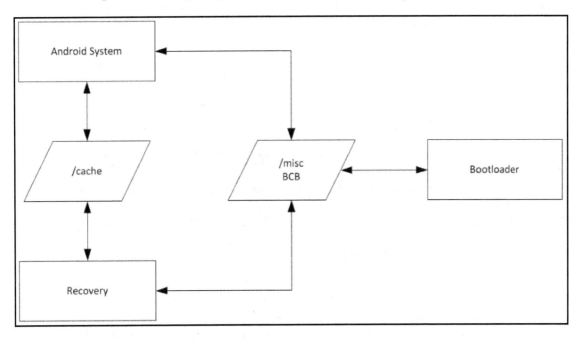

Interfaces of the Android system, recovery, and bootloader

In the preceding diagram, bootloader uses **BCB** in the **/misc** partition to communicate with the Android system and recovery. The Android system and recovery use the information in the **/cache** partition to talk to each other. Let's look into the details of these two communication channels.

BCB

BCB is the communication interface of bootloader to the main system and recovery.

> The Android system is also referred to as the main system in the recovery source code. We use the term main system as equivalent to Android system in this chapter.

BCB is stored in the /misc partition in a raw partition format, which means this partition is used just like a binary file without any filesystem.

Recovery uses a recovery.fstab file to mount all partitions in the system. If we look at the filesystem type of the /misc partition in recovery.fstab, it is emmc that is one of the raw filesystems used in recovery:

```
/dev/block/by-name/misc    /misc    emmc    defaults    defaults
```

There are five supported filesystem types in recovery including two raw filesystems and three normal filesystems.

The two supported raw filesystems are:

- mtd: This is the partition used in old Android devices. These devices use NAND flash and MTD partitions.
- emmc: This is a raw eMMC block device used in the recent Android devices.

The partitions for boot, recovery, and misc can be the mtd or emmc filesystem types.

The supported normal filesystem types are:

- yaffs2: A yaffs2 filesystem is usually used for MTD devices for system, userdata, or cache partitions. This is usually used in older Android devices.
- ext4: In the latest Android devices, the eMMC block devices are used. The standard Linux ext4 filesystem is usually used on top of eMMC block devices. The same as the yaffs2 filesystem type, system, userdata, or cache partitions can use the ext4 format.
- vfat : This is the filesystem type used for external storage such as SD card or USB.

Let's come back to the topic of BCB. BCB is defined as a data structure as follows in the $AOSP/bootable/recovery/bootloader.h file:

```
struct bootloader_message {
    char command[32];
    char status[32];
    char recovery[768];
    char stage[32];
    char reserved[224];
};
```

The `command` field is used by the main system when it wants to reboot the device into recovery. This can be the case when users select factory reset from the settings or an OTA update is available. This field can be used by bootloader as well, when the bootloader completes the firmware update it may want to boot to recovery for any final clean up.

The `status` field is updated by the bootloader after it completes the firmware update.

The `recovery` field is used by the main system to send a message to recovery or the recovery may use this field to send a message to the main system.

The `stage` field is used to indicate the stage of an update. In some cases, the installation of an update package may require restarting multiple times. The recovery UI can use this field to show the current stage of the installation:

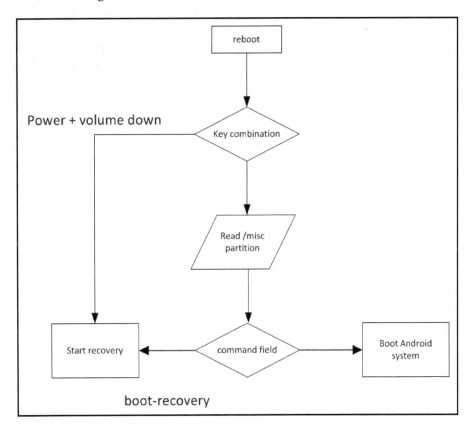

In the preceding diagram, the bootloader logic related to the checking of key combination and BCB is shown. The implementation can be vendor specific as long as the bootloader processes BCB according to the AOSP recovery definition. Usually, the bootloader checks the key combination first to decide whether the users want to enter the recovery mode. If there is no key combination pressed, it checks the BCB to decide the boot path.

Cache partition

There are three files in the cache partition, which can be used as the communication channels between the main system and recovery tool. These three files are:

- `/cache/recovery/command`: This is a file for input parameters from the recovery point of view. There is one command per line in this file. The arguments that may be supplied in the file are:
    - `-send_intent=anystring`: The main system may use this command to send a message back to itself after recovery exit
    - `-update_package=path` : This command specifies a path to install an OTA package file
    - `-wipe_data`: This command tells recovery to erase user data (and cache), and then reboot

- -wipe_cache: This command tells recovery to wipe cache (but not user data), then reboot
- -set_encrypted_filesystem=on|off: Enables/disables encrypted filesystems
- -just_exit: Does nothing; exits and reboots

- /cache/recovery/log: The runtime log file of recovery is at /tmp/recovery.log. Before recovery exits, it will back up the old log file and move the current log file to /cache/recovery/log.

- /cache/recovery/intent: Before recovery exits, it will check if there is any intent that needs to be sent to the main system using this file. The intent can be the message that the main system sends to recovery using the -send_intent command in the /cache/recovery/command file.

Main flow of recovery

After we have all the background knowledge about recovery and the components related to recovery, let's have a look at the main workflow of recovery. We will use the following diagram to explore the workflow of recovery:

1. When recovery is started, it will set the log file to /tmp/recovery.log first.
2. After that, it checks the --adbd option. If this option is specified, it will run a daemon for the sideloading using adb. You can refer to the source code at $AOSP/bootable/recovery/adb_install.cpp about how to launch recovery as adb daemon.
3. It retrieves and processes the arguments from cache partition and BCB by calling the get_args function.
4. Based on the commands retrieved from get_args, it may call the install_package function to install an update, or call the wipe_data or wipe_cache functions to erase user data or cache partition.
5. If there is no command for either updating a package or erasing data, it will call the prompt_and_wait function to enter the recovery user interface. Based on the user input, it may call apply_from_adb or apply_from_sdcard to update packages from USB or SD card. It may call the wipe_data or wipe_cache functions to erase user data or cache partition, and so on.

6. After all the tasks are completed or the users select entries to exit from recovery, it will call the cleanup function, `finish_recovery`, to do the final clean up. After that, it will reboot or shut down the system:

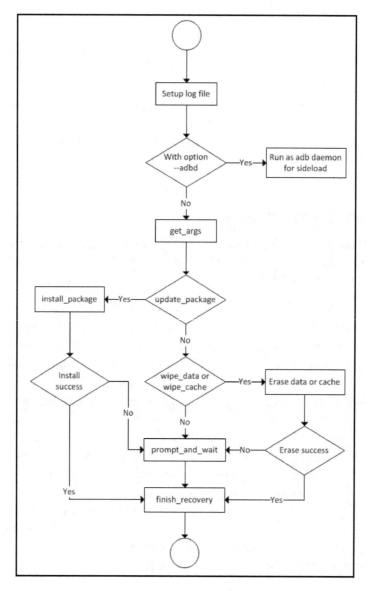

Recovery workflow

Based on the preceding flow analysis, we can look at the code snippet of the `main` function at `$AOSP/bootable/recovery/recovery.cpp` as follows:

```
int
main(int argc, char **argv) {
    time_t start = time(NULL);

    redirect_stdio(TEMPORARY_LOG_FILE);


    ...
    if (argc == 2 && strcmp(argv[1], "--adbd") == 0) {
        adb_main(0, DEFAULT_ADB_PORT);
        return 0;
    }

    printf("Starting recovery (pid %d) on %s", getpid(),
    ctime(&start));

    load_volume_table();
    get_args(&argc, &argv);

    ...
    ui->Print("Supported API: %d\n", RECOVERY_API_VERSION);

    int status = INSTALL_SUCCESS;

    if (update_package != NULL) {
        status = install_package(update_package, &should_wipe_cache,
        TEMPORARY_INSTALL_FILE, true);
        if (status == INSTALL_SUCCESS && should_wipe_cache) {
            wipe_cache(false, device);
        }
    ...
    } else if (should_wipe_data) {
        if (!wipe_data(false, device)) {
            status = INSTALL_ERROR;
        }
    } else if (should_wipe_cache) {
        if (!wipe_cache(false, device)) {
            status = INSTALL_ERROR;
        }
    } else if (sideload) {
    ...
    Device::BuiltinAction after = shutdown_after ? Device::SHUTDOWN :
    Device::REBOOT;
    if ((status != INSTALL_SUCCESS && !sideload_auto_reboot) || ui-
    >IsTextVisible()) {
        Device::BuiltinAction temp = prompt_and_wait(device, status);
```

```
            if (temp != Device::NO_ACTION) {
                after = temp;
            }
        }

        // Save logs and clean up before rebooting or shutting down.
        finish_recovery(send_intent);

        switch (after) {
            case Device::SHUTDOWN:
                ui->Print("Shutting down...\n");
                property_set(ANDROID_RB_PROPERTY, "shutdown,");
                break;

            case Device::REBOOT_BOOTLOADER:
                ui->Print("Rebooting to bootloader...\n");
                property_set(ANDROID_RB_PROPERTY, "reboot,bootloader");
                break;

            default:
                ui->Print("Rebooting...\n");
                property_set(ANDROID_RB_PROPERTY, "reboot,");
                break;
        }
        sleep(5); // should reboot before this finishes
        return EXIT_SUCCESS;
    }
```

After we have an overview of the recovery workflow, we will look at how recovery retrieves arguments from either BCB or cache files in the `get_args` function. After that, we will look at the two important workflows, factory reset and OTA update, from the user's perspective.

Retrieving arguments from BCB and cache files

As we can see in the main function of recovery, it calls to the `get_args` function to retrieve arguments from the main system or bootloader. The following is the flow diagram of `get_args`. It is in the same `$AOSP/bootable/recovery/recovery.cpp` file as the `main` function of recovery.

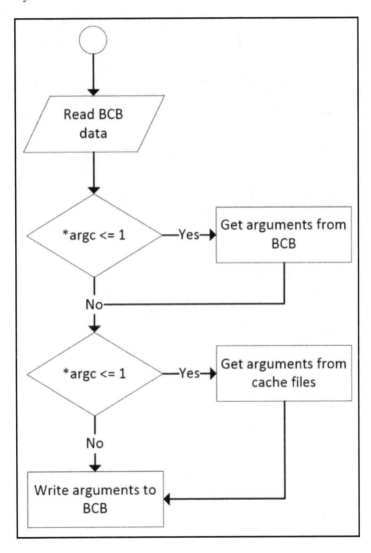

Flow diagram of get_args

From the following code snippet, we can see that it calls to the `get_bootloader_message` function to get the BCB data structure, `boot`:

```
static void
get_args(int *argc, char ***argv) {
    struct bootloader_message boot;
    memset(&boot, 0, sizeof(boot));
    get_bootloader_message(&boot);   // this may fail, leaving a zeroed
                                     //structure
    stage = strndup(boot.stage, sizeof(boot.stage));
    ...
```

If there are no arguments, the value of `argc` will be less or equal to 1. It will try to get the arguments from BCB, as in the following code snippet. In the `recovery` field of BCB, the command will start with `recovery\n`. The content after `recovery\n` is the same format as the cache command file, `/cache/recovery/command`:

```
if (*argc <= 1) {
    boot.recovery[sizeof(boot.recovery) - 1] = '\0';
    const char *arg = strtok(boot.recovery, "\n");
    if (arg != NULL && !strcmp(arg, "recovery")) {
        *argv = (char **) malloc(sizeof(char *) * MAX_ARGS);
        (*argv)[0] = strdup(arg);
        for (*argc = 1; *argc < MAX_ARGS; ++*argc) {
            if ((arg = strtok(NULL, "\n")) == NULL) break;
            (*argv)[*argc] = strdup(arg);
        }
        LOGI("Got arguments from boot message\n");
    } else if (boot.recovery[0] != 0 && boot.recovery[0] != 255) {
        LOGE("Bad boot message\n\"%.20s\"\n", boot.recovery);
    }
}
```

If the arguments can be retrieved from BCB, it will skip the cache command file. Otherwise, it will try to read arguments from the cache command file as follows:

```
if (*argc <= 1) {
    FILE *fp = fopen_path(COMMAND_FILE, "r");
    if (fp != NULL) {
        char *token;
        char *argv0 = (*argv)[0];
        *argv = (char **) malloc(sizeof(char *) * MAX_ARGS);
        (*argv)[0] = argv0;  // use the same program name

        char buf[MAX_ARG_LENGTH];
        for (*argc = 1; *argc < MAX_ARGS; ++*argc) {
            if (!fgets(buf, sizeof(buf), fp)) break;
```

```
            token = strtok(buf, "\r\n");
            if (token != NULL) {
                (*argv)[*argc] = strdup(token);
            } else {
                --*argc;
            }
        }
    }

    check_and_fclose(fp, COMMAND_FILE);
    LOGI("Got arguments from %s\n", COMMAND_FILE);
}
}
```

After processing both BCB and the cache command file, it will write the BCB block to the /misc partition so that if there is any error during the process of update or erase, the same process will continue after the reboot:

```
strlcpy(boot.command, "boot-recovery", sizeof(boot.command));
strlcpy(boot.recovery, "recovery\n", sizeof(boot.recovery));
int i;
for (i = 1; i < *argc; ++i) {
    strlcat(boot.recovery, (*argv)[i], sizeof(boot.recovery));
    strlcat(boot.recovery, "\n", sizeof(boot.recovery));
}
set_bootloader_message(&boot);
```

From the preceding code analysis, we can see that the cache command file is just a normal text file. It can be accessed by just using the standard C functions. To access the /misc partition for BCB data structure, the get_bootloader_message function is used to read BCB and the set_bootloader_message function is used to write BCB. The BCB data structure bootloader_message is defined in the bootloader.h file and related functions are implemented in the bootloader.cpp file.

The /misc partition is a raw partition and it is used by the code in bootloader.cpp as a normal file instead of a filesystem volume.

We can have a quick look at the get_bootloader_message function and its support function, get_bootloader_message_block, as follows:

```
int get_bootloader_message(struct bootloader_message *out) {
    Volume* v = volume_for_path("/misc");
    if (v == NULL) {
      LOGE("Cannot load volume /misc!\n");
      return -1;
    }
    if (strcmp(v->fs_type, "mtd") == 0) {
```

```
        return get_bootloader_message_mtd(out, v);
    } else if (strcmp(v->fs_type, "emmc") == 0) {
        return get_bootloader_message_block(out, v);
    }
    LOGE("unknown misc partition fs_type \"%s\"\n", v->fs_type);
    return -1;
}
```

In the `get_bootloader_message` function, it will call another function according to the type of partition, `/misc`. As we can see, the supported raw filesystem types are `mtd` and `emmc`. We can look at the `emmc` version, `get_bootloader_message_block`, as follows:

```
static int get_bootloader_message_block(struct bootloader_message *out,
const Volume* v) {
    wait_for_device(v->blk_device);
    FILE* f = fopen(v->blk_device, "rb");
    if (f == NULL) {
        LOGE("Can't open %s\n(%s)\n", v->blk_device, strerror(errno));
        return -1;
    }
    struct bootloader_message temp;
    int count = fread(&temp, sizeof(temp), 1, f);
    if (count != 1) {
        LOGE("Failed reading %s\n(%s)\n", v->blk_device,
        strerror(errno));
        return -1;
    }
    if (fclose(f) != 0) {
        LOGE("Failed closing %s\n(%s)\n", v->blk_device,
        strerror(errno));
        return -1;
    }
    memcpy(out, &temp, sizeof(temp));
    return 0;
}
```

As we can see, in the `get_bootloader_message_block` function, it accesses the `/misc` partition as a normal file using C functions `fopen`, `fread`, and `fclose`.

Now we have done the analysis of BCB and cache file processing. We will look at the following two most important workflows of recovery in the next two sections:

- Factory data reset
- OTA update

Factory data reset

One of the major functions of recovery is to support factory data reset. The factory data reset can usually be selected by users from **Settings** on the device, as shown in the following screenshot:

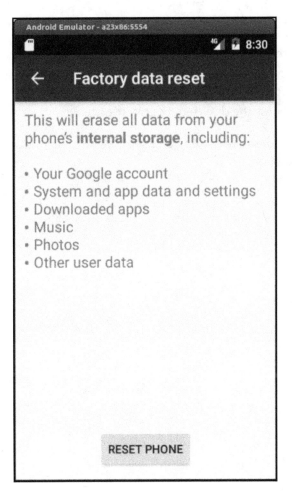

Factory data reset

The entire process can be divided into the following steps:

1. The user selects **Factory data reset** from **Settings**.
2. Main system writes `--wipe_data` to `/cache/recovery/command`.

3. Main system reboots the device into recovery. We have done the analysis about this when we talked about BCB in the previous section.

4. Recovery retrieves arguments from BCB or `/cache/recovery/command` in `get_args()`. After read arguments, recovery will write BCB with `boot-recovery` and `--wipe_data`.

5. Recovery erases both `/data` and `/cache` partitions. After this point, any following reboots will continue this step until the erase can be completed or the user takes other actions from recovery user interfaces to exit from recovery.

6. After erasing `/data` and `/cache` partitions, recovery calls to the `finish_recovery` function to erase BCB.

7. Recovery reboots the device to the main system.

We have analyzed most of the preceding steps except `finish_recovery`. Let's look at the `finish_recovery` function:

```
static void
finish_recovery(const char *send_intent) {
    // By this point, we're ready to return to the main system...
    if (send_intent != NULL) {
        FILE *fp = fopen_path(INTENT_FILE, "w");
        if (fp == NULL) {
            LOGE("Can't open %s\n", INTENT_FILE);
        } else {
            fputs(send_intent, fp);
            check_and_fclose(fp, INTENT_FILE);
        }
    }

    if (locale != NULL) {
        LOGI("Saving locale \"%s\"\n", locale);
        FILE* fp = fopen_path(LOCALE_FILE, "w");
        fwrite(locale, 1, strlen(locale), fp);
        fflush(fp);
        fsync(fileno(fp));
        check_and_fclose(fp, LOCALE_FILE);
    }

    copy_logs();

    struct bootloader_message boot;
    memset(&boot, 0, sizeof(boot));
    set_bootloader_message(&boot);

    if (ensure_path_mounted(COMMAND_FILE) != 0 ||
        (unlink(COMMAND_FILE) && errno != ENOENT)) {
```

```
        LOGW("Can't unlink %s\n", COMMAND_FILE);
    }

    ensure_path_unmounted(CACHE_ROOT);
    sync();   // For good measure.
}
```

In the `finish_recovery` function, it writes the intent to `/cache/recovery/intent`. Then, it processes the local file and creates the log file backup. Finally, it erases BCB by calling `set_bootloader_message` and removes `/cache/recovery/command` to restore the normal boot process.

OTA update

OTA update is another major function of recovery. OTA packages can be updated using the recovery user interface after entering the recovery mode manually. It can also be updated automatically after an update notification is received. In both cases, the path of the update package may be different, but the installation process is the same. In this section, we will look at the flow after the device received an OTA update notification. Then, we will look into the details of the installation process:

1. After an OTA update notification is received by the device, main system downloads the OTA package to `/cache/update.zip`.
2. Main system writes a `--update_package=/cache/update.zip` command to `/cache/recovery/command`.
3. Main system reboots the device into recovery.
4. Recovery retrieves arguments from BCB or `/cache/recovery/command` in `get_args()`. After read arguments, recovery will write BCB with `boot-recovery` and `update_package=...`.
5. Recovery calls `install_package` to install the update. At this step, any following reboots will continue this step until the installation can be completed.
6. If the installation is failed, the `prompt_and_wait` function is called to show an error and wait for user action. If the installation completes successfully, it will move to the next step.
7. Recovery calls to the `finish_recovery` function to erase BCB and remove the `/cache/recovery/command` file.
8. Recovery reboots the device to the main system.

Once the update package is downloaded, the installation is done by the `install_package` function:

```
int
install_package(const char* path, bool* wipe_cache, const char*
install_file, bool needs_mount)
{
    modified_flash = true;

    FILE* install_log = fopen_path(install_file, "w");
    if (install_log) {
        fputs(path, install_log);
        fputc('\n', install_log);
    } else {
        LOGE("failed to open last_install: %s\n", strerror(errno));
    }
    int result;
    if (setup_install_mounts() != 0) {
        LOGE("failed to set up expected mounts for install;
        aborting\n");
        result = INSTALL_ERROR;
    } else {
        result = really_install_package(path, wipe_cache, needs_mount);
    }
    if (install_log) {
        fputc(result == INSTALL_SUCCESS ? '1' : '0', install_log);
        fputc('\n', install_log);
        fclose(install_log);
    }
    return result;
}
```

In the `install_package` function, it sets the installation log file first. The log file path is `/tmp/last_install`. Then, it calls to `setup_install_mounts` to mount the relevant partitions. The actual installation is done in the `really_install_package` function, as shown in the following code snippet:

```
static int
really_install_package(const char *path, bool* wipe_cache, bool
needs_mount)
{
    ui->SetBackground(RecoveryUI::INSTALLING_UPDATE);
    ...

    MemMapping map;
    if (sysMapFile(path, &map) != 0) {
        LOGE("failed to map file\n");
```

```
        return INSTALL_CORRUPT;
    }

    int numKeys;
    Certificate* loadedKeys = load_keys(PUBLIC_KEYS_FILE, &numKeys);
    if (loadedKeys == NULL) {
        LOGE("Failed to load keys\n");
        return INSTALL_CORRUPT;
    }
    LOGI("%d key(s) loaded from %s\n", numKeys, PUBLIC_KEYS_FILE);

    ui->Print("Verifying update package...\n");

    int err;
    err = verify_file(map.addr, map.length, loadedKeys, numKeys);
    free(loadedKeys);
    LOGI("verify_file returned %d\n", err);
    if (err != VERIFY_SUCCESS) {
        LOGE("signature verification failed\n");
        sysReleaseMap(&map);
        return INSTALL_CORRUPT;
    }

    /* Try to open the package.
     */
    ZipArchive zip;
    err = mzOpenZipArchive(map.addr, map.length, &zip);
    if (err != 0) {
        LOGE("Can't open %s\n(%s)\n", path, err != -1 ? strerror(err) :
        "bad");
        sysReleaseMap(&map);
        return INSTALL_CORRUPT;
    }

    /* Verify and install the contents of the package.
     */
    ui->Print("Installing update...\n");
    ui->SetEnableReboot(false);
    int result = try_update_binary(path, &zip, wipe_cache);
    ui->SetEnableReboot(true);
    ui->Print("\n");

    sysReleaseMap(&map);

    return result;
}
```

In the `really_install_package` function, it initializes the user interface and shows the package location on the screen. Then, it creates a memory map for the update package. This is needed by the `zip` functions. After that, it verifies the update package using its signature. Finally, it calls to another function, `try_update_binary,` to do the installation.

The `try_update_binary` function performs three tasks:

1. Extracts `update_binary` from the update package.
2. Prepares the environment to execute `update_binary`.
3. Monitors the progress of installation.

Let's look into the details of these three tasks:

```
static int
try_update_binary(const char* path, ZipArchive* zip, bool* wipe_cache) {
    const ZipEntry* binary_entry =
            mzFindZipEntry(zip, ASSUMED_UPDATE_BINARY_NAME);
    if (binary_entry == NULL) {
        mzCloseZipArchive(zip);
        return INSTALL_CORRUPT;
    }

    const char* binary = "/tmp/update_binary";
    unlink(binary);
    int fd = creat(binary, 0755);
    if (fd < 0) {
        mzCloseZipArchive(zip);
        LOGE("Can't make %s\n", binary);
        return INSTALL_ERROR;
    }
    bool ok = mzExtractZipEntryToFile(zip, binary_entry, fd);
    close(fd);
    mzCloseZipArchive(zip);

    if (!ok) {
        LOGE("Can't copy %s\n", ASSUMED_UPDATE_BINARY_NAME);
        return INSTALL_ERROR;
    }
```

It tries to extract `update_binary` from the update package. The path of `update_binary` in the update package is predefined at `META-INF/com/google/android/update-binary`.

If `update_binary` can be extracted successfully, it will be copied to
`/tmp/update_binary`:

```
int pipefd[2];
pipe(pipefd);
const char** args = (const char**)malloc(sizeof(char*) * 5);
args[0] = binary;
args[1] = EXPAND(RECOVERY_API_VERSION);    // defined in Android.mk
char* temp = (char*)malloc(10);
sprintf(temp, "%d", pipefd[1]);
args[2] = temp;
args[3] = (char*)path;
args[4] = NULL;

pid_t pid = fork();
if (pid == 0) {
    umask(022);
    close(pipefd[0]);
    execv(binary, (char* const*)args);
    fprintf(stdout, "E:Can't run %s (%s)\n", binary, strerror(errno));
    _exit(-1);
}
```

As we can see from the preceding code snippet, after extracting `update_binary`, it will
prepare the environment to execute `update_binary`. The installation of the update
package is actually done by `update_binary` using a script. The following parameters are
passed to `update_binary` for the execution:

- The path of `update_binary`
- Recovery version
- A pipe for the communication between the parent and child processes
- The path of the update package

After the environment is ready, it will fork a child process to run `update_binary`. The
parent process will monitor the installation progress by talking to the child process through
a pipe:

```
close(pipefd[1]);

*wipe_cache = false;

char buffer[1024];
FILE* from_child = fdopen(pipefd[0], "r");
while (fgets(buffer, sizeof(buffer), from_child) != NULL) {
    char* command = strtok(buffer, " \n");
```

```
        if (command == NULL) {
            continue;
        } else if (strcmp(command, "progress") == 0) {
            char* fraction_s = strtok(NULL, " \n");
            char* seconds_s = strtok(NULL, " \n");

            float fraction = strtof(fraction_s, NULL);
            int seconds = strtol(seconds_s, NULL, 10);

            ui->ShowProgress(fraction * (1-VERIFICATION_PROGRESS_FRACTION),
            seconds);
        } else if (strcmp(command, "set_progress") == 0) {
            char* fraction_s = strtok(NULL, " \n");
            float fraction = strtof(fraction_s, NULL);
            ui->SetProgress(fraction);
        } else if (strcmp(command, "ui_print") == 0) {
            char* str = strtok(NULL, "\n");
            if (str) {
                ui->Print("%s", str);
            } else {
                ui->Print("\n");
            }
            fflush(stdout);
        } else if (strcmp(command, "wipe_cache") == 0) {
            *wipe_cache = true;
        } else if (strcmp(command, "clear_display") == 0) {
            ui->SetBackground(RecoveryUI::NONE);
        } else if (strcmp(command, "enable_reboot") == 0) {
            ui->SetEnableReboot(true);
        } else {
            LOGE("unknown command [%s]\n", command);
        }
    }
}
fclose(from_child);

int status;
waitpid(pid, &status, 0);
if (!WIFEXITED(status) || WEXITSTATUS(status) != 0) {
    LOGE("Error in %s\n(Status %d)\n", path, WEXITSTATUS(status));
    return INSTALL_ERROR;
}
```

As we can see from the preceding code snippet, the parent process will receive commands from the child process to show the progress, print out information to the screen, or set the clean up configuration after the installation.

Building recovery for x86vbox

After analyzing the workflow and key elements in the recovery source code, we can now start to build it for our x86vbox device.

The changes to support the recovery build include the changes to x86vbox devices and the changes to `recovery` and `newinstaller`.

Building configuration

Before we look at the changes for this chapter, let's look at the configuration files first. As usual, we have a manifest file for each chapter. We make changes for this chapter based on the source code of `Chapter 11`, *Enabling VirtualBox-Specific Hardware Interfaces*. The following are the projects that we are going to change:

```xml
<?xml version="1.0" encoding="UTF-8"?>
<manifest>

  <remote   name="github"
            revision="refs/tags/android-7.1.1_r4_x86vbox_ch12_r1"
            fetch="." />

  <remote   name="aosp"
            fetch="https://android.googlesource.com/" />
  <default  revision="refs/tags/android-7.1.1_r4"
            remote="aosp"
            sync-c="true"
            sync-j="1" />

  ...
  <project path="bootable/newinstaller"
  name="platform_bootable_newinstaller" remote="github" />
  <project path="device/generic/common" name="device_generic_common"
  groups="pdk" remote="github" />
  <project path="device/generic/x86vbox" name="x86vbox" remote="github"
  />
  <project path="bootable/recovery" name="android_bootable_recovery"
  remote="github" groups="pdk" />
  ...
```

We can see that we need to change four projects: `recovery`, `newinstaller`, `common`, and `x86vbox`. We use an `android-7.1.1_r4_x86vbox_ch12_r1` tag to baseline the source code in this chapter.

We can get the source code from GitHub and AOSP using the following command:

```
$ repo init -u https://github.com/shugaoye/manifests -b
android-7.1.1_r4_ch12_aosp
$ repo sync
```

After we get the source code for this chapter, we can set the environment and build the system as follows:

```
$ source build/envsetup.sh
$ lunch x86vbox-eng
$ make -j4
```

To build `initrd.img`, you can run the following command:

```
$ make initrd USE_SQUASHFS=0
```

Changes to x86vbox

For the x86vbox device, we need to change the Makefiles device first. Since we inherited x86vbox from the common Android-x86 device, we have only the following Makefiles:

```
$ ls *.mk
AndroidProducts.mk   BoardConfig.mk   x86vbox.mk
```

`AndroidProducts.mk` is the entry of the Android build system, which includes our `x86vbox.mk` Makefile. In `x86vbox.mk`, we add the following recovery related files:

```
PRODUCT_COPY_FILES += \
...
device/generic/x86vbox/recovery.fstab:recovery/root/etc/recovery.fstab \
device/generic/x86vbox/recovery/root/init.recovery.x86vbox.rc:root/init.rec
overy.x86vbox.rc \
device/generic/x86vbox/recovery/root/sbin/network_start.sh:recovery/root/sb
in/network_start.sh \
device/generic/x86vbox/recovery/root/sbin/create_partitions.sh:recovery/roo
t/sbin/create_partitions.sh \
...
```

These changes include two parts. The first part is related to the environment setup specific for VirtualBox, since we run recovery on the virtual hardware of VirtualBox. The x86vbox specific init script, `init.recovery.x86vbox.rc`, will be executed by the init process during the system startup.

The second part is related to the partitions of the storage device. As we discussed in previous chapters, we won't be able to use recovery with a single partition as we did in Chapter 8, *Creating Your Own Device on VirtualBox,* to Chapter 11, *Enabling VirtualBox-Specific Hardware Interfaces*. The partition table is defined in the recovery.fstab file. Let's look at the startup script, init.recovery.x86vbox.rc, first:

```
on init
    exec -- /system/bin/logwrapper /system/bin/sh /system/etc/init.sh

service network_start /sbin/network_start.sh
    user root
    seclabel u:r:recovery:s0
    oneshot

service console /system/bin/sh
    class core
    console
    disabled
    user shell
    group shell log
    seclabel u:r:shell:s0

on property:ro.debuggable=1
    start console
```

As the init script of Android, recovery also has a device specific init script, init.recovery.${ro.hardware}.rc. In our case, it is init.recovery.x86vbox.rc. Inside init.recovery.x86vbox.rc, it calls to the Android-x86 HAL initialization script, /system/etc/init.sh. In the HAL initialization during the Android start up section of Chapter 8, *Creating Your Own Device on VirtualBox,* we had a detailed explanation about the /system/etc/init.sh script.

We added two services, network_start and console, in init.recovery.x86vbox.rc. With these two services, we are able to enable VirtualBox-specific network interfaces and we can also have a console after boot up. With this debug console, we are able to debug recovery much easier later in this book.

Another important part in `x86vbox.mk` is we add a `recovery.fstab` partition table for recovery as follows:

```
/dev/block/sda1 /system  ext4  ro           wait
/dev/block/sda2 /data    ext4  noatime,...  wait
/dev/block/sda3 /sdcard  vfat  defaults     voldmanaged=sdcard:auto
/dev/block/sda5 /cache   ext4  noatime,...  wait
/dev/block/sda6 /misc    emmc  defaults     defaults
/dev/block/sda7 /recovery emmc defaults     defaults
```

As we can see, we have six partitions now. We don't really have a bootloader that can support fastboot protocol and recovery BCB now, so we don't really use `/boot` and `/recovery` partitions. However, we do have a two stage boot process from Android-x86 and we can have a workaround without bootloader support. We will see this in a moment when we look at the changes to `newinstaller` later in this chapter.

The `recovery.fstab` partition table is used by recovery and we need to change the related partition table for the Android main system as well, which is the file at `device/generic/common/fstab.x86`.

We need to add two entries in `device/generic/common/fstab.x86`, as follows:

```
/dev/block/sda3  /sdcard  vfat  defaults  voldmanaged=sdcard:auto
/dev/block/sda5  /cache   ext4  noatime,... wait
```

This `fstab.x86` file will be copied to the system image as `fstab.x86vbox` during the build process. The init process will process it to mount partitions. You may be wondering why we don't have `/system` and `/data` in the partition table. We use two stage boots and they are mounted in the first stage boot before Android starts. The source of both `/system` and `/data` can be configured through kernel parameters, as we discussed in previous chapters when we explained the two-stage boot process.

Be aware that both recovery and main system should mount the same block device partitions. For example, if recovery and main system mount different partitions for `/cache`, they won't be able to communicate with each other using the command file at `/cache/recovery/command`.

That's all about the changes to `x86vbox.mk`, so now let's look at another Makefile, `BoardConfig.mk`. To enable the build of recovery, we need to add the following two macros in `BoardConfig.mk`:

```
TARGET_NO_KERNEL := false
TARGET_NO_RECOVERY := false
```

The default values for both macros are set to true, which means both kernel and recovery are not built in the default configuration.

We added another macro that is related to the changes of recovery source code and we will look at the source code changes later:

```
# Double buffer cannot work well on virtualbox
RECOVERY_GRAPHICS_FORCE_SINGLE_BUFFER := true
```

The `RECOVERY_GRAPHICS_FORCE_SINGLE_BUFFER` macro is borrowed from the latest code of **Team Win Recovery Project (TWRP)**. With the changes to x86vbox Makefiles, we can actually build TWRP as well. This is a third-party recovery commonly used by many third-party ROMs, such as LineageOS/CyanogenMod, Omnirom, and so on.

Changes to recovery

The AOSP recovery code can work quite well on VirtualBox. There is only an issue related to the display. To fix the display issue, we need to change two files in the recovery source code.

We use the `RECOVERY_GRAPHICS_FORCE_SINGLE_BUFFER` macro as we mentioned earlier to configure the frame buffer changes. We need to add it to the recovery Makefile `minui/Android.mk` first as follows:

```
ifeq ($(RECOVERY_GRAPHICS_FORCE_SINGLE_BUFFER), true)
LOCAL_CFLAGS += -DRECOVERY_GRAPHICS_FORCE_SINGLE_BUFFER
endif
```

Since double buffer cannot work well on VirtualBox for the time being, we have to disable it as follows:

```
...
    /* check if we can use double buffering */
#ifndef RECOVERY_GRAPHICS_FORCE_SINGLE_BUFFER
    if (vi.yres * fi.line_length * 2 <= fi.smem_len) {
        double_buffered = true;

        memcpy(gr_framebuffer+1, gr_framebuffer, sizeof(GRSurface));
        gr_framebuffer[1].data = gr_framebuffer[0].data +
            gr_framebuffer[0].height * gr_framebuffer[0].row_bytes;

        gr_draw = gr_framebuffer+1;

    } else {
#else
```

```
    {
        printf("RECOVERY_GRAPHICS_FORCE_SINGLE_BUFFER := true\n");
#endif
        double_buffered = false;

        gr_draw = (GRSurface*) malloc(sizeof(GRSurface));
        memcpy(gr_draw, gr_framebuffer, sizeof(GRSurface));
        gr_draw->data = (unsigned char*) malloc(gr_draw->height *
        gr_draw->row_bytes);
        if (!gr_draw->data) {
            perror("failed to allocate in-memory surface");
            return NULL;
        }
    }
    ...
```

With a similar change to TWRP, TWRP can be built for x86vbox as well. The branch for building TWRP is included in the source code at GitHub and you can try it yourself.

Changes to newinstaller

As we discussed in the BCB section, bootloader decides the boot path according to the arguments stored in BCB. The recovery command stored in BCB is the same as the one in the /cache partition at /cache/recovery/command. We can actually move the same logic to the first stage boot in initrd.img. In this case, we can achieve the same result with the help of the first stage boot. The logic for factory data reset and OTA update will become the following steps:

1. The user chooses factory data reset or an OTA update available.
2. Main system writes a command --wipe_data or -- update_package=/cache/update.zip to /cache/recovery/command.
3. Main system reboots the device.
4. In the first stage boot, the init script will check whether the /cache/recovery/command file exists in the /cache partition.
5. If /cache/recovery/command exists, it will load ramdisk-recovery.img, otherwise, it will load ramdisk.img.
6. The rest of the steps will be the same as the normal boot process or the recovery boot process.

To implement the preceding logic, we added a shell function, `find_ramdisk`, to the `$AOSP/bootable/newinstaller/initrd/init` file as follows:

```
find_ramdisk()
{
    busybox mount /dev/sda5 /hd
    if [ ! -e /hd/recovery/command ]; then
            busybox umount /hd
            if [ "$RECOVERY" = "1" ]; then
                    RAMDISK=/mnt/$SRC/ramdisk-recovery.img
            else
                    RAMDISK=/mnt/$SRC/ramdisk.img
            fi
    else
            busybox umount /hd
            RAMDISK=/mnt/$SRC/ramdisk-recovery.img
            return
    fi
    echo boot using $RAMDISK ...
}
```

In this function, we mount the cache partition to `/hd` and check whether `/hd/recovery/command` exists or not. If it exists, we set the `RAMDISK` variable to `ramdisk-recovery.img`; otherwise, we set it to `ramdisk.img`. The init script will extract the ramdisk contained in the `RAMDISK` variable to the memory later as follows:

```
...
    zcat $RAMDISK | cpio -id > /dev/null
...
```

There is another variable called `RECOVERY` that is defined in `find_ramdisk`, which can be passed to the init script from the kernel command line. With this variable, we can force to boot to recovery.

Testing recovery

After we build the recovery and AOSP images, we can test them in VirtualBox. As we learnt from `Chapter 9`, *Booting Up x86vbox using PXE/NFS*, we can use PXE boot to boot the system and use NFS to access the AOSP images. To test recovery, we can add an option in the `$HOME/.VirtualBox/TFTP/pxelinux.cfg/default` file to boot using `kernel` and `ramdisk/recovery.img`. Even though we can boot the system to recovery now, we won't be able to update the system using the recovery in this chapter. We will find out more in the next two chapters.

Summary

We have done all the analysis and implementation of recovery for the x86vbox device. We have analyzed the workflow and key elements in the recovery source code in the first part of this chapter. In the second part of this chapter, we applied the knowledge that we gained in the first part to the implementation of the recovery for the x86vbox device. We changed the x86vbox device itself to add the recovery support. We also changed recovery source code to fix the display issue. Finally, we modified newinstaller so that we can have a complete boot flow for both main system and recovery.

In the next chapter, we will discuss how to create a recovery package and explain what is inside a recovery package.

13
Creating OTA Packages

In the last chapter, we analyzed the internals of recovery and learnt how it works. As we saw, one of the major functionalities of recovery is to support OTA update. In this chapter, we will look at the OTA package and study the process of the OTA package update. We will cover the following topics:

- We will look at what is inside an OTA package. We will study the internals of `updater` and `updater-script`.
- We will learn the process about how to build an OTA package.
- Finally, we need to improve recovery to remove the dependencies from the Android system.

What is inside an OTA package

Before we start to build an OTA package, let's look at what's inside an OTA package. The OTA package can be used to update the system to a new release. The new release can be a major release or a minor release. For example, it could be a minor update to the existing Android version to fix critical issues or security flaws. It could also be the major update from Android 6 to Android 7. Let's look at the content of the OTA package that we are going to create in this chapter to find out what is inside an OTA package. The OTA package that we are going to create in this chapter is an OTA update package of our entire ROM. We can use recovery to flash the OTA package to our VirtualBox device. This is another way to install the system image that we build to the virtual device.

Let's look at the content of the OTA package that we will build in this chapter. The OTA package itself is a ZIP file. After we extract the ZIP file, we can list the content of the ZIP file as follows:

```
$ ls -F
boot.img*  file_contexts*  META-INF/  recovery/  system/
```

We can see that it includes two files and three folders. After we flash this update package using recovery, it will update the `/boot` partition and the `/system` partition:

- `boot.img`: The image of the `/boot` partition, which includes kernel and ramdisk.
- `file_contexts`: This file is used to assign labels to files according to SELinux policy. SELinux is enabled by default in the latest Android system. After the recovery updates the system partition, it must apply labels using this file.
- `META-INF`: This folder includes the signature of the OTA package, the updater, and updater script. We will look at the details of this folder later.
- `recovery`: This folder includes an `install-recovery.sh` shell script and a `recovery-from-boot.p` patch file.
- `system`: This is the `system` folder that recovery will update to the `/system` partition.

OTA packages are usually used to update `/boot` and `/system` partitions. It does not update itself. The update of the `/recovery` partition is in the normal boot up process. During the boot up, the init will execute `install-recovery.sh` in the `init.rc` script through the following `flash_recovery` service:

```
service flash_recovery /system/bin/install-recovery.sh
    class main
    oneshot
```

The `install-recovery.sh` script installs recovery using the `recovery-from-boot.p` patch file as follows:

```
#!/system/bin/sh
if ! applypatch -c
EMMC:/dev/block/sda7:7757824:853301871de495db2b8c93f7a37779b9eeccb169; then
   applypatch -b /system/etc/recovery-resource.dat
EMMC:/dev/block/sda8:6877184:2f58cc1a4035176c8fefc19be70c00e625acc16b
EMMC:/dev/block/sda7 853301871de495db2b8c93f7a37779b9eeccb169 7757824
2f58cc1a4035176c8fefc19be70c00e625acc16b:/system/recovery-from-boot.p &&
log -t recovery "Installing new recovery image: succeeded" || log -t
recovery "Installing new recovery image: failed"
else
   log -t recovery "Recovery image already installed"
fi
```

In our environment setup, the `/recovery` partition is in the `/dev/block/sda7` partition. This script will check the `sha1` hash of the `/dev/block/sha7` partition. If the `sha1` hash value is not the same, it will update the `/recovery` partition.

Now let's look at the `META-INF` folder, as shown in the following screenshot:

```
$ls
boot.img  file_contexts  META-INF  recovery  system
$tree META-INF/
META-INF/
├── CERT.RSA
├── CERT.SF
├── com
│   ├── android
│   │   ├── metadata
│   │   └── otacert
│   └── google
│       └── android
│           ├── update-binary
│           └── updater-script
└── MANIFEST.MF

4 directories, 7 files
$
```

As we can see, the signature of the update package, updater, and updater script are included in the META-INF folder. Before the recovery applies the update, it will verify the package signature in the META-INF folder against the trusted certificates at /system/etc/security/otacerts.zip.

The updater is an executable at META-INF/com/google/android/update-binary. It interprets a script in the META-INF/com/google/android/updater-script file. The script is written in an extensible scripting language (edify) that supports commands for typical update related tasks.

Since the updater and the updater script are the key components in the OTA package to support an OTA update, we will look into the details of them.

Updater

updater is an individual executable for the target device in the AOSP source tree. It can be found in the $AOSP/bootable/recovery/updater folder. Let's look at the main function in the updater.cpp file. Since the main function is a little long, let's look at it in several paragraphs:

```
#include <stdio.h>
#include <unistd.h>
#include <stdlib.h>
#include <string.h>

#include "edify/expr.h"
#include "updater.h"
#include "install.h"
#include "blockimg.h"
#include "minzip/Zip.h"
#include "minzip/SysUtil.h"

#include "register.inc"

#define SCRIPT_NAME "META-INF/com/google/android/updater-script"

extern bool have_eio_error;

struct selabel_handle *sehandle;

int main(int argc, char** argv) {
    setbuf(stdout, NULL);
    setbuf(stderr, NULL);
```

```
    if (argc != 4 && argc != 5) {
        printf("unexpected number of arguments (%d)\n", argc);
        return 1;
    }

    char* version = argv[1];
    if ((version[0] != '1' && version[0] != '2' && version[0] != '3')
    ||
        version[1] != '\0') {
        // We support version 1, 2, or 3.
        printf("wrong updater binary API; expected 1, 2, or 3; "
                    "got %s\n",
                argv[1]);
        return 2;

    }
```

The updater has four arguments. The first thing it will do is check whether there are four arguments passed to it. As we can see from the code, these four arguments are:

- The first argument is the executable name, which is update-binary here
- The second argument is the updater version
- The third argument is the pipe that can be used to communicate to the recovery
- The fourth argument is the OTA package path

It will check the updater version before it continues:

```
// Set up the pipe for sending commands back to the parent process.

int fd = atoi(argv[2]);
FILE* cmd_pipe = fdopen(fd, "wb");
setlinebuf(cmd_pipe);

// Extract the script from the package.

const char* package_filename = argv[3];
MemMapping map;
if (sysMapFile(package_filename, &map) != 0) {
    printf("failed to map package %s\n", argv[3]);
    return 3;
}
ZipArchive za;
int err;
err = mzOpenZipArchive(map.addr, map.length, &za);
if (err != 0) {
    printf("failed to open package %s: %s\n",
            argv[3], strerror(err));
    return 3;
```

```
    }
    ota_io_init(&za);

    const ZipEntry* script_entry = mzFindZipEntry(&za, SCRIPT_NAME);
    if (script_entry == NULL) {
        printf("failed to find %s in %s\n", SCRIPT_NAME, package_filename);
        return 4;
    }

    char* script = reinterpret_cast<char*>(malloc(script_entry->uncompLen+1));
    if (!mzReadZipEntry(&za, script_entry, script, script_entry->uncompLen)) {
        printf("failed to read script from package\n");
        return 5;
    }
    script[script_entry->uncompLen] = '\0';
```

The next thing to do is to open the pipe to establish the communication channel with recovery. Then it extracts `updater-script` from the OTA package to prepare for the execution of the script:

```
    // Configure edify's functions.

    RegisterBuiltins();
    RegisterInstallFunctions();
    RegisterBlockImageFunctions();
    RegisterDeviceExtensions();
    FinishRegistration();

    // Parse the script.

    Expr* root;
    int error_count = 0;
    int error = parse_string(script, &root, &error_count);
    if (error != 0 || error_count > 0) {
        printf("%d parse errors\n", error_count);
        return 6;
    }

    struct selinux_opt seopts[] = {
      { SELABEL_OPT_PATH, "/file_contexts" }
    };

    sehandle = selabel_open(SELABEL_CTX_FILE, seopts, 1);

    if (!sehandle) {
        fprintf(cmd_pipe, "ui_print Warning: No file_contexts\n");
    }
```

```
// Evaluate the parsed script.

UpdaterInfo updater_info;
updater_info.cmd_pipe = cmd_pipe;
updater_info.package_zip = &za;
updater_info.version = atoi(version);
updater_info.package_zip_addr = map.addr;
updater_info.package_zip_len = map.length;

State state;
state.cookie = &updater_info;
state.script = script;
state.errmsg = NULL;

if (argc == 5) {
    if (strcmp(argv[4], "retry") == 0) {
        state.is_retry = true;
    } else {
        printf("unexpected argument: %s", argv[4]);
    }
}

char* result = Evaluate(&state, root);

if (have_eio_error) {
    fprintf(cmd_pipe, "retry_update\n");
}

if (result == NULL) {
    if (state.errmsg == NULL) {
        printf("script aborted (no error message)\n");
        fprintf(cmd_pipe, "ui_print script aborted (no error
        message)\n");
    } else {
        printf("script aborted: %s\n", state.errmsg);
        char* line = strtok(state.errmsg, "\n");
        while (line) {
            if (*line == 'E') {
                if (sscanf(line, "E%u: ", &state.error_code) != 1) {
                    printf("Failed to parse error code: [%s]\n", line);
                }
            }
            fprintf(cmd_pipe, "ui_print %s\n", line);
            line = strtok(NULL, "\n");
        }
        fprintf(cmd_pipe, "ui_print\n");
    }
```

```
        if (state.error_code != kNoError) {
            fprintf(cmd_pipe, "log error: %d\n", state.error_code);
            if (state.cause_code != kNoCause) {
                fprintf(cmd_pipe, "log cause: %d\n", state.cause_code);
            }
        }

        free(state.errmsg);
        return 7;
    } else {
        fprintf(cmd_pipe, "ui_print script succeeded: result was [%s]\n",
        result);
        free(result);
    }

    if (updater_info.package_zip) {
        mzCloseZipArchive(updater_info.package_zip);
    }
    sysReleaseMap(&map);
    free(script);

    return 0;
}
```

Before it can start to execute the update script, it needs to register functions to interpret edify language inside the update script. As we can see from the preceding code, these functions include the following four categories:

- Built-in functions to support the edify language syntax. These functions are implemented in `bootable/recovery/edify/expr.cpp`.
- Package installation related functions. These functions are implemented in `bootable/recovery/updater/install.cpp`.
- Functions to handle block-based OTA packages. In Android 4.4 and earlier versions, the file-based OTA updates are used. In Android 5.0 and later versions, the block-based OTA updates are used. Refer to the following URL about file versus block OTAs:
  `https://source.android.com/devices/tech/ota/block.html`
  The block-based functions are implemented in
  `bootable/recovery/updater/blockimg.cpp`.
- The developers can extend recovery and updater to provide device-specific OTA extensions.

After it registers all functions, it calls the `parse_string` function to parse the script. Finally, it calls the `Evaluate` function to execute the script.

The updater script

After we explore the implementation of updater, we will look at the updater script in this section. The updater script is the one that performs the update operations in the target device. The updater script is written in a simple script language called edify. An edify script is a list of expressions, one expression per line. It supports the following operators:

- The comparison operators, such as == (string equal) and != (string not equal)
- The logical operators, such as || (logical or), && (logical and), and ! (logical not)
- The concatenation operator +

The only reserved keywords are conditional keywords if, then, else, and endif.

All values in edify are strings. Empty strings are false in a Boolean context and all other strings are true.

 You can refer to the following URL to learn more about edify syntax:
https://source.android.com/devices/tech/ota/inside_packages

Edify functions

The major functionalities of the edify language are implemented as edify functions and the edify functions are registered in the preceding updater source code. To support the OTA update, the edify functions include built-in functions, installation functions, block image functions, and device extensions. We will look at each category in the following sections.

Built-in functions

The built-in functions are used to support edify language syntax. The built-in functions are registered by RegisterBuiltins. We can look at the following source code:

```
void RegisterBuiltins() {
    RegisterFunction("ifelse", IfElseFn);
    RegisterFunction("abort", AbortFn);
    RegisterFunction("assert", AssertFn);
    RegisterFunction("concat", ConcatFn);
    RegisterFunction("is_substring", SubstringFn);
    RegisterFunction("stdout", StdoutFn);
    RegisterFunction("sleep", SleepFn);
```

```
    RegisterFunction("less_than_int", LessThanIntFn);
    RegisterFunction("greater_than_int", GreaterThanIntFn);
}
```

The `RegisterBuiltins` function registers the following built-in functions:

- `ifelse(cond, e1[, e2])`: Evaluates `cond`, and if it is true it evaluates and returns the value of `e1`, otherwise it evaluates and returns `e2` (if present).
- `abort([msg])`: Aborts execution of the script immediately, with the optional `msg`. If the user has turned on text display, `msg` appears in the recovery log and on screen.
- `assert(expr[, expr, ...])`: Evaluates each `expr` in turn. If any is false, it immediately aborts execution with the message `assert failed`.
- `concat(expr[, expr, ...])`: Evaluates each expression and concatenates them.
- `is_substring(substring, string)`: Returns true if a substring can be found.
- `stdout(expr[, expr, ...])`: Evaluates each expression and dumps its value to `stdout`. This is useful for debugging.
- `sleep(secs)`: Sleeps for `secs` seconds.
- `less_than_int(a, b)`: Returns true if and only if `a` (interpreted as an integer) is less than `b` (interpreted as an integer).
- `greater_than_int(a, b)`: Returns true if and only if `a` (interpreted as an integer) is greater than `b` (interpreted as an integer).

Installation functions

The installation-related functions are registered by `RegisterInstallFunctions`. The following is the source code of it:

```
void RegisterInstallFunctions() {
    RegisterFunction("mount", MountFn);
    RegisterFunction("is_mounted", IsMountedFn);
    RegisterFunction("unmount", UnmountFn);
    RegisterFunction("format", FormatFn);
    RegisterFunction("show_progress", ShowProgressFn);
    RegisterFunction("set_progress", SetProgressFn);
    RegisterFunction("delete", DeleteFn);
    RegisterFunction("delete_recursive", DeleteFn);
    RegisterFunction("package_extract_dir", PackageExtractDirFn);
    RegisterFunction("package_extract_file", PackageExtractFileFn);
    RegisterFunction("symlink", SymlinkFn);
```

```
    RegisterFunction("set_metadata", SetMetadataFn);
    RegisterFunction("set_metadata_recursive", SetMetadataFn);
    RegisterFunction("getprop", GetPropFn);
    RegisterFunction("file_getprop", FileGetPropFn);
    RegisterFunction("write_raw_image", WriteRawImageFn);
    RegisterFunction("apply_patch", ApplyPatchFn);
    RegisterFunction("apply_patch_check", ApplyPatchCheckFn);
    RegisterFunction("apply_patch_space", ApplyPatchSpaceFn);
    RegisterFunction("wipe_block_device", WipeBlockDeviceFn);
    RegisterFunction("read_file", ReadFileFn);
    RegisterFunction("sha1_check", Sha1CheckFn);
    RegisterFunction("rename", RenameFn);
    RegisterFunction("wipe_cache", WipeCacheFn);
    RegisterFunction("ui_print", UIPrintFn);
    RegisterFunction("run_program", RunProgramFn);
    RegisterFunction("reboot_now", RebootNowFn);
    RegisterFunction("get_stage", GetStageFn);
    RegisterFunction("set_stage", SetStageFn);
    RegisterFunction("enable_reboot", EnableRebootFn);
    RegisterFunction("tune2fs", Tune2FsFn);
}
```

As we can see, most functions are registered here; we will now have a look at them:

- mount(fs_type, partition_type, name, mount_point): This function mounts a filesystem of fs_type at mount_point. The partition_type argument must be one of MTD or EMMC. The name argument is the name of a partition (system, userdata or cache, and so on). Recovery does not mount any filesystems by default and the updater script must mount any partitions it needs to modify.

- is_mounted(mount_point): Returns true if there is a filesystem mounted at mount_point.

- unmount(mount_point): Unmounts the filesystem mounted at mount_point.

- format(fs_type, partition_type, location, fs_size, mount_point): This function formats a given partition. The fs_type argument can be yaffs2, ext4, or f2fs. The partition_type argument can be MTD or EMMC. The location argument is either the name of the partition or device. The fs_size argument is the filesystem size and mount_point is the mount point name.

- `show_progress(frac, secs)`: Advances the progress meter over the next `frac` of its length over the `secs` seconds. The `secs` argument may be zero, in which case the meter is not advanced automatically, but by the use of the `set_progress` function defined as follows:
  - `set_progress(frac)`: This function sets the position of the progress meter within the chunk defined by the most recent `show_progress` call.
- `delete([filename, ...])`: Deletes all the filenames listed. Returns the number of files successfully deleted.
- `delete_recursive([dirname, ...])`: Recursively deletes `dirname` and all their contents. Returns the number of directories successfully deleted.
- `package_extract_dir(package_dir, dest_dir)`: Extracts all files from the package underneath `package_dir` and writes them to the corresponding tree beneath `dest_dir`. Any existing files are overwritten.
- `package_extract_file(package_file[, dest_file])`: Extracts a single `package_file` from the `update` package and writes it to `dest_file`, overwriting existing files if necessary.
- `symlink(target[, source, ...])`: Creates all sources as symlinks to target.
- `set_metadata(filename, key1, value1[, key2 , value2, ...])`: Sets the keys of the given filename to values.
- `set_metadata_recursive(dirname, key1, value1[, key2, value2, ...])`: Recursively sets the keys of the given `dirname` and all its children to values.
- `getprop(key)`: Returns the value of the system property key (or the empty string, if it's not defined).
- `file_getprop(filename, key)`: Reads the given filename, interprets it as a properties file (for example, `/system/build.prop`), and returns the value of the given key, or the empty string if the key is not present.
- `write_raw_image(filename_or_blob, partition)`: Writes the image in `filename_or_blob` to the MTD partition.
- `apply_patch(src_file, tgt_file, tgt_sha1, tgt_size, patch1_sha1, patch1_blob, [...])`: Applies a binary patch to `src_file` to produce `tgt_file`.
- `apply_patch_check(filename, sha1[, sha1, ...])`: Returns true if the contents of `filename` or the temporary copy in the cache partition (if present) have a SHA1 checksum equal to one of the given `sha1` values.

- `apply_patch_space(bytes)`: Returns true if at least bytes of scratch space is available for applying binary patches.
- `wipe_block_device(block_dev, len)`: Wipes the `len` bytes of the given block device, `block_dev`.
- `read_file(filename)`: Reads `filename` and returns its contents as a binary blob.
- `sha1_check(blob[, sha1])`: The `blob` argument is a blob of the type returned by `read_file` or the one-argument form of `package_extract_file`. With no `sha1` arguments, this function returns the SHA1 hash of the blob. With one or more `sha1` arguments, this function returns the SHA1 hash if it equals one of the arguments, or the empty string if it does not equal any of them.
- `rename(src_filename, tgt_filename)`: Renames `src_filename` to `tgt_filename`.
- `wipe_cache()`: Causes the cache partition to be wiped at the end of a successful installation.
- `ui_print([text, ...])`: Concatenates all text arguments and prints the result to the UI.
- `run_program(path[, arg, ...])`: Executes the binary at `path` with arguments `arg`. Returns the program's exit status.
- `reboot_now(name[, arg, ...])`: Reboots the device immediately. The `name` argument is the partition name passed to the Android reboot property.
- `get_stage(name)`: This function returns the value saved by the `set_stage` function. The `name` argument is the block device for the `/misc` partition.
- `set_stage(name, stage)`: This function stores a string value that future invocations of recovery can access. The `name` argument is the block device for the `/misc` partition. The stage is the string to store.
- `enable_reboot()`: Sends the `enable_reboot` command to recovery through the pipe.
- `tune2fs(arg, ...)`: Changes the filesystem parameters on an ext2/ext3 filesystem.

Block image functions

In Android 5.0 or above, the block-based OTA packages can be used. The block-based OTA packages treat the entire partition as a single file and update it at block level. The functions for block-based OTA packages are registered by the `RegisterBlockImageFunctions` function:

```
void RegisterBlockImageFunctions() {
    RegisterFunction("block_image_verify", BlockImageVerifyFn);
    RegisterFunction("block_image_update", BlockImageUpdateFn);
    RegisterFunction("range_sha1", RangeSha1Fn);
}
```

The block-based update implementation includes three functions:

- `block_image_verify(partition, transfer_list, new, patch)`: The `partition` argument is the device that the update will do. Usually, it is the `/system` partition. The `transfer_list` argument is a text file containing commands to transfer data from one place to another on the `target` partition. This command only performs a dry run without writing to test if an update can proceed.
- `block_image_update(partition, transfer_list, new, patch)`: This function is the same as `block_image_verify` except it performs the actual update.
- `range_sha1(partition, range)`: This function checks the SHA1 hash of a partition in the specified range.

Device extensions

As Android system developers, we can extend the edify language to meet our device-specific requirements. To extend the edify language with our own functions, we can register our functions using the following function call:

```
RegisterDeviceExtensions();
```

We will explain how to extend the edify language in the next chapter.

Preparing an OTA package for x86vbox

We have understood updater and the updater script inside an OTA package so far. We can build an OTA package for our x86vbox device now. To build an OTA package, we can use the following commands:

```
$ mkdir -p dist_output
$ make dist DIST_DIR=dist_output
```

The default OTA package build in Android 5 or above is to build the block-based OTA package, but we will get an error building block-based OTA packages for x86vbox. There are a lot more configurations that are needed to be done to support block-based OTA packages in our environment. All the third-party recovery packages cannot use block-based update packages as well.

To avoid this error, we need to change the following build/core/Makefile file to remove the --block option:

```
$(INTERNAL_OTA_PACKAGE_TARGET): $(BUILT_TARGET_FILES_PACKAGE) $(DISTTOOLS)
        @echo "Package OTA: $@"
        $(hide) PATH=$(foreach
        p,$(INTERNAL_USERIMAGES_BINARY_PATHS),$(p):)$$PATH
        MKBOOTIMG=$(MKBOOTIMG) \
            ./build/tools/releasetools/ota_from_target_files -v \
            --block \
            -p $(HOST_OUT) \
            -k $(KEY_CERT_PAIR) \
            $(if $(OEM_OTA_CONFIG), -o $(OEM_OTA_CONFIG)) \
            $(BUILT_TARGET_FILES_PACKAGE) $@
```

After the build is completed, we can check the OTA package as follows:

```
$ ls dist_output/**-ota-*.zip
dist_output/x86vbox-ota-eng.sgye.zip
```

Let's take a look at the updater script inside the OTA package that we just built:

```
(!less_than_int(1482376066, getprop("ro.build.date.utc"))) || abort("Can't
install this package (Thu Dec 22 11:07:46 CST 2016) over newer build (" +
getprop("ro.build.date") + ").");
getprop("ro.product.device") == "x86vbox" || abort("This package is for
\"x86vbox\" devices; this is a \"" + getprop("ro.product.device") + "\".");
ui_print("Target: Android-
x86/x86vbox/x86vbox:7.1.1/MOB30Z/roger12221103:eng/test-keys");
show_progress(0.750000, 0);
format("ext4", "EMMC", "/dev/block/sda1", "0", "/system");
mount("ext4", "EMMC", "/dev/block/sda1", "/system",
```

```
"max_batch_time=0,commit=1,data=ordered,barrier=1,errors=panic,nodelalloc")
;
package_extract_dir("system", "/system");
symlink("../../gm200/acr/bl.bin",
"/system/lib/firmware/nvidia/gm204/acr/bl.bin",
        "/system/lib/firmware/nvidia/gm206/acr/bl.bin");
...
symlink("wl127x-nvs.bin", "/system/lib/firmware/ti-connectivity/wl1271-
nvs.bin",
        "/system/lib/firmware/ti-connectivity/wl12xx-nvs.bin");
set_metadata_recursive("/system", "uid", 0, "gid", 0, "dmode", 0755,
"fmode", 0644, "capabilities", 0x0, "selabel",
"u:object_r:system_file:s0");
set_metadata_recursive("/system/bin", "uid", 0, "gid", 2000, "dmode", 0755,
"fmode", 0755, "capabilities", 0x0, "selabel",
"u:object_r:system_file:s0");
set_metadata("/system/bin/app_process32", "uid", 0, "gid", 2000, "mode",
0755, "capabilities", 0x0, "selabel", "u:object_r:zygote_exec:s0");
...
set_metadata("/system/xbin/su", "uid", 0, "gid", 2000, "mode", 04751,
"capabilities", 0x0, "selabel", "u:object_r:su_exec:s0");
show_progress(0.050000, 5);
package_extract_file("boot.img", "/dev/block/sda8");
show_progress(0.200000, 10);
unmount("/system");
```

In the updater script, it checks the build information of the current system first. If the current system is newer than the OTA package, it won't update the system. After that, it also checks the device name of the running system and the OTA package, both should match each other. Otherwise, we may update the system using a wrong OTA package.

After all verification work has been done, the script will format the /system partition and create a new system folder from the OTA package. Once the system files are installed, the script will create all necessary soft-links and apply properties for SELinux.

Finally, it will update the /boot partition with a new kernel and ramdisk.

Once we build the OTA package for the x86vbox device, and we also build recovery in Chapter 12, *Introducing Recovery*, we can update our system to the OTA package. We should be able to update the system using this OTA package, but the system may not be able to boot up at the moment. We have two issues that need to be resolved before we can do more.

Recalling how we built recovery for x86vbox, we reuse the source code that we developed from `Chapter 8`, *Creating Your Own Device on VirtualBox*, to `Chapter 11`, *Enabling VirtualBox-Specific Hardware Interfaces* as much as possible. This means we inherited the following features in the recovery build in `Chapter 12`, *Introducing Recovery*:

- The first problem inherited from the two stages boot is that we use the components in the Android `system` folder to boot recovery. Ideally, the recovery should not depend on anything else. It should be a self-contained system. For example, the recovery should work properly, even though the system image is damaged. We can repair the system using recovery.
- We use the two stages boot process from the Android-x86 project. As we can see from the previous chapters, the system disk layout for a two stages boot is different from the standard Android system. The system that we create using the OTA package is the standard Android system disk layout. We can only use the standard boot process to boot the system after the OTA update. This means we have to boot the system using `ramdisk.img` instead of `initrd.img`.

Removing dependencies on /system

The dependencies to the Android `/system` folder include two parts:

- All kernel modules for device drivers are located at:
  `$OUT/system/lib/modules/4.x.x-android-x86`.
- We need to run some basic Linux commands during the recovery boot process. For example, we do hardware initialization using the following command:
  ```
  on init
  exec -- /system/bin/logwrapper /system/bin/sh
  /system/etc/init.sh
  ```

Let's work on the preceding two points one by one in the following sections.

Hardware initialization in recovery

To load the minimum device drivers needed by recovery, we have to change the execution of the shell script for Android system start. This is a customization process from general to specific, which is different from the goal of the Android-x86 project. In the Android-x86 project, all possible device drivers are available, while we should only include the drivers needed by recovery for VirtualBox here. As we can see when we introduce a two stages boot, all possible device drivers are compiled and available in the `$OUT/system/lib/modules/4.x.x-android-x86` folder.

The kernel modules will be loaded to the system depending on the hardware found by the kernel dynamically. In our case, we will remove the dynamically loading process and keep the minimum kernel modules only necessary for the recovery boot up. Let's look at the original startup script for x86vbox:

```
on init
    exec -- /system/bin/logwrapper /system/bin/sh /system/etc/init.sh
```

During the startup, the `init` process will run the preceding command line to execute the `/system/etc/init.sh` script. The commands `/system/bin/logwrapper` and `/system/bin/sh` are both part of the Android system in the `/system/bin` folder. They are not available to recovery, since the `/system` partition is not mounted after recovery boot up.

To resolve this issue, we will use the `busybox` binary in `initrd.img` to provide a minimum environment to execute Linux shell commands in recovery environments. We cannot execute the `/system/etc/init.sh` script either, since it is stored in the `/system/etc` folder, which is also not available to recovery. We will replace it by creating another script, `init.x86vbox.sh`, in `/sbin` in the recovery environment.

We changed `init.recovery.x86vbox.rc` to the following one to remove the dependency from `/system`:

```
on early-init
    # for /bin/busybox
    symlink /bin/ld-linux.so.2 /lib/ld-linux.so.2
    symlink /bin/busybox /bin/sh

on init
    mkdir /vendor
    exec -- /bin/sh /sbin/init.x86vbox.sh

service network_start /sbin/network_start.sh
    user root
```

```
    seclabel u:r:recovery:s0
    oneshot

service console /bin/sh
    class core
    console
    group shell log
    seclabel u:r:shell:s0

on property:ro.debuggable=1
    start console
```

During the `early-init` stage, we create the soft-links to make `/bin/sh` available. We replaced `/system/bin/sh` with `/bin/sh` residing in recovery ramdisk.

In the `init.x86vbox.sh` script, we load the device drivers needed by recovery as follows:

```
#!/bin/busybox sh

echo -n "Initializing x86vbox hardware ..."
PATH=/bin:/sbin:/bin; export PATH

cd /bin;busybox --install -s

cd /x86vbox
insmod atkbd.ko
insmod cn.ko
insmod vboxguest.ko
insmod vboxsf.ko
insmod uvesafb.ko mode_option=${UVESA_MODE:-1024x768}-32

/sbin/mount.vboxsf sdcard /vendor
```

As we can see, in the shell script `init.x86vbox.sh`, we created all soft-links for `busybox` first. Then, we loaded all necessary device drivers. We also mounted a shared folder of VirtualBox under the `/vendor` folder so that we can exchange data between the host and the guest. We will use this folder in the next chapter.

Minimum execution environment in recovery

As we can see from both scripts, `init.recovery.x86vbox.rc` and `init.x86vbox.sh`, we need to execute some Linux commands so that we can perform our tasks during the boot up process.

We need to include all these Linux commands in `ramdisk-recovery.img` so that they are available to recovery. However, the problem is not as simple as we think so far. Most of the commands are dynamically linked instead of static linked in AOSP build output.

In our case, we have two sets of shared libraries that we need to include in `ramdisk-recovery.img`. The `busybox` binary in `initrd.img` from Android-x86 is prebuilt out of the AOSP tree, so they have their own dependencies. If we go to the `newinstaller` folder `bootable/newinstaller/initrd`, we can see the list of executable and shared libraries:

```
$ ls -1 lib
libcrypt.so.1
libc.so.6
libdl.so.2
libm.so.6
libntfs-3g.so.31
libpthread.so.0
librt.so.1
$ ls -1 bin
busybox
ld-linux.so.2
lndir
```

There are eight shared libraries besides the `busybox` binary, as we can see in the preceding snippet.

Besides `busybox`, we also have some executables that are built as part of the AOSP source tree. They have a different set of shared libraries, which need to be included in `ramdisk-recovery.img` as well. For example, the display `uvesafb` driver needs a user space daemon `/sbin/v86d`, which is built as part of the AOSP tree. Without a set of shared libraries in place, it won't be able to work properly. To allow us to run these executable files, we need to include the following shared libraries in `ramdisk-recovery.img`:

```
$ ls -1 recovery/root/system/lib
libc.so
libc++.so
libcutils.so
libext2_uuid.so
liblog.so
libm.so
```

```
libpcre.so
libselinux.so
```

You may be wondering how to find the shared library dependencies. One way that we can do this is to get the linkage information using the following command:

```
$ readelf -d $OUT/recovery/root/sbin/v86d

Dynamic section at offset 0x3e68 contains 29 entries:
  Tag        Type                      Name/Value
 0x00000003 (PLTGOT)                   0x4f7c
 0x00000002 (PLTRELSZ)                 240 (bytes)
 0x00000017 (JMPREL)                   0x5b0
 0x00000014 (PLTREL)                   REL
 0x00000011 (REL)                      0x5a8
 0x00000012 (RELSZ)                    8 (bytes)
 0x00000013 (RELENT)                   8 (bytes)
 0x00000015 (DEBUG)                    0x0
 0x00000006 (SYMTAB)                   0x1a0
 0x0000000b (SYMENT)                   16 (bytes)
 0x00000005 (STRTAB)                   0x3d0
 0x0000000a (STRSZ)                    324 (bytes)
 0x6ffffef5 (GNU_HASH)                 0x514
 0x00000001 (NEEDED)                   Shared library: [libc++.so]
 0x00000001 (NEEDED)                   Shared library: [libdl.so]
 0x00000001 (NEEDED)                   Shared library: [libc.so]
 0x00000001 (NEEDED)                   Shared library: [libm.so]
 0x00000020 (PREINIT_ARRAY)            0x4e50
 0x00000021 (PREINIT_ARRAYSZ)          0x8
 0x00000019 (INIT_ARRAY)               0x4e58
 0x0000001b (INIT_ARRAYSZ)             8 (bytes)
 0x0000001a (FINI_ARRAY)               0x4e60
 0x0000001c (FINI_ARRAYSZ)             8 (bytes)
 0x0000001e (FLAGS)                    BIND_NOW
 0x6ffffffb (FLAGS_1)                  Flags: NOW
 0x6ffffff0 (VERSYM)                   0x540
 0x6ffffffe (VERNEED)                  0x588
 0x6fffffff (VERNEEDNUM)               1
 0x00000000 (NULL)                     0x0
```

As we can see from the preceding output, we can find the shared libraries needed by /sbin/v86d using the readelf command. We also need to verify the dependencies through the testing in the recovery environment, which we will discuss more in the next chapter.

To include all the discussed kernel modules and shared libraries in `ramdisk-recovery.img`, we changed a part of `x86vbox.mk` as follows:

```
PRODUCT_COPY_FILES += \
    device/generic/x86vbox/vbox/vboxguest.ko:system/vendor/vbox/vboxguest.ko \
    device/generic/x86vbox/vbox/vboxsf.ko:system/vendor/vbox/vboxsf.ko \
    device/generic/x86vbox/vbox/vboxvideo.ko:system/vendor/vbox/vboxvideo.ko \
    device/generic/x86vbox/fstab.x86:root/fstab.x86 \
    device/generic/x86vbox/recovery.fstab:recovery/root/etc/recovery.fstab \
    device/generic/x86vbox/recovery/root/init.recovery.x86vbox.rc:root/init.recovery.x86vbox.rc \
    device/generic/x86vbox/recovery/root/sbin/network_start.sh:recovery/root/sbin/network_start.sh \
    device/generic/x86vbox/recovery/root/sbin/init.x86vbox.sh:recovery/root/sbin/init.x86vbox.sh \
    device/generic/x86vbox/recovery/root/sbin/create_partitions.sh:recovery/root/sbin/create_partitions.sh \
    device/generic/x86vbox/recovery/root/sbin/mount.vboxsf:recovery/root/sbin/mount.vboxsf \
    device/generic/x86vbox/recovery/root/sbin/gdbserver:recovery/root/sbin/gdbserver \
    device/generic/x86vbox/recovery/root/x86vbox/atkbd.ko:recovery/root/x86vbox/atkbd.ko \
    device/generic/x86vbox/recovery/root/x86vbox/cn.ko:recovery/root/x86vbox/cn.ko \
    device/generic/x86vbox/recovery/root/x86vbox/uvesafb.ko:recovery/root/x86vbox/uvesafb.ko \
    device/generic/x86vbox/recovery/root/x86vbox/drm.ko:recovery/root/x86vbox/drm.ko \
    device/generic/x86vbox/recovery/root/x86vbox/ttm.ko:recovery/root/x86vbox/ttm.ko \
    device/generic/x86vbox/recovery/root/x86vbox/drm_kms_helper.ko:recovery/root/x86vbox/drm_kms_helper.ko \
    device/generic/x86vbox/recovery/root/x86vbox/fb_sys_fops.ko:recovery/root/x86vbox/fb_sys_fops.ko \
    device/generic/x86vbox/recovery/root/x86vbox/sysimgblt.ko:recovery/root/x86vbox/sysimgblt.ko \
    device/generic/x86vbox/recovery/root/x86vbox/sysfillrect.ko:recovery/root/x86vbox/sysfillrect.ko \
    device/generic/x86vbox/recovery/root/x86vbox/syscopyarea.ko:recovery/root/x86vbox/syscopyarea.ko \
    device/generic/x86vbox/vbox/vboxguest.ko:recovery/root/x86vbox/vboxguest.ko \
    device/generic/x86vbox/vbox/vboxsf.ko:recovery/root/x86vbox/vboxsf.ko \
    device/generic/x86vbox/vbox/vboxvideo.ko:recovery/root/x86vbox/vboxvideo.ko \
    device/generic/x86vbox/recovery/root/lib/libc.so.6:recovery/root/lib/libc.so.6 \
    device/generic/x86vbox/recovery/root/lib/libcrypt.so.1:recovery/root/lib/libcrypt.so.1 \
    device/generic/x86vbox/recovery/root/lib/libdl.so.2:recovery/root/lib/libdl.so.2 \
    device/generic/x86vbox/recovery/root/lib/libm.so.6:recovery/root/lib/libm.so.6 \
    device/generic/x86vbox/recovery/root/lib/libntfs-3g.so.31:recovery/root/lib/libntfs-3g.so.31 \
    device/generic/x86vbox/recovery/root/lib/libpthread.so.0:recovery/root/lib/libpthread.so.0 \
    device/generic/x86vbox/recovery/root/lib/librt.so.1:recovery/root/lib/librt.so.1 \
    device/generic/x86vbox/recovery/root/bin/busybox:recovery/root/bin/busybox \
    device/generic/x86vbox/recovery/root/bin/ld-linux.so.2:recovery/root/bin/ld-linux.so.2 \
    device/generic/x86vbox/recovery/root/bin/lndir:recovery/root/bin/lndir \
    device/generic/x86vbox/recovery/root/system/bin/linker:recovery/root/system/bin/linker \
    device/generic/x86vbox/recovery/root/system/lib/libc.so:recovery/root/system/lib/libc.so \
    device/generic/x86vbox/recovery/root/system/lib/libc++.so:recovery/root/system/lib/libc++.so \
    device/generic/x86vbox/recovery/root/system/lib/libcutils.so:recovery/root/system/lib/libcutils.so \
    device/generic/x86vbox/recovery/root/system/lib/liblog.so:recovery/root/system/lib/liblog.so \
    device/generic/x86vbox/recovery/root/system/lib/libm.so:recovery/root/system/lib/libm.so \
    device/generic/x86vbox/recovery/root/system/lib/libpcre.so:recovery/root/system/lib/libpcre.so \
    device/generic/x86vbox/recovery/root/system/lib/libselinux.so:recovery/root/system/lib/libselinux.so \
    $(LOCAL_KERNEL):kernel \
```

Building and testing

After we have done all the analysis in this chapter, we can build and test our code now.

As usual, we have a manifest file for each chapter. We make changes for this chapter based on the source code of Chapter 12, *Introducing Recovery*. The following are the projects that we changed in this chapter:

```xml
<?xml version="1.0" encoding="UTF-8"?>
<manifest>

  <remote  name="github"
           revision="refs/tags/android-7.1.1_r4_x86vbox_ch13_r1"
           fetch="." />

  <remote  name="aosp"
           fetch="https://android.googlesource.com/" />
  <default revision="refs/tags/android-7.1.1_r4"
           remote="aosp"
           sync-c="true"
           sync-j="1" />

  <!-- github/android-7.1.1_r4_ch13 -->
  <project path="kernel" name="goldfish" remote="github" />
  <project path="bootable/newinstaller"
  name="platform_bootable_newinstaller" remote="github" />
  <project path="device/generic/common" name="device_generic_common"
  groups="pdk" remote="github" />
  <project path="device/generic/x86vbox" name="x86vbox" remote="github"
  />
  <project path="bootable/recovery" name="android_bootable_recovery"
  remote="github" groups="pdk" />
  . . .
```

We can see that we need to change four projects: `recovery`, `newinstaller`, `common`, and `x86vbox`. We have an `android-7.1.1_r4_x86vbox_ch13_r1` tag as the baseline of the source code for this chapter.

To get the source code from GitHub and AOSP directly, the following command can be used:

```
$ repo init -u https://github.com/shugaoye/manifests -b
android-7.1.1_r4_ch13_aosp
$ repo sync
```

After the source code is ready for use, we can set the environment and build the system as follows:

```
$ . build/envsetup.sh
$ lunch x86vbox-eng
$ make -j4
```

To build initrd.img, we can run the following command:

```
$ make initrd USE_SQUASHFS=0
```

To build the OTA package for the x86vbox device, we can run the following command:

```
$ mkdir -p dist_output
$ make dist DIST_DIR=dist_output
```

To test the AOSP images in VirtualBox, we need to use PXE boot and NFS as we introduced in Chapter 9, *Booting Up x86vbox Using PXE/NFS*.

After the build is completed, we can add an entry in the PXE boot configuration file, $HOME/.VirtualBox/TFTP/pxelinux.cfg/default, as follows to test recovery:

```
label 3. Recovery - x86vbox
menu x86vbox_ramdisk_recovery
kernel x86vbox/kernel
append ip=dhcp console=ttyS3,115200 initrd=x86vbox/ramdisk-recovery.img
androidboot.hardware=x86vbox
```

After the recovery is started, we can see the following screen of recovery on the x86vbox device:

The user interface of recovery for x86vbox looks the same on any Android device.

Before you download the source code and build everything by yourself, you can also download and test the pre-built image in this chapter at https://sourceforge.net/projec ts/android-system-programming/files/android-7/ch13/ch13.zip/download.

Summary

In this chapter, we learnt about the workflow of updater, which is the one actually to do the work of the OTA update. The updater interprets the updater script inside the OTA package to perform the update. We don't have to create the updater script by ourselves. It is created during the build process automatically. You may have some questions here, since you may use some recovery packages created by open source developers or ROM developers. You may even use recovery distributed by LineageOS/CyanogenMod or TWRP. How do they relate to the topics that we discussed in this chapter? These are the topics that we will cover in the next chapter.

14
Customizing and Debugging Recovery

In the last chapter, we created an OTA package for our x86vbox device. We also improved the recovery to remove all dependencies from the Android system so that it becomes a self-contained environment. We can run recovery and update the system using the OTA package we created. After the system is updated, we cannot use a two stages boot since the system becomes a standard Android system image layout.

In this chapter, we will enhance both recovery and the updater to support both standard and two stages boot using one system image. We will also enhance recovery to resolve one issue that we haven't talked about, which is how we pick up the OTA package in the recovery environment. In this chapter, we will cover the following topics:

- Introducing the Android native application debug skill, which we can use to debug both recovery and the updater
- Extending recovery and the updater to support the enhanced system image and load the OTA package via the shared folder of VirtualBox
- Exploring the famous third-party recovery packages such as Xposed, GApps, and so on

Debugging and testing native Android applications

Since the recovery environment is a self-contained environment, both recovery and the updater are static linked so they don't depend on the C runtime shared libraries. We talked about the C runtime shared libraries in the last chapter, when we removed the dependencies from the /system folder. In such an environment, the production release may contain only recovery itself, so it is very difficult to debug the recovery or updater in such an environment.

The only way that we can identify the potential issues is to look at the log files stored in the cache partition. At runtime, recovery prints the debug messages to the /tmp/recovery.log log file. Before it prepares to reboot the system, it will store the log file to the cache partition at /recovery/last_log. If the updater is executed to update the system, it will store the log file at /recovery/last_install in the cache partition.

To debug recovery or the updater in the production release, the developers can build the new version and flash it to the recovery partition. After that, the system needs to be rebooting to recovery to perform the test cases. Then, the developers need to check the log files in the cache partition to identify any potential issues. This process is very tedious and not efficient.

To make life easier, the developers may add a console service to the debug environment and remove it later in the production release. This is exactly what we do in our recovery build. We can add the following console service in the init.recovery.x86vbox.rc script:

```
service console /bin/sh
    class core
    console
    group shell log
    seclabel u:r:shell:s0
```

To have a console service, we need to include a shell environment. We can choose the toolbox or toybox in AOSP. We can also use the more powerful tool, busybox, which is the common tool used in many embedded systems.

After we have a debug console, we have a lot of flexibility to do many things. We can monitor the log messages at runtime instead of checking them offline. We can even include the gdbserver to the debug environment so that we can do source level debugging using gdb.

In this chapter, I will introduce how to do source-level debugging of both recovery and the updater. I will also introduce how to integrate the source-level debugging into Eclipse so that we can have an environment that is similar to the normal native Android application development, which is highly efficient for the developers who work on Android recovery.

Debugging with GDB

To use GDB to debug recovery and the updater, we need to tweak the start up script a little so that it won't start the recovery automatically. With this change, after the system boot up, we can start it using gdbserver in the debug console. To do this, we need to make a change to the $OUT/recovery/root/init.rc script as follows:

```
service recovery /sbin/recovery
    seclabel u:r:recovery:s0
    disabled
```

We add the disabled option to the recovery service. After the system boot up, we can start it manually or we can execute the recovery from the command line directly.

Both AOSP and Android NDK include gdb and gdbserver, so the developers can do source-level debugging for native applications.

In AOSP environments, gdb can be found at the following path:

$AOSP/prebuilts/gdb/linux-x86/bin/gdb

gdbserver is included in the system image by default. It can be found at:

$OUT/system/bin/gdbserver

We can copy gdbserver from the system image to ramdisk-recovery.img in the recovery debug environment.

In the embedded system or Android, gdbserver and gdb work in client/server mode. On Android devices, gdbserver invokes the debug target as a server. On the host side, gdb can connect to gdbserver through the network protocol. The network protocol is TCP over the adb connection.

To debug recovery, we can run the following command in the debug console:

```
# gdbserver :10000 /sbin/recovery
```

The debug port of the TCP protocol is `10000` here. We need to use `adb` to forward this port to the host side, since the network ports on the device side are invisible to the host. On the host side, we can run the following command to do the port forwarding:

```
$ adb forward tcp:10000 tcp:10000
```

After this, we can start `gdb` on the host side to establish the connection. We use `gdb` to debug recovery as an example here:

```
$ gdb $OUT/recovery/root/sbin/recovery
```

Pay attention to the fact that we use the `gdb` command from AOSP here and use the `$OUT` environment variable to locate the executable for the build output. Set up your environment variables correctly or use the absolute path. All our commands in this chapter are executed in the AOSP build environment. To set the AOSP build environment, we can run the following commands:

```
$ source build/envsetup.sh
$ lunch x86vbox-eng
```

After we start `gdb` to debug recovery, we may find an error message to complain that there are no debugging symbols in the executable. We need to load the debugging symbols and set the paths so that `gdb` can find the symbols for both recovery and any libraries loaded. We need to execute the following three commands in the `gdb` command line:

```
(gdb) symbol-file
$OUT/obj/EXECUTABLES/recovery_intermediates/LINKED/recovery
(gdb) set solib-absolute-prefix $OUT/symbols
(gdb) set solib-search-path $OUT/symbols/system/lib
```

For convenience, I use the `$OUT` environment variable to represent the output folder of the AOSP build. We can use it in the AOSP build shell console, but we cannot use it in the `gdb` command line. Convert it to the absolute path in your environment.

We can connect to `gdbserver` now. To connect to `gdbserver`, we can run the following command in the `gdb` command-line prompt:

```
(gdb) target remote :10000
```

The port `10000` tells `gdb` to connect to the localhost port `10000`, which we forward from the device using the `adb` command. We can debug recovery at source code level now.

To make the debugging process more convenient, we can put the symbol loading to the `gdb` start up script so that we don't have to do this every time. When `gdb` starts, it will look for a `.gdbinit` file at the `Home` directory. If `gdb` can find this file, it will run the command inside this file automatically. We can put the previous symbol loading in `.gdbinit` as follows for recovery:

```
python
import os
gdb.execute('symbol-file ' + os.environ['OUT'] +
'/obj/EXECUTABLES/recovery_intermediates/LINKED/recovery')
gdb.execute('set solib-absolute-prefix '+ os.environ['OUT'] + '/symbols')
gdb.execute('set solib-search-path ' + os.environ['OUT'] +
'/symbols/system/lib')
end
```

As we can see, we actually create a short Python script in `.gdbinit`. The `gdb` command line supports Python binding, so we can run `python` in the `gdb` command line. With `python`, we can use the `$OUT` environment variable, so we can make this script portable.

Even though this script is portable, without using the absolute paths, this script is for recovery only. We need to change it when we debug the updater. We will integrate `gdb` into Eclipse later. With Eclipse integration, we can run different `gdb` start up scripts for different debugging targets. We can create two `gdb` start up scripts, one for recovery and one for the updater. We can name them `recovery.gdb` and `updater.gdb`. The content of `recovery.gdb` is the same as the previous content. `updater.gdb` looks as follows:

```
python
import os
gdb.execute('symbol-file ' + os.environ['OUT'] +
'/obj/EXECUTABLES/updater_intermediates/LINKED/updater')
gdb.execute('set solib-absolute-prefix '+ os.environ['OUT'] + '/symbols')
gdb.execute('set solib-search-path ' + os.environ['OUT'] +
'/symbols/system/lib')
end
```

Before we move to the next topic on Eclipse integration, we still have one last issue that needs to be resolved for the source-level debugging. To run recovery, we can just execute it without any command-line arguments. For the updater, we need to provide the following three command-line arguments; if we recall, we talked about the internals of the updater in the last chapter:

- Updater version
- Pipe to communicate with recovery
- Path of OTA package

We can run the updater in the debug console as follows to start `gdbserver`:

```
# gdbserver :10000 {path of updater}/updater 3 1 {path of OTA package}
```

From the preceding snippet, we can see that we need to resolve two paths. Where do we store the updater and where do we store the OTA package?

When the users perform an update in recovery, recovery extracts the updater to the `/tmp` folder from the OTA package and starts it from there. In the normal debugging of recovery and the updater, the developers use the sideloading methods provided by recovery. There are two ways to load the OTA package using sideloading. One way is to load from an SD card and the other one is to load the OTA package from the `adb` connection in sideloading mode. In our configuration, we have a separate partition--the virtual hard disk for SD card if we refer to `recovery.fstab`:

```
...
/dev/block/sda3 /sdcard vfat defaults voldmanaged=sdcard:auto
...
```

We can find a way to load both the updater and the OTA package to this SD card partition, but it is not convenient for us. In our case, since we use VirtualBox, we can use the shared folder between the host and the guest of VirtualBox to resolve this problem very easily. If you don't remember this, you can refer to Chapter 11, *Enabling VirtualBox Specific-Hardware Interfaces*, as we discussed this topic in detail there. We can map the shared folder to the `/vendor` folder in our recovery environment. We can copy the updater and the OTA package to this folder or we can even map the AOSP build output to this folder directly. After we set up this folder, we can invoke the updater using `gdbserver` as follows:

```
# gdbserver :10000 /vendor/sbin/updater 3 1 /vendor/update-x86vbox-ch14.zip
```

We can debug both recovery and the updater now.

Integration with Eclipse

As we use Eclipse as the **Integrated Development Environment** (IDE) in this book, we can integrate the source-level debugging to the Eclipse environment so we can have a much better user interface compared to the command line-based `gdb`.

Before we can debug recovery or the updater in Eclipse, we need to import projects x86vbox and recovery to Eclipse. Refer to Chapter 4, *Customizing the Android Emulator*; there is a section called *Integrating with Eclipse* that shows how to do this.

As we know, Eclipse uses different plugins to support different programming languages. Google used to provide the **Android Development Tooling** (**ADT**) plugin for Eclipse as the Android application development environment. For the Android native applications, we usually use **C/C++ Development Tooling** (**CDT**) for the C/C++ language development. To integrate the source-level debugging of recovery and the updater with Eclipse, we need to configure CDT to do so. This configuration process is general to all Android native application developments. You can use any latest Eclipse with CDT to follow the instructions in this section. In our case, we use the Eclipse version that comes with the ADT bundle. It may still be available at the following URL:

```
https://dl.google.com/android/adt/adt-bundle-linux-x86_64-20140702.zip
```

To configure CDT to use `gdb` from AOSP, we can select the menu **Run** and **Debug Configurations** to create a new debug configuration in the **C/C++ Application** item called **recovery debug**, as shown in the following screenshot. We will use this debug configuration to debug recovery. We can create the debug configuration for the updater to use the same setup process:

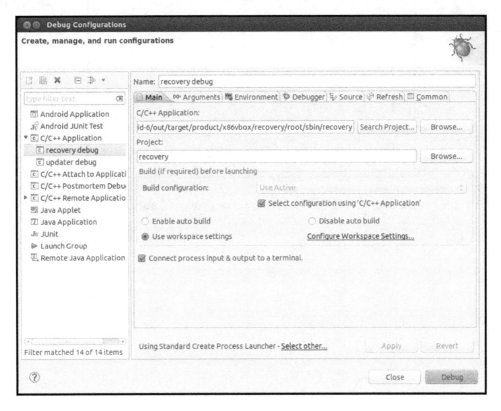

In the **Main** tab, we can set **Project** to recovery, which we import to Eclipse from the AOSP source code. We can set **C/C++ Application** to recovery or updater in the AOSP output folder using the **Browse...** button.

At the bottom of the dialog box, we can select the launcher to use. If we click the highlighted text **Select other...**, we will see the following dialog box:

We should choose the launch type **Standard Create Process Launcher**.

Next, we should go to the **Debugger** tab, as shown in the following screenshot, to set the debugger configuration. In this **Debugger** tab, we should set **Debugger** as **gdbserver**. In the **Debugger Options** group, there are multiple tabs as well. We should set **GDB debugger** as `x86_64-linux-android-gdb` for Android 6 or `gdb` for Android 7. In both cases, `gdb` in the `prebuilts/` folder of AOSP should be used. For **GDB command file**, we should set `recovery.gdb` for recovery and `updater.gdb` for the updater. The GDB command file is the GDB script that we talked about in the *Debugging with GDB* section. We start Eclipse from the AOSP build console so that all the paths for the AOSP prebuilt tools have been set up properly in the AOSP build console. Otherwise, we should use the absolute path:

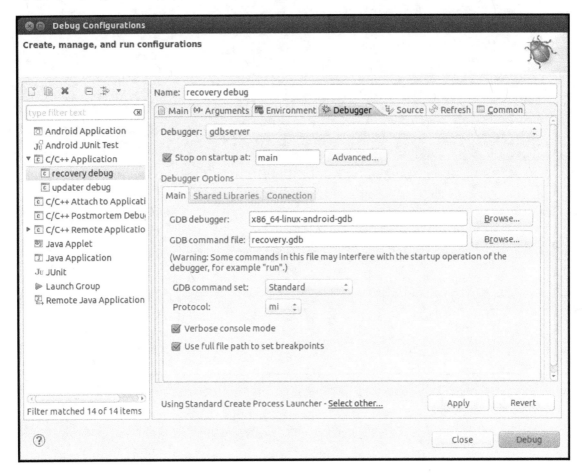

To configure the connection with `gdbserver`, we need to go to the **Connection** tab in the **Debugger Options** group, as we can see in the following screenshot. The **Type** should be set to **TCP**. The **Host name or IP address** should be `localhost`. We set the **Port number** to `10000`:

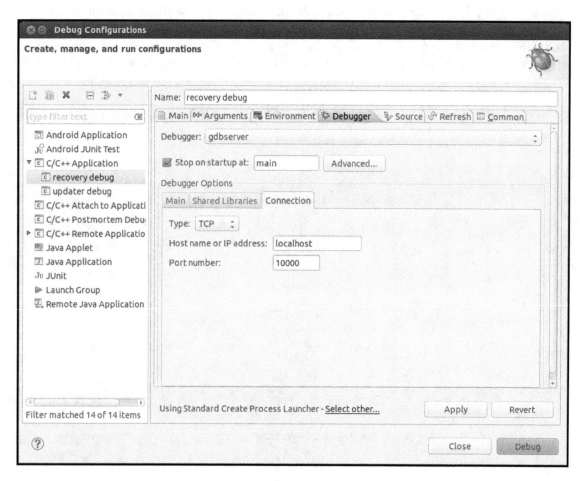

Now we have set up all the necessary configurations in CDT for `gdbserver`. We can start to debug recovery or the updater from the device console using the following command:

```
# gdbserver :10000 /sbin/recovery
```

Or:

```
# gdbserver :10000 /vendor/sbin/updater 3 1 /vendor/update-x86vbox-ch14.zip
```

Once we start `gdbserver` on the device, we need to forward the TCP port `10000` to localhost using the following command:

```
$ adb forward tcp:10000 tcp:10000
```

After this, we can click the **Debug** button in the preceding screenshot to start a debugging session, and we will see the following screen in the Eclipse debug perspective:

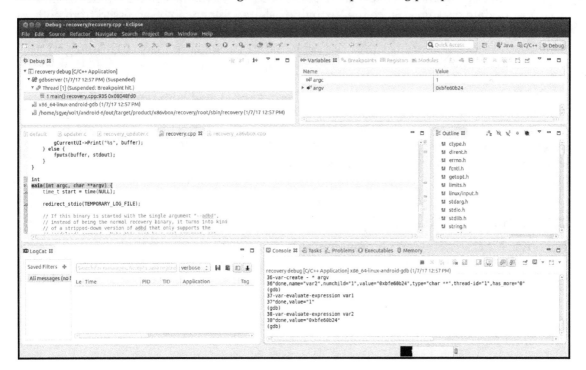

Extending recovery and the updater

After we have set up the debug environment for both recovery and the updater, we will extend both in this chapter to achieve the following goals:

- **Customized update package**: We will create a single system image that can be used for a standard Android boot and a two stages boot.
- **Creating partitions**: We introduced how to install x86vbox images to hard disk using NFS in Chapter 9, *Booting Up x86vbox Using PXE/NFS*. We will use recovery as a method to install x86vbox images in this chapter. To install x86vbox images on a blank hard disk, we need to add an option to allow the users to create partitions on the hard disk.
- **VBox shared folder**: In order to access the x86vbox update images conveniently, we will enhance recovery to be able to use the VirtualBox shared folder to store update packages. Since the VirtualBox shared folder can be accessed from both the host and the device, the developers can choose to map the AOSP output folder as shared storage or can copy update packages to the shared storage manually.

The AOSP recovery system has defined a proper way to extend both recovery and the updater to perform device-specific tasks. The third-party recovery programs such as TWRP or Cyanogen use a similar way to extend the AOSP recovery. The method introduced in this chapter is a good reference for manufacturing or ROM developers about how to extend or enhance the original AOSP recovery and updater.

Extending recovery

The original AOSP recovery is written in C++ language. The implementation of key functionalities is encapsulated in two classes. In the documentation of AOSP, it is recommended to extend recovery to create your own classes by inheriting these two classes.

The first class that we will extend is class `Device` defined in `$AOSP/bootable/recovery/device.h` and the second one is the `ScreenRecoveryUI` class defined in `$AOSP/bootable/recovery/screen_ui.h`. The `ScreenRecoveryUI` class is inherited from another class, `RecoveryUI`, which is used by recovery to perform user interaction functions. The AOSP recovery uses the polymorphism of C++ so that we can extend both the `Device` and `RecoveryUI` classes to let recovery use our version of these two classes to include additional features as we want. We can look at the code of recovery initialization as follows:

```
...
RecoveryUI* ui = NULL;
...
    Device* device = make_device();
    ui = device->GetUI();
    gCurrentUI = ui;

    ui->SetLocale(locale);
    ui->Init();
...
```

During the initialization, recovery creates an instance of the `Device` class by calling the `make_device` function. Inside the `device` instance, a `RecoveryUI` class instance is initialized as well. Recovery gets it by calling the `device->GetUI()` function and stores it in the `ui` global variable. To initialize the graphic system, it calls to the `ui->Init()` function to do the graphic system initialization.

The AOSP recovery allows the developers to overwrite the `make_device` function to extend the `Device` and `RecoveryUI` classes through inheritance.

Let's come back to the goals that we want to achieve to extend recovery. We want to add the following two enhanced features to the recovery of the x86vbox device:

1. Create partitions according to the `recovery.fstab` file.
2. Enable to apply updates from the VirtualBox shared folder.

We start with the changes to extend the `ScreenRecoveryUI` class as follows:

```
#include <linux/input.h>
#include <sys/types.h>
#include <sys/wait.h>

#include "common.h"
#include "screen_ui.h"
#include "device.h"
```

```
// defined in "roots.h"
int unmount_format_volumes(int format);

class X86vboxUI : public ScreenRecoveryUI {
public:
    virtual KeyAction CheckKey(int key) {
      if (key == KEY_HOME) {
        return TOGGLE;
      }
      return ENQUEUE;
    }
};
```

The `X86vboxUI` class is created in the file under the device `x86vbox` folder as follows:

`$AOSP/device/generic/x86vbox/recovery/recovery_x86vbox.cpp`

As we can see, we overwrite a `CheckKey` virtual function to handle the key press. We use the methods from the parent class, `ScreenRecoveryUI`, for all other functions.

Next, we extend the `Device` class to add our features as follows:

```
class X86vboxDevice : public Device {
private:
    X86vboxUI* ui_;

public:
    X86vboxDevice(X86vboxUI* ui) : Device(ui), ui_(ui)  { }

    virtual const char* const* GetMenuItems();
    virtual BuiltinAction InvokeMenuItem(int menu_position);
    X86vboxUI* GetUI() { return ui_; }
    int CreatePartitions();
};
```

In our `X86vboxDevice` class, we overwrite the `GetMenuItems`, `InvokeMenuItem`, and `GetUI` methods to change the menu items and support sideloading from the VirtualBox shared folder. We add a new method, `CreatePartitions`, to allow the users to create partitions on hard disk:

```
static const char* MENU_ITEMS[] = {
    "Reboot system now",
    "Reboot to bootloader",
    "Apply update from VBox shared storage",
    "Apply update from SD card",
    "Wipe data/factory reset",
    "Wipe cache partition",
```

```
    "Mount /system",
    "View recovery logs",
    "Create partitions",
    "Power off",
    NULL
};

const char* const* X86vboxDevice::GetMenuItems() {
  return MENU_ITEMS;
}
```

As we can see from the preceding code, we changed the original menu item "Apply update from ADB" to "Apply update from VBox shared storage" and we added an additional menu item "Create partitions". When the users select an action from the preceding menu item, the following InvokeMenuItem function will be called eventually:

```
Device::BuiltinAction X86vboxDevice::InvokeMenuItem(int menu_position) {
  switch (menu_position) {
    case 0: return REBOOT;
    case 1: return REBOOT_BOOTLOADER;
    case 2: return APPLY_ADB_SIDELOAD; // Apply update from VBox shared
                                       // storage
    case 3: return APPLY_SDCARD;
    case 4: return WIPE_DATA;
    case 5: return WIPE_CACHE;
    case 6: return MOUNT_SYSTEM;
    case 7: return VIEW_RECOVERY_LOGS;
    case 8:
        // Create partition
        CreatePartitions();
        return NO_ACTION;
    case 9: return SHUTDOWN;
    default: return NO_ACTION;
  }
}
```

As we can see, there are a set of default actions that are defined in the BuiltinAction enum as follows. These actions are handled by recovery itself:

- NO_ACTION: Do nothing.
- REBOOT: Exit recovery and reboot the device normally.
- REBOOT_BOOTLOADER: Exit recovery and reboot the device to bootloader.
- APPLY_EXT, APPLY_CACHE, and APPLY_ADB_SIDELOAD: Install an update package from various places. It can be a storage on an SD card or a connection from adb.

- WIPE_DATA: Reformat the user data and cache partitions, also known as a factory data reset.
- WIPE_CACHE: Reformat the cache partition only.
- MOUNT_SYSTEM: Mount the System folder.
- VIEW_RECOVERY_LOGS: View recovery logs.
- SHUTDOWN: Power off the device.

We reuse the APPLY_ADB_SIDELOAD member of the BuiltinAction enum to install an update package from the VirtualBox shared folder for the x86vbox device. The changes were made in the bootable/recovery/recovery.cpp file and we will talk about this in a moment.

To create partitions, we call the CreatePartitions member function and return NO_ACTION. There is no action needed to be done in the upper layer:

```
static const char *X86VBOX_PARTITION_SCRIPT = "/sbin/create_partitions.sh";
static char* const x86vbox_argv[] = {"create_partitions.sh", NULL};
int X86vboxDevice::CreatePartitions() {
    int status;
    pid_t child;

    status = unmount_format_volumes(0);
    if (status != 0) {
        LOGE("failed to un-mount the partitions; aborting\n");
        return status;
    }

    if ((child = vfork()) == 0) {
        execv(X86VBOX_PARTITION_SCRIPT, x86vbox_argv);

        status = unmount_format_volumes(1);
        if (status != 0) {
            LOGE("failed to format the volumes; aborting\n");
            return status;
        }
        ._exit(-1);
    }
    waitpid(child, &status, 0);
    if (!WIFEXITED(status) || WEXITSTATUS(status) != 0) {
        LOGE("%s failed with status %d\n", X86VBOX_PARTITION_SCRIPT,
        WEXITSTATUS(status));
    }
    return WEXITSTATUS(status);
}
```

In `CreatePartitions`, we call the `unmount_format_volumes` function to unmount hard disk volumes first, if there are any of them in use. Then, we execute a `/sbin/create_partitions.sh` shell script to create partitions. Finally, we call the `unmount_format_volumes` function again to unmount and format hard disk volumes. The argument of the `unmount_format_volumes` function tells us whether we want to format the partition after we create it. Let's look at this function as follows:

```
#ifdef X86VBOX_RECOVERY
//
// Unmount or format volumes
// format - if it is not zero, format the volume.
//
int unmount_format_volumes(int format) {
  if (fstab == NULL) {
      LOGE("can't set up install mounts: no fstab loaded\n");
      return -1;
  }
  for (int i = 0; i < fstab->num_entries; ++i) {
      Volume* v = fstab->recs + i;

      if (strcmp(v->mount_point, "/tmp") == 0) {
        if (ensure_path_mounted(v->mount_point) != 0) {
            LOGE("failed to mount %s\n", v->mount_point);
            return -1;
        }
      } else {
        if (ensure_path_unmounted(v->mount_point) != 0) {
            LOGE("failed to unmount %s\n", v->mount_point);
            return -1;
        }
        if (format) {
         if(strcmp(v->mount_point, "/system") == 0 ||
                    strcmp(v->mount_point, "/data") == 0 ||
                    strcmp(v->mount_point, "/cache") == 0) {
              int result = format_volume(v->mount_point);
              if (result != 0) {
                LOGE("failed to format volume:%s; aborting\n", v-
                    >mount_point);
                return result;
              }
          }
        }
      }
  }
  return 0;
}
#endif
```

We changed the `bootable/recovery/roots.cpp` recovery code to add this function, so we add an `X86VBOX_RECOVERY` macro to enable or disable it.

Now, let's look at how we implement the installation of an update package from the VirtualBox shared folder. We reuse the `APPLY_ADB_SIDELOAD` action to call our `apply_from_x86vbox` function to do this. After `InvokeMenuItem` is returned, it returns to a recovery function, `prompt_and_wait`. This is where recovery waits for user input and takes the corresponding actions:

```
...
case Device::APPLY_ADB_SIDELOAD:
case Device::APPLY_SDCARD:
    {
      bool adb = (chosen_action == Device::APPLY_ADB_SIDELOAD);
      if (adb) {
        #ifdef X86VBOX_RECOVERY
        status = apply_from_x86vbox(device, &should_wipe_cache);
        #else
        status = apply_from_adb(ui, &should_wipe_cache,
        TEMPORARY_INSTALL_FILE);
        #endif
      } else {
        status = apply_from_sdcard(device, &should_wipe_cache);
      }
...
```

We changed the `bootable/recovery/recovery.cpp` recovery code, so we conditionally compile the code using the `X86VBOX_RECOVERY` macro.

The `apply_from_x86vbox` function is also implemented in the same file, as follows:

```
#ifdef X86VBOX_RECOVERY
static const char *X86VBOX_ROOT = "/vendor";

static int apply_from_x86vbox(Device* device, bool* wipe_cache) {
    modified_flash = true;

    char* path = browse_directory(X86VBOX_ROOT, device);
    if (path == NULL) {
        ui->Print("\n-- No package file selected.\n");
        return INSTALL_ERROR;
    }

    ui->Print("\n-- Install %s ...\n", path);
    set_sdcard_update_bootloader_message();
    void* token = start_sdcard_fuse(path);
```

```
    int status = install_package(FUSE_SIDELOAD_HOST_PATHNAME,
    wipe_cache, TEMPORARY_INSTALL_FILE, false);

    finish_sdcard_fuse(token);
    return status;
}
#endif
```

As we can see, we reuse the code from the `apply_from_sdcard` function and change the path to `/vendor`, which is the mount point for the VirtualBox shared folder.

Finally, we overwrite the `make_device` function to create an instance of the `X86vboxDevice` class instead of the `Device` class:

```
Device* make_device() {
    return new X86vboxDevice(new X86vboxUI);
}
```

After we make all the changes, we can run the code in the `gdb` debugger as we explained in an earlier part of this chapter.

After we start `gdb` and connect to the target device, we can set the debug point at:

(gdb) b make_device
(gdb) b X86vboxDevice::InvokeMenuItem

We can trace and debug our code now.

Extending the updater

We have three goals in this chapter to support additional features for the x86vbox device. We implemented VirtualBox shared folder support and created partitions in recovery code. The last one is that we want to create a customized update package. We can use this image to support both the standard Android boot process and the two stages boot.

If we want to create an image that can support both boot up processes, let's look at the following diagram:

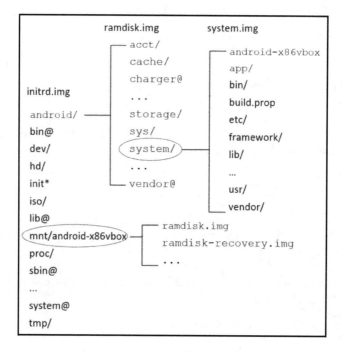

Layout of images for two stages boot

In the preceding diagram, we show the layout of three image files involved in both the normal boot up process and the two stages boot up process.

In the normal boot up process, there are only `ramdisk.img` and `system.img` involved. When `kernel` and `ramdisk.img` are loaded into memory, the layout of `ramdisk.img` is used as the root filesystem. The init process is in charge of mounting the rest of the filesystems to the root filesystem. `system.img` is mounted at the `/system` folder.

In the two stages boot up process, there are four image files involved: `initrd.img`, `ramdisk.img`, `system.img`, and the image file for the first stage boot. The image file for the first stage is an image like the `x86emu_x86.img` that we introduced in Chapter 6, *Debugging the Boot Up Process Using a Customized ramdisk*. The image files `ramdisk.img` and `system.img` are included inside `x86emu_x86.img`. At the beginning, `kernel` and `initrd.img` are loaded into memory. The layout of `initrd.img` is the root filesystem of the first stage boot. A separate image file containing both `ramdisk.img` and `system.img` is mounted at the `/mnt/android-x86vbox` folder.

The init script inside `initrd.img` extracts `ramdisk.img` to the `/android` folder. This folder will be used as the root filesystem of the second stage boot. The init script will do a bind mount of `system.img` to the `/android/system` folder, so we will have a complete Android filesystem layout under the `/android` folder.

To combine the first stage image file like `x86emu_x86.img` to `system.img`, we can create an `android-x86vbox` folder in the `system.img` and put both `ramdisk.img` and `ramdisk-recovery.img` in this folder. In the two stages boot, `system.img` is mounted at `/mnt`. The init script in `initrd.img` can find `ramdisk.img` or `ramdisk-recovery.img` at `/mnt/android-x86vbox`, which is the same as before. For `system.img`, we need to change the init script a little. Instead of doing a bind mount from `/mnt/android-x86vbox/system.img` to `/android/system`, we need to move the mount point `/mnt` to `/android/system`. The following figure shows the layout of images after we combine the two stages boot into `system.img`:

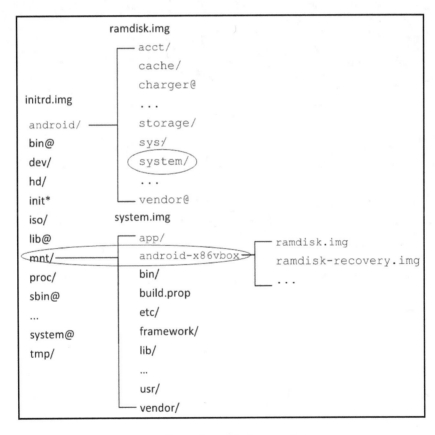

Layout of images using system.img for two stages boot

We can change the `check_root` function in the init script as shown in the following code snippet. This function is in the `bootable/newinstaller/initrd/init` file. We move the mount point using the `mount` command with the `--move` option. We also use an `X86VBOX` kernel argument to handle this. If this variable is not defined, the behavior of the init script won't change:

```
check_root()
{
    if [ "`dirname $1`" = "/dev" ]; then
        [ -e $1 ] || return 1
        blk=`basename $1`
        [ ! -e /dev/block/$blk ] && ln $1 /dev/block
        dev=/dev/block/$blk
    else
        dev=$1
    fi
    try_mount ro $dev /mnt || return 1
    find_ramdisk
    if [ -n "$iso" -a -e /mnt/$iso ]; then
        mount --move /mnt /iso
        mkdir /mnt/iso
        mount -o loop /iso/$iso /mnt/iso
        SRC=iso
    elif [ ! -e $RAMDISK ]; then
        return 1
    fi
    zcat $RAMDISK | cpio -id > /dev/null
    if [ -e /mnt/$SRC/system.sfs ]; then
...
    else
        if [ -n "$X86VBOX" ]; then
          mount --move /mnt /android/system
        else
          rm -rf *
          return 1
        fi
    fi
    mkdir mnt
    echo " found at $1"
    rm /sbin/mke2fs
    hash -r
}
```

In the standard build of the OTA package, we won't be able to include `ramdisk.img` and `ramdisk-recovery.img` into the `system.img`. Luckily, the AOSP recovery provides a way to support this kind of situation. To make this change we need to provide additional functions in our code, and the build system will include the code in the build process automatically.

To support this, we need to do two things. The first one is we need to add additional steps to the OTA build process so that we can create a data file that we can apply to the system during the OTA update. To do this, we can add an additional Python script that will be invoked during the OTA build. This Python script will add our customized edify function to the updater script.

The second one is we need to enhance the updater to process our edify functions during the OTA update. If we recall, we covered the `RegisterDeviceExtensions` function when we walked through the implementation of the updater in Chapter 13, *Creating OTA Packages*. This is how the updater can register device extensions during the initialization.

To extend the updater, we can create a file in our `device` folder at `device/generic/x86vbox/recovery/recovery_updater.c`

We add a device-specific `edify` function, `x86vbox.reprogram`, in this file as follows:

```
#include <stdlib.h>
#include <string.h>

#include "edify/expr.h"
#include "minzip/Zip.h"
#include "minzip/SysUtil.h"

extern struct selabel_handle *sehandle;

Value* ReprogramX86vboxFn(const char* name, State* state, int argc, Expr*
argv[]) {
  bool success = false;

  if (argc != 2) {
    return ErrorAbort(state, "%s() expects 2 args, got %d", name,
    argc);
  }

  char* zip_path;
  char* dest_path;
  if (ReadArgs(state, argv, 2, &zip_path, &dest_path) < 0) return NULL;

  /* Start to extract files. */
  MemMapping map;
```

```
    if (sysMapFile(zip_path, &map) != 0) {
        printf("failed to map package %s\n", zip_path);
        goto done;
    }

    ZipArchive za;
    int err;
    err = mzOpenZipArchive(map.addr, map.length, &za);
    if (err != 0) {
        printf("failed to open package %s: %s\n",
                    zip_path, strerror(err));
        goto done;
    }

    struct utimbuf timestamp = { 1217592000, 1217592000 };  // 8/1/2008
                                                            // default

    success = mzExtractRecursive(&za, "android-x86vbox", dest_path,
                                &timestamp,
                                NULL, NULL, sehandle);
    /* End to extract files. */
    done:
    mzCloseZipArchive(&za);
    sysReleaseMap(&map);
    unlink(zip_path);
    free(zip_path);
    free(dest_path);

    return StringValue(strdup(success ? "t" : ""));
}

void Register_librecovery_updater_x86vbox() {
    RegisterFunction("x86vbox.reprogram", ReprogramX86vboxFn);
}
```

We can see that we register this edify function in
`Register_librecovery_updater_x86vbox`.

The implementation is done in the `ReprogramX86vboxFn` function. The
`ReprogramX86vboxFn` function has a list of standard arguments of all edify functions:

- name: This is the name of the edify function
- state: This is the context that the edify function is working at
- argc: This is the number of arguments that pass to the edify function from the updater script
- argv: This is the list of arguments

What this function does is that it takes the path of a ZIP and the path of the destination folder as the arguments. It extracts the contents of this ZIP to the destination folder. The ZIP file is the one that includes both `ramdisk.img` and `ramdisk-recovery.img` so that they can be used by the init script of `initrd.img`. The destination folder is `/android-x86vbox`, which the init script will search for.

In the preceding function, both the ZIP file path and the destination folder are retrieved by calling the `ReadArgs` function. After that, an instance of the data structure `ZipArchive` is created to be used to extract files.

With all the code changes, we need to create an Android Makefile at:

    device/generic/x86vbox/recovery/Android.mk

The following is the code of the Makefile. We will build `recovery_x86vbox.cpp` as the `librecovery_ui_x86vbox` library and `recovery_updater.c` as the `librecovery_updater_x86vbox` library:

```
LOCAL_PATH := $(call my-dir)
include $(CLEAR_VARS)

LOCAL_MODULE_TAGS := eng
LOCAL_C_INCLUDES += bootable/recovery
LOCAL_SRC_FILES := recovery_x86vbox.cpp

# should match TARGET_RECOVERY_UI_LIB set in BoardConfig.mk
LOCAL_MODULE := librecovery_ui_x86vbox

include $(BUILD_STATIC_LIBRARY)

include $(CLEAR_VARS)
LOCAL_MODULE_TAGS := eng
LOCAL_C_INCLUDES += bootable/recovery
LOCAL_SRC_FILES := recovery_updater.c

LOCAL_MODULE := librecovery_updater_x86vbox
include $(BUILD_STATIC_LIBRARY)
```

We also need to add the following two macros in `BoardConfig.mk` so that both recovery and the updater will link to these two libraries:

```
# device-specific extensions to the recovery UI
TARGET_RECOVERY_UI_LIB := librecovery_ui_x86vbox

# add device-specific extensions to the updater binary
TARGET_RECOVERY_UPDATER_LIBS += librecovery_updater_x86vbox
```

We have extended both recovery and the updater to support the additional features we need so far, but we still have two things missing. We need to create the ZIP file that will be used by `ReprogramX86vboxFn` during the OTA update. We also need to add a few lines of `edify` script in the updater script so that the `ReprogramX86vboxFn` function will be called during the update.

To add the ZIP file to the OTA package, we can add a new Android Makefile, `AndroidBoard.mk`, to our x86vbox device as follows:

```
LOCAL_PATH := $(call my-dir)
include $(CLEAR_VARS)

$(call add-radio-file,images/x86vbox.dat)
```

These are called **radio files** for historical reasons. They may have nothing to do with the device radio. The Android build system simply includes this `x86vbox.dat` file in the OTA package.

To generate this `x86vbox.dat` file, we do this in our x86vbox device `Makefile` to avoid the changes to the AOSP code:

```
X86VBOX_BOOT_IMAGES_DIR := images/android-x86vbox

...

dist:
    if [ -d "images" ]; then \
    echo "Find images folder."; \
    rm -rf images; \
    fi
    mkdir -p ${X86VBOX_BOOT_IMAGES_DIR}
    cp ${OUT}/ramdisk.img ${X86VBOX_BOOT_IMAGES_DIR}
    cp ${OUT}/ramdisk-recovery.img ${X86VBOX_BOOT_IMAGES_DIR}
    cp ${OUT}/kernel ${X86VBOX_BOOT_IMAGES_DIR}
    cd images; zip x86vbox.dat android-x86vbox/*
    cd ../../..;mkdir -p dist_output
    cd ../../..;make dist DIST_DIR=dist_output 2>&1 | tee x86vbox-`date
    +%Y%m%d`.txt
```

The preceding lines are added to `device/generic/x86vbox/Makefile`, so we will build the OTA package in the `device/generic/x86vbox` folder as follows:

```
$ make dist
```

Now the only thing that we need to do is add the `edify` script to `updater-script` inside the update package.

Extending the Python module

To extend the release tools, we can create a Python module named `releasetools.py` in our `device` folder. The build system will check this file in the `device` folder. If it presents, it will be called:

```python
import common

def FullOTA_InstallEnd(info):
  info.script.Print("Full OTA update, Writing x86vbox images...")
  # copy the data into the package.
  x86vbox_dat = info.input_zip.read("RADIO/x86vbox.dat")
  common.ZipWriteStr(info.output_zip, "x86vbox.dat", x86vbox_dat)

  # emit the script code to install this data on the device
  info.script.AppendExtra(
    """package_extract_file("x86vbox.dat", "/tmp/x86vbox.zip");"""
    info.script.AppendExtra(
    """x86vbox.reprogram("/tmp/x86vbox.zip", "/system/android-
    x86vbox");""")

def IncrementalOTA_InstallEnd(info):
  info.script.Print("Incremental OTA update, Writing x86vbox
  images...")
  # copy the data into the package.
  source_x86vbox_dat = info.source_zip.read("RADIO/x86vbox.dat")
  target_x86vbox_dat = info.target_zip.read("RADIO/x86vbox.dat")

  if source_x86vbox_dat == target_x86vbox_dat:
    # x86vbox.dat is unchanged from previous build; no
    # need to reprogram it
    return

  # include the new x86vbox.dat in the OTA package
  common.ZipWriteStr(info.output_zip, "x86vbox.dat",
  target_x86vbox_dat)

  # emit the script code to install this data on the device
  info.script.AppendExtra(
    """package_extract_file("x86vbox.dat", "/tmp/x86vbox.zip");"""
    info.script.AppendExtra(
    """x86vbox.reprogram("/tmp/x86vbox.zip", "/system/android-
    x86vbox");""")
```

We implemented two Python functions that will be called by the build system. Both `FullOTA_InstallEnd` and `IncrementalOTA_InstallEnd` will be called at the end of the script generation. At this point, we can do additional things on top of the normal OTA update. As we can guess from their names, `FullOTA_InstallEnd` is called for the full OTA update and `IncrementalOTA_InstallEnd` is used for the incremental OTA update.

In both functions, we use Python to generate the following lines of `edify` script in `updater-script`:

```
package_extract_file("x86vbox.dat", "/tmp/x86vbox.zip");
x86vbox.reprogram("/tmp/x86vbox.zip", "/system/android-x86vbox");
```

The first line, `package_extract_file`, is the `edify` function that we introduced in Chapter 13, *Creating OTA Packages*. We use it to extract the `x86vbox.dat` ZIP file to `/tmp/x86vbox.zip`. The second function, `x86vbox.reprogram`, is our extension of the `edify` function that extracts files from `/tmp/x86vbox.zip` to `/android-x86vbox`.

Building and testing the extended recovery and updater

With all the preceding changes, we can build and test the enhanced recovery and updater now.

As usual, we have a manifest file for each chapter. We make changes for this chapter based on the source code of Chapter 13, *Creating OTA Packages*. The following are the projects that we changed in this chapter:

```
<?xml version="1.0" encoding="UTF-8"?>
<manifest>

  <remote  name="github"
           revision="refs/tags/android-7.1.1_r4_x86vbox_ch14_r1"
           fetch="." />

  <remote  name="aosp"
           fetch="https://android.googlesource.com/" />
  <default revision="refs/tags/android-7.1.1_r4"
           remote="aosp"
           sync-c="true"
           sync-j="1" />

  <project path="kernel" name="goldfish" remote="github" />
  <project path="bootable/newinstaller"
```

```
      name="platform_bootable_newinstaller" remote="github" />
<project path="device/generic/common" name="device_generic_common"
 groups="pdk" remote="github" />
<project path="device/generic/x86vbox" name="x86vbox" remote="github"
/>
<project path="bootable/recovery" name="android_bootable_recovery"
remote="github" groups="pdk" />

...
</manifest>
```

We can see that we need to change four projects: recovery, newinstaller, common, and x86vbox.

To get the source code from GitHub and AOSP directly, we can check out the android-7.1.1_r4_ch14_aosp branch as follows:

```
$ repo init https://github.com/shugaoye/manifests -b
android-7.1.1_4_ch14_aosp
$ repo sync
```

After the source code is ready for use, we can set the environment and build the system as follows:

```
$ source build/envsetup.sh
$ lunch x86vbox-eng
$ make -j4
```

To build initrd.img, we can run the following command:

```
$ make initrd USE_SQUASHFS=0
```

After we build the system and generate initrd.img, we can create the OTA update package. Since we need to generate x86vbox.dat, we should build OTA inside the x86vbox device folder to call our own Makefile as follows:

```
$ cd device/generic/x86vbox
$ make dist
```

As x86vbox is built for VirtualBox, in this book we use the PXE/NFS setup to test our images. You may refer to Chapter 9, *Booting Up x86vbox Using PXE/NFS* for the test environment setup. After the build is completed, we can use the following PXE boot configuration file to test recovery. The PXE configuration file can be found at $HOME/.VirtualBox/TFTP/pxelinux.cfg/default:

```
prompt 1
default menu.c32
timeout 100

label 1. x86vbox (2 stages boot)
menu x86vbox_debug
kernel x86vbox/kernel
append ip=dhcp console=ttyS3,115200 initrd=x86vbox/initrd.img
androidboot.hardware=x86vbox DEBUG=2 SRC=/android-x86vbox ROOT=/dev/sda1
VBOX_GUEST_ADDITIONS=1 SDCARD=vendor DATA=sda2 X86VBOX=1

label 2. x86vbox
menu x86vbox_ramdisk
kernel x86vbox/kernel
append ip=dhcp console=ttyS3,115200 initrd=x86vbox/ramdisk.img
androidboot.hardware=x86vbox

label 3. Recovery - x86vbox
menu x86vbox_recovery
kernel x86vbox/kernel
append ip=dhcp console=ttyS3,115200 initrd=x86vbox/ramdisk-recovery.img
androidboot.hardware=x86vbox
```

After we power on the virtual device, we can see the following boot menu from PXE bootloader. We have three options:

- The first option is the two stages the boot of x86vbox
- The second option is the normal Android boot of x86vbox
- The third option is the recovery boot of x86vbox

As we discussed before, we don't have a bootloader that can support recovery. For example, we cannot support the case if the user selects the factory reset--the system will boot to recovery to clear the user data automatically.

With the two stages boot, we can do it in our environment as well. The default boot option is x86vbox two stages boot. If the init script in `initrd.img` finds the recovery command in the `/cache` partition, it will boot to recovery automatically:

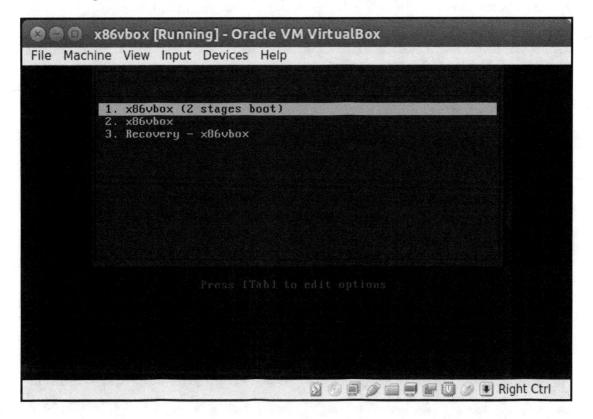

To test recovery, we will select option 3 manually to start recovery. After the recovery has started, we will see the following screen of recovery on the **x86vbox** device. We can see that there is an option for us to apply updates from VirtualBox shared storage. There is another option to create partitions. These are the options that we added in this chapter:

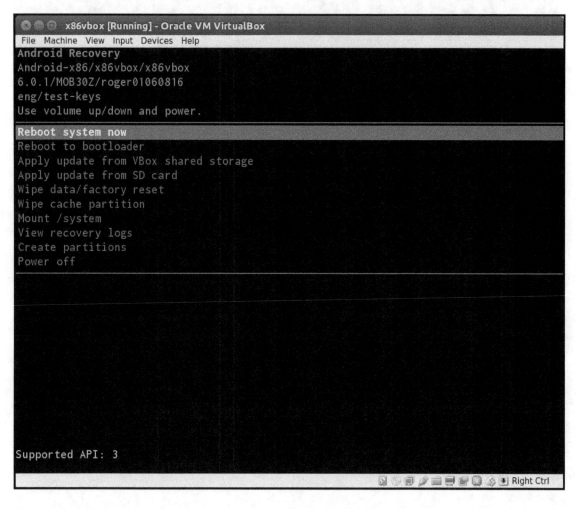

If we select the option to apply updates from VirtualBox shared storage, we will see the following screen, which allows us to select an update package.

The `update-x86vbox-ch14.zip` update package is the OTA package that we built in this chapter. This package can be downloaded from the following SourceForge link, so you can download it and test it right away:

https://sourceforge.net/projects/android-system-programming/files/android-7/ch14/ch14.zip/download

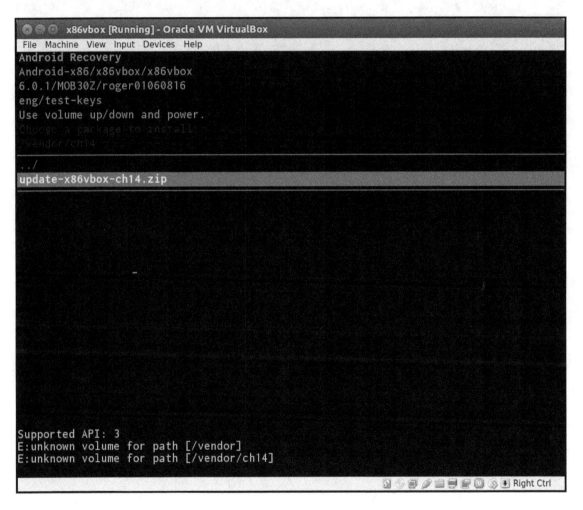

Once the update package is selected, the update process is started as shown in the following screenshot:

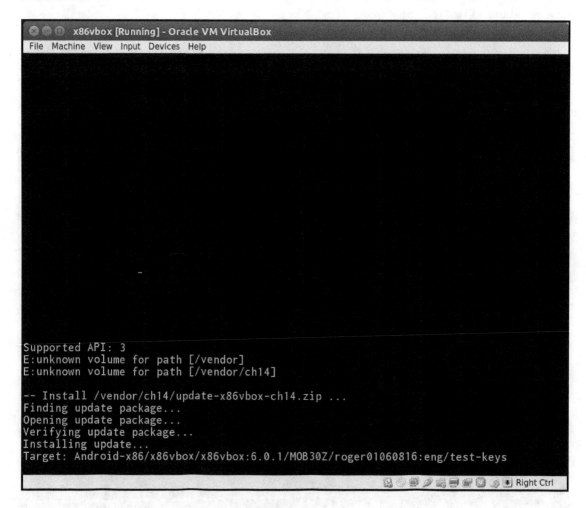

When the update is completed, we will see the following screenshot with a successful message:

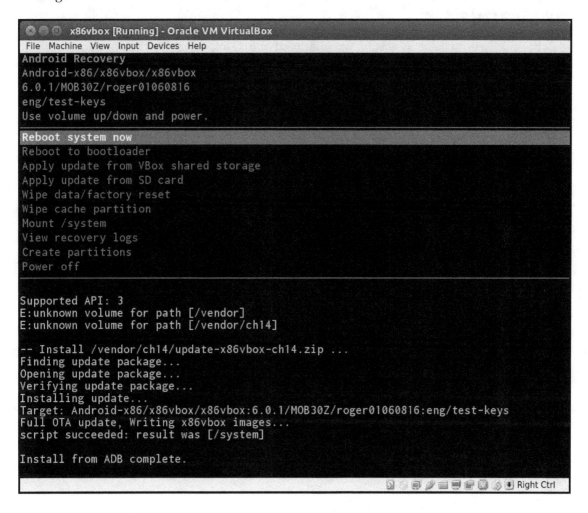

Supporting the third-party recovery packages

In `Chapter 12`, *Introducing Recovery*, we mainly give the detailed introduction about the recovery from the original AOSP. There are many open source recovery projects derived from the AOSP recovery such as TWRP or Cyanogen Recovery (CMR). They allow the users to update various update packages which cannot be done using the original recovery.

Internally, there is not too much difference between these recovery projects and the original one. They extend the original one in many different ways to meet various needs. We won't talk about these recovery projects in this book, but we can explore some third-party update packages to find out what we can do to support these famous update packages. From testing these and minor fixes, we know how to improve our recovery to suit the needs of various open source update packages.

If the third-party recovery packages are written using edify, we should not have any problem applying them. The problems come from the way that they update their data. To be convenient for their development, they may not use edify language to write their `updater-script`. This is because recovery can execute any `update-binary` and `updater-script` as long as it follows the same packaging method documented by Google.

Xposed recovery package

The first third-party recovery package that we are going to look at is the famous Xposed recovery package. To install Xposed on our devices, we can install it after we root our device or we can apply an update package using recovery.

The Xposed update packages can be downloaded from the following URL:

`http://dl-xda.xposed.info/framework/`

The version that we will use in this section is version 87 (`xposed-v87-sdk23-x86.zip`).

Since the update package is a ZIP file, we can extract it to a temporary space and look at the internal details inside the update package:

```
$ ls -1F META-INF/com/google/android/
flash-script.sh
genymotion-ready
update-binary
updater-script
$ cat META-INF/com/google/android/updater-script
# this is a dummy file, the magic is in update-binary and flash-script.sh
```

As we can see, the updater-script is just a dummy file; updater-binary actually executes the flash-script.sh script, which is a shell script.

If we power on our x86vbox device and enter recovery to apply this package, we will get the following error message in /tmp/recovery.log:

```
...
*****************************
Xposed framework installer zip
*****************************
- Mounting /system and /vendor read-write
I:1 key(s) loaded from /res/keys
Verifying update package...
I:comment is 1738 bytes; signature 1720 bytes from end
I:whole-file signature verified against RSA key 0
I:verify_file returned 0
Installing update...
*****************************
Xposed framework installer zip
*****************************
- Mounting /system and /vendor read-write
mount: can't find /system in /proc/mounts
! Failed: /system could not be mounted!
E:Error in /sideload/package.zip
(Status 1)

Installation aborted.
```

We can see from the error message that the flash-script.sh script cannot mount the /system partition.

To find out the issue, we can look at the following code snippet of this script and compare it to the preceding error message:

```
...
echo "*******************************"
echo "Xposed framework installer zip"
echo "*******************************"

if [ ! -f "system/xposed.prop" ]; then
  echo "! Failed: Extracted file system/xposed.prop not found!"
  exit 1
fi

echo "- Mounting /system and /vendor read-write"
mount /system >/dev/null 2>&1
mount /vendor >/dev/null 2>&1
mount -o remount,rw /system
mount -o remount,rw /vendor >/dev/null 2>&1
if [ ! -f '/system/build.prop' ]; then
  echo "! Failed: /system could not be mounted!"
  exit 1
fi
...
```

As we can see, the reason it fails is because this script assumes the mount command is available when it executes. In our environment, we do have the mount command available, but it is not in the execution path by default. The mount command in our environment is a symbolic link of busybox. This version of mount needs the standard Linux mount table, /etc/fstab, instead of /etc/recovery.fstab.

With the preceding analysis, we can just simply update our start script to fix the issues as follows:

On early init:

```
# for /bin/busybox
symlink /bin/ld-linux.so.2 /lib/ld-linux.so.2
symlink /bin/busybox /bin/sh
symlink /bin/busybox /sbin/sh
symlink /etc/recovery.fstab /etc/fstab
```

On init:

```
export PATH /bin:/sbin:/system/bin
mkdir /vendor
exec -- /bin/sh /sbin/init.x86vbox.sh
...
```

In the `init.recovery.x86vbox.rc` script, we add the `/bin` path for `busybox` to the `PATH` environment variable. We create a `/etc/fstab` symbol link to `/etc/recovery.fstab`. With these changes, we build recovery and apply the Xposed package again. We can see from the following screenshot that the package is applied successfully:

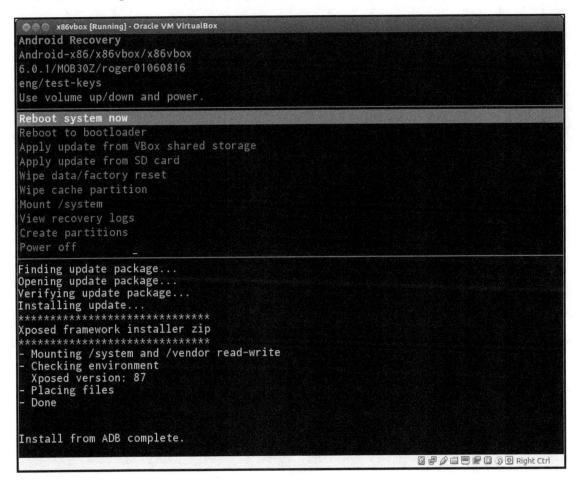

Opening GApps

Let's look at another famous open source update package, GApps. The GApps project provides **Google Mobile Services** (**GMS**) replacement using its update packages. There are many Android devices shipped without GMS. If the users of these devices want to use Google applications, GApps is one of the major choices for them. They can download a version of a GApps package suitable for their device and flash an update package using recovery.

The GApps packages can be downloaded at the following URL:

```
http://opengapps.org
```

There are many choices of GApps packages at their website based on platform, Android version, and variant of packages (super, stock, full, mini, micro, nano, or pico, and so on).

We will use a small size pico variant to test in our environment. As we did for the Xposed update package, we want to look at update-binary and updater-script first. After we extract the package to a temporary space, we can see that the updater-script is just a dummy file and update-binary is a shell script:

```
$ cat updater-script
# Dummy file; update-binary is a shell script.
```

If we look at update-binary in the following snippet, we can see that it is a shell script using /sbin/sh to interpret it. We will create a symbolic link, /sbin/sh, to the busybox in the start up script so we don't have any problems with running it:

```
#!/sbin/sh
...
export OPENGAZIP="$3"
export OUTFD="/proc/self/fd/$2"
export TMP="/tmp"
case "$(uname -m)" in
  *86*) export BINARCH="x86";;  # e.g. Zenfone is i686
  *ar*) export BINARCH="arm";; # i.e. armv7l and aarch64
esac
bb="$TMP/busybox-$BINARCH"
l="$TMP/bin"
setenforce 0
for f in app_densities.txt app_sizes.txt bkup_tail.sh gapps-remove.txt
g.prop installer.sh busybox-x86 tar-x86 unzip-x86 zip-x86; do
  unzip -o "$OPENGAZIP" "$f" -d "$TMP";
done
for f in  busybox-x86 tar-x86 unzip-x86 zip-x86; do
  chmod +x "$TMP/$f";
```

```
done
if [ -e "$bb" ]; then
  install -d "$1"
  for i in $($bb --list); do
    if ! ln -sf "$bb" "$1/$i" && ! $bb ln -sf "$bb" "$1/$i" && ! $bb
    ln -f "$bb" "$1/$i" ; then
      # create script wrapper if symlinking and hardlinking failed
      because of restrictive selinux policy
      if ! echo "#!$bb" > "$1/$i" || ! chmod +x "$1/$i" ; then
        echo "ui_print ERROR 10: Failed to set-up Open GApps' pre-
        bundled busybox" > "$OUTFD"
        echo "ui_print" > "$OUTFD"
        echo "ui_print Please use TWRP as recovery instead" > "$OUTFD"
        echo "ui_print" > "$OUTFD"
        exit 1
      fi
    fi
  done
  PATH="$1:$PATH" $bb ash "$TMP/installer.sh" "$@"
  exit "$?"
else
  echo "ui_print ERROR 64: Wrong architecture to set-up Open GApps'
  pre-bundled busybox" > "$OUTFD"
  echo "ui_print" > "$OUTFD"
  exit 1
fi
```

This script expects the same list of arguments, which recovery will pass to `update-binary`.
It uses the arguments to find the update package ZIP file and extracts a setup of files to
`/tmp`:

```
# ls -1 /tmp
app_densities.txt
app_sizes.txt
bin
bkup_tail.sh
busybox-x86
g.prop
gapps-remove.txt
installer.sh
last_install
recovery.log
tar-x86
unzip-x86
update_binary
zip-x86
```

These files are the tools that the GApps package needed for the next stage of installation, as we can see in the preceding snippet. It includes its own version of `busybox` and compression tools. After it extracts all the files, it fixes the permission for executables and installs the symbol links for `busybox`. After that, it executes the real installation script, `installer.sh`. This is a very complicated shell script, so we won't do further analysis on it. We can apply the GApps package to our system without any problem, as we can see from the following screenshot:

The following screenshot shows the screen after we install GApps successfully:

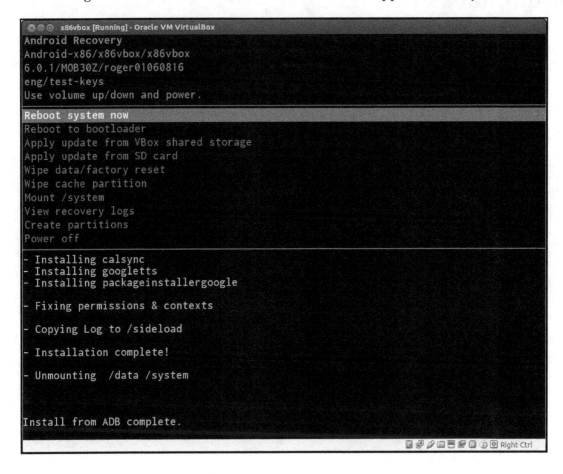

Summary

In this chapter, we started with an introduction of debugging tips for recovery and the updater. The same method can be used for other native applications as well. After that, we enhanced both recovery and the updater to support our customized system image, which can be used as a normal system image and also can be used to support a two stages boot. We also added features such as apply image from the VirtualBox shared folder and created partitions in recovery. Finally, we analyzed two famous open source update packages: Xpose and GApps. We can apply them to x86vbox devices without any problems.

We have concluded the entire book now. I hope as a system developer you can benefit from the concepts, hands-on practices, and source code in this book. If you can build and test the two devices, x86emu and x86vbox, in this book yourself, you should be able to get enough experience to start your own Android system projects without too many issues.

Finally, you can visit my GitHub repository frequently while you read this book. I will consistently update the source code to fix any issues found:

```
https://github.com/shugaoye
```

Index

www.ingramcontent.com/pod-product-compliance
Lightning Source LLC
LaVergne TN
LVHW081328050326
832903LV00024B/1064